GLIMPSING
HEAVEN

*A father's journey through his children-inspired transformation
to discover, fall in love with and fight for mother-nature*

MARTIN A. LOPEZ

iUniverse®

GLIMPSING HEAVEN
A FATHER'S JOURNEY THROUGH HIS CHILD-INSPIRED TRANSFORMATION
TO DISCOVER, FALL IN LOVE WITH AND FIGHT FOR MOTHER-NATURE

iUniverse books may be ordered through booksellers or by contacting:

iUniverse
1663 Liberty Drive
Bloomington, IN 47403
www.iuniverse.com
844-349-9409

ISBN: 978-1-5320-9444-6 (sc)
ISBN: 978-1-5320-9445-3 (e)

Library of Congress Control Number: 2021904997

Print information available on the last page.

iUniverse rev. date: 05/27/2022

CONTENTS

PART 2: FACING HELL ON EARTH, THE FRIEND, THE ENEMY, ANALYSIS AND SOLUTIONS

THANK YOU TO MY BIRTH FAMILY

Throughout this book I highlight and have even been critical of Dave, my blood brother, when addressing my brother's position on the environment. Let me make it clear: If it were not for him and everything he has done for me and my family, I would never have been able to write this book! By being the moving force in the family's invitation to Las Vegas to join my blood family, and giving us a house near the river, he created the conditions that enabled me to be close to my children and ultimately to see the world through their eyes. From a struggling private law firm in Albuquerque, he brought my family to a small town where he was quite influential in facilitating Sally and I obtaining employment.

There is just not enough room in this book to identify all the successes that my family experienced because of Dave. He even lent me money so I could afford to publish this book.

As for Pete, my other blood-brother, although I am told he investigated me to see that I was the real thing, he has been there for us whenever we needed any help regarding the house. He watched the house when we were gone and was there to greet us when we returned from Hobbs, NM. Most amazing about Pete is that since Molly, our birth mother has been unable to take care of herself, he has been there for her. Now that she is at a nursing home, he visits her four times a day. What a son!

Pete so reminds me of the George Bailey character in the movie – *'It's a Wonderful Life'*. I am told by my birth-mother, Molly, that when Pete was going to college and making very high grades, his father became ill and was unable to run the business. They asked Pete to run the business. Like George Bailey, Pete had to forgo all the dreams he ever had, to return to run the family Sand and Gravel business. Like George Bailey, he married a beautiful and intelligent woman. (Carla is a college professor.) I won't give away the ending of the movie, except to say that, in this context, Pete can be forgiven for most anything.

Regarding Molly, my birth mother, she could have easily said that she did not want it known that she gave up a child. She was quite brave to publicly acknowledge me as her son and all the criticism that would bring. I am eternally grateful.

So, if I seem a bit critical on some issues, I do not think I am an ingrate! I am just overly candid about my opinions regarding the environment. The difficult truth is that there are many good people who have yet to recognize and accept, that by our failure to change and take action, we are enabling the polluters to destroy us. Thank you Dave, Pete and Molly for everything you have done for the Lopez family. It has been life-changing!

ACKNOWLEDGEMENTS

MILGRACIAS (THANK YOU VERY MUCH) & 'DE NADA'S' (YOUR WELCOME'S)

I hereby thank the following:

- Sally, my dear, loving and tolerant wife for being the greatest wife and mother in the world. Thank you for never giving up hope that we would have children.
- Ali' and Amadeo, my dear children, for inspiring me to become what I would never have been without you.
- Mom and dad, (Gregoria and Martin Lopez), for adopting and raising me with compassion, love and in an environment that encouraged education and a respect for all human beings.
- Maye, (Susie Silva), my dear grandma, for loving me unconditionally and demonstrating how remarkable a woman could be.

- *There are so many I would like to thank and so many responsible for my successes, big and small. There are not enough pages to do so.*

A SPECIAL ACKNOWLEDGEMENT AND THANK YOU TO MY CHILDREN

Both Ali' and Amadeo made this book possible, not only by way of their inspiration but because of their wonderful writing and artistic contributions. I have thanked them in more than just words for their contributions.

DE NADAS ('YOUR WELCOMES')

ABOUT THE AUTHOR

*At Robertson High School, Amadeo had an assignment in his English class in which he was to ask me fifty questions to find out as much as he could about me. Consistent with the theme of this book, I could think of no better way to introduce myself. Here it is in an abbreviated version with updates **bolded and italicized**.*

-Lopez, Amadeo / Ms. Maestas /ENG IV / 20 November, 2011

FIFTY QUESTIONS TO MY FATHER

1. **Name?** Martin Lopez
2. **Age?** 60 years old. **(70)**
2.5 **Education?** Graduated from Cathedral High School in Gallup, New Mexico in 1968. Graduated from the University of New Mexico in 1973. Graduated from the George Washington National Law Center in 1977.
3. **Occupation?** New Mexico Legal Aid Staff Attorney. *(Public Defender and now semi-retired.)*
4. **Who is your family?** My wife, Sally Lopez and my two children, Amadeus (Amadeo) and Alizandra (Ali') Lopez.
5. **Do Ali' and I have other family besides the Lopez family?** Yes. The Lopez family is through adoption. Your grandparents are Martin and Gregoria Lopez from Gallup, **NM.** You have two aunts, Theresa Lopez, my sister, and **Christine Julius, my deceased sister.** Then you have the Romero/Gutierrez family as my birth/blood family. Dave Romero Sr. and Molly (Amelia) Gutierrez, Romero are your grandparents. You have two uncles from the Romero family: Dave and Peter Romero, *my blood brothers*.
6. **Why did you wait so long to have kids, 'grandpa'?** We tried for ten grueling years to have children. (Joke.) With the help of modern science Ali' arrived and then without the aid of science you, magically, were born.
7. **What kind of attorney are you and what do they do?** An attorney that represents and advises poor people in civil matters: Divorce, Custody, Domestic Violence, Landlord Tenant, Consumer and Social Security cases. *(Post 2011, I joined Public Defender in Hobbs, NM. I represented poor people charged with crimes.) (As of April 22, I am temporarily retired.) Update: I now represent my brother Dave against the City of Las Vegas.*
8. **What other kind of attorney have you been?** Civil Rights attorney, Prosecutor and Criminal Defense lawyer.
9. **What were the highlights?** As a Civil Rights lawyer, I argued and prevailed in the Tenth Circuit Court of Appeals. I proved to the court that my client, Candido Martinez, had a valid Civil Rights action against the City of Albuquerque police department. Phil Davis and I negotiated a Civil Rights settlement against a City in New Mexico in an action wherein a police officer literally held my client, a Mexican American, while a cowboy assaulted him.

Recently at the Public Defenders, I represented a black man charged with Possession of Methamphetamine with Intent to Distribute. He was facing serious time in the penitentiary. Interestingly, a few years previously, a black electrician, had sued the same investigating and arresting officer and received a significant monetary judgment from a jury. The Electrician had claimed that the officer had forced him to take a blood test. Through some work and research, I discovered that the police officer had a tainted background and should not be trusted. He had been forced to resign from the Midland Police Department after he had kept the drug evidence of 30 defendants, mostly blacks and Hispanics, in his car and house, instead of the Police locker. Imagine what he was doing with that drug evidence?

From my client, I learned that there had been a search by a drug-sniffing dog who had gone into the house and had detected no drugs. Then the officer in question went into the house. Walla! He finds a big bag of methamphetamine or so he testified. No report had been turned over regarding this failed dog search. I was able to use this information to convince a jury that my client was not in possession of methamphetamine, notwithstanding the officer alleging he had found a very large bag of meth in my client's house. The jury found my client not guilty.*1

As a Public Defender in Hobbs, NM, I also represented a Mexican Immigrant in a jury trial who was charged with a Felony DWI. A white female witness had said she saw him in a local convenience store, nearly falling down drunk and that when he drove away, he nearly hit her. On the stand she conveniently was unable to recall the facts. She did testify that a member of her family was killed by a drunk Mexican Immigrant. The jury found him not-guilty in 4 minutes.*2

As a prosecutor, there were too numerous victories to mention. The last one I recall is getting a conviction in a jury trial against a guy who became a preacher in the penitentiary. He had shot his girlfriend in the groin and claimed the devil made him do it.

10. **Have you enjoyed being a father?** Yes.
11. **What are the highlights?** -Your birth. You were a big baby, 8 lbs15 oz. even though you were born caesarian two weeks early. You peed on the doctor as he took you out of mom's stomach. I figured that with that big chest of yours and your big hands and long fingers, you would be a wrestler or a boxer or a piano player. Mmm!

- Ali's birth. She looked like me, poor thing! *But she grew into a beautiful girl and woman.*
- Your piano recital and Ali's.
- The wonderful interaction and adventures you and Ali' have had with the dogs. The four dogs have become part of the family. Fluffy, Number Eight, Agent Orange and Blue.
- The great camping and fishing experiences we have had.
- Sally and I coaching you to # 5 in the Southwest and coaching Ali' to the top of the rankings.
- You winning the Southwest Closed tournament.
- Ali's comeback win in the Finals of the District tournament against remarkable odds. Even her coach had deserted her.
- Ali' speaking her mind to the coach in front of the team, to let her and Raven challenge the coach's daughter and Miranda for the number one position.
- Ali' speaking her mind to the newspaper about police harassing the students on the Plaza.

- Ali' having a mind of her own, in spite of all the pressures to conform.
- Ali' being student of the month numerous times.
- Ali' exiting High School as a Freshman, passing her GED and enrolling in college.
- Amadeo - You winning the tournament in Roswell when you were down 5-2 in the third set and the whole crowd was against you.
- Seeing the magnificent paintings, drawings and sculptures that you and Ali' put together.
- You badly beating Sandia Preps' Michael Atkins in the Team State Finals after he had trounced you in your two matches with him during the season.
- You winning the Silver Gloves State Championship.
- **You going to college and being on the Honor roll your first year in college**.
- *Ali's remarkable dedication to her new job which often requires her to work three 16-hour days in a week.*
- *Ali's hard work to obtain her Certified Nurses Assistant (CNA) certificate.*
- *Your graduation, in December, 2018 (and now the graduation party at Betty's house.).*
- *Every moment I have been fortunate enough to spend with you, Ali' and your mom.*

12. **What kind of tennis instructor are you and what are the highlights of your career?**
    - Just an ordinary tennis instructor who has played competitive tennis at the 4.5-5.0 levels and who decided to start a tennis program in Las Vegas in 1999. The highlights are as follows:
    - Working with Sally to do the following:
    - Starting a low-income tennis program for Housing children in Las Vegas.
    - Having a summer program that enabled children who may have never picked up a racket otherwise, to learn tennis and travel all over the country to play tennis.
    - Twice receiving the award of Best Tennis Program in the Southwest.
    - Coaching the West tennis team and doing what had never been done before. Sally and I qualified boys' and girls' team into the district tournament and 5 single qualifiers in 2005.
    - One of our 'housing' students is now an assistant Pro at the Highpoint Swim and Tennis Club.

13. **Hobbies?** Reading, writing, keeping a diary, poetry, *and now, walking the dogs, composting, growing a garden, and watering and caring for the many plants that will go to our garden.*

14. **What do you write?** Mostly a diary and commentaries on values that end up in my family Christmas letter and once in a while I may submit them to the newspaper.

15. **Why do you write poetry?** It's in my genes. I forgot to wash them. Seriously! Sister Helen Francis, my high school English teacher got me started and I was hooked. It is therapeutic. It clarifies the important emotional and intellectual events that are emerging and converging in my life. In a sense, poetry addresses these matters and to a certain extent resolves them. As related to you and Ali', your birth and your lives became my greatest inspiration and writing became a way of *celebrating your lives and* passing on my values to you.

16. **What have been the most important things in your life?** Having wonderful parents. Meeting and falling in love with your mom; the birth and lives of you and Ali'; your successes and our tennis program's successes *and reuniting with my birth family. (Read 'Glimpsing Heaven' and you will find out what is now most important in my life.)*

17. **What lessons from your life can you give me?** Discover that what you do well, what makes the world a better place and that what you enjoy. Then develop it.

18. **What mistakes did you make?** Not checking the 'updated' draw at the state tournament, the morning of the state tournament.

19. **Did you ever write a poem that encompasses your philosophy about how to live?** Yes.

20. **Could you relate it to us?** Yes. *(See **THE JUMPROPE SONG** in Ch. II – Roots of The Book.** I amended this poem considerably but the essence is still the same.*

21. **Is this the one we used to say at bedtime every night?** Yes.

22. **What do you mean–Don't forget the light?** "Light" is the symbol for knowledge and wisdom.

23. **What do you mean – Don't forget to fight?** To stand up for your beliefs at risk to your reputation and life. "Fight" means battling for what you believe in and against injustice. It doesn't necessarily mean physical fighting.

24. **What do you mean- Don't forget your brother who is reaching up to you?** This is a biblical concept and is a tenet of other religions. (Matthew 25:26 **NIV**) I was a stranger and you did not invite me in, I needed clothes and you did not clothe me, I was sick and in prison and you did not look after me." Also (See Matthew 25:45 **NIV**) "… I tell you the truth, whatever you did not do for one of the least of these, you did not do for me."

25. **Is this about empathy?** Yes.

26. **Do you think I am empathetic enough?** Before you condemn another, ask yourself what you would have done or said in the other person's shoes?

27. **What do you mean: …the final portrait of your soul depends on what you drew?** Your actions and omissions will ultimately either haunt you or allow you to live and die with the belief that you have lived a good life.

28. **What do you mean – Redemption is justice rendered to all?** It means we all have a duty to treat humanity, particularly the powerless, to fair treatment. The failure to the least of humanity, impacts us all.

29. **What do you mean – Don't bury your soul in a world of desire, a house full of things fuels a funeral pyre.** Love of things and not humanity, will destroy you. *I have now realized that failing to embrace nature as family, is destroying us. The 'funeral pyre' now burns hotter than ever.*

30. **Do you think I am too obsessed with things?** To some extent we all are. Just remember people come before things **and those without come before those with.**

31. **What do you mean – Don't allow your gifts to be stifled by the world, just let them flow, a bright flag unfurled?** Find out what comes natural to you and refine that ability or talent. Don't hide it or be embarrassed about it.

32. **What do you think my gifts are?** Musical, **mechanical,** language, athletics, artistic, lyrical, farming, **fishing, investigative, hunting and an innate sense for nature.**

33. **So how should I develop my gifts?** Recognize what they are with the assistance of your teachers and your father. Let them direct you in that development.

34. **What do you mean – Boldly cast your net on the sea of life and it will return to bring beauty or strife?** Don't be afraid of life, particularly now when your parents can help.

35. **Who is the mentor?** I am the mentor. *You will need to look inside yourself and discover your essence and learn from it. Enlighten yourself by seeking out the wisdom around you and inside you. Never forget your connection to nature and treat her like family.*

36. **Have I been listening to the mentor?** Sometimes. Better now than a year ago.

37. **What does it mean – "As Jesus lived so we must"?***3 Read about Jesus' life in the Bible, the Nag Hammadi discoveries and Deepak Chopra's, "The Third Jesus".

38. **But isn't Jesus, God?** In the Churches' view, yes. But more important than believing whether he is God is whether you are following in his footsteps and in what he has told you to do for your neighbor.

39. **What are** your **regrets?** Too few to mention.

40. **Do your worry about dying?** No.

41. **What do you worry about?** I worry about how I should live with the little time remaining. I worry if I will be able to do what I need to do so my children will be prepared to lead moral and successful lives. *I worry about the world you and your children will be entering. If nothing is done to stop pollution, you and your kids will inherit an earth that is devastated by pollution.*

42. **Anything else you want to add that I have not asked that you think is important to mention?** Thank you, Ms. Maestas, for providing a vehicle that allowed me to relate, and compelled Amadeo to listen, to important matters we would not otherwise have talked about.

1. Unbelievably, my supervisor, to whom I had inquired about this particular officer, told me that he was a very nice guy and he got along with him well. Not exactly what the facts turned out to be. Thank goodness I disregarded his assessment of the officer. Remarkably two of my fellow Public Defenders to whom I had told the facts, thought I had done a disservice to the police department by taking this case to trial. They believed that by taking the case to trial I had ruined our relationship with the police department. Wow! How did they forget to whom we owed a Constitutional duty of representation! It was not the police!

2 Racism was alive and well in this southern New Mexico city.

3. Regarding question 37, I have changed the poem since I wrote it for Amadeo and Ali' and eliminated the reference to 'Jesus'.

PREFACE

THE ESSENCE OF PART 1 AND PART II OF GLIMPSING HEAVEN

After a magical transformation once my children were conceived and born, I searched for a reason why I had been filled with this mountainous emotional connection to my children, humanity and the wonder of nature surrounding and permeating my entire being. *

This book was initially about inspirational poems and essays about my children. (One of the early book titles was going to be 'Let the Children Take Your Heart'.) Once I began a search for the reasons for the change, it became clear that nature had worked its magic on me by just becoming a father and being with my children. But as time went on, I realized the change went well beyond the maternal instinct. The transformation affected my view of the world and my concern for children, my fellow man and nature. I wondered why no one else was experiencing this or seeing the world as I was taking it in. Certainly, others had been fathers to children. Why had they not undergone this transmogrification?

After a search and journey through the Bible and two churches, the answer was discovered in The Lost Gospels. Specifically, my children's inspiration and my new-found connection to mankind, was best explained in *The Gospel According to Thomas, Logion 22.* (**See Ch. III: 'Lost Gospels Explain Jesus' Main Message and my Transformation Better Than Any Accepted Church Doctrine.** (The mother nursing a child symbolizing our oneness with mankind.) The connection had an explanation that matched my circumstances. My children transforming my being was explained.

The transformation that allowed me to see the wonders of nature as never before, was best explained again, in the Lost Gospels, specifically, ***The Sayings of Jesus #3 of the Gospel of Thomas.*** *(See Ch. III,* under the same title supra.) I was able to absorb and appreciate the message of the Lost Gospels. *(Heaven is in us and all around us)*. This was critical for me. Heaven on earth, rather than somewhere in the sky and only after we die, was a powerful and immediate message. It followed perfectly that we are directly responsible for our fellow man in this heaven on earth rather than living a life motivated by a Heaven after death and only if we followed the Church beliefs correctly.

I could come to no other conclusion that this heaven on earth was, not only how we treated our fellow man, but how we treated nature. My poems, I believe, are infused with this feeling and belief. This new outlook changed the title again to Glimpsing Heaven/Facing Hell on Earth.

I did not want this book to become a 'how to' book but my moral imperialism could not be hidden. The second part of the book is *Part 2-Facing Hell on Earth, the Friend, the Enemy, A Review and Solutions ; Chapter 10 – DON'T FORGET TO FIGHT ……….. FOR NATURE.)* Here, I briefly analyze and provide some 'solutions' to resolve the disaster we find ourselves in. You will also find 'source' materials at the end of the book. I certainly have ideas that will offend many.

However, I believe my ideas are well-founded and will lead us to where we need to go. Please read on and decide for yourself.

Ultimately I settled on the title 'Glimpsing Heaven' since it best and briefly encapsulated the idea of the book.

Paul Campos, a good friend and the best man at my wedding, referred me to 'BABIES', on Netflix. It reveals that scientifically, we males are chemically changed by having a child.

PART 1

Glimpsing Heaven

MY JOURNEY AND TRANSFORMATION

CHAPTER 1

INTRODUCTION TO
'LET THE CHILDREN TAKE YOUR HEART'

Children throughout history seem to have received little praise, recognition or respect. The attitude has been what can they do or teach us. It is presumed that they have to 'grow up' to gain any respect or recognition. Only until they have learned to become a bread-winner or mothers, do we recognize them.

This book is premised on the belief that a baby or a child, can be life-changing. My experience with my children tells me that when Jesus acknowledged the importance of children and told the apostles to let the children come to Him, He was saying that children can inspire you to find heaven on earth.

The poem, 'Let the Children Take Your Heart', should reveal that children can be life-changing. The rest of this book, I hope attests to this belief. Their existence can be transforming and yes even miraculous. They certainly were for me.

*1. My first-cousin Pia, (a lawyer), reminded me the other day that there was a time when I was not appreciative of the significance of children in our lives. She recollected when I first had children and had told her about my pre-children attitude. I would get annoyed when I went to a restaurant and parents would obliviously let their kids run around the restaurant. As bad, they would bring their baby to a restaurant and ruin my peace and quiet by allowing him or her to cry the entire time. She recalled that I had told her that now that I have kids, 'I had become them', (Those parents).

His followers said to him, "When will the kingdom come?" "It will not come by watching for it. It will not be said, 'Look here it is, 'Rather, the father's kingdom is spread out upon the earth, and people do not see it." Saying 113 of The Gospel of Thomas.
"If you love a being for his beauty, you love none other than god, for he is the Beautiful Being."
The mystic Muid ad-Din ibn al-Arabi (1165-1240)

MY CHILDREN UNLOCKED HEAVEN'S DOOR

A window, a wormhole, a portal, a path, a way, an opening, was created. A gaze from the eyes of God returned my searching view. The light through the opening shone brightly and breathtakingly. That which was hidden was now revealed. The foreboding, dark and heretofore impenetrable curtain of death was lifted. My being was transformed. I could see, feel, hear and touch as if I were the liquid light of wisdom and compassion.

The light emanated from and through the eyes and the hearts of my two little children. My windows to the world have now been opened to the plight of all children. The delivery and existence of Ali and Amadeo were the vehicles of my journey beyond death. The fullness and brightness of their being, delivered me beyond the corporeal reality which had so long locked me to the material and the physical which had muddied and distorted the pathways to wisdom, light and love.

I am now free to fully love, to fail, to be a fool and to risk dying because I now know, through my children, that there is a beauty and love that supersedes all else. They will carry on my light into the future.

My children were and are the inspiration for my senses to take in the "beauty", to see "the light", to be able to "love" and the motivation "to fight" against the injustices of this world.

BIRDIE FLYING IN CLOUDS BY ALI

CHRISTMAS BY ALI'

"…and if you take my hand my son, all will be well when the day is done." Tell me why you are smiling my son? Is there a secret that you can tell everyone? Do you know more than men that are wise? Can you see what we all must disguise through your loving eyes? **'Day is Done' written and composed by Peter Yarrow and sung by Peter Paul and Mary**

Now they were bringing the babes also to him that he might touch them; but when the disciples saw it, they rebuked them. But Jesus called them together and said, "Let the little children come to me, and do not hinder them, for of such is the kingdom of God. Amen I say to you *whoever does not accept the kingdom of God as a little child will not enter into it." **Luke 18:15-17 NIV***

*-Jesus said, "The person old in days will not hesitate to ask a little child seven days old about the place of life, and he shall live. For many of the first will be last and become a single one." **Saying # 4 of The Gospel of Thomas.***

*His followers said, "When will you appear to us and when shall we see you?" Jesus said, "When you strip without being ashamed and you take your clothes and put them under your feet like little children and trample them, then [you] will see the child of the living one and you will not be afraid." **The Sayings of Jesus # 17 of The Gospel of Thomas.***

LET THE CHILDREN TAKE YOUR HEART

G   B   E   E   E   D C
Let the children come to me
C   B   A   A   A G F
His words there for all to see
G   B   E   E   E   D   C
Let the children take your heart
C B   A   A   A   D F
To the Promised Land depart
G   B   C   E   EE   D   C
Their hearts and eyes reflect pure light
C   C   B   A   A   A G   F
That leads us out from desperate night.
G   G   A   A   G   B   C
Let the children take your heart.

G   BEE   EDC
From a journey incomplete
C   BA   AA   G F
They are wings beneath" my feet.
G   G BEE   ED C
They lift me up where eagles soar
C   BA   A   AG F
There we glimpse through Heaven's door.
CC DE E   ED C
I sing of children in my home.

C C B A A A G F
I revel in bliss never known.
G G A A G B C
Let the children take your heart.

G C   E E E   D C
If you've not received these gifts,
C B A A A G F
You may never heal the rift.
G B E   E   E   D C
As our Lord heals heart and soul,
C C B A A   A G F
My babies now make me whole.
G C E   E   E   D C
As the drought transforms to rain
C B   A   A A   G F
Luscious green is God's terrain.
G G A A G B C
Let the children take your heart.

REFRAIN

C   D E F F   F E D
With the connection to the divine
E D C C C   B A
We create the words and rhyme,
A   C   E E E D C
With the Spirit as our muse,
C B A   A A   A G F
O'er time's mountains we peruse.
G   C E E   E D C
When the children take our eyes,
A   C C C   B A
Their vision makes us wise.
G G A A B B C
Let the children take your heart.

G C E   E E   D C
If your heart's not touched the sky,

C C B A A A G F
A baby's never filled your eye.
C D E   E E D C
If you've searched but not found,
C B   A A   A G F
Listened, but heard no sound,
C D E E E E D C
Hear the children and what they say
C C B A   A A G   F
Get on your knees and with them play.
B B C C D   E   C
Let the children take your heart.

C D E   F   F F   E D
If your blind heart has turned to stone,
F   E D D D   C A
Let the children guide you home.
C E   F   F F E D
If death's sting you seek to steal*,
C   C B A A   G F
Then to yourself you must not kneel.
C   D E E   E D C
Love the children in your life
C   B A A A   G A F
And eternal blessings will be rife.
C C D D C B   C
Let the children take your heart.

C D E E   E D C
To see inward look outside.
C B A A   A G F
Love the children at your side.
B   C D E E D C
Tune in the music of the soul,
C B   A   A   A G F
A loving parent must be your goal.
C D E   E   E DC
A child loved turns hearts aglow
C C B A A   A G F
So love for life you'll finally know.
C C D D C B C
Let the children take your heart.

C E F   F F E D
Jesus walked upon the waters
C B A   A A G F
Jesus sailed upon the sea.
C D E E E D C
He has given us the power
E   D C C C   B A
Through the Holy Ghost to see.
C   D   E E E D C
My kids led me to the doorway
C B A   A   A   G F
To the light, they hold the key.
G B A A   G   B   C
Let the children take your heart.

Let the children come to me
His words there for all to see
Let the children take your heart
To the Promised Land depart
Their hearts and eyes reflect pure light
That leads out from desperate night.
Let the children take your heart.

(See The Nag Hammadi Library, The Gospel of Thomas: These are the secret sayings that the living Jesus spoke and Didymos Judas Thomas recorded. 1. And he said, "Whoever discovers the interpretation of these sayings will not taste death."

CHAPTER II

THE ROOTS OF THE TRANSFORMATION TREE

INTRODUCTION

I think most of us have a template on how to live, i.e., what is good and what is evil. It used to be called a conscience. For most of us this belief is contained in our religious education. As a kid who seemed to have more questions than my religious teachers had answers, I formulated my own views on good and evil. From my search for truth, it sure seemed, that as a country, we were devoid of a conscience. My being was so much formed and held together by a comfortable trust in empire-building, war-making, Jesus-distorting, racism-tolerating, mind-managing, money-making-justifies-evil, nature-ignoring, nature-destroying and technology trumping everything else. Maintaining power and profits seemed to justify most any action. Once I had children, I felt compelled to put together an outline that I could use to teach my children what is good and what is evil. The Jumprope prayer/song is that poem.

Moreover, you will notice that this poem became the outline for this book.

THE JUMPROPE SONG

ASHES TO ASHES, DUST TO DUST?
OR
ARE WE MORE
THAN A MERE SOUL-BEARING HUSK,
LIVING BY MAN-INSCRIBED PAGES
OF A PRE-ENLIGHTENMENT TRUST?

ARE WE:
BLINDLY AND HEARTLESSLY RAMPAGING
THROUGH OUR NATURAL HOME
WITH EYES ON A HEAVEN ABOVE,

OBLIVIOUS TO THE DEVASTATION DONE
TO OUR HEAVEN-ON-EARTH BELOW.

HAVE WE NOW BECOME:
A LOVELESS AND FLIGHTLESS DOVE
DEVASTATED WITHOUT LOVE,
WITHOUT WINGS TO FLY,
WITHOUT A HEART TO FEEL
POISONED BY OUR GREED,
SO ALL WE HAVE LEFT
IS THE TECHNOLOGY PLANTS
FROM OUR TOXIC HUMAN SEED.

WE MUST NOW HEAL THE DOVE:
BECOME HER WINGS AND HER HEART
REFUSE TO BECOME A PART
OF THIS BLIND AND RECKLESS TREK
OBLIVIOUS TO OUR EARTH AWRECK.

LET US
BEGIN TO SOW ON EARTH
THE VIBRANT SEED OF VERITY
AND BEGIN TO GROW THE FRUIT
OF WHAT IS RIGHT AND JUST.

WE EMBARK
BY DARING TO ASK THE LAND,
RIVERS, OCEANS AND SKY
THE IMPORTANT REASON WHY.

THEN
DEFY THE DARKNESS
OF MERE OBEDIENCE AND TRUST:
RISE FROM THE ASHES,
AS THE PHOENIX, WE MUST.

UP
INTO HEAVEN ON WINGED FLIGHT,
UP PAST THE STARS, TO ETERNAL LIGHT

TO RETURN ENLIGHTENED AND READY
TO FIGHT THE DEVOURING NIGHT.

SO KNOW THIS:
EVERY MOMENT IS A GRAIN OF SAND,
SLIPPING THROUGH THE GLASS TO ANOTHER LAND.
DON'T TRY TO CATCH IT, KISS IT GOODBYE,
LEST ANOTHER GRAIN PASSES YOU BY.

BUT DON'T FORGET THE BEAUTY
DON'T FORGET THE LIGHT,
DON'T FORGET TO LOVE
AND DON'T FORGET TO FIGHT.

AND DON'T BURY YOUR SOUL
IN A WORLD OF DESIRE
A HOUSE FULL OF THINGS
FUELS A FUNERAL PYRE.

AND DON'T ALLOW YOUR GIFTS
TO BE STIFLED BY THE WORLD.
JUST LET THEM FLOW
A BRIGHT FLAG UNFURLED.

DON'T FORGET YOUR BROTHER
WHO IS REACHING UP TO YOU.
THE FINAL PORTRAIT OF YOUR SOUL
DEPENDS ON WHAT YOU DREW.

THE GREATEST WRONG
IS TO IGNORE EVIL IN YOUR MIDST.
IF THEY ARE ATTACKING THE INNOCENT
YOU MUST RESIST.

REDEMPTION IS JUSTICE
RENDERED TO ALL.
CONDEMNATION TO THOSE
WHO FAIL TO HEED THE CALL.

SO BOLDLY CAST YOUR NET
ON THE SEA OF LIFE
AND IT WILL RETURN
TO BRING GLORY OR STRIFE.

GOODNESS OR EVIL
WHAT IS YOUR CHOICE?
CAN YOU HEAR
THE MENTOR'S VOICE?

ALL THROUGH THE DOOR
OF DEATH MUST PASS.
LIVE THIS MOMENT
AS YOU WOULD LIVE THE LAST.

SO DARE THE WORLD!
DON'T LET THEM DESTROY YOUR ESSENCE!
SEARCH INSIDE, DOWN, ABOVE AND AROUND
TO ACHIEVE YOUR FULL FLORESCENCE.

INTERPRETATION OF FIRST STANZA OF JUMPROPE SONG

The Jumprope Song is the essence of what I thought were the most important beliefs and values that I could pass on to my children at a young age. It is also poetry which speaks in symbols rather than any literal interpretation. The rhyme scheme, I hope, made it easy to memorize. I remember my daughter (when she was quite young) and I, presenting the Jumprope Song at a poetry get-together at our local library. It was well received.

The introduction of this book contains the simpler of the interpretations of the Jumprope Song. See 'About the Author – 50 Questions to my Father.' The following supplements those interpretations.

Ashes to Ashes, Dust to Dust: This is a Catholic term used at funerals to let everyone know that our bodies were but disposable vehicles to deliver our soul to its ultimate destination. Depending on how we followed the Catholic rules and directives, the soul would continue after death in an eternity of Heaven or Hell. It is a message that reinforces the belief in an afterlife and a critical requirement of abiding by tenets of the faith. We dare not believe our heart or mind should interfere with this directive.

Don't Let Them Destroy Your Essence. Don't Forget the Beauty. The Jumprope Poem rejects this limited *Catholic* viewpoint in favor of searching to find one's unique essence and our connection to nature.

Dare the Darkness of Mere Obedience and Trust. Rise From The Ashes. For me, the 'darkness' and the ashes address and symbolize the daily attacks and deaths within each of us of the spiritual, the creative, the maternal and the very ability to love. These 'deaths' are a consequence of parental control, cultural influences, religion, our job, the economic system, the media, the government and the vast pressures to fit in just to function. These influences are all at work to destroy that uniqueness that distinguishes us. These influences continually work to mold and shape us so, in the assembly line of human widgets, we fit into the bigger machine. So we are talking about the deaths of our inner self.

This notion is articulated in the Lost Gospels. See Chapter III – *LOST GOSPELS EXPLAIN JESUS' MAIN MESSAGE & MY TRANSFORMATION BETTER THAN ANY ACCEPTED CHURCH DOCTRINE.* I submit that if we have continually allowed what is part of us to be destroyed or conformed until the original is gone, we will find nothing when we look within, only *poverty*. (See quotes as part of the introduction of *Let The Children Take Your Heart in Chapter 1* and Ch. 4.4)

Religion is one of the more powerful of the influences that destroy our inner unique being. What cannot be controlled, is punished or destroyed. This was literal in the dark ages. Post-enlightenment, Judeo Christian religion is compelled to be subtler about control. But, ultimately it is directed at destroying that uniqueness, that spiritual, that creative, the maternal and the love for mankind, which does not conform with a One-God Faith. With the devil as the boogieman, we are disliked, insulted, separated, berated, shunned and threatened with eternal damnation for not conforming. Yes, many suffer a million small deaths for their uniqueness and their failure to get on board. *(See Chapter 9 -First Communion Nightmare Revisited.)*

So these deaths, (*the ashes*) are the daily consequence of outside control. The poem, '*The Ashes*' in Chapter VIII, is the extreme of this manner of control. Chapter 10, *"To fight"*, contains some examples of a system attempting to compel conformity. Throughout the book I address how our government, religion and politics have attempted to conform us to the belief that there is no emergency related to our pollution of the environment. *(See Ch. 10 - **A DIAGNOSIS OF THE ENEMY, A REVIEW OF THE ISSUES, A BATTLE PLAN, AND SOLUTIONS**).*

RISE FROM THE ASHES, AS THE PHOENIX, WE MUST: As you know the Phoenix was the mythical creature which, after its destruction, regenerated itself, to live again. My poetic 'directive' follows from what I am talking about in the first line. We must continually regenerate. We must rise from the ashes of the death that the world inflicts on our inner being on a daily basis. We must fight the 'fit in' culture and government with continual regeneration of our maternal, our loving instincts and unique abilities and talents.

I have devoted an entire Chapter (IX - *Don't Allow Your Gifts to be Stifled by the World*) to this idea. Chapter VI – *(Don't Bury Your Soul in a World of Desire)* is again about how we must live to continually rise from the ashes of daily deaths in our being.

So, the poetic line is not tied to our actual physical deaths, but the daily destruction of that unconformed part in us that distinguishes us from the outside world.

UP INTO HEAVEN ON WINGED FLIGHT: If taken religiously or literally, this would mean upwards, away from the earth. The 'Winged Flight', if read literally, would suggest that the Phoenix is literally flying. That would not be accurate. Upwards refers to an elevated state of being. 'Heaven' refers to the tremendous beauty and joy to be found in that heavenly state. The 'Winged Flight' refers to the vehicle – The Phoenix or the embodiment of regeneration from death that I referred to above.

UP PAST THE STARS, TO ETERNAL LIGHT (*If they say to you: 'Where do you come from?' (then) say to them: 'We have come from the light, the place where the light has come into being by itself, has established [itself] and has appeared in their image.'"* (See Saying 50 of the Gospel of Thomas)

Again, this is not literal. However there has been discussion about a place in the universe that houses all the wisdom of time. I am told that the geniuses on earth who have made advanced discoveries, somehow, tapped into this repository of wisdom. I don't know if there is a literal place of enlightenment. I am saying that if we, like the Phoenix, continually regenerate what the world is daily destroying in us, we will find that heaven that is in us and around us. Our 'journey to the light' (towards wisdom and compassion), will enlighten and enhance the 'heavenly' and enable us to see and feel that heaven within and surrounding us.

I have provided this explanation because I believe that the most severe of the evils in our country can be traced to the destruction of our unique inner being. So that now when we look within, all we find is *'poverty'*.

This inner poverty would explain why we would elect a president whose inner being is vacuous. This, I would suggest, is why we incarcerate more people than any other country in the world. This is why we incarcerate far more blacks than their numbers in the population. This is why the rich and the big corporations have controlled production and have polluted to the point of heating up the world and changing the climate patterns for the worse. This is why politicians have become pawns of big money and have sold the public what the public wants to hear. This death of our inner being explains why we tolerate the damage to our environment, the death therefrom and the catastrophe that has already begun and will have dire consequences for our children and grandchildren.

So now you know how a simple sounding poem with such an unthreatening title could say so much. And that is just one part of the poem.

CHAPTER III

DON'T FORGET THE BEAUTY

A. *REMEMBERING NATURE AND CHILDREN*

ON COMMUTING NEAR THE NEW MEXICO BOSQUE IN AUTUMN
On this quiet Sunday
When the world seems tranquil,
My soul is stirred
And my eyes are showered
By the river bank's color-fest of leaves,
Autumn's earth-rainbow
For mother-nature-searching eyes.
I am taken and enthralled
By the breathtaking spectacle
Of the colorful cascade of leaves,
The vivid yellows, once green
Now parading the bosque
Forming a flood
Of bright colored dreams.

It is shortly dusk and
The sun will heed its timely call
And the shadows will silence the colors.
Leaves will yawn silently
As their night whispers:`
It is time to dream.
The early winter wind hums a lullaby
And supple and seemingly secure

Green shades of summer
Whisper a last supplementation.

As they dream of spring
And shutter from the cold,
They hold onto their mother
But as the carriage of life begins to stir,
They signal the sun a sad adieu,
Shut their tired eyes and
Peacefully slip into their autumn nap.
From a life-green,
To a vivid yellow,
Then to a bright orange,
The cool breath of mother night
Will paint them tan,
Then to a dull rust.
And with the gentle and cool fall breath
Even the strongest succumb
And their tenuous hold will break
From what bore and briefly fed them.
Feather-like they will fall
And float to the leaf-filled ground
To dry, crumble and crackle
Neath your children's feet
As nature's soft shawl
O'er the rio's dank skin.

Heaven's radiant illuminator
Dims and fades sooner now.
The subtle message
Signals to the slumbering
That their light,
Whether bright or dull,
Will fade and fall
And join with earth
And with once green tongues,
Now laid soft and silent.
They will blend as fertile
Firmament and food

So more and grander
Alveoli of ancient wood
Can reach to the sun,
Breathe life to the sky
And give birth to petals
Of glorious green,
So children
And their children
Can breathe
And forever bask in the glow
Of timeless color-filled streams
Of children's dreams
Of romping carefree
In the playground
That is the beauty and brilliance
Of autumn in the Bosque.

CANADIAN RIVER IN SABINOSO, NM

RIO (My Childhood Memories)

At three New Mexico cities,
North to south,
I had glimpsed the long
Wet and winding mouth
Of the Rio Grande river.
And each time,
I reveled in the river's splendor,
Its fullness and its depth.
From the distant and high mountains
Of the City of Holy Faith,
From the bridges and banks
Of the dusty City of the Duke
And from the Bosque of Los Lunas,
I saw the grand swath
That its fury had slowly
And subtly carved.
My eyes smiled to caress
It's jagged and winding contours.

I grew up near the Rio Puerco
That we called the "Perky", for short.
It was my playground, my hiking trail,
My camp-site and companion.
I knew its violence in the summers
When its angry rushing waters
Carried away all that was untethered.

And within a stone's throw
From this part-time river,
Lived the most memorable of women
Who I knew as "Maye".
She was my grandma,
My mother's mom
And my babysitter
Who watched me
While my parents worked.
Her first residence was in San Marcial
Whose last residents' homes
Were buried in a graveyard
Of cold water and darkness.
Maye left in time but other families
Did not fare so well.
Their belongings, ornaments and treasures
Lay quietly buried and at rest at the bottom
Of the consuming path
Of this unrelenting robber of a river
That respected the rights of no resident
Who lucklessly happened to live
In its devouring pathway.
All that these forlorn folks had left

Was rendered useless.
Like a sunken Spanish galleon
On the losing side of a battle
With an enemy as treacherous
As pitiless pirates without a conscience,
Bent on total devastation,
Homes and valuables
Were buried in a watery grave
Never to be joined with the living.

Like the sailor that returns to the sea,
When Maye moved to my home town of Gallup,
She moved next to the Rio Puerco.
Once again, the impulsive and dangerous one
Had become her neighbor.
Though it would rage only in July and August,
In Maye's magnificent mind,
The moving dark memory of San Marcial
Must have remained
In some deep hidden part of her.
Like the deadly tidal wave
Of the Spanish Flu epidemic
That took her husband
And father in 1918,
Leaving her mom and her alone
To raise four young daughters,
The seasonal threat of mad rushing waters
Escaping their fragile dirt walls
Must have been permanently etched
In my Maye's marvelous memory.

I am recollecting a unique day
In my childhood in Gallup, New Mexico,
Right across Sullivan street from Maye's yard
Where I and scores of others
Stood on the threshold
Of God's greatest natural gift and punishment.

Like naïve soldiers
Viewing the first atomic bomb blast,
Adults and children stood gawking
At a river gone mad.

We were transfixed by the power
Of a roaring wall of undammed fury,
Now madly flowing passed us and
Growing, ever higher,
Daring to devour my Maye's footbridge,
Whose wooden bottom was a safe 25 feet
From what was usually
The sandy bed of the Perky's path.
And now, frighteningly,
This roaring wall of water,
A mere hundred and fifty feet from
Maye's house and yard,
Threatened another San Marcial nightmare.
Six feet from the precipice of the raging river,
Standing only on a bank made of sand
We were riveted and were witnessing
The long twisting mouth of life
Suddenly disgorge its overflow
In what we called a flash-flood.

It was relentlessly fed upstream
By a wailing wall of tears of a tormented heaven.

All of us should have known
From experience and good sense
That it's unbridled anger would rip and carry away
The unsuspecting or oblivious
Who dared near its furious path.
And we heard about them on the news, the next day,
Those who fell asleep, on a cool outdoor soft bed;
Those who drank to a deep slumber
One nightcap too many,
To die in a watery grave in the morn.
They were those
Who did not care or who trusted life
To remain the same, and never learned
Until too late,
That furious nature has its own plan.
Those who were unfortunate enough
To live beneath the level of the river's banks,
Would find these waters
Rushing into their yard, front rooms and basements
And like a bold burglar, who fears not to be caught,
This wicked water's intrusion
Would change Gallupians' lives forever.

As the rushing and unrelenting waters rose
And flowed over the wooden walking path of the bridge
And now when the waves
Were perilously close to the wooden hand rail
That spanned the length of the bridge

And violently threatening
Maye's wood and metal
Connection with the rest of the town,
Some insane teenager actually
Leaped onto the flat hand-railing
And in a bizarre display of bravado,
Dangerously dared the mad river,
Now just inches from his foolish feet
To take him home.
He walked the entire length of the bridge
And jumped onto dry land on the other side.
And just as the waves threatened to reach
The wide flat wooden hand rails of the bridge
That had miraculously allowed its last passenger,
And just as the mad youngster jumped
From the vehicle of his death,
A bridge securely connected to ground
At each end,
A permanent fixture of so many years,
Was violently torn from its metal moorings.
A loud screeching sound could be heard by all,
Causing the less daring to jump back.
We then witnessed the roaring and roiling waters
Convert our walking bridge into a sailing barge
And see it, Fellini-like, be ferried downstream
as a prisoner of nature's angry and wild whim.
As I jumped back, I knew for sure
That, like a magician's tablecloth act
The dirt we stood on
Would be yanked away beneath us
And we would be sucked into the monster river.

Didn't anyone else realize this?
Why were we even standing here?

Suddenly, violently and unexpectedly,
The illusion of permanence and life's continuity
Was rudely ripped away.
It was my first moving lesson about nature's
Power, passion and unpredictability.
Does the world still believe that a wall
Will stop a mad and raging ocean?
In some way I sensed and felt the same awe
Of our most ancient ancestors
Who respected nature by worshiping it.
Now I too had learned of nature's God-like powers.
Here, nature had stunningly reached out to me
And in a show of power,
Threatened my being
And forever grabbed my respect.

Here, in rushing waters, unbridled and violent,
Was the same matter that flooded through
Our bodies and our planet of liquid blue.
It was neither evil nor good.
It was nature.
It was the very essence of our being.
The rage and the serene
And all the unpredictable consequences.
It was life and death
Separated by a few feet of earth.
I marveled and I shuttered.
When the heavens cried no more

And the river lost its ire,
And mud evaporated back into sand,
Brave explorers were again drawn
Into the magnificent snaking swath,
Now dry and sandy, the only beach
We Gallupians had.
Like pirates and treasure hunters,
Oblivious to the dangers lurking therein,
We returned to the now waterless hollow
Across from my Maye's street
To again become noble adventurers in a trip
Up the winding and exposed belly of the beast.

Our playground was now
Newly tailored by the storm.
Who knew what discoveries were to be unearthed!
We fool-heartedly ignored the hidden quicksand
Our mothers warned us about.
Because somewhere we would discover
The lost and discarded treasure
That would make us kings.
Or at least contain the secrets of the universe.

On these adventures,
I always had one eye to the sky and up-river,
Lest the white fluffy face of God
Were to turn dark and gloomy
And direct its diluvian message downward
And a giant wall of water would come rushing down
To sweep us away and we would never be found.
Nah! I would see it coming and sprint to climb up

The sometimes steep perky walls
Or so my child-mind figured.
We were always a moment,
A few feet away
From becoming a part of the fury
That a worried working mother warned us about.
A warning unheeded.
Such is my memory
Of New Mexico rivers as a child.

RIO GALLINAS IN LAS VEGAS, NM FLOODING

MY COMMENTARY ON 'RIO'

In Las Vegas, one of my children's favorite things to do is the "river-walk". We are about a football field away from the Gallinas River, a bit further than my grandma Maye's house was from the Rio Puerco in Gallup. On these walks, the children have fished, spotted snakes, been bitten by a snake, floated rafts, thrown rocks, searched for cool rocks, 'discovered' alien bugs and just enjoyed trekking through nature's beauty.

Recently we were flooded and spent three days bailing the water out of the basement. So now we have experienced both faces of the Rio – the rage and the serene.

The poem, 'Rio' should reveal how my child-self and now, how my children and children everywhere, love an adventure, even if it is risky. They love the experience of living in the middle of nature without walls to limit the feel or their view.

And then we get older and become tired and afraid of the unpredictability of nature. 'Rio' was my effort to travel back to the days when my neighbor and childhood buddy, Jimmy Ramsey and I dared to challenge our bi-polar pal, the Rio Puerco.

My kids' experiences reminded me of those days of the last century and reignited my love and respect for nature.

MONSTER STORM BUILDING between VEGAS and SANTA FE BY MARTIN LOPEZ

NEW MEXICO STORM

Memory send me to an August storm,

Where thunderheads build till plumbed giants form.

Show me a beautiful and silent white fluffed explosion

Upwards and outwards in tantalizing slow motion.

I see one o'r the Sandias, blooming and billowing white,

Warriors and angels, fragile facades of dream light.

So awesome, so bright, this elegant alluring lie

Of beauty and form, Greek gods brought nigh.

Then, Heaven's soft white feathers on azure slowly fade,

Grey curtains fall like an ominous shade.
Power to enthrall, power to delight,
As pillowed fluffs of light darken, God's face turns fright.

I see sharp and jagged messages of white streaking lights,
A neighbor reminding – Don't ignore this sight!
Is this His beautiful creative mind we see?
Or the magical show that nature gives for free?

Downward dripping, snow-white panther casing his prey,
White powdered paws reaching, teasing, then melting away.
Riveted by the cinema of haunting shapes,
Captured and raptured, your mind can't escape.
Entranced and awed by the theater of light,
Thor's hammer rocks you from your skyward delight.
You're pummeled by cool drops, quickening their pace,
And thoughts turn to deluge, biblical rage.

What spectacle of the sky could ever compare?
Save streams of colors now arcing dusk's air.
As the bold eye of God burns red into night,
Flaming crimsons, golds and purples glorify God's good night.

Is this Heaven we touch, night, its refrain?
Will this spectacle of the sky forever remain?
Will our children and grandchildren be dazzled
By the pageantry and theater in the sky?
Or will the future show of splendor from above
Be a tragedy of poison and drought brought nigh?

So please take in that beauty.
Become the storm, become the lightning in the night.

Spread the warning like the pre-storm breeze.
Alert all - Become the bold,
Frightening thunderous call to fight.
Shake the world with your words,
Wake up the sleeping night sky.
Save your children from the poison,
Hear earth's wailing cry!
Open your heart to the beauty.
Let the heavens touch your soul.
Look around and upwards.
The beauty to inspire will find
Your searching and loving eye.

Photo by author

Each kind of tree is a sort of musical instrument: the apple a cello, the old oak a bass viol, the cypress a harp, the willow a flute, the young pine a muted violin. Put your ear close to the whispering branch and you may catch what it is saying.
Guy Murchie, Jr.

Granma's Tree by Ai'

THE THE KIDS IN THE TREES
SONG: GREEN GRASS GROWS ALL AROUND
Sung by Pete Seeger and many others
Lyricist - William Jerome. Melody by Harry Von Tilzer

TO LOVE A TREE

In A Hating Sea

With No Empathy

I had always loved our rivers

And the bridges that spanned their void

And the thrill of the water rushing near.

But I'd never loved a tree.

I'd never had a treehouse,
Nor much liked to climb.
Nor would mom ever approve of it.
You might fall on your head, you know!

The poor Chinese Elms
Were derided by all
For destroying foundations
And ruining pipes.
Could this have been a racial antipathy?
Would they have been loved more
If named American Elms or USA trees?
Could it have been a 'Communist' fear?
The Chinese were trying to destroy
The very foundation of our society!
No domino theory needed here.
The Communists had already
Planted their roots
In the very foundation of our lives.

I thought of those roots
Like the snakes from Pandora's head,
Reaching out and strangling
All who dared near.

Sure, I had heard
That only God could make a tree,
And I'd seen the giant redwoods in a postcard.
And of late, I had become aware

Of the mass of giant wood alveoli
Around the Rio Grande, we call the Bosque.
My vision soared to glimpse the majesty
Of the tall pine trees of McGaffe, near Gallup.
Never had I seen so many, towering so high
Like giant soldiers, all at attention,
Saluting the sacred sky.

But I could not come to love them.
I could not see them for what they were.
They were there...like earth we trample on,
The abundant water we drink,
The omnipresent air that we breathe...
For me, they were all mere props,
Not-so-fancy green shades
On the makeshift outdoor stage of my child-life.

Trees were nice for protection from the sun,
But I could always go inside.
When it came time for raking the lawn,
I hated those messy trees.
Just as my mother hated
The incessant dust on the furniture
That she insisted on cleaning daily.
Why can't we just get rid of the source-
The leaf-shedding trees?

And now, wasted years later,
I realize why

My dire and deadly disconnect
From earth, sky and sun
And the mother that provides all:
I grew up in Gallup, New Mexico
'Indian Capital of the World'!
No one told them that
Columbus didn't discover India!

The Native Americans
Who loved and respected
A Mother-Earth that was part of them,
Were now ravaged and relegated
To reservations.
The children of those who lived close to nature,
Were torn from their families
And forced to attend Christian boarding schools
To 'civilize and Christianize' them.
These vicious transformation centers
Operated on the racist premise and plan:
'Kill the Indian...Save the Man'*
They were but 'savages' to the white victor.
These 'schools' were worse than penitentiaries.
'Educated' meant everything 'Indian'
Was demeaned, demolished and removed -
Their appearance, their language, their habits, their clothing,
Their beliefs, cultural and religious,
And even their names.

The cruel consequence was a Native American
Whose essence of goodness and the love of nature
Was terrorized, tortured and anything 'Indian'
Was ruthlessly rooted out — *
All part of the racist policy
Directed to the vanquished red-man,
The inferior of the superior white Christian!
The Native-Americans
Were once a proud people,
Who lived close to and respected the earth.
They were now brainwashed and decultured
By believers in a Judeo Christian God
Who had long been divorced from mother earth
And now resided at a non-earth location
Allegedly accessible by a prayer-line,
If you were on the right faith network.

These Gallupians who fully accepted
The white man's superiority
Over those who lived close to the earth,
Understood all through the eyes
Of how much it could make them.
They saw the soil, it's fruits, sun and trees
As heartless and soulless, a mere means,
A supply, a material and cold capital.

The tree was but a means to build a house.
It had no value, unless cut down

To shelter us from the bipolar
And unpredictable whims of nature —
Hot to cold, wet then dry,
Snow, then hail then sleet
Windy then calm,
Hardly a loving mom!

The dead tree-wood
Was but an insulating balm
From nature's inhuman harangues.
The lifeless wood from the tree
Was merely the wall and cover to protect us
From the serial assaults of dastardly nature.
Otherwise, the tree was valueless.

The 'Indians' were not much more
Than the coal from Gallup's coal mine
Or the uranium ore from the uranium mines,
Or that idle tree in the forest.
They had worth only
If we could profitably use them
To build our wealth and to make money.
Otherwise all the above was nice
But valueless if not consumed for profit.
Native Americans were treated no differently -
They were but the main attraction
To lure and build Gallupian's wealth.

To the vicious victor went the supremacist spoils:
The vanquished native
Whose essence of goodness and the love of nature
Suffered the cruelest of consequences:
Like their children in the racist schools,
They were inhumanely treated
And anything 'Indian'
Was callously removed. —*
All part of the racist policy of demeaning the vanquished,
The inferior of the superior white Christian!

To the above, add further humiliation:
Those who had long been in contact
With Mother Earth
Were now callously compelled
By the cold Gallupian capitalists
To publicly demonstrate and dance
That which was sacred to them-
Their religious ceremony.

And all this
For a crass people and country
That, without a second thought,
Had relegated Native-America
To second-class citizenship.

I grew up in this callous country
Where nature and those who loved earth

Had been heartlessly reduced
To the earth-covered, asphalt-paved street stage
Where they were tastelessly transformed
Into dancers for dollars
To parade their religious ceremonial wares
And to advertise the *'Indian Capital of the World.'*
It was through these unfeeling eyes
And insensitive hearts,
I was expected
To see and feel the world.
In this town, that severely suffered
From a case of nature-disconnect,
The poor trees never had a chance
To reach out and touch my soul.
Gallup painted the arboreal portrait
So it's worth was measured in dollar bills,
The more money it made,
The more beauty it portrayed!

Then, I left Gallup for a degree
And I thought Gallup had left me.
I fell in love in Albuquerque.
Sally and I married
And after we sadly thought
That we would never conceive life —
We Did!
Alizandra and Amadeo were born.
I suddenly had my eyes opened.

I could finally see the trees
And they were so beautiful!

No longer were they scary haunts
And witches' claws
At dusk in leafless fall.
They now beckoned to my children,
And my children to them.
They asked to be seen,
To be climbed, to be a friend.
Trees were born to me through my kids.

With the new-found antennae
God had given me
Through my children,
I could feel and hear
The deafening screams
Of the dying and disappearing rain forests
Being razed with blazing speed.
I listened to the buzz saw,
The scream of "timberrr"
And the deafening sound
Of fresh-felled wood -
Another lung exploding!

I could smell the smoke
Coming from the arboreal family
Of tall powerful brown
And green camouflaged sentinels

Whose job was to diligently transform
Human poison to life's sustaining breath.
They were now ablaze
From the searing heat ignited by
The big-brained beasts
Who chose comfort and wealth
In a country that was content to live
In a technologically transformed matrix,
Deaf to the sounds of death,
Devoid of empathy to see, hear and feel
The scream of a mother
Whose lungs were being torn
And burned out from her tender bosom.

On wings of my children's
Miraculous birth
I soared eagle-like
To the elevated perch
Of my comfortable nest
In the new-found giant tree,
Secluded on the lofty mountain-top,
Beyond the darkening shadows
I touched the luminous sunlight
And it enlightened my view.

I could now see over mountain ranges;
I could see beyond the present;
I could now connect with the future.

My children were my wings
And through their hungry innocent eyes
I cringed to see us racing to the future
Of plastic trees and plants
And pavement instead of grass,
Cement and steel skyscrapers
And vast cattle ranges
In place of the natural majesty
Of arboreal splendor.
I could see a world choking
And dying, devoid of the magic
Of our mother's saving lungs
Because no one respected
The invisible life's-breath,
The gift our heavenly trees endow.

And like that branch
You trim from the big tree
And plant in the desert,
And for years you think
It is just a lifeless stick in the ground,
Just deadwood, so stiff and dry,
One day, Pinocchio-like
It comes to life!
A real tree!
It actually turns green and blossoms.
That branch was me.
My children were the rain, the sun

And the mystical magic of love
That made the wood come alive
And changed me, so now
I can love a tree.

*According to Col. Richard Pratt's speech in 1892: 'A great general has said that the only good Indian is a dead one, and that high sanction of his destruction has been an enormous factor in promoting Indian massacres. In a sense, I agree with the sentiment, but only in this: that all the Indian there is in the race should be dead. Kill the Indian in him, and save the man." On March 3, 1819, the Civilization Fund Act ushered in an era of assimilationist policies, leading to the Indian boarding-school era, which lasted from 1860 to 1978. The act directly spurred the creation of the schools by putting forward the notion that Native culture and language were to blame for what was deemed the country's "Indian problem." (See 'the Atlantic' EDUCATION Death by Civilization by Mary Annette Pember March 8, 2019

*"Investigations of the later twentieth century have revealed many documented cases of sexual, manual, physical and mental abuse occurring mostly in church-run schools." See Wikipedia American Indian boarding schools

Martin with Ali', Sally and Amadeo

AN ADVENTURE THROUGH CARLSBAD CAVERNS WITH MY SON AT AGE 56

My son and I descend by an elevator
Directly down into the earth, miles deep
To glimpse a hidden ancient treasure.
Concerned about what I had read,
I had asked about atomic testing nearby
And we were assured by the tour guide
That in this deep cave, we are safe.

After the deep descent we arrive
In the promised secure and buried bowels
Beneath the New Mexico desert
And begin the trek into
A giant frame of
A frozen moment of time.

My son and I gawk and gasp
At the immense space of a hidden underground church,

Replete with vast domed ceilings and grand grottos,
Deftly decorated with saintly etchings of an ancient artist.
We are told of a place once with water and reefs
That now is transformed into an expertly chiseled church.

We gaze totem poles tracing to an ancient tribal religion
That tell us of an artist with an eternity of time
Who knew not to rush this masterpiece.
Behold the spires spawned of
An ancient and foreign architect.
Giant and vast rounded pillars,
Like gargantuan bloated grey appendages
Expanding skyward from the ground
And downwards from the distant ceiling.
At an undetectable rate
They grow towards each other
Like Heaven's giant limbs
Reaching downwards
And Hells' frozen swollen searching figures
Dreaming upwards,
As if to one day, greet and grasp
And in gazing their sameness, recognize
They are mere manifestations
Of each other.

In this slow-motion world,
Hope is a drop of lime water
That will one day,
A very long day,
Seal the grasp between
The searching lost appendages,
One painstakingly slow drop at a time,
Hundreds of millions of years slow.

Ama and I are both in awe
As we survey and struggle to digest
The genius of the handiwork.
We are surrounded by a cool and eerie calm
Like the silence of a sacred setting

As during the offering of the body and blood
In the solemn miraculous moment of the Catholic mass.

In a stark reversal of
The Old Testament God, Jehovah
Whose face you dared not gaze*
Or name you dared not say in vain,
Lest you wished to die,
In this church, merely touching
The face and treasures of the creator,
Infects the eyes of the maker
And ultimately destroys the creations.

What a trusting design-maker, this artist,
To design a shelter so delicate,
Like a house made of bubbles
That empowers all living creatures
To massacre its masterpieces by simple touch.
Perhaps a designer/architect
That has bestowed free will
Or just the work of nature
That always whispers:
Enjoy the beauty
Do not devour it
As it will never return.

Behold buried in the bowels of the earth
The bizarre behavior of bacteria
That survives without food;
That feast on rocks
And lives without sunlight.
They have the power to destroy other bacteria.
From what dimension is this deviant life form?

Maybe the future creature,
More hardy than humanity
That patiently waits to replace us
Once we corrupt all the beauty.

Behold the beauty and peace of the hidden Heaven
And one does not have to die to delight in its splendor!
The majesty is now spread out before our voracious eyes,
Where the frozen fox gazes peacefully at its home.
See the giant dragons and gorgons,
Lion tales linger, and fairies frolic free.
Popcorn-shaped food
Grows and delicately details the ceiling and walls.

What is the meaning of this miraculous marvel of nature?
What dimension of time and space?
What nature the planet
That hides these DaVinci-like sculptures?
Is this underground castle, a creation,
So beautiful and complex,
That only a divine mind could design it?
Or could the genius of mother nature
Be solely responsible for this creation?
What remarkable seed to spawn such a sight?
Or astonishing mind to create such a seed?
Or is this the cave house of the oracle
That predicts that man will soon devour and infect
All the beauty that feeds, inspires and sustains him?

Exodus 33:20 ESV But," he said, "you cannot see my face, for man shall not see me and live."

AMADEO'S SECRET FISHING HOLE

AMADEO CATCHING FISH IN CANADA

ALI', CAMICE AND AMADEO FISHING by Ali' at age 7

"The kingdom is inside you and it is outside you."
The Gospel of Thomas

I AM A FISHERMAN
By Amadeus Reed-Lopez and Martin Lopez

I am the son of my mother's family
Who were poor and who fished
For food, for fun and reveled in the warming sun.
The lakes, rivers and streams
Flow powerfully in my blood.
There is no separation from these liquid dream streams
That flow around my being.
We are one.

I am a distant descendent of the Apostle Peter
Who was a fisherman, and becoming Jesus-inspired,
Became a fisher of men.

In the dry deserts of New Mexico
The rivers and lakes call me.
Storrie, Murphy, Bluewater, Conchas Lake,
Lake 13, Sabinoso, Gallinas, Gila, Pecos…..
They are like family
That demand my time and attention.
And I could not and can never deny their call.

I was heavenly hooked
At my family's very first fishing trip.

My baptism by earth's waters
Miraculously transformed me into a new person.
God-like, the mere casting of rod, string, hook and bait
Brought forth life at my fingertips and control.
Alleluia! Did no one else know about this miracle?
Others did come, but at the water's edge,
I was always in my own world…….
Until you asked what was inside of me.

I recollect at seven, the discovery of a tennis racquet
And my near-perfect connection to the tennis ball.
I shed my shyness in exchange for control of my world.
My miraculous stringed tennis staff

Consumed snakelike all opponents' sorcerer-sourced snakes,
And lifted me to the podium of victory.

A State Championship and a scholarship
Were the fruits
Of this mystically stringed-racquet of control.
But now, with fishing, I experienced an epiphany:
Could the miraculous message of my mystical rod
With string and hook
Open a path to the Promised Land,
Just as Moses parted the Red Sea with his staff?
Could my dry words, a lifeless rock, be transformed
By the baptism of my rod, line and hook
Into the flowing and moving water of an idea?
Could this humble message touch a world,
Now blinded by bright lights, high tech and the dazzle of a dollar?

The rod and reel entwines me with the earth.
Nature's bounty in rivers, streams and lakes
Have connected me with my mother, planet blue.
Not merely, as the racquet and tennis ball
Gave me control,
But, in discovering my place and role
In the bigger sacred scheme of life
Where fishing is but a small but enlightening part
Of the greater masterpiece we call earth.

It is about a mother that will
Give unto death
To protect me
So I will never starve.
The other powerful inspiration, was the daunting
And silent scream from the choking and sorrowful sky!
Was my little fishing hole next?
What was to become of my finned friends?
Do I have some duty to preserve
This living breathing liquid monument of life and joy
For my children and grandchildren, yet unborn?
Must I too act like the mother salmon
Who risk their existence
By swimming upstream
Through dangerous rivers and streams
To lay their eggs and then die?
Must I preserve the lake and stream
And keep it dream-clean

For all the mother salmons of the world?
For if there is no stream, there is no future life.

I have learned that I must act as if
My little lake is like the last of the liquid fishing grounds.
Its' death destroys mine and everyone's godly gift
To delight and survive from the fruits born of
The ever so thin protective skin
Of our skies, earth and waters of life.

I have rediscovered the original holy truth about existence:
God is that sacred perfection in nature
And the divine complex connections that
Sustain the glorious and regal gift of the planet.
We, the beneficiaries of this godly gift,
In this ingeniously intertwined creation,
Must discover and actively direct
Our maternal love for the planet
Even unto death.
We forever lose our earthly paradise
By ignoring the delicate connections
Between nature and man that permeate our being.
We must re-entwine with our earthen mother,
Or see, feel, hear and touch her, never more.

Earth is not a mere techno-stage upon which
We construct our techno-industrial toys
And then cast away the left-overs!

Stop destroying my family's playground!!
I want to fish forever!!
I want my future families to fish forever!!
So as you see,
I, the fisherman, have become
One of the fishers of men,
Or maybe
Fishers of nature's family of friends.
Nature's example has, like the sun,
Warmed my cactus flowers to blossom
So I have finally found my maternal side.
So every time I fish, it is a prayer:
Revel in your gift, but protect it.
Every act of destruction of our gift
Of the waters of life,
Severs our connection with God.
Our disregard for this plentiful bounty of nature

Destroys our descendant's future gifts.
Closing our eyes to damaging this planet of blue
Will bring nature's miracle to a turbulent end.
We will no longer embrace this verdure bestowal
With a planet bereft of its natural state.
We will never suckle from
The beauty and sustenance
Of that magnificent and glorious stream
Of heavenly delights of our earthly river of life.

We, nature's fishers of men
Cannot and will not fail
To heed nature's desperate and dying call!

By Amadeus Reed-Lopez and Martin Lopez

(Around the time this was written, my brother Dave had initiated a search to determine our ancestral roots by tracing our appellations. Amadeo's grandma Mollie, my birth mother, submitted her blood to be analyzed. Among many surprises, we all discovered that we had, amongst other roots, Jewish roots from Spain. We were all delighted and, as you can see by the poem, inspired!)
(Caveat: Since I had the final draft, the picture of my son may be more of how I would like him to be than the actuality. His life was the first draft.

A NEW MEXICO CACTUS BLOOMING (Photo taken by author)

B. NATURE, CHILDREN AND THE END OF LIFE

Don't you understand what I' trying to say?
And can't you feel the fears I'm feeling today?
....
And you tell me over and over and over again my friend.
Ah, you don't believe we're on the eve of destruction.

Eve of Destruction
Lyricists P.F. Sloan and Steve Barri
Sung by Barry McGuire

"Earth could turn into a hothouse planet like Venus with boiling oceans and acid rain, if humans don't curb irreversible climate change. Trump's decision to pull us out of the Paris Accords could be the tipping point."
Stephen Hawking, in a recent interview before his death

Dear Grandpa

Dear Grandpa:
Wherever you might be
Or are you anywhere?
They say you were a trial lawyer;
That you could even write
And would always try to do the right thing
And your brother was a trial lawyer,
Student body president and Harvard educated
And your other brother was a very smart businessman
And great-great grandma Mollie had a Masters in education.
Impressive blood family from which I come!
So, what did any of you do
To save:
The trees
And the wonderful smell
After the rain kissed the leaves;
The sky with a sun we could see;
Water we could drink
And air that didn't stink?

And you knew the dirty air and water
Was killing millions when you lived.
It is far worse now!
What did you and your family
Do to stop it grandpa?
Did you not think about your grandkids
And the family that came after you?

Although I never met you,
I've read your book and saw the pictures
That you never published before you died.
You knew so much about our country
And you learned to appreciate the beauty,
Albeit, late in your life.
I am so grateful that your children inspired you
To write the book that has connected me to you.
Thank you for sharing this inspired book
And Uncle Amadeo for bringing it to me.
But what took you so long?

You showed me many and different trees
That your children played on or around!
They were all so beautiful!

To me they were our life-emanating
Giant and silent wooden protectors
That would keep us safe from the sun and bad air.
They would spread their branches and leaves
Like a giant umbrella to protect us from the heat
So the breezes were cool
And I learned that these thoughtful trees
Filtered out the bad air for good air
So you could care-freely inhale
The sweetness of the earth.

That was when the air was clean.
Now it is but a dream!

Then,
Our friends, the trees existed in abundance.
One teacher uncomfortably shared with me
That the trees use to clean the air
Before they were either cut or burned down
Or were the scorched victims of a fevered earth.
But now they are gone grandpa!

We are left with big and growing deserts
That have replaced our friends the trees
And the plants we need to survive.

That dust-bowl you had in the Thirties…
It's starting here and is growing…
Everywhere in the world!
And the big machines that industry said
Could take the place of the trees,
Cannot seem to do what natures' wonders could do.
There is talk about moving to Mars
But only the billionaires can afford it.
Oh great! Leave everybody else to suffer and die!

So grandpa, tell me:
You and Dave could convince juries of 12
But didn't think the future of your children
Was important enough
To do everything in your power to
Convince the State and country
That their children and grandchildren
Would suffer and die if we did nothing
To fight the scourge of pollution?
Did Great Uncle Pete figure

It was just a bad investment
To make an issue of the environmental catastrophe,
Even though his family would be victims?
Or was he saving his money
To afford their escape to Mars?

I am gazing out my window at noon
And can feel
The debilitating dry heat of the drought
And see only a dreary darkness.
I smell a sickly-sweet stench of decay
And a worsening spoiled smell.
So many things are dying, different animals too.
The News says we can't go outside today
Lest we want to breath in
The poison and the smoke and get sick.
It has been that way for a month!

Since the devastating diluvial destruction
By storms, hurricanes and tornados
To our coasts and the world's low-lying coasts,
The United States and everywhere else
Have been in the greatest economic depression ever.
Mass migrations to livable land
Are occurring everywhere and causing chaos.
Seems with the increasingly hot temperatures,
The bugs are reproducing faster than ever
And guess what they are eating?
Anything that tries to grow.
Farming communities everywhere in the world
Have been devastated.
Nobody has enough food.
And if that wasn't enough,
New diseases are sickening and killing
All around the world,
Connected to destroying the forests,
That make your Covid pandemic
Look like nothing.

It wasn't supposed to be this way grandpa.
It seems that you knew the problem
And you had family that could get it done
But you didn't do enough to stop the polluters
And their oppression of nature.
You lived luxuriously and benefitted

From all of the polluter-provided comforts
While millions were dying!
Now your family is dying!

You didn't do enough
To save our passive protective arbors.
And now it is too late!
Didn't anybody understand that
There are consequences for destroying nature?
That there are deadlines
For getting the earth's temperature lower
To avoid devastation?
Even I know that when I have a high temperature
I better act to get it down or I will die.
How could they not know
That same idea was true for the earth's health?

It seems as if even God
Has contracted a fatal disease
Or worse yet, has died.
Wouldn't He have fixed this,
Or inspired us to fix it?
Or did He know that
When he endowed the perfect world of nature
To us for safekeeping,
He was condemning it and mankind.
And now He is punishing us?

He could have given us some better direction,
Like, nature is sacred and god-like
Love it and treat it like family.
But He didn't
And here we are!
The Church people seem content.
They say it's time to repent
For the apocalypse is drawing near
And we best get our house in order
Or we will have eternal hell to fear.
They must not have looked outside
And seen that hell has long-ago
Begun burning here
In our once earthly heaven
To all we hold near and dear.

.

How blind would people have to be!
Yet they almost seem smug
As if to say that they had it right.
Well I don't think I'll be raptured.
I just never believed like them.

In your days shouldn't the church-people
Have been talking about how particularly devastating
A heated-up earth would be for poor people?
Did the church people forget Jesus' essential lesson:
What you do unto the least of my brethren,
You do unto me?

The church-people say I should be excited
About this horrendous mess
Since I will see you that much sooner
In their Heaven in the sky.
I have this awful feeling grandpa
That their Heaven in the sky
Has now been transformed
Into a fiery oven.
If it is any part of earth's scorching sky,
I see only a hell to look forward to.

So should I be happy
Like the church-people tell me, grandpa?
Or has it all been a pathetic hoax
That the government,
Big business, the rich guys
Their buddies, the churches
Our parents and teachers
Sold us, to keep us
Quiet, obedient and content,
Hooked on your meat and dairy
And addicted to buying unnatural
And deadly consumer crap
And discarding our garbage everywhere,
Raping nature in the process?

So, did no one do anything
Because God was to take care of it all?
And nature was there
For whatever we wanted to do with it?
Or because people thought it was impolite
To disagree or make a scene
Or look stupid if they were wrong?

When we were still able to go to school
My teacher chided me when I asked:
Why we waited until it was too late
To clean up the earth and save the trees?
There was nothing that could be done!
She sternly sounded
As if I was the one who was at fault.

She told me:
You should not be asking questions like that!
It is unpatriotic.
It was obviously God's will
And she ended the class,
Leaving us all to digest what happens
When you question God's will.
I know you wouldn't tell me that!
But did that explanation work with everyone else?
And wasn't there a Pope
Who shamed Capitalists
For putting the dollar
Over taking care of the earth and the poor?
And why didn't they listen
To the Holy Man grandpa?

And wasn't there a losing president named Gore
Who warned you of the coming tragedy
If we did not stop polluting our earth?
Why did no one listen to this wisdom?
Why would they have voted for the other guy?
And what about that brilliant Barry Commoner guy
Who made it clear that everything is connected in nature?
That when you throw your garbage into nature and
Pollute the earth, air and water,
The consequences to humanity are disastrous.
Why didn't we elect him for president?
So now, I guess
We are having the silent spring!
If it were just silence,
I would be okay!

Maybe it is true what they say:
That humanity is just a deadly virus
That needs to be cured by extinction.
But I don't want to die!
When we had a yard with one tree,

We used to have a tree-house
Until they made us take it down
Because it was against the law to deface nature.
Is that pathetically funny grandpa?
Did they punish people then
For crimes that didn't hurt anyone?
Funny gramps, that you were punished
For enjoying nature's feel-good flower
But they let the big industries
Destroy the flowers, trees, earth's creatures
And humanity
As if there were no consequences.
I guess greed and apathy did us in.

Or was the government too busy
Putting black, brown and poor white folks behind bars
For smoking weed and other feel-good drugs
And then making them work for practically nothing?
Sounds like slavery to me!
Is it really true grandpa that the United States
Jailed more people
Than any other country?
Is that why nobody did anything?
They feared being incarcerated
Or stigmatized or ostracized
If they spoke their mind
And then they would not be able to get a job
To support their family?
Is it true grandpa that the elected politicians
Were bought out by the big Corporate Interests
And the corporations made money polluting the environment
And the politicians made a fortune for their service to the SuperPacs?
And that even the Supreme Court jumped in
And said that was just fine… First Amendment rights!

Is that why nobody did anything?
They felt powerless?
That is how I feel grandpa.

And wasn't your generation - the baby-boomers,
Touted for standing up to the establishment
Speaking your mind in spite of the consequences,
Bringing a bad war to an end and forcing a president to resign?
Did you just lose your energy to fight what was wrong?
What was stopping you grandpa?

I feel so alone grandpa
And so very hungry!

You know our polar ice caps are all gone!
And deadly viruses hidden for eons
Have now been uncovered
And are causing great sickness.
I know you knew because the book,
Climageddon told you about this.

The oceans are getting hotter and rising.
Our cities on the east, south and west coasts
Were destroyed by devastating storms
And great flooding.
Everyone tried to move more inland.
But, unless you are rich,
There is no room.
States have border police
To keep people from entering from other states.

It has been how I think it would be
Where desperate and dying citizens
Of a foreign war-torn country
Were trying to escape to another country,
But there are too many desperate people
And too few resources to accommodate them
And they are being turned away
But they have no place to go.
So many people
Are suffering and dying grandpa!

It is getting even darker and harder to breathe grandpa.
And I am so thirsty!
There is a forest fire nearby
In one of our last forests.
There has been no rain for so long
And it is getting hotter and hotter.

If I go through hell here will I go to Heaven later?
What if there is no later?
What if earth is our only heaven?
What then grandpa?

I am waiting for Uncle Amadeo to come.
I don't know how, but he has managed
To grow a garden so we can eat

And somehow, he keeps us supplied with water.
I don't know how he is doing this.
All around us,
People are starving and dying of thirst.
But his great skills in living off the grid
And being in tune with nature
Have made it possible for my survival.

I only know
I would be dead without him.
He is getting older now.
I just hope he has not been ambushed
By starving people
Who now have my food and water.

Can you even hear me?
Speak to me dear grandpa!
Tell me what to do now.
I need help.
I just don't understand
Why you would have let this happen?

Love, Your Granddaughter, Amali'

SALLY, MY WIFE, AND HER FATHER, CHARLES REED, (CHUCK).

TO MY WIFE ON HER DAD'S DEATH
(Written 1989)

THE DAY HE GAVE YOUR HAND TO ME,
COAT OF BROWN AND PEACH SHIRT WORE HE.

HE DANCED, HE LAUGHED, HE WAS SO HIGH
TO SEE HIS SEEDLING BLOSSOM NIGH.

BUT AS CHRISTMAS TREE TURNS CROSS OF WOOD,
SO FATHER'S PATHS VEER AWAY FOR GOOD.

ONCE A TOAST TO LIFE WITH RICH RED WINE,
NOW, HALF-EMPTY CUP, WITH TASTE OF BRINE.

A SEA OF MEMORIES, TURNED MIST BY TIME,
TO THUNDERHEADS, THEN SOOTHING RAIN SUBLIME.

NOW, ONCE TEARS OF JOY, WITH GRIEF, CONVERGE,
FROM WEDDING MARCH, TO FUNERAL DIRGE.

THROUGH VESTIBULE, TO PALL, AND THEN TO PEW,
ALL SADLY FILE, TOWARDS THE PALE DEBUT

OF CORPSE, WHERE ONCE RED RIVERS DID FORM,
A STIFF STALK, OF WOULD-BE DREAMS, NOW SHORN.

SAME BRIGHT COAT, PEACH SHIRT, AND WEDDING TIE,
NOW FADED COLORS, DIMMED, NEATH DARK DREARY SKY.

FROM SOFT PINK, TO HARD BLUE, THEN BURIED DEEP
IN SILENT RICH SOIL, A DREAM POD ASLEEP,

TO REST FOREVER, WHILE LIFE'S LIGHT TAKES FLIGHT,
ON DREAM RAINBOWS ARC, IT'S NEXUS THROUGH THE NIGHT.

SO LOOK UPWARDS, BREATH THE COLORS, OF HOPE AND LOVE
GLIMPSE THE GLORIOUS FLIGHT, OF THE MORNING DOVE.

IT DELIVERS TO YOU, YOUR FATHER'S RICH BOUQUET
FULL OF SEEDS OF DREAMS FROM HIS BRIEF STAY.

SO PLANT IT IN RICH EARTH, STILL COLD
AND SEE YOUR FATHER'S DREAMS TAKE HOLD.

THE RAINBO GOD SPIRIT
(SHALAKO DIST. CO. ALBUQUERQUE, NM)

*The Rainbow God was the first creation of Father-Mother Earth who represents
perfect balance within the great god spirit. He is the protector guardian of all things
that are divinely created, and appears in all four corners of the earth plane.
In Navajo tradition, the rainbow is the path of the Yei (holy spirits).*

ON THE WINGS OF A SNOW-WHITE DOVE
HE SENDS HIS PURE SWEET LOVE
A SIGN FROM ABOVE
ON THE WINGS OF A DOVE
Written by Bob Ferguson
Sung by Felin Husky and Ferlin Husky

COMMENTARY ON 'TO MY WIFE ON HER DAD'S DEATH'

Written on 7/3/18. As I was reviewing the poem "To My Wife on Her Dad's Death", I remembered something about a day over twenty-five years ago, that we thought was going to be the day our daughter was born. We were anxiously traveling from Los Lunas to Albuquerque to the hospital where Ali' was ultimately born. Although Ali' was not born that day, ('false labor' I guess), something unusual happened.

As we were driving on the highway that takes us from Los Lunas to Albuquerque, (1993), I glanced to the right and in the distance, far above us, I barely detected a bird that seemed to be flying in the same direction that we were going. Because of the distance away from the car, I cannot say it was a dove, but it was close to the color white. It is a trip of about thirty minutes to the hospital. As I continued to look, the bird continued to fly in the same direction we were going, as if it were flying on the same path that we were taking. This lasted for at least 20 minutes and I lost sight of it. It was unique enough, that I pointed it out to Sally and told her kiddingly, that this bird was guiding us to the hospital. Because of the labor pains she was somewhat distracted from everything else.

Years later, I ask: Was Ali' the bouquet from Sally's father, on wings of a dove?

AUTUMN'S MESSAGE TO SPRING

TO THE YOUNGER GENERATION:
SOMEDAY THE SUN WILL DISAPPEAR
AND THE MOON WILL CAREEN FROM YOUR HEAVENS.
WHERE ONCE THERE WAS A VAST OCEAN – YOUR PLAYGROUND,
YOU WILL WAKE SADLY TO A DESERT,
YOUR WORLD, BLED DRY.
THERE, STARS WILL WEEP SLOWLY TO A SLUMBER
AND WINTER WILL NEVER AGAIN REACH OUT TO SPRING.

SO
IF THIS NIGHTMARE
YOU'D RATHER NOT KNOW,
THEN, TODAY
ASK THE BRILLIANT STARS FOR GUIDANCE
AND LIKE A YOUNG ISLAND EXPLODING THROUGH THE SEA,
DARING TO SPIT FIRE AT THE STAID AND STODGY SKY,
THE ANSWERS WILL ECHO THUNDEROUSLY WITHIN YOU.
YOU WILL HEAR THEM.....

BUT ONLY, BUT ONLY,
IF IN SPRING, YOU HEEDED WINTER'S WORRIED DREAMS.

SO
BEFORE THE POISONED SKY ROILS A ONCE FRIENDLY SEA
AND RAVAGES THE NEIGHBORING LAND WITH MUCH MISERY;
BEFORE OUR WOODEN-LEAVED PROTECTORS OF BREATH
BECOME A MERE MEMORY FORETELLING OUR DEATH
AND MOTHER EARTHS' ONCE FERTILE FIELDS OF FOOD
DETERIORATE INTO A DESERT
WHERE HELLISH HEAT SUCKS THE LIFE
FROM EVEN THE PRICKLY TONGUES OF THE CACTUS CLAN
WHO THEN SADLY WITHER TO DUST AND DIE;
BEFORE THE SIRENS SING THEIR LAST CHORUS
OVER THE GARBAGE-STREWN GRAVES OF A LIFE-GUTTED SEA;
BEFORE THE MOURNING MOON TEETERS
THEN TUMBLES FROM ITS PRECARIOUS PERCH
AND TIRED TEARY EARTH ROLLS TO A STOP
WITH THE BITTER OF WHAT COULD HAVE BEEN;
BEFORE YOU BECOME THIS BLEAK NIGHT,

LISTEN
TO THE ANCIENT TONGUE OF AUTUMN
AS IT REACHES OUT AND SCREAMS TO SPRING:

WARM WAVES OF IDEAS WILL STILL DANCE
LONG AFTER LOVERS AND RULERS HAVE RAGED
AND THE ETERNAL VOICE OF SACRED SOULS
WILL STILL SOUND SOFTLY IN THE NIGHT'S SILENCE,
AND
THE BRILLIANT EYE OF LOVE WILL STILL PEER
OVER THE HORIZON TO WARM HEARTS
THAT CAN SEE AND HEAR.

SO
BEFORE YOU BECOME PART OF
HOLLOW HOPELESS EYES THAT DO NOT SEE
AND CAULIFLOWERED EARS THAT DO NOT HEAR
IN THE COLD, BARREN AND PREDATOR-FILLED
DESERT OF DARKNESS,
LISTEN!
FOR IN THE FRIGID WEE MORN OF BRITTLE YOUTH
IF YOU HAVE STOOD IN THE SUN'S LIGHT,
YOU ARE BOUND TO BUTTERFLY BECOME
THE BRILLIANCE OF DAYBREAK
AND THE MAJESTIC GLOW OF WARMTH AND LIGHT
ON AN EARTH OF MANY AND BEAUTIFUL TOMORROWS,
WHERE YOU WILL BE ENDOWED
WITH THE SENSITIVITY OF A MOTHER
AND THE COURAGE TO PROTECT YOUR YOUNG
FROM HARM THAT THREATENS TO BEFALL THEM.

LIKE A VISIT OF A VAST FIREBALL FROM AN UNKNOWN GALAXY,
YOUR EXISTENCE
WILL WARM SOULS, IMPASSION HEARTS
AND FIRE IMAGINATIONS
SO THE WORLD WILL SURELY SEE
THEIR CONNECTION TO OUR EARTH HOME.

THE DEVASTATION WE HAVE DONE
AND THE DUTY TO MEND OUR MISTAKE,
IS OURS ALONE.
THE DREAM WILL LIVE
ONLY IF YOU ARE
THE SINGULAR, THE COMPASSIONATE,
THE SEEKER OF TRUTH
WHOSE EYES, EARS, MIND AND HEART,
DID NOT SHUT DOWN
AND IN THE CACOPHONY OF YOUTH

AND IN FICKLE AND FRENZIED SPRING,
YOU ROSE ABOVE THE TUMULT
AND DARINGLY TUNED IN
TO THE SYMPHONY OF WISDOM
PLAYED BY THE FADING LIGHT OF AUTUMN.

C. A MORAL VIEWPOINT

SUMMARY AND COMMENT ON POPE FRANCIS ENCYCLICAL, LAUDATO SI.

I had heard that Pope Francis, from Latin America, had actually addressed the issue of the environment in an extensive Encyclical - Laudato Si, (On Care For Our Common Home). I had heard too that he went by the name Pope Francis, after Saint Francis, the Saint of Nature or the Nature Mystic.

Historically, Popes were extremely conservative. So many were out of touch with what was going on or were just interested in being popular. So I wondered if we would finally have a spiritual leader in the world that actually was knowledgeable, truly cared about the poor and downtrodden and had the courage to speak up about it.

The environment, pollution and the ongoing disaster is truly an issue about the 'Haves' and 'Have-nots', i.e., moneyed interests who make money off their polluting products and the poor who suffer the effects of the pollution. Would Pope Francis tread gently so as not to hurt the feelings of the moneyed interests? No one likes contributing to the Church if you insult them! Would he pull a Pope Pius XII 'neutrality' approach in response to the slaughter of the Jews in Nazi Germany and look the other way as long as Catholics and wealthy donors were protected? Or would the new Pope step on some Capitalist toes?

In June of 2018, I asked a close family member, a practicing Catholic, what he thought of the Popes latest Encyclical on the environment? It had been published on June 18, 2015 so certainly on a topic so critical to our time, he had discussed it or it had been addressed from the Catholic pulpit. I was surprised that my highly educated, Catholic-church-attending family member, had not heard about the Encyclical. Was it just my family, just Las Vegas N.M. or was this obliviousness occurring in Catholic Churches throughout the country?

It should not have been a surprise to me. As a Catholic School kid attending school during a time of political turbulence, there lived a black man named Martin Luther King Jr. who was daringly leading the battle against racism. He paid the price with his life. A large segment of the black community were uniting, marching and fighting, non-violently for their rights to stand on the same footing with white people. The movement ultimately resulted in the famous Civil Rights Act. Do you think this was ever discussed at our high school? These critical moral issues of our country depriving a group of people from being treated as human beings was never addressed at Cathedral High school. The other issue of great political import, going on during that time, was the Vietnam War. The only thing I recall hearing the priest tell anyone was to 'support your troops!' I so much wanted to stand up and ask: Why Father? Why would we sanction murder of the Vietnamese and the poisoning and destruction of the Vietnamese land by Napalming it? But I wasn't that gutsy!

As I look back at Gallup, N.M., racism was alive and practiced daily without a second thought. Gallup was surrounded by the Navaho and Zuni reservations. Guess which group of people were treated like Blacks were in the South? So maybe in Gallup, the issue of racism against Blacks was not discussed because Gallupians feared we might be told to start equality in your own backyard before you tell us about racism.

So I should not be surprised that things have not changed. Catholics in this country have always been of the persuasion that the Pope does not boss us. But maybe and finally, morality has joined hands with religious dogma. (Unfortunately, this has come at a time when the priest-pedophilia issue is the front page news.)

So I was excited to hear about a pope who addressed the critical issue of our time – the polluting of the environment and its impact. He suffered from no religious denial. Amazingly, he had an opinion that even identified the bad guys and had bold recommendations to address it.

*He was careful not to reveal how the Judeo Christian religious culture had contributed to the pollution problem. He borrowed from Genesis, "till and keep", without the anti-nature language of **Genesis 1:28-30 <u>NIV</u>:** God blessed them and said to them. Be fruitful and increase in number, fill the earth and **<u>subdue</u>** it. **Rule over** the fish of the sea and the birds of the air and over every living creature that moves on the ground. However, overall, the Pope spoke knowledgeably about pollution, it's danger, those who were responsible and whether their acts were evil.*

Finally, a Pope dares address the question of morality as part of the Catholic faith! Finally, a Pope who has a science background – he studied Chemistry prior to entering the seminary. Finally a Pope from Latin America, the first. Maybe now the issue of poverty will be taken more seriously. Finally, a Pope who is daring enough to address the crucial issue of our time – the pollution of the environment, and even address moral culpability! Finally, a holy man who puts destruction of our ecological system on the same level as injuring or killing our fellow man. Moreover, he is a Pope daring enough to point the finger of blame at the countries that have fallen below a standard of goodness because of greed.

As you might have suspected, this environmental encyclical was opposed by Vatican conservatives, Catholic conservatives, and the US evangelical movement. Yet he still pursued it.

I have fallen asleep and must be dreaming! As a former Catholic, I have always paid attention to the leaders of the Catholic Church. Far from Holy men, they seemed to be afraid to address morality outside the narrow confines of ancient Catholic doctrines. I had given up attributing any credence to what they said, until now.

Remarkably, Pope Francis directs us to the examination of conscience to include a new dimension. Not only should we live in communion with God, with others and with oneself, but also with all creatures and with nature. This is gigantic!

Who would have imagined it? In a world that seems as conservative as ever, a man of the Catholic cloth dares to be identified as a 'radical' and loudly sends the message to ensure the continued existence of the earth and mankind. Ecology finally joins religion and religion acts morally! This skeptic is shocked! My faith in mankind is renewed. I think the inspiration begun by my children, has now reached a new apex of hope out of formerly dashed expectations. Praise be to Pope Francis!

*Please review my summary and commentary of Pope Francis' Encyclical – Laudato Si, in which he actually addresses, analyzes, makes moral conclusions and directs blame at those responsible. Yes, he points to us! (**Bolded parts are my emphasis.**)*

SUMMARY AND COMMENT

(The following is the outline of the Encyclical, with Chapter pages, to facilitate a comparison to the original: (A 16 part Introduction), *CHAPTER ONE,* **WHAT IS HAPPENING TO OUR COMMON HOME,** *(17-61) CHAPTER TWO,* **THE GOSPEL OF CREATION** *(62-100) CHAPTER THREE,* **THE HUMAN ROOTS OF THE ECOLOGICAL CRISIS,** *(101-136) CHAPTER FOUR,* **INTEGRAL ECOLOGY,** *(137-162), CHAPTER FIVE,* **LINES OF APPROACH AND ACTION,** *(163-201) and CHAPTER SIX,* **ECOLOGICAL EDUCATION AND SPIRITUALITY** *(202-246)).*

Laudato Si Introduction. The Encyclical takes its name from the invocation of Saint Francis of Assisi, "Praise be to you, my Lord" which in the *Canticle of the Creatures* reminds us that the **earth,** our common home **"is like a sister** with whom we share our life **and a beautiful mother who opens**

her arms to embrace us" (1). We ourselves "are dust of the earth" (cf. Gen 2:7); our very bodies are made up of her elements, we breathe her air and we receive life and refreshment from her waters" (2). "This sister now cries out to us because of the harm we have inflicted on her by our irresponsible use and abuse of the goods with which God has endowed her" (2). Her cry, united with that of the poor, stirs our conscience to "acknowledge our sins against creation" (8). Taking the words of the "beloved" Ecumenical Patriarch Bartholomew, the Pope reminds us: **"For human beings... to destroy the biological diversity of God's creation; for human beings to degrade the integrity of the earth by causing changes in its climate, by stripping the earth of its natural forests or destroying its wetlands; for human beings to contaminate the earth's waters, its land, its air, and its life – these are sins".15 For "to commit a crime against the natural world is a sin against ourselves and a sin against God". (8)**

If there was one paragraph that could capture the spirit and message of the encyclical, it is the approach to the world taken by St. Francis:

"If we approach nature and the environment without this openness to awe and wonder, if we no longer speak the language of fraternity and beauty in our relationship with the world, our attitude will be that of masters, consumers, ruthless exploiters, unable to set limits on their immediate needs. By contrast, if we feel intimately united with all that exists, then sobriety and care will well up spontaneously. The poverty and austerity of Saint Francis were no mere veneer of asceticism, but something much more radical: a refusal to turn reality into an object simply to be used and controlled." (See # 11 of the Intro.)

Comments: The analogy to a mother and sister humanizes nature for those who believe nature deserves less respect than humanity. Remarkable is that, finally a leader of a Christian Judeo organizations has identified pollution as a sin.

So if the polluter goes to 'confession' and confesses his 'sin', is he forgiven and entitled to go to Heaven? In my days at the Catholic Church, if one was truly contrite he would be forgiven. If not, he was doomed to Purgatory, or Hell, if the sin was 'Mortal'.

I am told by my knowledgeable sister-in-law that now, the only thing that sends you to Hell is turning away from God. So is knowingly polluting, evil enough, that it can be categorized as turning away from God? How about supporting the polluters by buying their products? How about contributing to the politicians that deny our destruction of the environment by pollution?

Or is 'turning away from God' merely a 'faith' mandate. I.e., You can pollute all you want as long as you believe in God? What if your vision of God is different from the traditional Catholic version of God? I don't know the answer to these questions. (I will talk to my catholic sister-in-law, a college professor, who used to teach 'catechism'.)

<u>Failing Our Environment Is Failure to Our Fellow Man.</u> In damaging our "common home", which is like our sister and our mother, by polluting, we are damaging our relationship with other humans, in particular, the poor and future generations. Thusly, we are not practicing good stewardship of the gift of creation.

Comment: Finally a church leader comments on the act of pollution impacting the poor and future generations. Finally, in this encyclical, a pope gives clarification and definition of 'good stewardship', which had been biblically ambivalent and missing everywhere else, until now.

The Encyclical, *Laudato si'* (Praised Be You) is developed around the concept of **'integral ecology'**, as a model able to articulate the fundamental relationships of the person: with God, with one's self, with other human beings, **and with creation.** The Pope explains in n. 15, of <u>Ch. I,</u> that this movement starts (by listening spiritually to the results of the best scientific research on environmental matters available today, "letting them touch us deeply and provide a concrete foundation for the ethical and spiritual itinerary that follows". **"Science is the best tool by which we can listen to the cry of the earth." "...** *A very solid scientific consensus indicates that we are presently witnessing a disturbing warming of the climatic system. In recent decades this warming has been accompanied by a constant rise in the sea level and, it would appear, by an increase of extreme weather events,.... a number of scientific studies indicate that most global warming in recent decades is due to the great concentration of greenhouse gases (carbon dioxide, methane, nitrogen oxides and others) released mainly as a result of human activity. As these gases build up in the atmosphere, they hamper the escape of heat produced by sunlight at the earth's surface." (P.18 and 19, under note 23 'Climate as A Common Good)*

Comment: *The Pope is on the same page as the scientists! Wow!*

<u>CHAPTER 1</u> asks the question? **WHAT IS HAPPENING TO OUR COMMON HOME? (17-61)**

<u>What Kind of Home Do We Want to Leave to Our Children?</u> (See Ch. I: (17-6 (See page 18 and 19 under note 1)) This chapter presents recent scientific findings on the environment as a way of listening to the cry of creation.

<u>**Comment on Sources:**</u> *The Pope in proposing methods for addressing and resolving the environmental problems, relies on numerous and varied sources. He refers to contributions by philosophers and theologians, not only Catholic but also Orthodox (the already cited Patriarch Bartholomew) and Protestant (the French thinker Paul Ricoeur) as well as the Islamic mystic Ali Al-Khawas.*

Comment: *Kudos to a Pope that does not fear to rely on sources outside the Church.*

He then addresses in Ch. 1, part 1: POLLUTION, WASTE AND THE THROWAWAY CULTURE (Ch 1 Part 1 POLLUTION AND CLIMATE CHANGE, 20-26) Pollution affects the daily life of people with serious consequences to their health, so much so that it causes millions of premature deaths (20), while "the earth, our home, is beginning to look more and more like an immense pile of filth" (21).

"There is also pollution that affects everyone, caused by transport, industrial fumes, substances which contribute to the acidification of soil and water, fertilizers, insecticides, fungicides, herbicides and agrotoxins in general. Technology, which, linked to business interests, is presented as the only way of solving these problems, in fact proves incapable of seeing the mysterious network of relations between things and so sometimes solves one problem only to create others."

My Comment. The Pope's belief that we have misplaced our faith in technology as the solution for any problem, is consistent with the position 'Glimpsing Heaven' has taken.

At the root of this situation we find the *"**throwaway culture**"*, which we have to oppose by introducing models of production based on **reuse and recycling and by limiting the use of non-renewable resources.** Unfortunately, "only limited progress has been made in this regard" (22).

"Climate change is a global problem with grave implications, environmental, social, economic, political and for the distribution of goods" (25). Climate changes afflict entire populations and are among the causes of migration movements, but **"many of** *those who possess more resources and economic or political power seem mostly to be concerned with masking the problems or concealing their symptoms...***"** (26). At the same time, *"our lack of response to these tragedies involving our brothers and sisters points to the loss of that sense of responsibility for our fellow men and women upon which all civil society is founded"* (25). **Climate change "represents one of the principal challenges facing humanity in our day"** (25).

(Cf. Rules of Ecology by Barry Commoner in the Closing Circle -Everything must go somewhere. There is no "waste" in nature and there is no "away" to which things can be thrown.)

My Comment: the above must be a reference to coal, gas and oil, a 'non-renewable resource'. One-use plastics also fall in this category.

<u>**Polluting the Water.**</u> (Part 2. THE ISSUE OF WATER [27-31] The Pope addresses the issue wherein **entire populations, and especially children, get sick and die because of contaminated water, while aquifers continue to be polluted by discharges from factories and cities.** The Pope clearly states that *"...access to safe drinkable water is a basic and universal human right, since it is essential to human survival and, as such, is a condition for the exercise of other human rights"* (30). To deprive the poor of access to water means *"they are denied the right to a life consistent with their inalienable dignity"* (30)

The Pope reminds us: "For human beings... to destroy the biological diversity ... by causing changes in its climate ...; *<u>to contaminate the earth's waters, its land, its air, and its life – these are sins</u>"*(Ch 1 #8).

My Comment: Interestingly, the Pope's reference to earth as our mother, is a reminder that Native Americans have viewed the earth and nature as their 'mother'. Should we not be looking more to them for guidance?

<u>**Failure to Preserve Biodiversity Equates to Destruction of Equilibrium and Life Everywhere.**</u> (Ch. 3 LOSS OF BIODIVERSITY [32-42] The great majority of the extinction of plant and animal species are caused by human activity. (3) *"Each year sees the disappearance of thousands of plant and animal species which we will never know, which our children will never see, because they have been lost forever"* (33). The diverse species are not just an exploitable "resource": they have a value in and of themselves, which is not in function of human beings. *"**All creatures are connected ..., for all of us, as living creatures, are dependent on one another**"* (42). The *care of richly biodiverse areas is necessary for ensuring the equilibrium of the ecosystem and therefore of life.*

*<u>Comment:</u> Again, the Pope refers to science: **integral ecology**. He is quite clear: Science is the best tool by which we can listen to the cry of the earth.*

(Cf. Rules of Ecology by Barry Commoner in the Closing Circle – Everything is connected to everything else.)

(Part 4.) DECLINE IN THE QUALITY OF HUMAN LIFE AND THE BREAKDOWN OF SOCIETY [43-47] The current model of development adversely affects the quality of life of most of humanity, showing *"that the growth of the past two centuries has not always led to an integral development and the improvement of the quality of life"* (46). *"Many cities are huge, inefficient structures, excessively wasteful of energy and water"* (44), becoming unlivable from a health point of view, while contact with nature is limited, except for areas reserved for a privileged few (45). *"**We were not meant to be inundated by cement, asphalt, glass and metal, and deprived of physical contact with nature."(44)**

(Ch 5, GLOBAL INEQUALITY) *"...the deterioration of the environment and of society affect the most vulnerable people on the planet" (48), the majority of the planet's population, billions of people." "...the gravest effects of all attacks on the environment are suffered by the poorest"* **(48) In international economic, political debates, they are considered as "an afterthought" or "merely as collateral damage".** (49).

Why is this so? The powerful opinion-makers often reside in the affluent urban areas, far removed from the poor and with little contact with their problems. Thus *"they live and reason from the comfortable position of a high level of development and a quality of life well beyond the reach of the majority of the world's population." This lack of physical contact and encounter, encouraged at time by the disintegration of our cities, can lead to a numbing of conscience and to tendentious analyses which neglect parts of reality.* At times this attitude exists side by side with a "green" rhetoric. (49) *"...we have to realize that **a true ecological approach always becomes a social approach: it must integrate questions of justice in debates on the environment, so as to hear both the cry of the earth and the cry of the poor."** (49)*

The solution is not reducing the birth rate, but counteracting *"an extreme and selective consumerism"* **of a small part of the world's population** (50).

My Comment: The Pope sides with Barry Commoner that population control is not the main issue. Moreover, "an extreme and selective consumerism" appears to be a jab at the United States.

Part 6. **WEAK RESPONSES**. Pope Francis shows himself to be deeply affected by the weak responses in the face of ongoing tragedies occurring to many people and populations. Even though there is no lack of positive examples (58), there exists a *"false or superficial ecology which bolsters* **complacency and a cheerful wrecklessness**" (59). *"Such evasiveness serves as a license to carrying on with our present lifestyles and models of production and consumption."* **Culture and adequate leadership are lacking** as well as the willingness to change life style, production and consumption (59).

My Comment: The Pope's comments look to be directed towards our country. Our form of Capitalism does seem to contribute to the avoidance of taking action against the dangerous consequences of pollution. That so large a group voted for a president that denies the existence of man-made global warming, speaks volumes in support of the pope's perception of our country.

*My Critical Comment: **CHAPTER II** - THE GOSPEL OF CREATION (62-100) and Comment: Interpretation of bible – 'collective good'. In spite of numerous biblical verses suggesting that a dominance of nature is acceptable, Pope Francis selects from the Judeo-Christian tradition. He states that the Biblical accounts offer a comprehensive view that expresses the **"tremendous responsibility"** (90) of humankind for creation, the intimate connection among all creatures and the fact that "the natural environment is a collective good, the patrimony of all humanity and the responsibility of everyone" (95).*

*Forgive me, but a full reading of the Bible, reflects at best, an ambivalence when it comes to the nature and quality of our duty to the environment. (See Ch. 10 of Glimpsing Heaven, Facing Hell on Earth - **A DIAGNOSIS OF THE ENEMY, A REVIEW OF THE ISSUES, A BATTLE PLAN, AND SOLUTIONS.**)*

Ch. II **THE LIGHT OFFERED BY FAITH** [63-64] The complexity of the ecological crisis calls for a multicultural and multidisciplinary dialogue that includes spirituality and religion. Faith offers "ample motivation to care for nature and for the most vulnerable of their brothers and sisters" (64); **"Christians"…"realize that their responsibility within creation, and their duty towards nature and the Creator, are an essential part of their faith."** (64)

Comment: Forgive me again, but one of the points of this book was that faith without actions has gotten us into the problem that we are now in. (See Ch. 10). However the Pope's tying our actions to science, (as well as to faith), mitigates this concern to some extent. I would submit, it is not faith, but empathy, (love thy neighbor as thyself) and following in Jesus' footsteps, that we need to discover and exercise.

Violation of Relationship with Earth Is Sin. (Part 2: THE WISDOM OF THE BIBLICAL ACCOUNTS [65-75]) The story of creation is key for reflecting on the relationship between human beings and other creatures and how sin breaks the equilibrium of creation in its entirety. These accounts **"suggest"** that *"**human life is grounded in three fundamental and closely intertwined***

relationships: with God, with our neighbour and with the earth itself." **"According to the Bible, these three vital relationships have been broken, both outwardly and within us. This rupture is sin"** (66).

My Comment: Although the Pope is treading on shaky ground in suggesting that the bible clearly tells us that destroying the earth is a sin, (at best it is ambiguous). Kudos to him for trying to enlist a whole segment of the world community to recognize an evil.

The Earth is a Gift, Not a Possession/ Duty of Care to Nature. (Part 3. THE MYSTERY OF THE UNIVERSE [76-83] (81); *"By the word of the Lord the heavens were made." (77). "This tells us that the world came about as the result of a decision, not from chaos or chance, and this exalts it all the more" (77) "...creation can only be understood as a gift from the outstretched hand of the Father of all...."(76) "God's love is the fundamental moving force in all created things; "For you love all things that exist, and detest none of the things you have made;"(77) "Nature is usually seen as a system which can be studied, understood and controlled, whereas creation can only be understood as a gift from the outstretched hand of the Father of all..." (76)*

My Comment: The 'Gift' analogy may be the best argument to show us that how we treat the earth reflects directly on our moral character. Everyone can understand that how we take care of a gift or how we disregard or destroy it, reveals how we feel or have no feelings for the gifting person. However, I submit that the Catholic belief that nature did not come about as a result of chance, (but created by God), in actual practice, seems to contribute to our tendency to study, understand and control nature. (76)

In fact, the opposite of the gift-from-God analogy is true. The belief in science and natures' eternal presence, its interrelatedness, its' delicate existence, and our inescapable intertwinement with nature, should compel us to take care of it. The suggestion that the belief in a God, makes us more careful with nature has not proven correct. Unfortunately, believers in God have quite often, been more totalitarian in their viewpoints and lacking in the real key to caring – empathy and love.

Relationship to All Creatures. (Part 4 THE MESSAGE OF EACH CREATURE IN THE HARMONY OF CREATION [84-88]) "God wills the interdependence of creatures. The sun and the moon, the cedar and the little flower, the eagle and the sparrow" "...Creatures exist only in dependence on each other, to complete each other, in the service of each other" (63) **"...each creature has its own purpose. None is superfluous."** (84)

My Comment: Again the Pope follows the line of ecological thinking in the four Rules of Ecology by Barry Commoner in the Closing Circle, particularly, 'Everything is connected to everything else.'

Part 5 - A UNIVERSAL COMMUNION [89-92] *"...called into being by one Father, all of us are linked by unseen bonds and together form a kind of universal family, a sublime communion which fills us with a sacred, affectionate and humble respect."* (89) **"A sense of deep communion with the rest of nature cannot be real if our hearts lack tenderness, compassion and concern for our fellow human beings"** *(91).*

Comment: We are certainly in sync as to this essential point! But how much compassion should we have for the polluters? Maybe nature's lesson is the best - the more appropriate emotion towards the polluters should be the one that compels mother-bears to fight to the death for their endangered cubs?

Duty to Share. Part 6: THE COMMON DESTINATION OF GOODS [93-95]. "...the earth is essentially a shared inheritance, whose fruits are meant to benefit everyone" (93) and those who possess a part are called to administer it with respect for a "social mortgage" that applies to all forms of ownership (93). *"That is why the New Zealand bishops asked what the commandment "thou shall* *not kill", means when "twenty percent of the world's population consumes resources at a rate that robs the poor nations and future generations of what they need to survive" (95)*

My Comment: The concept of capitalism and plutocracy is antithetical to the 'sharing' notion.

Part 7 - **THE GAZE OF JESUS** [96-100]. Jesus invited his disciples "to recognize the paternal relationship God has with all his creatures" (96) and to "live in full harmony with creation" (98), without despising the body, the material or pleasant things of life. "...the **destiny of all creation is bound up with the mystery of Christ**" (99) and, **at the end of time, all things will be consigned to the Father.** "In this way the creatures of this world no longer appear to us under merely natural guise because the risen One is mysteriously holding them to himself and directing them towards fullness as their end" (100).

Comment 1: The above section is based on these two biblical quotes: "Are not five sparrows sold for two pennies? And not one of them is forgotten before God" (Lk 12:6) "Look at the birds of the air: they neither sow nor reap nor gather into barns, and yet your heavenly Father feeds them" (Mt 6:26). I submit that the lesson that the sparrows and the 'birds' are being taken care of by God, directs the 'believer' away from the significance of Nature's role and our duty to preserve it. I.e., God is taking care of them, either now or after they die.

Comment 2: The Pope seems to be saying that all of nature will be with him in Heaven: "all things will be consigned to the father: or "holding them to Himself and directing them towards fullness at their end." He then qualifies it as 'mystery'. In light of ***Genesis 1:28-30 NIV's*** directive from God to *'subdue'* **nature,** it is not clear to me that nature has any priority in the bigger biblical scheme.

<u>**The Morality of Technology**</u> **CHAPTER III** - **THE HUMAN ROOTS OF THE ECOLOGICAL CRISIS** (101-136) This chapter analyzes the worlds' present condition. It addresses symptoms and deepest causes of the pollution problem. (15) The pope does this in a dialogue with philosophy and the social sciences.

Part 1 **TECHNOLOGY: CREATIVITY AND POWER** [102-105] It is right to appreciate and recognize the benefits of technological progress for its contribution to sustainable development. But our advanced "...***technology has given those with the knowledge, and especially the economic resources to use them, an impressive dominance over the whole of humanity and the entire world*** **(104).** "...***we cannot claim to have a sound ethics, a culture and spirituality genuinely capable of setting limits and teaching clear-minded self-restraint" (105).***

My Comment: Thank you Pope Francis for essentially saying the rich and powerful need to be restrained and technology is being used for evil.

<u>**Technology and Profit Motive Must be Restrained.**</u> Part 2 (THE GLOBALIZATION OF THE TECHNOCRATIC PARADIGM [106-114]) The dominant technocratic mentality perceives reality as something that can be manipulated limitlessly. It is a reductionism that involves all aspects of life. "We have to accept that technological products are not neutral, for "they create a framework which ends up conditioning lifestyles and shaping social possibilities along the lines dictated by the interests of certain powerful groups." (107)

The technocratic paradigm also dominates economy and politics. In particular, **"the economy accepts every advance in technology with a view to profit ...** Yet by itself the market cannot guarantee integral human development and social inclusion" (109). **Trusting technology alone to resolve every problem means "to mask the true and deepest problems of the global system" (111),** given "that scientific and technological progress cannot be equated with the progress of humanity and history" (113). **A "bold cultural revolution" (114) is needed "to recover the values and the great goals swept away by our unrestrained delusions of grandeur." (114)**

My Comment: Technology Should Not be our God. In Chapters 2 and 3 supra, the Pope addresses the egregious failure that underlies our present severe circumstances – the belief that technology will solve any problems that we have or may have in the future. This allows big business to continue to put dangerous products on the market because we have grown up to ignorantly destroy nature without concern that there are serious consequence to be paid that technology cannot timely fix.

Comment: The Pope is saying that we must have an alternative to our technologically advanced, pollution belching and poisoning machines and vehicles of death, just because it makes money for someone.

Recognize the Importance of Nature. (Part 3 THE CRISIS AND EFFECTS OF MODERN ANTHROPOCENTRISM [115-121]) *"**Putting technical reasoning above reality, modern anthropocentrism no longer recognizes nature as a valid norm and living refuge. We thereby lose the possibility of understanding the place of human beings in the world and our relationship with nature,** while "our 'dominion' over the universe should be understood more properly in the sense of responsible stewardship"* (116).

My Comment. The Pope does acknowledge that Christianity is in part to blame for our disrespect of nature: *"An inadequate presentation of Christian anthropology gave rise to a wrong understanding of the relationship between human beings and the world. Often, what was handed on was a Promethean vision of mastery over the world, which gave the impression that the protection of nature was something that only the faint-hearted cared about."* (116) The truth is that God has told us in the Old Testament to *'suppress'* nature when it suited us. See ***Genesis 1:28-30 NIV.***

'The need to protect employment': Integral ecology *"needs to take account of the value of labour"* (124). Everyone must be able to have work, because it is *"part of the meaning of life on this earth, a path to growth, human development and personal fulfilment"* (128), while *"to stop investing in people, in order to gain greater short-term financial gain, is bad business for society"* (128). In order that everyone can really benefit from economic freedom, *"restraints occasionally have to be imposed on those possessing greater resources and financial power"* (129). *"Civil authorities have the right and duty to adopt clear and firm measures in support of small producers and differentiated production.* ***To ensure economic freedom from which all can effectively benefit, restraints occasionally have to be imposed on those possessing greater resources and financial power (129)***

Comment: Unfortunately, many in our Country will dismiss this wisdom as 'Socialism' and reject it. That would be a gigantic mistake. We will need to use this idea to ensure that those put out of work by ending fossil fuel production are given employment in the recycling business.

Part 4. DECLINE IN THE QUALITY OF HUMAN LIFE AND THE BREAKDOWN OF SOCIETY [43-47] The current model of development adversely affects the quality of life of most of humanity, showing *"that the growth of the past two centuries has not always led to an integral development"* (46). *"Many cities are huge, inefficient structures, excessively wasteful of energy and water"* (44), becoming unlivable from a health point of view, while contact with nature is limited, except for areas reserved for a privileged few (45).

Comment: *The Pope's comment jibes perfectly with a country whose wealth is in the hands of fewer and fewer and cities are often synonymous with poverty and bad housing.*

Nature Cannot be Treated as Separate. (CHAPTER IV) INTEGRAL ECOLOGY (137-162) The heart of the Encyclical's proposals is integral ecology as a new paradigm of justice. It *"will help to provide an approach to ecology which respects our unique place as human beings in this world and our relationship to our surroundings"* (15). In fact, **nature cannot be regarded as something separate from ourselves or as a mere setting in which we live" (139).** *"Today, the analysis of environmental* *problems cannot be separated from the analysis of human, family, work-related and urban contexts, nor from how individuals relate to themselves..."* (141).

Everything is Connected. (ENVIRONMENTAL, ECONOMIC AND SOCIAL ECOLOGY [138-142]) Time and space, physical, chemical and biological components of the planet and "...living species are part of a network which we will never fully explore and understand." (138). (141), (142).

Part 2 **CULTURAL ECOLOGY** [143-146] "Ecology, then, also involves protecting the cultural treasures of humanity" (143) in the broadest sense. It is necessary to integrate the rights of peoples and cultures with the proactive involvement of local social actors from their own culture, with "particular concern for indigenous communities" (146).

Comment: Looking at our treatment of Native Americans, do we now see that stripping them of their culture, which was so closely connected to nature, was one of our greatest evils?

The Gift of our Bodies and the World From God Mandates Moral Action. (Part 3. ECOLOGY OF DAILY LIFE [147-155]) Integral ecology involves everyday life. Nevertheless, authentic development presupposes an integral improvement in the quality of human life: public space, housing, transportation, etc. (150-154). The human dimension of ecology also implies *"the relationship between human life and the moral law, which is inscribed in our nature"* (155). *"Our body itself establishes us in a direct relationship with the environment and with other living beings. The acceptance of our bodies as God's gift is vital for welcoming and accepting the entire world as a gift from the Father and our common home, whereas* **thinking that we enjoy absolute power over our own bodies turns, often subtly, into thinking that we enjoy absolute power over creation"** *(155).*

Comment: Has the bible, in clearly painting humanity as superior to nature, reinforced the notion that we have absolute power over creation?

The Duty to All. (Part 4 THE PRINCIPLE OF THE COMMON GOOD [156-158]) Integral or human ecology "is inseparable from the notion of the common good" (158). In the contemporary world, where "injustices abound and growing numbers of people are deprived of basic human rights and considered expendable", **working for the common good means to make choices in solidarity based on "a preferential option for the poorest" (158).**

The Duty to Future Generations. (Part 5 JUSTICE BETWEEN THE GENERATIONS [159-162]) **The common good also regards <u>future generations.</u>.** *"We can no longer speak of sustainable development apart from intergenerational solidarity."* (159), However we cannot forget the poor of today *"whose life on this earth is brief and who cannot keep on waiting"* (162).

Duty of Open Debate (**CHAPTER V:** LINES OF APPROACH AND ACTION (163-201)) We need proposals "for dialogue and action which would involve each of us individually no less than international policy" (15). For this, **dialogue is essential!**

Think 'One World, One Plan. Part 1 DIALOGUE ON THE ENVIRONMENT IN THE INTERNATIONAL COMMUNITY [164-175]. "Interdependence obliges us to think of one world with a common plan", proposing solutions "from a global perspective, and not simply to defend the interests of a few countries" (164).

Comment: Electing a President that reinstates our country as participants in the Paris Climate Accords, would be a nice start.

Part 2: DIALOGUE FOR NEW NATIONAL AND LOCAL POLICIES [176-181]) **"Local individuals and groups can make a greater sense of responsibility, a strong sense of community, a readiness to protect others, a spirit of creativity and a deep love for the land. (179) They are also concerned about what they will eventually leave to their children and grandchildren. These** values are deeply rooted in indigenous peoples" (179) Politics and economy need to abandon the logic of short-sighted efficiency, focused on profit alone and short-term electoral success.

"...on the national and local levels, much still needs to be done, such as promoting ways of conserving energy. These would include favouring forms of industrial production with maximum energy efficiency and diminished use of raw materials, removing from the market products which are less energy efficient or more polluting, improving transport systems, and encouraging the construction and repair of buildings aimed at reducing their energy consumption, and levels of pollution.

Comment: I hear the pope saying we must empower those at the local level over a system in which profit dominates all

Analysis Must Be From Environmental View. (Part 3: DIALOGUE AND TRANSPARENCY IN DECISION-MAKING [182-188]) It is essential to analyze and evaluate business proposals from an environmental and social point of view so as not to harm the most disadvantaged populations (182-188).

Capitalism and The Nanny State Is Not the Answer. (My title*)* (Part 4: POLITICS AND ECONOMY IN DIALOGUE FOR HUMAN FULFILMENT [189-198]) Starting from the global crisis, **"a new economy, more attentive to ethical principles, and new ways of regulating speculative financial practices and virtual wealth" (189), should be developed. "The environment is one of those goods that cannot be adequately safeguarded or promoted by market forces" (190).** "Efforts to promote a sustainable use of natural resources are not a waste of money, but rather an investment capable of providing other economic benefits in the medium term" (191). More radically, "redefining our notion of progress" (194) is necessary, linking it to improvements in the real quality of people's lives. (196). Together they are called to take on a new integral approach.

Religions Must Begin Talking About the Environment. *(My title)* (Part 5 RELIGIONS IN DIALOGUE WITH SCIENCE [199-201]) **Religions must enter into "dialogue among themselves for the sake of protecting nature, defending the poor, and building networks of respect and fraternity" (201).**

Educate Towards Ecological Wisdom (CHAPTER 6) ECOLOGICAL EDUCATION AND SPIRITUALITY (202-246) The roots of the cultural crisis are deep, and it is not easy to reshape habits and behaviour. Education and training are key. *"Change is impossible without motivation and a process of education"* (15). *All educational sectors are involved, primarily "in school, in families, in the media, in catechesis"* (213).

Comment: All of you religion instructors are now on notice to begin teaching the students about ecology.

Part 2: **EDUCATING FOR THE COVENANT BETWEEN HUMANITY AND THE ENVIRONMENT [209-215])** The **importance of environmental education cannot be overstated. It is able to affect daily actions and habits, the reduction of water consumption, the sorting of waste and even "turning off unnecessary lights" or wearing warmer clothes so as to use less heating** (211) "...avoiding the use of plastic and paper, cooking only what can reasonably be consumed, showing care for other living beings, using public transport or car-pooling, planting trees,.."

My Com*m***ent:** (Cf. with my recommendations to make Ecology mandatory in the school system.) Also see Ch. 4 E in this book: *'A POETIC EDUCATION WITH FOOTNOTES ABOUT POLLUTION, THE PROBLEM and THE CONSEQUENCES'*

Must Change Self-Centered Lifestyle to Common Good. Part 1: TOWARDS A NEW LIFESTYLE [203-208]) Despite practical relativism and the consumer culture, "all is not lost. Human beings, while capable of the worst, are also capable of rising above themselves, choosing again what is good, and making a new start, despite their mental and social conditioning… **Changes in lifestyle and consumer choices can bring much "pressure to bear on those who wield political, economic and social power"** (206). "If we can **overcome individualism,** we will truly be able to develop an alternative lifestyle and bring about *significant* changes in society" (208). See Part 5: CIVIC AND POLITICAL LOVE [228-232])

Part 7 **THE TRINITY AND RELATIONSHIPS BETWEEN CREATURES** [238-240]

"For Christians, believing in one God whose trinitarian communion suggests that the Trinity has left its mark on all creation" (239). The human person is also called to assume the trinitarian dynamism, going out of oneself "to live in communion with God, with others **and with all creatures"** (240).

Mary's Example. (Part 8 QUEEN OF ALL CREATION [241-242]) Mary, who cares for Jesus, now lives with him and is Mother and Queen of all creation. "All creatures sing of her fairness" (241).

My Comment: (Mary represents that maternal instinct that this book is so much a part. (See Ch. III of this book - THE APPEARANCES OF THE VIRGIN MARY AND HER MESSAGE - WHAT DOES IT MEAN?)

A Question: The Pope makes it clear that destroying nature is a sin. But how serious a sin is it? Is it Hell-rendering? Is responsibility diminished or nullified by ignorance, inadvertence, duress, fear, habit, inordinate attachments and other psychological or social factors. These are the factors that excuse, justify, mitigate or are a complete defense to sin. So is it a defense to sin that we must drive a car and, by necessity, pollute, to get to work to survive? How about eating meat and dairy? We should now know that the Animal agriculture industry is one of the biggest polluters in the world. We always have the option of becoming Vegan or Vegetarian. Or is our argument that our contribution is so insignificant that it cannot be a 'serious' sin. Or how about 'throwing away' our food scraps that end up in the landfill that are the cause for serious methane pollution? If we didn't know this, do we have some moral duty to find out? If we choose not to compost, is that a sin? If we are a business and we 'throw away' the left overs, is that a sin? Is it a sin to use and 'throw away' our plastic containers? Has 'convenience' become a defense to sin?

I submit that the consequences for our throwaway culture are so severe - world-ending, that, burying our head in the sand as to this consequence, and doing nothing, is a mortal sin. I will wait for the Pope's next encyclical to see if he will address this issue.

D. A SCIENTIFIC PERSPECTIVE

(I do not claim to be a scientist or anything close. Nor did I take any ecology classes. So, I felt compelled to address, at least, the basics of understanding nature. I have therefore included The Four Laws of Ecology by Barry Commoner in his book, The Closing Circle. Most is taken directly from his book.

'all progress in capitalistic agriculture is a progress in the art, not only of robbing the labourer, but of robbing the soil; all progress in increasing the fertility of the soil for a given time, is a progress towards ruining the lasting sources of that fertility.'
by
Karl Marx, Capital vol 1

'Man lives on nature – means that nature is his body, with which he must remain in continuous interchange if he is not to die. That man's physical and spiritual life is linked to nature means simply that nature is linked to itself, for man is a part of nature.'
by
Karl Marx
If we do not own the freshness of the air and the sparkle of the water, how can you buy them?
Chief Seattle, Leader of the Suquamish and Duwamish Native American tribes.

All things share the same breath – the beast, the tree, the man...
the air shares its spirit with all the life it supports.
by
Chief Seattle, Leader of the Suquamish and Duwamish Native American tribes.

Humans merely share the earth. We can only protect the land, not own it.
by
Chief Seattle, Leader of the Suquamish and Duwamish Native American tribes.

Take nothing but memories, leave nothing but footprints!
by
Chief Seattle, Leader of the Suquamish and Duwamish Native American tribes.

THE FOUR LAWS OF ECOLOGY
By
Barry Commoner

Everything is connected to everything else. There is one ecosphere for all living organisms and what affects one, affects all. Humans and other species are connected/dependent on other species.
Think cybernetics. The roots of the word are from helmsman. He is part of a system that also includes the compass, the rudder, and the ship. *'If the ship veers off the chosen compass course, the change shows up in the movement of the compass needle. Observed and interpreted by the helmsman this event determines a subsequent one: the helmsman turns the rudder, which swings the ship back to its original course. When this happens, the compass needle returns to its original, on-course position*

and the cycle is complete. ...In quite a similar way, stabilizing cybernetic relations are built into an ecological cycle. With this in mind it becomes hard to practice anything other than compassion and harmlessness.

For example, when any substance that is not metabolized, such as pesticides or mercury, enters the food chain, it becomes increasingly concentrated as it moves toward the top. As a chemical, it has no natural connection.

Everything must go somewhere. There is no "waste" in nature and **there is no "away"** to which things can be thrown. Instead, it is transferred from place to place, converted from one molecular form to another, and acting on the life processes of any organism in which it is lodged.

Everything such as wood smoke, nuclear waste, carbon emissions, etc., must go somewhere.

In every natural system, what is excreted by one organism as waste is taken up by another as food. Animals release carbon dioxide as a respiratory waste; this is an essential nutrient for green plants. Plants excrete oxygen, which is used by animals. Animal organic wastes nourish the bacteria of decay. Their wastes, inorganic materials such as nitrate, phosphate, and carbon dioxide, become algal nutrients. (*Algae possess chlorophyll, the green pigment essential for photosynthesis, ...Algae are primary producers of organic matter which animals depend on either directly or indirectly through the food chain (APHA, 1995)* **My addition for clarification.**

Where Does It Go? Consider a common household item which contains mercury. A dry-cell battery containing mercury is purchased, used to the point of exhaustion, and then 'thrown out." So where does it go *'First it is placed in a container of rubbish; this is collected and taken to an incinerator. Here the mercury is heated; this produces mercury vapor which is emitted by the incinerator stack, and mercury vapor is toxic. Mercury vapor is carried by the wind, eventually brought to earth in rain or snow. Entering a mountain lake, let us say, the mercury condenses and sinks to the bottom. Here it is acted on by bacteria which converts it to methyl mercury. This is soluble and taken up by fish; since it is not metabolized, the mercury accumulates in the organs and flesh of the fish. The fish are caught and eaten by a man and the mercury becomes deposited in his organs, where it might be harmful. And so on."*

Nature Knows Best. Humankind has fashioned technology to improve upon nature, but such change in a natural system is, says Commoner, "likely to be detrimental to that system." The Creation, one can argue, has an intelligence, and to tinker with that 'unintellectually' we get global warming pollution, etc.

"...living things accumulate a complex organization of compatible parts; those possible arrangements that are not compatible with the whole are screened out over the long course of evolution. Thus, the structure of a present living thing or the organization of a current natural ecosystem is likely to be "best" in the sense that it has been so heavily screened for disadvantageous components that any new one is very likely to be worse than the present ones.

The artificial introduction of an organic compound that does occur in nature is very likely to be harmful when man synthesizes an organic substance with a molecular structure that departs significantly from the types occurring in nature. The probability is that no degradable enzyme exists and that the material will accumulate.

There is No Such Thing as a Free Lunch. Exploitation of nature will inevitably involve the conversion of resources from useful to useless forms. In nature, both sides of the equation must balance, for every gain there is a cost, and all debts are eventually paid. This ecological law embodies the previous three laws. Because the global ecosystem is a connected whole, in which nothing can be gained or lost and which is not subject to over-all improvement, anything extracted from it by human effort must be replaced. Payment of this price cannot be avoided; it can only be delayed. The present environmental crisis is a warning that we have delayed nearly too long. (Commoner refers us to Moby Dick.)

The introduction of nitrogen into the soil to increase agricultural yields may have its side effects. For example, Commoner points to the experience in Decatur, Illinois, where nitrogen was used to increase crop yield. Nitrate run-off got into the water system with the result that there was evidence that infant mortality was increased.

My comment: I think of this law when I think of all the trees that have been cut down to make buildings, intentionally burned down to prevent fire hazards or being burned because we have heated our atmosphere to the point that the dryness easily leads to fires. In any case, the 'free lunch' is over and mother nature is compelling us to repay. The first step in repayment is to plant more trees. As important, stop polluting the atmosphere, heating it up and causing more trees to burn! It should be clear that the bill has come due!

Our ignorance of the marvelous miracle of the earth's leafed lungs in transforming human exhalations into breathable life-sustaining oxygen is a basic that we must begin teaching our children and the world immediately.

(To help memorize these four laws, not that it will be difficult for anyone other than me to memorize these laws, I have used the following pneumonic device: **CABFare: Connected, Away, Best, Free.)**

A SELECTIVE SUMMARY OF 'THE CLOSING CIRCLE' AND COMMENTS THEREON

Nature is evenly balanced. We cannot disturb her equilibrium, for we know that the law of Cause and Effect is the unerring and inexorable law of nature; but we do fail to find our own equilibrium as nations and as individuals, because we have not yet learned that the same law works as inexorably in human life and in society as in nature-that what we sow, we must inevitably reap.
Sidney Bremer

What is happening now is of a geological and biological order of magnitude. We are upsetting the entire earth system that, over some billions of years and through an endless sequence of groping, of trials and errors, has produced such a magnificent array of living forms, forms capable of seasonal self-renewal over vast periods of time.
Thomas Berry, "The Universe and the University"

We are grossly wasting our energy resources and other precious raw materials as though their supply were infinite. We must even face the prospect of changing our basic ways of living. This change will either be made on our own initiative in a planned and rational way, or forced on us with chaos and suffering by the inexorable laws of nature.
Jimmy Carter, A Government as Good as Its People

It should not be believed that all beings exist for the sake of the existence of man. On the contrary, all other beings too have been intended for their own sakes and not for the sake of anything else.
Maimonides (Rabbi Moses ben Maimon)

The frog does not drink up the pond in which it lives.
Sioux Indian Proverb/ Chinese Proverb

Our most serious problem, perhaps, is that we have become a nation of fanaticists. We believe, apparently, in the infinite availability of finite resources.
Wendell Berry

Today's massive loss of species and habitat will be slowed only when the human community understands that nature is not an inferior to be exploited or an enemy to be destroyed but an ally requiring respect and replenishment. We are part of the web of life. Many strands already have broken. We must act quickly to repair what we can. Our lives and livelihood depend on it.
United Nations Environment Programme

I know we all have an aversion to reading a detailed book review. However, The Closing Circle, by Barry Commoner, captures and simplifies ecology so even I can understand it. Moreover, as a Biologist and a Presidential contender he has a keen sense of what we need to do with our political and economic system to deal with the problem. The essence of the book is about how our failure to recognize the importance of the ecosystem has put us in the middle of an ecological disaster that is already causing death and destruction. Since I am not a scientist and Barry Commoner is, my hope is that my words, ideas and inspiration will not seem outrageous in the light of science.

My brother, Dave, read my poem, 'Dear Granpa', about a fictional granddaughter in the future, slowly dying because of the severe pollution. His comment: You sound like one of those Jihadists! I realized then that my concerns about the environment would not be taken seriously unless supported by a scientist. Commoner is far more. He has a Masters and a PHD in Biology from Harvard. His book cover on the Closing Circle says: *He is widely regarded as American's best informed and most articulate spokesman for the safeguarding of man's environment.* He was a former presidential candidate. He has credentials. I do not think anyone would call him a Jihadist. Although when he ran for president in the 80's, I am sure they called him names. In any case, he is a scientifically educated witness to the worsening ecological disaster. The following is my selective summary of the book.

(The Bold parts are my emphasis.)

In the Closing Circle, Commoner summarizes the history of the environmental problem:

"Thus, since World War II, in the United States, private business has chosen to invest its capital preferentially in a series of new productive enterprises that are closely related to the intensification of environmental pollution."

Citing Heilbroner he answers the question of what has motivated this pattern of investment?

"...the touchstone of investment decisions is profit."

He addresses the dynamics of the problem. He identifies it is as an *'ecologist's nightmare':*

"thus, the extraordinarily high rate of profit of this industry appears to be a direct result of the development and production at rapid intervals of new, usually unnatural, synthetic materials—which, entering the environment, for reasons already given, often pollute it. This situation is an ecologist's nightmare, for in the four to five-year period in which a new synthetic substance, such as a detergent or pesticide, is massively moved into the market—and into the environment—there is literally not enough time to work out its ecological effects. Inevitably, by the time the effects are known, the damage is done and the inertia of the heavy investment in a new productive technology makes a retreat extraordinarily difficult. The very system of enhancing profit in this industry is precisely the cause of its intense, detrimental impact on the environment.

He states the size and urgency of the problem:

"Both the environmental and population crises are the largely unintended result of the exploitation of technological, economic, and political power. Their solutions must also be found in this same difficult arena. **This task is unprecedented in human history, in its size, complexity, and urgency."**

Commoner addresses the issue of our time, which if addressed by me, I would be called a 'radical' or, by some, 'unpatriotic':

"Far more serious than such objections is the question of whether a conventional 'market place" economy is fundamentally incompatible with the integrity of the environment."

He later reiterates this concern:

"Here it raises the fundamental question of whether the basic operational requirements of the private enterprise economic system are compatible with ecological imperatives."

Citing details in a list of synthetics technologies, including pesticides and DDT with attendant devastating results Commoner comments:

"Nor should we forget, in this connection, that the United States defoliation campaign has imposed on Vietnam concentrations of various herbicides—of still unknown toxicity to human beings—never achieved anywhere in the world on such a scale."

The Closing Circle author addresses the damaging effects of NTA in detergents and nitrogen fertilizer in the soil. He concludes:

This is evidence that a high rate of profit is associated with practices that are particularly stressful toward the environment and that when these practices are restricted, profits decline.

Mr. Commoner addresses the serious difficulty in our Capitalist system in making a low-powered car that has less of an impact on the environment. *

"As the size and selling price of a car are reduced, then, the profit margin tends to drop even faster. A standard United States sedan with a basic price of $3000, for example, yields something like $250 to $300 in profit to its manufacturer. But when the price falls by a third, to $2,000, the factory profit drops by about half. Below $2,000, the decline grows even more precipitous. ....."

.....It would therefore yield a smaller profit relative to sales price than the standard heavy, high-powered, high-polluting vehicle.

Commoner details the serious problem with our present system:

"In general, this argument has a considerable force, for it is certainly true that industrial pollution tends to destroy the very "biological capital" that the ecosystem provides and on which production depends.

Based on numerous illustrations, Commoner then opines:

*"Nevertheless, it is a fact that in this and other instances, **the industrial operation—until constrained by outside forces—has proceeded on the seemingly irrational, self-destructive course of polluting the environment on which it depends.**"*

In illustrating and explaining the paradoxical relationship between the profitability of a business and its tendency to destroy its own environmental base, the author cites a statistician, Daniel Fife, who uses the whaling industry, which has been drilling itself out of business by killing whales so fast as to ensure that they will become extinct. Fife points out that:

"even though the irresponsible business will eventually wipe itself out, it may be profitable to do so—at least for the entrepreneur, if not for society—if the extra profit derived from the irresponsible operation is high enough to yield a return on investment elsewhere that outweighs the ultimate effect of killing off the whaling business. "....the irresponsible" entrepreneur finds it profitable to kill the goose that lays the golden eggs, so long as the goose lives long enough to provide him with sufficient eggs to pay for the purchase of a new goose.

Fife concludes: *"Ecological irresponsibility can pay—for the entrepreneur, but not for society as a whole."*

Commoner opines:

"A business enterprise that pollutes the environment is therefore being subsidized by society; to the extent, the enterprise, though free, is not wholly private."

Commoner identifies the essential conflict:

*Therefore, **there appears to be a basic conflict between pollution control and what is often regarded as a fundamental requirement of the private enterprise system—the continued maximization of productivity.***

Commoner makes a recommendation, that is sure not to be appreciated by American businesses, on how to bring the world to environmental balance:

*"If the world is to return to environmental balance, the **advanced countries will need to rely less on ecologically costly synthetics and more on goods produced from natural products—a process which, on both ecological and economic grounds, ought to be concentrated in the developing regions of the world.***

Commoner specifically addresses 'cost' of pollution to the health of a wage earner vis-à-vis 'cost' of pollution in economic terms and the dangerous 'lag time' when the pollution continues to build up in the ecosystem or the employee's body:

"...chronic, low-level exposure to radiation mercury, or DDT may shorten a wage earner's life without reducing his income or even incurring extra medical costs during his lifetime. In this case, the

cost of pollution is not met by anyone for a long time; the bill finally paid by exacting the wage earner's premature death, which—apart from the incalculable human anguish—can be reckoned in terms of some number of years of lost income. In this situation, then, during the "free" period, pollutants accumulate in the ecosystem or in a victim's body, but not all the resultant costs are immediately felt. ....."...when the environmental bill is paid, it is met by labor more than by capital."

He addresses the environmental costs, based on the business assumption that there is no cost in destroying nature:

*"In the creation of this capital, **certain goods are regarded as freely and continuously available from nature: the fertility of the soil, oxygen, water—in general, nature, or the biological capital represented by the ecosphere. However, the environmental crisis tells us that these goods are no longer freely available, and that when they are treated as though they were, they are progressively degraded."***

My Comment: One example of natural or biological capital is carbon dioxide absorption.

This is done by trees and plants which take in carbon dioxide and give off oxygen. Guess what happens when you chop down trees or they are consumed by fire because of the heat of Global Warming?

Commoner recommends a solution and explains the limits of our exploitation of the ecosystem as the reason that our system must change:

*"The effect of the operation of the system on the value of its 'biological capital needs to be taken into account in order to obtain a true estimate of the over-all wealth-producing capability of the system. **The course of environmental deterioration shows that conventional capital has accumulated, for example in the United States since 1946, the value of the biological capital has declined. If the process continues, the biological capital may eventually be driven to the point of total destruction."** "...Thus despite its apparent prosperity, in reality the system is being driven into bankruptcy. **Environmental degradation represents a crucial, potentially fatal, hidden factor in the operation of the economic system."** "the total rate of exploitation of the earth's ecosystem has some upper limit,** which reflects the intrinsic limit of the ecosystem's turnover rate. If this rate is exceeded, the system is eventually driven to collapse."*

His recommendation: *"Thus there must be some limit to the growth of total capital, and productive system must eventually reach a "no-growth" condition, at least with respect to the accumulation of capital goods designed to exploit the ecosystem, and the products which they yield."*

He then addresses the different rates of the natural turnover of the soil systems and explains how our economic system must adjust:

"It follows, then that if these different ecosystems are to be exploited concurrently by the private enterprise system without inducing ecological breakdowns, they must operate at differential rates of economic return. However, the free operation of the private enterprise system tends to maximize rates of return from different enterprises."

He recommends a solution to the problem of non-exploitation of the ecosystem with the need to maximize profits:

*A corrective expedient is the provision of **subsidies**; but in some cases these **may need to be large enough to amount to nationalization**—a contradiction of private enterprise."*

Commoner dares to attribute some insight to Karl Marx author of Das Kapital, who he says points out:

".... that agricultural exploitation in the capitalist system is, in part, based on its destructive effects on the cyclical ecological process that links man to the soil."

Commoner then addresses the apparent incapacity of our economic system and the specific needs of the environment as viewed by Marx:

If, on these grounds (Marxian analysis), it is concluded that the private enterprise system must continue to grow, while its ecological base will not tolerate unlimited exploitation, then there is a serious incompatibility between the two."

Commoner asks the big question:

"....whether the private enterprise system can survive the environmental crisis without basic change."

He cites Robert Heilbroner with the answer:

"Ordinarily I do not see how such a question could be answered in any way but negatively, for it is tantamount to asking a dominant class to acquiesce in the elimination of the very activities that sustain it."

Commoner emphatically states:

"...the environmental crisis is not a theoretical danger, but a real and present one; it demands immediate social action."

He details **what must be done** if we are to survive economically as well as biologically:

*"...industry, agriculture, and transportation will have to meet the inescapable demands of the ecosystem. This will require the **development of major new technologies, including: systems to return sewage and garbage directly to the soil; the replacement of many synthetic materials by natural ones; the reversal of the present trend to retire land from cultivation and to elevate the yield per acre by heavy fertilization; replacement of synthetic pesticides, as rapidly as possible, by biological ones; the discouragement of power-consuming industries; the development of land transport that operates with maximal fuel efficiency at low combustion temperatures and with minimal land use; essentially complete containment and reclamation of wastes from combustion processes, smelting, and chemical operations (smokestacks must become rarities); essentially complete recycling of all reusable metal, glass, and paper products, ecologically sound planning to govern land use including urban areas."***

My comment: I suspect that today he would add the production of electric vehicles.

He then addresses **the cost** which he clarifies is in 1958 dollars:

"A very rough estimate of the existing capital equipment that would need to be replaced in order to remedy major ecological faults might be about one-fourth, or about six hundred billion dollars worth."..."*one half of the postwar productive enterprises would need to be replaced by ecologically sounder ones."*

"To this estimate must be added the costs of efforts to restore damaged sectors of the ecosystem, which would range in the area of hundreds of billion dollars.

He estimates that this amount of money would be needed over a twenty-five-year period.

"..then the cost of survival becomes about forty billion dollars annually over that period of time."

In other words,

"...most of the nation's resources for capital investment would need to be engaged in the task of ecological reconstruction for at least a generation.

He notes:

"...the process of environmental recovery will be an unprecedented challenge to the flexibility and strength of the economic system.

As far as specifics of the change, Commoner says:

"...this principle would favor the manufacturer who produced the more durable vehicle... "This same principle would favor the production of returnable bottles over nonreturnable ones, of a sparsely packaged product over one heavily encased in plastic of natural products over synthetic ones."

Comment: In another of his books, *The Politics of Energy (1979)*,Commoner called for

"a national policy for the transition from the present, non-renewable energy system to a renewable one"—a transition which he believed a traditional free market economy would be unable to accomplish. He wanted Americans to **use solar rather than conventional power, trains rather than automobiles, and methane or gasohol rather than gasoline**—proposals which ran not only up against powerful vested interests but also against some basic American habits and preferences.

Commoner then opines:

"...modern technology which is privately owned cannot long survive if it destroys the social good on which it depends—the ecosphere. Hence an economic system which is fundamentally based on private transactions rather than social ones is no longer appropriate and increasingly ineffective in managing this vital social good. The system is therefore in need of change."

Commoner gives his view of what needs to happen:

"...we can expect that in an ecologically sound economy, meaningful employment would become universally available. For once the principle is established—as demanded by the ecological imperative—that production is for social use rather than private profit or plan fulfillment," it would be clear that social good must begin with the welfare of the people who make up society. These considerations apply to all industrialized nations; all of them need to reorganize their economies along ecologically sound lines."

Commoner tells us what is the one major requirement for the ecological reconstruction of modern industry:

"...to reduce the present reliance on synthetic materials and power-consumptive processes and, wherever possible, to substitute for them natural materials and processes that rely relatively more on labor than on power.

On page 290, he daringly opines about the Military Industrial Complex:

"Thus, it is inconceivable that the United States could find the huge capital resources for the needed reconstruction of industry and agriculture along ecologically sound lines unless we give up our preoccupation with large-scale military activities—which since World War II have preempted most of the nations' disposable income"

On Chapter 13, entitled 'The Closing Circle', Mr. Commoner declares:

*"For we are in an environmental crisis because the means by which we use the ecosphere to produce wealth are destructive of the ecosphere itself. **The present system of production is self-destructive; the present course of human civilization is suicidal."***

The scientist who is usually optimistic, Commoner predicts some ominous consequences:

"The environmental crisis is somber evidence of an insidious fraud hidden in the vaunted productivity and wealth of modern, technology-based society. This wealth has been gained by rapid short-term exploitation of the environmental system, but it has blindly accumulated a debt to nature in the form of environmental destruction in developed countries and of population pressure in developing ones—a debt so large and so pervasive that in the next generation it may, if unpaid, wipe out most of the wealth it has gained us. In effect, the account books of modern society are drastically out of balance, so that, largely unconsciously, a **huge fraud has been perpetrated on the people of**

the world. **The rapidly worsening course of environmental pollution is a warning that the bubble is about to burst, that the demand to pay the global debt may find the world bankrupt."**

However, he is optimistically states:

"This does not necessarily mean that to survive the environmental crisis, the people of industrialized nations will need to give up their "affluent" way of life" ".....the needed productive reforms can be carried out without seriously reducing the present level of useful goods available to the individual; and, at the same time, by controlling pollution the quality of life can be improved significantly."

Then **he identifies 'certain luxuries' that the environmental crisis and the approaching Bankruptcy, will force us to give up:**

*"These are the political luxuries which have so long been enjoyed by those who can benefit from them: **the luxury of allowing the wealth of the nations to serve preferentially the interests of so few of its citizens; of failing fully to inform citizens of what they need to know in order to exercise their right of political governance; of condemning as anathema any suggestion which re-examines basic economic values; of burying the issues revealed by logic in a morass of self-serving propaganda. To resolve the environmental crisis, we shall need to forego, at last, the luxury of tolerating poverty, racial discrimination, and war."***

My Comment*:* He seems to be on the same page with the Pope.

Near the end of the book he gives us one of nature's biggest lessons:

"...that nothing can survive on the planet unless it is a cooperative part of a larger, global whole."

After telling us how nature 'healed' and completed the circle of life, three billion years ago when the cyanobacteria thrived, (the first photosynthetic organism) and turned sunlight into sugar and excreting oxygen as waste, he tells us:

"Human beings have broken out of the circle of life, driven not by biological need, but by the social organization which they have devised to "conquer" nature: means of gaining wealth that are governed by requirements conflicting with those which govern nature. The end result is the environmental crisis, a crisis of survival. Once more, to survive, we must close the circle. We must learn how to restore to nature the wealth that we borrow from it."

My Comment: And there you have my 'summary' of 'The Closing Circle'. And Commoner's book came out in 1971. Apparently no one was listening then! It is my hope that the rest of *Glimpsing Heaven* is given context and scientific support for the claim that pollution's danger is real, that we are the cause and that the need to respond is urgent! What we do or fail to do today, will have a severe impact on our children and grandchildren. Should that not be enough motivation to act?

*Commoner's book came out before electric cars appeared on the scene. I am sure that he would strongly support electric cars over gas powered cars if the book had been written later.

E. A POETIC EDUCATION ABOUT POLLUTION, THE PROBLEM and THE CONSEQUENCES, WITH FOOTNOTES,

The following is what happens when a poet with a teacher's mentality and a coach's heart, meets the mentality of a lawyer: Pollution facts meet poetic scheme with footnotes to verify there has been no distortion of truth's illuminating light beam. 'Solutions' savor and inspire the winning dream. It is part of my proposal to make 'Understanding Manmade Pollution & It's Dire Consequences' required reading from grade school through college.

This educerepoem is directed to kids and adults. It is a primer or a proem for those who want to enjoyably learn about the basics of ecology, the philosophy, the politics, the morality and the economics that complicate it. I also provide some solutions. I have provided 'footnotes' for those who want to search further for the truth of what is being said. It is in rhyme form so you can easily commit it to memory. Feel free to memorize parts of it by jump-roping, if you want some exercise. (That is the jock in me.) Patticaking would be fun too. In any case, this poem with footnotes is a method of introducing children and adults to our connection with the natural world and how we are destroying it. I want it to be fun and educational.

My bias is that I believe we are living in Paradise or what was once Paradise until we began thoughtlessly 'dumping' on it and spewing toxic gases into it as if it would not have an impact. The consequences are severe and worsening! So start patticaking for nature or get out that jump rope and begin jumping so our kids and grandkids get to enjoy the beauty, the wonders and sustenance of our earth mother.

97% of scientist agree that global warming is manmade.*.2 So please educate yourself about nature and how we must stop destroying it. Hope this helps.

POLLUTION DEVASTATION IN POETIC VERSE or JUMPEROPE FOR NATURE

I. The Facts

A fact that should bring tears: **CO2 HIGHEST IN 3 MILLION YEARS**
The concentration of CO_2 in our atmosphere
As of 2018, is the highest it has been
In almost 3 million years. *1

NASA and NOAA data show global averages in 2016
Were almost one degree centigrade warmer   **WE ARE HEATING UP QUICKLY**
Than the mid-20th century average *1
How's that for a wakeup alarmer? *1.2

The U.N. chief warns: Point of no return   **IRREVERSIBILITY MAY BE NEAR**
Is in sight and hurtling towards us
(*Like a nuclear rocket*)
But we refuse to learn.
Efforts to stop climate change
Have been utterly sparse.
What is lacking is political will

We must stop digging and put down the drill
Stop the bacon, eggs and steak,
Not one more cow should we kill
Stop using plastic
Not one more bottle or bag should we fill.
The effects of climate change
Are already being felt.
The rage against nature must be stilled. *1.5

You say you like it hot -   **HOTTEST DECADE EVER**
More time to play in the beach sand.
Well, seventeen of the 18 warmest years
Have occurred since the year 2000. *1

In a history of testing temperatures,   **GETTING HOTTER**
The last four years measured the most severe heat.*2
If you can't feel the swelter, you're at the North Pole
Or ensconced in an air-conditioned suite.

You think of Alaska, you think polar bears and ice cold.
In 100 years of Anchorage history,   **EVEN ALASKA HEATING UP**
Weather stations have never recorded 90 degrees.
Anchorage is facing a 4th of July like never before.
They expect the temperatures to rival a Miami shore. * 3

11 % of all global human-caused greenhouse gas emissions   **CUTTING DOWN TREES**
Are caused by deforestation, comparable to the emission   **RANKS WITH VEHICLE**
From all the cars and trucks on the planet. *1   **POLLUTION**
Time for the 'replanting-our-leafed-wooden-lung' decision.

The biggest extinction the planet has ever seen
Some 250 million years gone by   **ALL THE MARKINGS OF ANOTHER**
When a volcano erupted and spewed   **EXTINCTION**
Carbon dioxide and pollution into the sky.
It warmed the planet, acidified the seas
By robbing the O2
Sickening mother earth,
Bringing the threat of near-death nigh.
90% of species in the ocean
As did two-thirds of those on land, all deceased.
It was largely caused by greenhouse gases
And scientists are finding similarities
Between now and then. *
The current warming is déjà vu all over again

But this time
It is a human volcano spewing CO2
Through the techno-mountain made by man.

Australian climate experts warn
That climate change caused by a rapidly warming planet
Represents a threat to human civilization.
It could end by 2050
Due to the destabilizing
Societal and environmental devastation.

CIVILIZATION COULD END BY 2050

We are heading into a future where society could collapse
Due to instability set off by migration patterns
Of billions of people affected by drought,
Rising sea levels
And an environmentally caused rout. *4

**STARVING PEOPLE KNOW NO
BORDERS**

In 2018, the world's leading climate scientists
Made the starkest warning to date:
Our current actions are not enough
To meet our target of 1.5C of warming.
We must do more, before it is too late.

**WE ARE NOT DOING ENOUGH
TO STOP GLOBAL WARMING**

The World Health Organization
Identified and informed us all with certainty
Climate Change, is the greatest health challenge
Of the 21st Century. *5

**THE GREATEST CHALLENGE OF
OUR LIFE**

The hope of ending pollution
And saving the planet looks grim
If the Climate Summit in Madrid
Is any indication,
Where the U.S. and other big polluters
Made only promises but no concrete acceptations
To help small countries
Vulnerable to rising seas and powerful storm devastation.*5.5

**U.S. & BIG POLLUTERS
AT CLIMATE SUMMIT
BLOCK
REAL COMMITMENT TO STOP POLUTION**

So, like a pompous politician
That you might know,
Do you believe
This disastrous pandemic
Could not be foreseen…
It came out of nowhere,
No time to prepare for this dark scene.

**DESTROYING FORESTS PRECIPITATES
PANDEMICS**

Well sorry to burst your bubble clean,
But it has been known, at least, since 2016
That destroying forests
And the ecosystems of life's dreams,
Then moving next door,
Is the cause of pandemics
Including Corona 19. *5.55

A WARNING FROM A BRILLIANT SCIENTIST

Stephen Hawking, before he died said:
Earth could turn into a hothouse planet like Venus
With boiling oceans and acid rain,
If humans don't curb irreversible climate change.* 5.6

**EARTH BECOMING A
HOTHOUSE**

II.   MOTHER NATURE IS OUR FAMILY

Nature and man are family
So why are we recklessly devouring from the knowledge tree?
And despoiling and plundering our mother for easy money?
Say adios to paradise and all future humanity. *6

**STOP DESPOILING NATURE WITH
OUR WASTES**

Like a baby suckles milk from mama
We breathe oxygen from the tree.
We don't toss out our mama because
She got no chocolate milk in her mammary. *7

**DON'T DESTROY NATURE FOR YOUR
COMFORT**

Just as a mother's arms
Hold baby near her breasts,
Through the earth and sky
Our vulnerable beings are caressed.

EARTH IS OUR MOTHER

Just as the blood stream enters the heart
Through two large veins
Then leaves through the artery into the lungs
Where it becomes the breath of life
So earth's lungs, the trees,
Sustain mother's big-brained children
Transforming CO2 to oxygen
For them to breathe.

**OXYGEN/WATER – OUR LIFEBLOOD
TREES, MOTHER EARTH'S HEART**

And with the liquid flow
Of earth's life-giving rains,
On waiting thirsty terrain,
Then upwards from earth's leaf-lungs' roots
That rely on trees breathing out water vapor

THE WATER CYCLE

Providing humidity to the sky, forming clouds
Then life sustaining rains,
And the cycle begins again.

71% of the earth's surface is water
The ocean safeguards most of this liquid gift.
It also is in water vapor in the air
And our rivers, lakes, glaciers and in deep aquiferial rifts. *8
The deliverer of liquid life
Through our body, just like mother earth
Are the cherry-colored human streams and rivers
Composing 60% of our human girth.

Oceans, rivers and streams
Quench the thirst of the 'children' of mother earth
So take care of mother and her milk.
Abusing her is to relinquish our earthen berth.

Guess what is absorbing our carbon dioxide pollution?
Yes, acidity has increased 30% in our oceans
Since the Industrial Revolution.
This rate of change surpasses all chemistry changes
In 50 million years in our vast ocean.
Living in an acidifying sea
Is challenging for corals, oysters, lobsters
And others from the shell-building animal tree.* 8.5

And don't forget our mother's coral reefs,
The tropical rainforests of the sea.
Rising temperatures and warming acidic oceans
Will wipe them out by the end of the century.*8.7

And say adios to your finned ocean friends.
¾ of the world's fisheries are exploited or depleted.
40% of fish caught every year are discarded,
Right Whales are near extinction,
By 2048, Say hello to fishless oceans.*8.8

And don't forget mother's four-legged children.
They are not expendable for your palate's satisfaction
And ultimately, world devastation.
They too can feel pain and loss beyond measure.
Stop massacring them for your eating pleasure!

TAKE CARE OF YOUR WATER

OUR BODIES, LIKE EARTH, ARE MOSTLY WATER

FAILURE TO CARE FOR EARTH IS OUR DOOM

CO2 =ACIDITY IN THE OCEAN=DEATH & DEMISE OF CORALS AND SHELL

POLLUTION KILLING CORAL REEFS

WE ARE THE CAUSE OF FISH EXTINCTION

WE ARE KILLING AND EATING ANIMALS FOR OUR EATING PLEASURE

III. A SATIRIC LOOK ABOUT DESTROYING MOTHER EARTH

Mother has a fever and it is worsening.
Of course, we take her to the garage
Put her in the comfortable car,
Turn it on and close the doors and forget her.
This should make her better.

TRAPPING GREENHOUSE GASES & A FEVERED EARTH

Your baby daughter has a cold
What should you do?
Light a cigarette
And blow smoke in her face
Until she turns blue?

POLLUTION KILLING THE CHILDREN

Your mama is sick, what to do?
Cut out her lungs
And make delicious lung burgers for the fam.
Then start a chain store.
Call it – Lungalicious!

FORESTS ARE THE LUNGS OF THE EARTH

'Murdering Mother and Her Children'
Coming to your town in 2020.
Admission is free to the few who care
In a country that has plenty
And too few, brave enough to dare
To see the monster in their mirror.

DEATH & DESTRUCTION FROM POLLUTION HAS ARRIVED

IV. THE CASUALTIES, CONSEQUENCES AND CONNECTIONS,

Pollution kills nearly 4.6 million people per year.*9
The polluters have declared war
On the poorest and weakest in the world
Profiteers see not the light, through the Empath's door.

POLLUTERS CAUSE SUFFERING & DEATH

THE CONSEQUENCES

Before pollution, weather and climate changes
Came over hundreds of thousands of years slow.
Increasing heat from pollution, means drastic shifts
Will occur in a 200-year raging flow. *10
Extinction of humanity will occur in a significantly shorter time frame
Than is being presented by our world governors.
It is getting worse at a far faster rate
Than we are planning or preparing for.
We have been given inaccurate and incomplete predictions
For when the main consequences of global warming will occur,

HEATING SKY ACCELERATES WEATHER CHANGES

WE HAVE BEEN LIED TO IN ORDER TO APPEASE THE FOSSIL FUEL & ANIMAL AG INDUSTRIES

As well as how bad those consequences will be.
In part, this is happening to protect
Corporate fossil fuel and animal agriculture's
Overflowing pockets-full of money. *11

The most expensive and worst consequences of Global Warming will not occur
In 40 to 80 years as we are being told.
And much will occur in less than half that time.
The disaster is already beginning to unfold! *11

THE DISASTER IS HAPPENING NOW

A MASSIVE REMAKE NEEDED

A UN panel of scientists say
12 years to control global warming
Before we have hell to pay.
Needed is a revolutionary remake
To the global energy frame
To limit the global warming monster
To levels, moderate and tame.*11.5

IT'S HAPPENING HERE!

California has 149 million dead trees.
Until recently, 2018 was the worst year of record for wildfires. *12
From January 1 to September 8, 2019,
There were 35,386 wildfires
Compared with in the same period in 2019 -
41,051 wildfires, almost 6,000 higher!
That many fewer earth lungs means
Less breathable air in a future of earth mega-bonfires.

THE EARTH'S LUNGS ON FIRE

Even the Amazon Rain Forest,
The super lungs for earth-mother dearest
Which provides 20% of the earth's oxygen
Is now ablaze and at its severest. *13
An 83% increase since 2018
When there were fewer than 40,000 fires.
Now more than 72,000 since January 2019
A cataclysm most dire.
Worsened by illegal fires to deforest for cattle ranching.
Mother earth suffocates to keep the dollars dancing.

BURNING EARTH'S LUNGS FOR MONEY

The Amazon has been fire-resistant for much of its history
But now there are wildfires caused by drought and human activity.
The intensity and frequency of droughts is linked clearly
With increased deforestation and human-caused climate change
Costing us most dearly.

WILDFIRES FROM DROUGHTS DEFORESTATION & POLLUTION-CAUSED HEAT

Think of forests as water-fountains.
Taking water from the ground
And putting it in the air through their leaves,
Just like the CO2 to oxygen our lungs breath,
Take away the trees and the rains will cease.* 13.5

**'TRANSPIRATION'
DEFORESTATION LEADS TO
DROUGHTS**

About a billion more people might be exposed
To mosquito-borne diseases as temps continue to rise
As Zika, chikungunya and dengue move north
The U.S. is in for a bug-biting blood-sucking surprise. *14

**HOTTER MEANS MORE
MOSQUITO AILMENTS**

Or do you still believe the head blamer
Who simply says it is China we must abhor
Or do you know that deforestation
And destroying an ecosystem, then moving next door,
Makes you a target of deer ticks and Lyme disease disorder
Or worse, in a crowded world
Where we are all 'next door'
You become a victim
Of a displaced bat or snake or infected animal
And the killer corona virus they transfer*13.6
To one human being and then upon all humanity
A sea of hurt, will pour.

**CORONA VIRUS CAUSED BY
DEFORESTATION**

So you believe a planet warming
Will bring more days at the beach.
And nothing more than poor polar bears without ice
But you are unaffected – you are out of reach.
Think again my friend.
Our pollution colliding with nature
Is more than just a minor nature-bender
It is a giant pileup,
The start of a mother-earth-ender.

**THE CONSEQUENCES OF POLLUTION ARE
DISASTEROUS**

Deserts like Phoenix will get hotter
Water will become more scarce
Expect less food, more vegetationless land*15
Deaths tolls will grow, as will the desert sands.

**EXPECT LESS
FOOD/DEATH TOLLS TO
RISE WITH EXTREME HEAT**

As heatwaves intensify around the globe,
The human body will be overcome - that is sure!
Expect dehydration, heatstroke and organ damage
Particularly to the elderly, children and the poor. *16

**HEATWAVES AFFECT THE
WEAKEST**

Pollution from burning fossil fuels affects the air we breathe
Expect more wildfires and the fine particles
To penetrate your lungs, bringing death
Burning eyes, heart and lung disease. *17

**FOSSIL FUEL = MORE FIRES
=MORE DEATH**

If you love the winged creatures
That fill and raise our eyes to the beautified sky,
Then know that our polluted and heated air
Are the cause, in large numbers, for them to die. *18

**POLLUTION KILLING OUR
BIRDS**

V. THE CAUSATION, CONNECTION & CONSEQUENCES

The record temps in the sky
Are from our fossil fuels despoiling,
Our leafed lungs, logged, felled and burning
Our Cow Ag. causing toxic methane polluting
And our thrown-away food scraps
In the landfill
Maliciously methane maligning.
The sea absorbs the heat which means more evaporation. *19
So storms to hurricanes and cyclones are now a-roiling. *11
And they are stronger than ever before:
The destructive power of hurricanes has increased
By roughly 50% in the last 30 years. *11
Will we wake up to the reality of this destructive deluge
Before the devastating destruction leaves our family in tears.

**COAL, GAS & OIL, ANIMAL AG.,
TREES BEING CUT DOWN
FOOD SCRAPS THROWN AWAY
DESTROY DELICATE
BALANCE**

**MORE HEAT EQUAL
MORE EVAPORATION
EQUAL MORE & POWERFUL HURRICANES**

And forget not, our powerful polluting
Bureaucracy and industry of war –
The Pentagon and U.S. military
Are one of the biggest polluters in history.

**PENTAGON
ONE OF THE BIGGEST POLLUTERS**

EFFECTS OF ANIMAL AGRICULTURE

Did you know
That animal agriculture causes more pollution
Than all the cars, buses, planes and boats on the ocean
But we love our burgers, steaks, bacon, eggs and ice cream.
Our spoiled pallet, the politicians and big industry *1.3
Have joined to addict us to meat and dairy.
Say goodbye to life's future light beams.
With every cow we torture and kill,
We dig the grave, to inter our children's dreams
And bury our future
In the cowardly created cemetery
For the lovers of meat and dairy.

**ANIMAL AGRICULTURE
POLLUTES MORE THAN
VEHICLE POLLUTION**

With a tombstone that reads:
'O'd'd from a tasty dream, turned nature nightmare
About violent feelingless slaughter
Of our fellow voyagers
While we revel in our late night's I'ce Scream!'

One of the greatest contributors of methane,   **REARING COWS POLLUTES**
More deadly than CO2
To our already heated up atmosphere
Is the pollution beast of animal agriculture.
Enjoying your steaks, burgers,   **AG INDUSTRY ONE OF THE BIGGEST**
Eggs, cheeze milk and ice cream?   **POLLUTERS**
The industries that bring you these treats
Are one of the biggest polluters
On our small sphere of dreams!*.3

If that does not put you ill at ease,   **MEAT IS A CARCINOGEN**
Know that processed meats – cause a cancerous disease.
So eat your ham, salami, bacon and 'dogs'
Knowing that evidence is strong
That your life may not be as long
To finish singing your beautiful life's song.
So where do all the oats go   **COWS EAT THE OATS**
That could feed the poor and the hungry?   **THAT THE POOR COULD HAVE**
Of course they go to feed the cow   **EATEN**
Who then goes to a wealthy country
To feed the rich and well off.
So much for 'what we do to the least of our brethren…'
As we habituate on our carcinogenic meat and dairy heroin.

And where does all the excessive excrement go   **EXCREMENT & FERTILIZER=**
From the cows whose defecation is everywhere?   **DEADZONES IN THE SEA**
To the rivers and streams that lead to the sea.
Where, combined with fertilizer,
More than 400 dead zones worldwide, have formed
To create a lifeless sea.
Off someone's coast,
Once pollution free. *19.1

And what effect the enormous amounts of water   **ENORMITY OF WATER**
To raise livestock and poultry for meat?   **TO PRODUCE MEAT**
660 gallons of water to make a burger.
Not even scarce water depletion will inspire a retreat,

Nor will the thirst of the poor
Inspire us to stop eating meat.

So what does it say about us
That we allow billions of animals
To be prisoners their entire life,
To experience not the slightest affection
Or fellowship with another living being?
Could their existence have more severe strife?
What does it say about us to blatantly defile
The sacred bond between baby and mother,
Just when the maternal relationship
Is most craved for each other?
Some will never know a mother's touch or call
Nor taste mother's milk.
What does this say about our humanity?
Have we replaced compassion, kindness and mercy
With selfishness, silence and brutality?
Could we imagine a more perfect hell
For our fellow earth travelers?
Could we imagine any greater
Greed, cruelty and violence,
All for our steaks, eggs and burgers.
Not for our poor
But for the industrialized world to feast -
Those who need it the least. *

**FACTORY FARMING
OUR ANIMAL CRUELTY TO BENEFIT THE
WEALTHY REVEALS OUR INSENSITIVITY &
CRUELTY**

All the grains that poor humans could consume
Go to feeding cows to feed our wealthy commune.
While the poor go without
And we, the pampered pawns of Animal Ag Industry
Are the cause of the poor's death and misery.

**WE ARE THE CAUSE
OF THE MISERY OF
THE POOR**

We daily feed our family carcinogenic meat*32
Now cows replace
Where once life-breathing trees were replete.
Cows poison us and we inhale methane-poisoned air.
We commit slow suicide
With our meat and dairy-loving affair.

**COWS MEAN FEWER TREES
STOP TEARING OUR EARTH LUNGS OUT
FOR STEAK**

Red meat production requires more water and land than plants
And produces significant greenhouse emissions.
It further drives deforestation.

EATING MEAT KILLS

The wildlife losses in the last 50 years
Are a severe devastation
And include the insect Armageddon. *33
We must begin to eat
A larger variety of plants and vegetation.

EAT MORE VEGATABLES, SAVE THE WILDLIFE

How about the devastation of deforestation
To raise cows to feed the rich?
Look to the rainforests of Brazil
To find the murderous niche.

RAISING CATTLE DESTROYS MOTHER'S LUNGS

Have you heard of the 'Largest Living Thing'-
The Pando aspen forest in Utah is dying
Because cattle and deer are a-grazing
And we are cutting down the trees, *31.5
Part of Americas' earth-lung out-phasing.

ANOTHER SET OF LUNGS BITING THE DUST

Enjoying your McDee's hamburger today?
Overdosing cows with antibiotics will make you pay.
Anti-biotic resistant bacteria are on the rise.
Stop now, so a super-bug does not cause your child's demise. *32.5

DEATH IS THE FRUIT OF EXCESSIVE ANTIBIOTICS

Stop poisoning your mother
With garbage and technology-inspired debris.
And stop cutting earth's lungs down for pasture
For your carcinogenic steak spree.

STOP POISONING MOTHER

Raising cattle produces more
Global warming greenhouse gases
Than transportation, *32.6
as measured in CO2 equivalent,
and Methane emissions are 86 times more destructive
Than all vehicle emissions.

RAISING CATTLE IS A MAJOR POLLUTER

You don't think what you eat, affects animals or vegetation?
There has been a 60% decline in wildlife population
Since 1970 and the biggest driver is global farming
Where cows consume the oats that the poor aren't getting.

EATING MORE PLANTS SAVES WILDLIFE CHANGE YOUR DIET

The use of fertilizer and pesticides, when misused,
Hurts wildlife and damages their natural place of living.
Our heated air is melting the polar caps.*20
Guess what has been hidden for thousands of years?
Now bubbling up from the sea to add to our fears
Poison methane to add to the drear. *21

HOTTER AIR MELTING POLAR ICE CAPS RELEASING METHANE

High temperatures from greenhouse gases
Are melting the Greenland artic ice *21.5
Critical to maintaining global temperatures.
Now we have less cooling reflecting ice.
It is radically changing our weather patterns,
More severe storms and longer draughts
And more erratic weather all about. *22

**POLLUTION MELTING ARTIC ICE
EQUAL RADICAL WEATHER
PATTERNS**

And the melting is happening faster than we thought.*22.2
The cause is man-made Global Warming,
From fossil fuel, animal ag and forest destruction
Adding more water to already rising seas
An additional 30% to the yearly ocean rise,
Threatening coastal cities at risk of flooding during storms
And the ensuing cause of destruction and loss of lives. *23

**POLLUTION IS MELTING ICE CAPS
& CAUSING THE OCEAN TO RISE
=
FLOODING & DYING**

Nature and humanity
Are intricately entwined
Ignoring the assault on nature,
Ushers in a hellish and turbulent end-times.

**IGNORING
CONNECTION, INVITES DESTRUCTION**

Dumping garbage and poison in the rivers
And polluting the sky and our sacred sea,
Say goodbye to paradise as you know it
It's soon to be a bygone memory

POISONING PARADISE IS SUICIDE

VI. THE WEAPONS OF DESTRUCTION
An area of coastal ecosystems larger than New York City
Is destroyed every year, eliminating important protectors
From extreme weather for coastal communities
And releasing carbon dioxide into the atmosphere.*23.5
Time for coastal communities final eulogies.

**WE ARE POLLUTING AND
DESTROYING OUR COASTS**

As if gutting the earth and poisoning the sky
Was not enough to destroy a planet,
They fracture and poison the earth's foundation to get more oil
Mother Earth quakes and polluted water is left in the soil. *24

**FRACK'G POLLUTES & MAKES THE
EARTH QUAKE**

If you like your water and sand radon rich,
Then uranium mining is your niche.
It has big-time income for the business clique
But for downstream dwellers, people are gett'n sick. *25

**URANIUM MINING IS
DANGEROUS**

On June 20, 1969
The Cuyahoga River in Ohio caught fire.
It wasn't the first, there were a dozen other scorching pyres
In the late 1800's and 1900's sparked by pollution,
US EPA in 1970 was finally the resulting creation.

BURNING WATER INSPIRED EPA

If water burning 50 years ago didn't inspire to stop pollution?
How much of the earth must become a furnace
Before we learn fossil fuel, the Pentagon and Animal Ag
Are the matches that burns us?
And how soon will it take for America to act
Before the 'heater' can't be unplugged
And how long before the polluters are attacked.
With potent laws we must enact. *26

HOW LONG BEFORE WE ACT?

APPAREL & TEXTILE INDUSTRIES
So, it's fashion you say that makes you this way.
Well this piece of info should make your day:
Your beloved fashion industry
Is the 2nd biggest polluter in the world today. *27

DRESSING FOR DEATH

Did you know that those clothes you wear
Are one of the worst polluters anywhere.
5% of all landfill space
Is filled with textile wastes. *28
25% of the world's chemicals
Are used for textile production. *29
10% of the worlds' carbon emissions
Are from the apparel & textile industrialization. *30

CLOTHES DESTROY THE EARTH

STYLE POLLUTES AND KILLS

Many of our clothes contain plastics
Like polyester, nylon, acrylic and polyamide.
In most new fabrics - 64%,
The plastic polluter is now identified.

OUR CLOTHES ARE MADE OF PLASTIC

When you wash your clothes,
Millions of plastic fibres
End up in the wastewaters,
Then into the ocean and absorbed by sea creatures. *30.1,

WASHING YOUR 'PLASTIC' CLOTHES POLLUTES

Enjoy your fish and shrimp,
In oceans, now micro-plastic rife.
20% of all fresh water contamination
Is made by textile treatment & dyeing pollution. *31

TEXTILES & DYES DESTROY THE LAND

This pollutes the water & makes the land barren
And useless to those plann'n on a-garden-grow'n.
So when you dress fancy today,
There are human beings that will pay
With their life and health
In their, oh so brief stay.

FAST FASHION KILLS

So, do you feel pretty today
Contributing to mankind's death and decay
Or does feeling contrite
Show you in a bad light?

**OBSESSIVE NEED FOR BEAUTY
KILLS**

Maybe being naked in paradise had a good reason.
With pollution-free skin, hair, trees and leaves for protection.
In Paradise, USA, you fashion fanatics can claim
Your choice in clothes is a 'killer' selection.

**CLOTHES ARE CULPRITS/
POLLUTION HELL IS THE
PRICE
(WRITTEN BEFORE THE FOREST FIRE IN
PARADISE)**

VII.   THE THREAT TO POLLUTERS

So stop dumping your plastic in the sea*34
And your damaging and deadly debris
Go find another planet to destroy
With your callous regard for humanity.

**DO NOT TOLERATE THE
POLLUTERS**

Stop acting like an ingrate child
And treating earth like your personal junkyard
By destroying her with garbage and polluting debris
We are ailing and dying in this poisoned earth sea.

**STOP TREATING EARTH AS LESS
THAN HUMANITY**

DON'T BUY THE DECEPTION OF BUSINESS

All was fine until farmers and workers
Began getting ill and dying
Asking what could be the cause,
Was there someone who was lying?

**TECHNOLOGY & PROFITS BREED
DECEPTION**

In 1982, Exxon knew how high global emissions would be today.
And they knew then how bad the consequences would be.
And instead of changing and telling the truth for earth's survival
They invested heavily in a disinformation campaign,
Promoting Climate Science Denial. *35

**THEY KNEW AND THEY LIED
TO US**

DUTY & DIRECTIVE TO PROFITEERS: MAINTAIN THE BALANCE OF NATURE

Nature's cycles sustaining life **RESPECT NATURE'S CYCLE OF**
Don't jibe with the profiteer's advice. **LIFE**
We must interact with nature at its own pace
What we steal from the earth, we must replace. *36

THE BIGGIST POLLUTERS

The biggest polluters in the world **ANIMAL AG & FOSSIL FUEL**
Are the Fossil Fuel industry **ARE THE BIGGEST POLLUTER**
And Animal Ag. -
The meat and dairy companies. *37

As of Nov, 2018, animal ag companies
Are the biggest water and air polluters in the world.*37.5
So when are we going to do what is right?
Stop eating meat & dairy, stop this earth blight.

The Pentagon is one of the biggest greenhouse gas polluter in the world,*37.6
But is exempt from the Paris Accords. *38 **PENTAGON BIGGEST**
Beware the Military Industrial Complex, said Ike, **GREENHOUSE GAS**
We must tell the pollution king, **POLLUTER IN WORLD**
We will plug the hole in the pollution dike.

VIII.   THE POLLUTANTS AND THE PAIN

Enjoy your favorite pollutants **THE KILLERS**
In the air and sky outside:
Carbon Monoxide, Sulphur Dioxide,
Methane and Nitrogen Dioxide. *39

Pesticides used by farm workers **PESTICIDES SICKEN &**
Are killing and making field workers ill. *40 **KILL**
Stop sickening and killing employees
Stop being the cause of their disease.

Arsenic ending up in ground water
From Petroleum Refineries **PETROLEUM, MINING AND SMELTING**
And Mining and Smelting Industries. **REFINERIES POLLUTE**
Insure terminal maladies. *41

Revel as you drown in your industrial waste, **CAR BATTERY POLLUTES**
Polluting our precious water to drink.
In landfills lay toxins like lead oxide, led and mercury,
Nickel and cadmium from your disposable battery. *42

We are sickening from the Chromium in our dyes,
The Mercury and Arsenic from fossil fuel combustion
And from our coal power plants, poisoning the air
All for business profits, our comfort and outward impressions. *43

Coal Mining and tanneries cause lung cancer,
Asthma, Emphysema and bronchitis –
The costs of business?
Sickness and dying, the answer. *44

We got chemicals for every job:
Pesticides to kill the pests,
Herbicides to kill the pesky weeds,
Insecticide to rid us of the insect breeds.
Benzene and Vinyl hydrochloride
Are toxic chemicals from plastic production
They cause cancer by polluting our air and soil
And never breaking down, causing a deadly turmoil. *45

Think you just get water from your plastic bottle?
Enjoy your estrogen-like chemicals,
In addition to BPA
That comes with the plastic water bottle you drink today. *46
Plastics' phthalates evaporate into the air
Affecting fertility and causing birth defects.
So, as you put groceries in your convenient plastic bag
Don't sniff it! 'Phthalates destroy' should be the danger tag. *45
Micro-plastics are reaching every corner of our little sphere,
Blown from the big cities to land formerly pristine and pure.
Like all the mussels with microplastics around the UK,
Nanoplastics get into an organisms' tissue, most every day.

These plastics absorb chemicals in the environment.
They have become disease transmitters in the coral reefs
So look up and breathe and be all you can be
You are now living in a poisoned plastic sea.*47
Plastics have now made their way to the oceans
Animals and birds think it is food.
Thank humanity for the sea animals' last supper
Yes! Using plastic bags is more than just rude! *45
Microplastics have invaded the largest habitat for life on earth –
In the deep ocean and the food chain, with life, they are now wound
From jellyfish to giant blue-fin tuna.
Small plastic pieces in every larvacean they found.

**CLOTHES-MAKING DYES
POLLUTE
COAL POLLUTES**

**COAL MINING AND
TANNERIES KILL**

**ARRAY OF CHEMICALS FOR
EVERY NATURE-KILLING JOB**

**CHEMICALS COME WITH
PLASTIC
PHTHALATES ARE
SICKENING**

PLASTIC KILLS

**PLASTIC KILLING WILDLIFE IN THE
OCEAN**

So they confirmed that what we introduce
To the habitat passing through these creatures of the deep
Is incorporated into the food web
That leads to marine animals people eat. *48

THE CHEMICAL'S DAMAGING EFFECTS

These chemicals are attacking people,   **CHEMICALS KILL**
Destroying their neurological system,
Causing Parkinson's disease
And damaging the source of cerebral wisdom. *49

Insecticides give you headaches   **KILLING NATURE, WE KILL**
Fungicides affects your skin   **OURSELVES**
Herbicides destroy your digestion
And the skin problems begin.
2 million metric tons used annually on fields   **SICKNESS FROM POISON IN THE**
Causing simple skin irritation,   **FARM FIELD**
To hurting, to nervous system disorders
To causing cancerous devastation. *50

Killing your plants with 'Roundup' weed killer?   **WEED KILLERS KILL MORE THAN**
Wonder if glyphosate kills just plants and not you? *51   **WEEDS**
It certainly disrupts the 'good' bacteria in your digestive system.
If you don't think it's probably dangerous, better ask W.H.O.

Hope you like your poisons and pollution   **A CULTURE OF CONSUMABLE**
Served without a warning   **DEATH**
Mercury in your fish
Carcinogenic meats, for your main dish;

Organic wastes from municipalities   **DROWNING IN OUR OWN WASTES**
And food processing manufactories,
Wastes from pulp and paper factories,
Industrial chemicals and metals,
Oil spills and drainage of fertilizer
Now poisoning your once-heavenly rivers, lakes and seas.

You thought diabetes was caused by genetics,   **AIR POLLUTION CAUSES DIABETES**
Bad diets and lack of exercise?
Adding air pollution, meat and dairy
To the sickening list
Should bring tears to your caring eyes! *52
14% of diabetes in the world
Is caused by air pollution.

8.2 million years of healthy lives lost
In the world in 2016, such a cost!
150,000 cases in the U.S. alone,
Of pollution-linked diabetes, are now known. *52

IX. CONSEQUENCES OF MANMADE POLLUTION HAVE ARRIVED

Climate change is now causing
More frequent and severe weather in our United States.
Death and massive damage is our fiery fate.   **POLLUTION IS ALREADY HURTING US**
Include damage to infrastructure, ecosystems, health and the economy
According to the most comprehensive climate report to date. *53
The top climate scientists in the country
Say that global warming, with no sight of turnabout,
Is already affecting American communities
From hurricanes to wildfires to floods and drought. *53

It is going to hurt cities, people in the countryside   **IT WILL GET WORSE**
And as the world continues to warm,
Things are going to get worse.
And the president fails to sound the alarm. *53

The Global Change Research Program says
Humans are driving climate change   **WE ARE THE CAUSE**
And already suffering from its effects.   **THE THREAT IS IMMEDIATE**
Climate change is "an immediate threat,
Not a far-off possibility" or distant prospect *53

Because of climate change,   **WILDFIRES MORE FREQUENT DUE TO**
Large wildfires are increasingly recurring.   **CLIMATE CHANGE**
The area burned in wildfires nationwide each year,
For the past 20 years, has been upsurging. *53

Unless efforts to improve air quality are implemented,   **FAILURE TO CLEAN THE AIR =**
Climate change will worsen existing air pollution levels.   **DEATH**
This will increase health effects: adverse cardiovascular and respiratory,
Including an early unplanned trip to the mortuary. *53

Those most economically and physically vulnerable   **WE ARE RESPONSIBLE**
Will be most severely impacted by climate change,   **FOR OTHERS' DISEASE**
Whether it's air pollution, disease, floods or fire disasters. *53   **AND DEATH**
We are the pollution and death spell-casters
Quickly becoming the world's disease and death-delivering masters.
Successful adaption has been hindered   **PUBLIC STILL THINKS CLIMATE**
By the dangerous and faulty assumption   **WILL BE THE SAME**

That climate conditions are and will be similar
To those bygone days of times golden. *53

The scientific findings are in stark contrast to policies
Put forward by the Trump administration,
Which include announcing this countries'
Climate Agreement termination. *53

PRESIDENT IGNORES THE SCIENCE

X. POLLUTION IS IMMORAL
And we thought we learned the lesson that
Mass production of death by gas and fire
Was the nightmare we no longer had to fear.
Our elected head tells us it's a hoax. It's not dire.

THIS IS A HOLOCAUST

Killing our fellow man is certainly immoral
How about destroying nature, is that a sin?
Finally, a holy man who has chimed in.
The Pope said clearly without doubt,
We have infected God's gift of nature,
Our closest next-of-kin.
Yes, we have a duty to future humanity
That now must, in earnest, begin. * 54

POPE FRANCIS: DESTROYING NATURE IS A SIN

The Pope and the scientist read
From the same book and same cover
All creatures are connected
And dependent on one another.

SCIENCE MEETS GOD IN LAUDATO SI' & THEY AGREE

And what about wasting food
That could feed all the poor.
Instead it ends up in landfills
Violating the Savior's admonition
What you do to the least of thy brethren…..
It is reckless, immoral and inane
To pollute our world with polluting methane? *53.5

WASTING FOOD IS IMMORAL

XI. THE FOUR LAWS OF NATURE *53.6
Everything is connected with everything else
Is the first rule of Ecology.
With the wisdom of a holy man's Encyclical,
Should we now add it to the biblical:
"What we do to the least of our brethren…"
What we do to mother nature….
As an appropriate analog to save our earthly heaven.

WE ARE INEXTRICABLY CONNECTED WITH NATURE

Everything must go somewhere is the second law.
So if you smoke a cigarette and blow it in your child's face
Are you acting immorally, knowing
Second-hand smoke will cause a cancerous fate.

**OUR CONTRIBUTION
TO POLLUTION IS EVIL**

And that 'somewhere', is it known?
Yes! We have created a 'Dead Zone':
The oxygen-depleted water In the Gulf of Mexico.
This is but one of many in the world
That are now known.
I.e., not enough oxygen to support marine life.
It is about the size of New Hampshire.
It is caused by animal waste and over-use of fertilizer
On agricultural fields during the blooming splendor.

**EXCESS NITRATES IN
FERTILIZER KILL**

Nutrients such as nitrogen flow from the corn belt
Are now ending up in the Gulf
Where life once dwelt.
Say adios to fish, shrimp and crabs
If that was your fishing home.
We will never reduce the dead zone
Until more serious actions are taken
To reduce fertilizers into this dying system. *55

**STOP OVER-
FERTILIZING**

Nature knows best is the third ecological law.
So respect the delicate complicated evolution
Of hundreds of thousands of years.
It is a sin to destroy it for your own satisfaction.

**STOP ACTING
LIKE YOU ARE BETTER THAN
NATURE**

There is no free lunch is the fourth natural law.
Exploitation of nature, transforms resources
From useful to useless,
Destroying nature's balance equation.
Ultimately ejects mankind
From the circle of living relations.

REUSE, RECYCLE, REPAY

We robbed nature's carbon bank in the ground,
Transformed it to carbon dioxide in the air;
We mass-murdered cows and ravaged our greenwood giants
For our meat and dairy affair, releasing deadly methane everywhere;
We packaged most all with poisonous plastic
And tossed it to the garbage, rivers and seas to cause death and disease;
We dumped garbage everywhere;
We unleashed poisonous methane into our once clean air

THERE IS NO 'AWAY'

And now our sentence is earth decimation
With no appeal for our devil-may-care affair.

XII.   THE CULTURAL CAUSES

"Waste and the throw-away culture"
Are at the heart of the sickness of pollution.
Those with the money and power
Are invested in hiding the solution.
An attitude of recklessness and of devil-may-care
Prevents the leadership and lifestyle change
That would avoid the requiem for humanity
And the destruction
Of our once-clean water and air.

**THROWAWAY CULTURE =
POLLUTION/
THE
POWERFUL HIDE THE
SOLUTION**

**WRECKLESSNESS & DEVIL-MAY-CARE
ATTITUDE - SOURCE
OF THE PROBLEM**

.

FOOD WASTE

So you say you don't pollute,
You hardly even drive your car that much.
Well yeah, maybe you throw left-overs away.
How does that ruin anybody's day?

**WASTING FOOD HEATS THE
PLANET**

95% of the food we throw away *55.5
Ends up in landfills at the end of the day.
Guess what happens then?
It breaks down to form methane
A potent greenhouse gas
Causing more pollution pain.

WASTED FOOD BECOMES POISON

In the U.S. alone,
31% of the available food supply
Went uneaten…so what, you say?
16% of the world's methane pollution
Comes from rotting wasted food, thrown away
So compost your wasted food
For that garden you start today.

WASTED FOOD KILLS

So give your edible food away to those in need,
Compost that upon which no one can feed
Over a hundred billion pounds of food wasted this year.
Our moral duty could not be made more clear

**MORAL DUTY NOT TO
WASTE**

Death from pollution has arrived
Yet we refuse to see
We are blinded with our comforts
Recklessly consuming from the knowledge tree

**TECHNOLOGY HAS MADE US
BLIND TO DEATH**

We are self-centered and devoid of empathy
So we refuse to teach & learn basic ecology.
Our hard heart and uneducated ear mean
We don't hear mother's wailing plea.

TURN AN EDUCATED EAR TO NATURE/HEAR HER WAIL

XIII.   A PLEA TO TAKE ACTION TO STOP THE POLLUTION KILLERS

Stop killing mother earth   **PROTECT EARTH, DON'T BELIEVE THE LIES**
Just because you can
Stop believing the business lies
That it is nature we must ban.

We are the 2nd biggest polluter on the planet.*56
We love our meats, dairy, plastics, cars, coal, oil and gas.
We're the biggest earth bakery
Start planning Mother Earth's funeral mass.

WE ARE THE 2ND BIGGEST POLLUTER

TIME IS OF THE ESSENCE/CROSSING THE LINES, HASTENS A CATASTROPHIC TIME *11, *57 and *63

So you think you have an abundance of time
To reverse this cataclysmic crime
We must act now!
We've already crossed many critical lines.

THE LONGER WE WAIT, THE MORE DIFFICULT THE JOB

Further transgressions, hastens exponentially
The global warming wrecking machinery
Leading to destabilization
& a planet devoid of a breathable sky.
So recognize now the tipping points of the accelerated disaster.
When one is reached, hell will heat much faster
Suffering, devastation and disaster
Will follow soon after.

CROSSING THE TIPPING POINTS ACCELERATES THE DISASTER

More melting ice, *58
More water in our oceans,
Higher sea levels,
Thus begins the deadly progression

MORE MELTING ICE = HIGHER SEA = COASTAL FLOODING

Our ice reflects heat away from the earth.
The darkness of the water absorbs it
And mother's temperature
May never recover or reverse it.

ICE IS OUR AIR COOLER

And don't forget the escaping methane
From the permafrost and tundra.
It heats 20 to 100 times that of carbon dioxide.
This might be enough to precipitate
An irreversible permafrost melting slide.

**ESCAPING METHANE
FROM MELTING ICE KILLS**

Water vapor is the most important greenhouse gas
Because it warms whatever it touches.
More vapor, more heat, more water from our seas,
Equals more water vapor in an endless cycle
Towards exponentially progressive planetary disease.

**WATER VAPOR DANGEROUSLY
WARMS**

Sea Plankton produce 50 to 80% of the worlds' oxygen supply.
The death of these carbon-eating and oxygen-producing creatures of the sea
Because of carbonization, acidification & warming,
Bode death and destruction to an endless degree.

**POLLUTION
KILLS OXYGEN-PRODUCING
PLANKTON**

The more heat from the sky and captured by the sea
Can suddenly rise to the sea surface
Releasing massive heat into the heaven's
Ensuring a helliferous lesson to the nth degree

**HEAT FROM THE SKY
CAPTURED BY THE SEA
MAY TRIGGER DEVASTATING
HEAT RELEASE**

Losing our carbon-capturing forests
By heat, droughts, wildfires and harvesting
Increases carbon and heat in the sky
Potentially triggering an exponential progress
Of heat and unbreathable air, for to die.

**ALLOWING FORESTS TO DIE
TRIGGERS
EPIDEMIC HEATING OF PLANET**

And don't forget your soils
That normally absorb carbon
When they begin releasing it back into the sky
Because of escalating heat
Another tipping point to make us cry!

**SOARING HEAT SENDS CARBON IN
SOIL BACK TO THE SKY**

Major ocean currents stabilize
Our weather and seasons.
If the North Atlantic current
Were slowed down or diverted
It would create
Very significant changes in weather patterns
And strongly impact our vital crop production.

**CHANGE IN CURRENTS =
CHANGE IN WEATHER
AFFECTING CROP PRODUCTION**

And don't forget
The global warming-caused pandemic potential
By still-living bacteria and viruses never seen by our eyes
When ancient ice glaciers melt
And release their deadly surprise.

MELTING ICE RELEASES DISEASE-CAUSING BUGS

And if we haven't learned that Fracking
Creates havoc in earth's foundations,* 59
We may discover that the weight of rising seas and
Melting ice shifting can move tectonic plates
Causing super volcano-like eruptions
Blocking the sun for years
Killing off most of the human population.

MELTING ICE SHIFTING, RISING SEAS, MAY MOVE TECTONIC PLATES = SUPER VOLCANO, BLOCKING THE SUN = HUMANITY ENDING

We may have a decade to prevent a total climate disaster.
We must keep global warming
To within 1.5 degrees Celsius of the pre-industrial ranges.*60
Or face a tipping point towards irreversible catastrophic changes. *61

**TIME IS RUNNING OUT
ACT NOW!**

XIV. MEET & GET TO KNOW YOUR NATURE NEIGHBOR
WHAT TO DO TO STOP THE DISASTER:

Goodness or evil
What is your choice?
Can you hear
Creation's dying voice?

HEAR CREATIONS DYING VOICE

Nature is not
A stage upon which we play.
It is both mother & family,
Our moral responsibility!

OUR DUTY

Respect the natural beauty
Intricately woven through our being
The trash you discard today
Will be your child's death and sickening.

TOLERATING POLLUTION KILLS YOUR CHILDREN

EDUCATE YOURSELF
Our schools demand a basic core
Of English and Math for a degree
But require no course to save the world
No school prereq., for basic ecology.
So we send them into a world
Where they pollute without knowing

SCHOOLS MUST TEACH ECOLOGY

IGNORANCE BREEDS WRECLESSNESS = DEATH

They are being poisoned with a smile
Your death is now being served in # 9 aisle.

We refuse to teach & learn basic ecology,
Though our life and health depend on it
And businesses lie because they don't care.
We trust technology to save our derriere.
So please learn
Your polluters and poisons.
Demand Ecology 101!
First you must know what's killing you,
Then outrage and action,
Before this deadly web is further spun.

**WE REFUSE TO LEARN WHAT WILL
SAVE US BECAUSE
BUSINESS LIES & WE TRUST
TECHNOLOGY**

**FIGHT FOR KNOWLEDGE & A
FUTURE**

We need to stop this disaster!
So what do we do to address the problem?
Reuse, recycle and limit non-renewables,
A critical cause of the pollution devastation.

**REUSE, RECYCLE & LIMIT NON-
RENEWABLES**

THE CARBON CYCLE*61.5

Plants use carbon from the air, to make the food we eat
Animals eat the plants and we store the carbon
In our heads, torso, legs and feet.
Animals eat smaller animals and the carbon transmission repeats.
All living creatures breathe
And carbon is freed into the air as carbon dioxide.
When animals die, the carbon marries, buries
and honeymoons with the soil, its new-found bride.
After millions of years, it transforms to diamonds, coal or fossil fuel.
So in vain, they have not died.
The sea has so much stored carbon, it is called a carbon sink.
It is getting hotter because humans disturb the carbon cycle, of this big drink.
As we burn more coal oil and gas, more carbon corrupts the once-clean air.
Our leafed sentinels tirelessly absorb and consume the carbon
But we continue to callously burn and cut, because we don't care.
This leaves a lot of carbon in the air
Which leads to catastrophic global heating everywhere.
We have broken the delicate carbon cycle.
So our tree-cutting, technologically comforting
Throw-away, devil-may-care lifestyles
Have doomed the dream of clean water and air
Along with all humanity's welfare.

REUSABLE ENERGY

Renewable energy is not a mere dream.
Iceland runs on nearly 100% renewable energy.
Electricity is by hydropower and geothermal steam.
Proof that the clean power of nature is ours to redeem.*61.6

REUSIBLE ENERGY IS FOR REAL

And who knew we could put the wind to work
Just insert a wind mill to catch the breeze
And nature does our work with ease.
No pollution, no death, no disease.

PUT THE WIND TO WORK

How about hiring the sun who works for free?
We just capture its light and heat in our solar array
And whalla! Inside our house the sun's rays are channeled.
Adios to those pollution vandals, Hello to the comforting solar ray!

HEAT YOUR HOUSE WITH THE SUN

Did you know that underwater tides can produce energy?
Just install wind-mill like blades on the ocean floor or river bed.
With the magic of a gear box it's like underwater wind-mills with water
So you don't need coal and oil to make your house warmer.

PUT THE TIDES TO WORK

Have you heard of geothermal energy
Where the heat of the earth
Converts to steam to spin turbines
To produce electricity to warm our indoor environs?

GEOTHERMAL ENERGY

And isn't it time to invest in electric vehicles
And put the poison belching metal dinosaurs out to pasture?
Our government could help avoid the pollution disaster
By imposing subsidies to make it happen faster.

GO ELECTRIC CARS!

XV. TAKING ACTION

The assault on nature
Is an attack on us all.
If you care about family
It is time to heed nature's call.

DUTY TO FAMILY

Forests and terrestrial soils combined
Store more than two and half times as much carbon as the sky.
So let's stop cutting these carbon-storing trees
And begin programs to grow
More wooden lungs with leaves. *62

FIGHTING POLLUTION WITH NATURE

Point the finger at the culprits
Make sure your politicians are aware.
Don't pretend it is not world-ending
Lest your grandchildren think you did not care.

ACT! YOUR CHILDREN ARE AT STAKE

So intricate the ties to mother nature
We are the child breastfeeding from our mom.
Stop feeding mother the waste from
Animal ag, fossil fuels, plastics and garbage.
Her death is humanities' last breath drawn.

STOP KILLING MOTHER NATURE

Preserving mother nature is our untapped solution
Tropical forests superbly store carbon.
And provide 30% of action
To prevent the worst climate change devolution
But they receive only 2% of all climate funding. *63
We must save the world
By a radical rethinking.
Denial and words will not save
This Titanic ship quickly sinking.

NATURE: THE UNTAPPED SOLUTION

An ocean of garbage as big as
Europe, India and Mexico,
Contaminates all the sea creatures we eat.
So, if you like sea food, you're eating poisoned meat. *45

OUR GARBAGE POLLUTING SEA ANIMALS

So take your non-plastic bag to Wal-Mart
Don't use their plastic bag because it's 'free'.
Stop using drive-up fast-food to pollute
Park, go in and know: you've saved some pollution misery.

DON'T USE PLASTIC OR DRIVEUPS

Insist in your community
That Ecology be taught your child
Without that basic eco-training
Your sending a baby into the wild.

MANDATE ECOLOGY BE TAUGHT

And who said kids don't rule?
Thousands in Italy walked out of school
Demanding action on climate change
As part of a global strike of the schools.

ITALIAN KIDS STRIKE THEIR SCHOOLS

And don't forget Greta Thunberg,
Hero and leader of the young.
You are never too young to lead the charge.

NEVER TO YOUNG TO SAVE THE PLANET

The world will surely listen
As you speak loudly and your numbers enlarge.

And bear in mind what Obama began   **REJOIN THE**
And Trump removed from the earth-saving plan: **PARIS**
Get us back as partners to the 2015 Paris Agreement.   **AGREEMENT**
Let's work together to save our heaven-on-earth endowment!

Ending deforestation and restoring degraded forests   **STOP CUTTING, START**
Could create 80 million jobs and bring a billion people out of poverty   **PLANTING TREES =**
And add 2.3 trillion in productive growth.   **GIGANTIC JOB**
How's that for a save-the-planet itinerary. *57   **INVESTMENT**
So take the sixteen-year-old Greta Thunberg boat to your community.
Become a climate activist; become an eco-warrior   **BECOME AN ACTIVIST**
And seize the opportunity to spread knowledge and unity
Around the notion that we must act now
Against the Global Climate calamity.

XVI   THE LEGAL REMEDIES
And don't forget the remedy   **SUE THE DASTARDS**
As American as apple pie.
Sue the dastardly company
Poisoning your earth, water and sky!

In the State of cars and movie stars,   **GET THE LED OUT**
Led paint-makers got a surprise.
The U.S. Supreme court has ruled:
Clean your multi-million dollar lie-ridden led mess! *64
No more death and sickness to pay for your monetary success.

And you think kids don't have any say   **'THE BIGGEST CASE ON THE**
They've sued the government   **PLANET'**
To make them pay
For failing to stop climate change
By using fossil fuels for 50 years
This violated their basic right
To a climate system able to continue the human light. *65

And in Pennsylvania, three families sued the frackers   **THE POISONING/**
For poisoning and sickening their family and pets   **FRACKERS PAID**
And after fighting the injured family for six years,
The gas drillers paid three million for their pollution debt. *66

And in the State of the Rocky Mountain high
John Denver can write one more song about the sky
Government set a limit:
It's practically free to have solar energy from on high.

GIVE CREDITS FOR SOLAR ARRAYS

Exxon now sued by the N.Y. A.G.
Because they misled investors
About resulting climate change
And the resulting financial jeopardy. *67

HOW TO ADDRESS OIL COMPANY DECEPTION

And in Albuquerque and Santa Fe, New Mexico,
Two tiny threads in the mother-earth's grand web,
The cities have banned plastic bags.
So is it now time for all our states to do the same?
An example, small as it may be
But a mighty step to heal the weakening world web
And a powerful example and message
That we can all move to save humanity.

ALBUQUERQUE& SANTA FE NM BAN PLASTIC BAGS

TIME TO TAKE ACTION

XVII. THE GAMBIT LAID, YOUR NEXT MOVE
We know how this could end
If we don't stop our reckless revelry.
Respect the natural gift you've received
Don't end this glorious life symphony.

RESPECT NATURE, TAKE ACTION, SAVE LIVES

----

1 CONSERVATION INTERNATIONAL 'CLIMATE CHANGE: 11 FACTS YOU NEED TO KNOW www.conservation.org. NASA and NOAA show that global averages in 2016 were 1.78 degrees F (0.99 degrees C) warmer than the mid-20th century average.; Australia has its hottest day on record as Sydney residents brace for heat, fires and smoke – 105.6 degrees (12/18/19 The Washington Post.)

6-5-2020:'Heat-trapping carbon dioxide in air hits new record high' by Seth Borenstein, Associated Press Science Dept.:'The world hit another new record high for heat-trapping carbon dioxide in the atmosphere, despite reduced emissions because of the coronavirus pandemic, scientist announced Thursday, June 4, 2020. Measurements of carbon dioxide, the chief human-caused green house gas, averaged 417.1 parts per million at Mauna Loa, Hawaii... Carbon dioxide can stay in the air for centuries...'

*1.2 The average global temperature for May (2020), was 1.71 degrees F (0.95 of a degree C) above the 20th century average, tying with May 2016 as the hottest May on record. May (2020)was the hottest May on record worldwide, a European climate agency has reported.

*1.3 See footnotes from Animal Ag in this book, Ch 10

*1.5 SLATE: 'U.N. Chief Warns "Point of No Return" on Climate Change "Is in Sight" by Daniel Politi, Dec. 01, 2019. U.N. Secretary-General Antonio Guterres: "The point of no return is no longer over the horizon. It is in sight and hurtling towards us".

BBC NEWS: 'Brazil's Amazon deforestation highest since 2008, space agency says. 18 November 2019

*2 *NASA GISS & NOAA NCEI (www.giss.nasa.gov) National Aeronautics and Space Administration: '2018 Fourth Warmest Year in Continental Warming Trend, According to NASA, NOAA, posted Feb 6, 2019*

*3 *The New York Times 7-4-19 "Anchorage Has Never Reached 90 Degrees. That Could Change this Week" by Mike Baker*

*4 *The NPR Daily Newsletter "The 'Great Dying' Nearly Erased Life On Earth. Scientists See Similarities To Today'*

*5 npr Has Your Doctor Talked To You About Climate Change? 7/13/19; COP24 SPECIAL REPORT: HEALTH & CLIMATE CHANGES World Health Organization

*5.5 The New York Times: U.N. Climate Talks End With Few Commitments and a "Lost' Opportunity. Dec 15, 2019.

*5.55 See Part 2 of the this book: '*Facing Hell on Earth, the Friend, the Enemy, Analysis and Solutions,* **A.** WHO/WHAT IS THE FIGHT FOR? OUR FORESTS! X. **DON'T FORGET TO FIGHT FOR NATURE** 1. DESTRUCTION OF FORESTS IS CAUSING POLLUTION, DROUGHTS AND PANDEMICS, INCLUDING THE CORONA VIRUS

*5.6 'A runaway greenhouse effect turned Venus into 'hell.' Could the same thing happen here?'(Michael Parkin for the Washington Post) By Sarah Kaplan March 20 at 6:40 pm.; Citing Giada Arney in article Sciences and Exploration Directorate at National Aeronautics and Space Administration; Citing 'the Carbon Cycle by Holli Riebeek – 'earth observatory' of NASA 'The Carbon Cycle' at https://earthobservatory.n

*6 Tree of *Knowledge of Good and Evil is from the bible. (Genesis) Our use of technology without concern for the consequences is what I believe it is talking about.*

*7 *Author's poetic take.*

*8. USGS *water.usgs.gov*

*8.5 Sarah Cooley, Ocean Conservancy Blog, Ocean Currents: 'Corals, Lobsters and Oysters—Oh My! 'Seeking solutions for our favorite shell-builders

*8.7 See 'Climate change and pollution could eliminate nearly all coral reefs by the end of the century' By Chris Ciaccia/Fox News;

NBC News:'Great Barrier Reef hit by third major bleaching event in five years' by Denise Chow on March 23, 2020 ('Coral bleaching occurs as a response to abnormal conditions, such as when ocean temperatures are cooler or warmer than usual or when ocean water is more acidic than normal.' '…the reefs are subsequently more susceptible to disease.' '…In the 2016 bleaching event, 27 percent of the great Barrier Reef's corals died, and the following year, 22 % were lost, meaning nearly half the famed reef's corals died in just two years."

8.8. See ftnts 49, 50, 51, 52, 53, 54, 55, 56, and 56.1 Factory Farming /Animal Agriculture/Cattle Industry/Meat and Dairy Industry, *in Chapter 10*

9 The Lancet Commission on pollution and health, Published: October 19, 2017

Executive Summary: For decades, pollution and its harmful effects on people's health, the environment, and the planet have been neglected both by Governments and the international development agenda. Yet, pollution is the largest environmental cause of disease and death in the world today, responsible for an estimated 9 million premature deaths.

10 See the Global Changes Research Program which published a report in 2009 entitled Global HYPERLINK "http://www.globalchange.gov/what-we-do/assessment/previous-assessments/global-climate-change-impacts-in-the-us-2009" Climate Change HYPERLINK "http://www.globalchange. gov/what-we-do/assessment/previous-assessments/global-climate-change-impacts-in-the-us-2009" Impacts in the US. March 6, 2019 by Sarah Cooley

11 CLIMAGEDDON The Global Warming Emergency and How to Survive It by Lawrence Wollersheim

11.5 Vox 'Report by Unmair Irfan Oct 8, 2018: we have just 12 years to limit devastating global warming. (www.google.com)

12 Vox 'California has 129 million dead trees. That's a huge wildfire risk. But no one can afford to cut them all down' By Umair Irfan on Sep 4, 2018; THE VERGE 'The California fires show how unprepared we are for climate change Climate disasters require a new kind of preparedness by Russell Brandom on Oct. 29, 2019 12:32 pm

13 EXPRESS 'Amazon rainforest fire: How did the Amazon fire start? How long has it been on fire? By Amalie Henden Published 12.11 Wed Aug 21, 2019 (INPE National Institute for Space Research)

13.5 'Rivers in the sky: the devastating effect deforestation is having on global rainfall' South China Morning Post Magazine Published Nov. 8, 2019, https://wwwgoogle.com

13.6 THINK AGAIN, Opinions, Analysis, Essay by Andrew Stern (https.//www.nbcnews.com) Amy Vitor.

14 CNN health 8-3-19; How climate change could expose new epidemics by Amelie Bottollier-Depois. See Earth/Environment at PHYS ORG (https://phys.org)

15 WOWT Claim: Future heat waves pose threat to global food supply by Anthony Watts, March 19, 2014. From the Institute of Physics: Heat waves could significantly reduce crop yields and threaten global food supply if climate change is not tackled and reversed. This is according to a new study led by researchers at the U of East Anglia and published today, 20 March, in IOP Publishing's journal Environmental Research Letters….

*16 CBS News June 4, 2019. Human civilization faces "existential risk" by 2050 according to new Australian climate change report. See report written by David Spratt, research director for Breakthrough National Centre for Climate Restoration in Melbourne and Ian T. Dunlop,

*17 "Air Pollution More Deadly than Smoking, new Study Finds by Ann W. Schmidt; Fox News, Published in the European Heart Journal.

*18 WILDLIFE & BIODIVERSITY: 'As temperatures continue to rise, birds struggle to survive' 'Record-breaking temperatures reduce bird population and are behind absence of insectivorous birds by Harshita Alok Sharma Updated June 12, 2019; "'The Blob' blamed for largest Pacific NW seabird die-off in history" by Karina Mazhukhina, KOMO News;

*19 Latest research finds a large buildup of heat in the oceans, suggesting a faster. rate of global warming. (The Washington Post 10-31/18) The findings mean the world might have less time to curb carbon emissions; wwwnpr.org. 'Earth's Oceans Are Getting Hotter and Higher, And It's Accelerating, Sep 25, 2019 by Rebecca Hersher (As the world's climate changes, ocean warming is accelerating and sea levels are rising more quickly, warns a new report by the U.N. Intergovernmental panel on Climate Change.); 'Oceans are warming at the same rate as if five Hiroshima bombs were dropped in every second' By Ivana Kottasova, CNN, January 13, 2020. See 'ADVANCES IN A ATMOSPHERIC SCIENCES, VOL. 37.,February 2010, 137—142.

*19.1 See 'Dead zones, facts... (https://www.natonalgeogr) 'Dead zones, explained'

*19.5 (See ftnt. 69 from Animal Ag. In Ch 10)

*20 www.livescience.com LIVESCI=NCE 'Upside-Down Rivers' of Warm Water Are Carving Antarctica to Pieces' by Brandon Specktor October 10, 2019

*21 See The Washington Post, entitled 'Arctic Cauldron' by Chris Mooney

World Health Organization

*21.5 Greenland is losing ice seven times faster than in the 1990s and is tracking the Intergovernmental Panel on Climate Change's high-end climate warming scenario, which would see 400 million more people exposed to coastal flooding by 2100. See PHYS.ORG, University of Leeds, published in December 2019

*22.2 CNN Climate Change: Scientists find another threat to Greenland's glaciers lurking beneath the ice. See the study in the journal Nature Geoscience.

*23 Article: Global Warming is Shrinking Glaciers Faster Than thought by Associated Press, Apr. 08, 2019. Author Michael Zemp, Director of the World Glacier Monitoring Service, Danish Meteorological Institute.; CBS NEWS "11 BILLION TONS OF ICE MELTED IN Greenland-in just one day by Sophie Lewis Aug 2, 2019; 'Greenland ice losses rising faster than expected' Dec 10, 2019 (phys. org); 'Upside-Down Rivers' of Warm Water Are Carving Antarctica to Pieces' Oct 10, 2019; (www. livescience.com)

*23.5 CONSERVATION INTERNATIONAL wwwconservation.org, 'CLIMATE CHANGE: 11 FACTS YOU NEED TO KNOW. (See fact # 7)

*24 food&waterwatch 'Fracking and Earthquakes' (In Oklahoma, the Oklahoma Supreme Court has permitted Plaintiffs to sue the Oil Companies for earth quake damages caused by fracking. "Induced Earthquakes"-USGS Earthquake Hazards Program https://earthquake.usgs.gov.myths

*25 Potential Environmental Effects of Uranium Mining, Processing, and Reclamation by The National Academics of SCIENCES ENGINERING MEDICINE NAP

*26 See Google News 'Business Insider' by Hilary Brueck June 22, 2019, 9"08am

*27 Eileen Fisher#Vision 2020 (Sep 3, 2015) and One Green Planet

*28 Council for Textile Recycling

*29 Science Direct

*30. Forbes (Dec. 3, 2015 'Making Climate Change Fashionable – The Garment Industry Takes On Global Warming.)

*30.1 Vox: 'More than ever, our clothes are made of plastic. Just washing them can pollute the oceans' by Brian Resnick on January 11, 2019.

*31 Science Direct

*31. See journal PLOS One and UNIVERSE 'A Single Giant Organism 107 Acres Wide is Dying Fast by Yasmin Tayag on Oct. 17, 2018

*31.5 See journal PLOS One and UNIVERSE 'A Single Giant Organism 107 Acres Wide is Dying Fast by Yasmin Tayag on Oct. 17, 2018

*32 CDC (Centers for Disease Control and Prevention 'National Antimicrobial Resistance Monitoring System for Enteric Bacteria (NARMS)

*32.5. World Health Organization (WHO) says processed meat causes cancer. The International Agency for Research on Cancer (ARC) has classified processed meat as a carcinogen, something that causes cancer. And it has classified red meat as a probable carcinogen, something that probably causes cancer...Processed meat includes hot dogs, ham, bacon, sausage and some deli meats. It refers to meat that has been treated in some way to preserve or flavor it. Processes include salting, curing, fermenting, and smoking. Red meat includes beef, pork lamb, and goat.,

*32.6 See UN News Centre Nov 29, 2006

*33 npr FOOD FOR THOUGHT For a Healthier Planet, Eat These 50 Foods, Campaign Urges, Martch 24, 2019, Eleanor Beardsley

*9.250 Vox by Unmair Irfan on Dec 10, 2018

*34 MARINE LITTER SOLUTIONS AND WWW.FAUNA-FLORA.ORG, article by Abigail Entwistle, 9th November 2017

*35 2015 investigation by Inside Climate News into what Exxon knew about the impact of fossil fuels on climate change. 'Exxon Mobil misled the public about the climate crisis. Now they're trying to silence critics' by Geoffrey Supran and Naomi Oreskes of The Guardian (https://amp.the guardian.com)

*36 See The Closing Circle by Barry Commoner and Global Footprint Network, Advancing the Science of Sustainability, 'How the Footprint Works'

*37 Home/Latest Energy News by Tsvetana Paraskova (July 18, 2018) GRAIN and the Institute for Agriculture and Trade Policy (IATP)

*37.5 https://vegnews.com 'REPORT:MEAT COMPANIES ARE OFFICIALLY THE WORLD'S BIGGEST WATER POLLUTERS by Nicole Axworthy Nov 18, 2019

*37.6 The Guardian: The pentagon emits more greenhouse gases than Portugal, study finds;(theguardian.com)

*38 See Global Research. First published by International Action Center and Global Research in September 2014. (globalresearch.ca); See 8/1/18 article U.S. Military is World's Biggest Polluter by Whitney Web for EcoWatch I the USA

*39 NSW Government

*40 Farmworker Justice: "Pesticide Safety"

*41 American Academy of Pediatrics (September 19, 2012)

*42. Earth Day CANADA. earthday.ca

*43 EPA 'Mercury' 'Basic Information about Mercury NIH U.S. National Library of Medicine 1-888-FIND-NLM

*44 Ghose. MK, et al. Environ Int. 2000 Authors Ghose Mi, Majeee SR Environ Int. 2000 Aug.26(1-2)81-5

*45 THE WORLD COUNTS, Article: Pollution from Plastic 'Plastic is Forever'(www.theworldcounts. com),Environmental Investigation Agency: The Shocking Impact of Plastic Solution in our oceans. Huff Post Green: How to Solve the Plastic Pollution Problem and Poverty at the Same Timecoastal Care: Plastic Pollution.

*46 NPR at www.npr.org (See estrogen-like chemicals): 'Study: Most Plastics Leach Hormone-Like Chemicals

47 Scientist Deonie Allen of the EcoLab, part of the National Center of Scientific Research for France, coauthor on a new paper in NatureGeoscience. 'A Shocking Find Shows Just How Far Wind Can Carry Microplastics by Matt Simon on 4/14/19

*48 "Microplastics Have Invaded The Deep Ocean – And The Food Chain". The Monterey Bay findings appear in the Journal Nature Scientific Reports June 6, 2019

*49 Parkinson's Foundation 'Environmental Factors' parkinson.org

*50 Food&waterwatch 'Monsanto Manipulates Science to Make Roundup Appear Safe' *Foodandwaterwatch.org*

*51 *PubMed.gov; US National Library of Medicine, National Institutes of Health 'Major pesticides are more toxic to human cells than their declared active principles.; In 2015, the World Health Organization (WHO) declared glyphosates "probably" carcinogenic to humans"*

*52 *The Atlantic 'A Frightening New Reason to Worry About Air Pollution' by Olga Khazan July 5, 2018. The study published in the The Lancet Planetary Health.*

*53 *Article: Climate Change is Already Hurting U.S. Communities, Federal Report Says by 'THE FOURTH NATIONAL CLIMATE ASSESSMENT. The culmination of years of research and analysis by hundreds of top climate scientists in the country. As of 2018 it is the most recent such assessment. NPR (www.npr.org) Dec 21, 2019: 'Catastrophic' Wildfires Continue To Rage Across Australia'*

*53.5 *See Google: 'Environmental Impact' (www.foodrescue.net) the environmental problem created by food waste is the methane gas it emits while in our landfills. The EPA has initiated the Food Recovery Challenge offering their full support to any schools donating their surplus food; Society of St. Andrew 'Resources to Understand Food Waste in America' (endhunger.org)*

53.6 The Closing Circle by Barry Commoner

54 See Pope Francis Encyclical on the Environment

*55 *USA Today 'Near-record 'dead zone' predicted in the Gulf of Mexico this summer by Doyle Rice. Forecast by researchers at Louisiana State University. Also se Gulf of Mexico hypoxia: https:// gulfhypoxis.net/*

*55.5 *Society of St. Andrew, Gleaning America's Fields – Feeding America's Hungry, (endhunger.org). This cite references numerous organizations and studies on this issue.;. The environmental problem created by food waste is the methane gas it emits while in land fills: www.foodrescue.net, 'up to 40% of all food ends up in landfills.*

56 Reuters/Lucy Nicholson

*57 www.conservation.org 'CLIMATE CHANGE: 11 FACTS YOU NEED TO KNOW'FACT # 12 "Fight climate change naturally."

*57 *Conlcusions based on book Climageddon, the Global Warming Emergency and How to Survive It. By Lawrence Wollersheim.*

*58 www.livescience.com LIVESCI=NCE 'The World's Thickest Mountain Glacier Is Finally Melting, and Climate Change Is 100% to Blame by Brandon Spector 07 November 2019

*59 KDKA: 'this Is Something We Need To Do': Pa. Gov. Wolf Authorizes $3 Million Study On Health Impacts Of Fracking', Author Andy Sheehan, Nov 22, 2019, Pittsburgh.cbslocal.com

*60 *The Report from the Intergovernmental Panel on Climate Change,*

*61 *NASA GLOBAL CLIMATE CHANGE: Is it too late to prevent climate change?*

*61.5 google 'Carbon Cycle'

*61.6 'Geotheral energy is poised for a big breakout' by David Roberts on Oct. 21, 2020 on VOX (https://www.vox.com) "...geothermal may hold the key to making 100% clean electricity available to everyone in the world. "The ARPA-E project AltaRock Energy estimates that "just 0.1% of the heat content of Earth could supply humanity's total energy needs for 2 million years."

*62 WORLD ECONOMIC FORUM There is a forgotten solution to climate that we must invest in nature;

*63 www.conservation.org 'CLIMATE CHANGE: 11 FACTS YOU NEEDTO KNOW' FACT # 9 "Nature is an untapped solution."; Center for Global Development: 'Tropical Forests Offer up to 24-30% of potential Climate Mitigation' Nov 4, 2015 by Jonah Busch and Jens Engelmann *97%

*64 See Sherwin Williams Conagra ordered to pay cleanup costs for led in the paint based on a 'public nuisance' theory. This opens the door to sue for environmental damages in t

*20.35 'A shocking Find Shows Just How Far Wind Can Carry Microplastics by Matt Simon 415/19 he other states. /

*65 See Juliana v. United States

*66 npr, Environment and Energy Collaborative. '$23 Million Settlement Revealed in High-Profile Fracking Case. See journalist Eliza Griswold book 'Amity and Prosperity', winner of the 2019 Pulitzer Prize winner in general nonfiction.

*67 See City New York v. Exxon Corp. 932 F2d 1020 – 1991 – court of Appeals, 2nd – Cited by 322 City New York v. Exxon Corp, 633 F. Supp. 609 – Dist. Court SD New York. Cited by 243

F. THE SPRING OF LIFE

Here comes the sun, doo-doo-doo-doo, here comes the sun
And I say it's all right
Little darling, it's been a long cold lonely winter
Little darling, it feels like years since it's been here
Little darling, the smiles returning to the faces
"Here Comes the Sun"
by
The Beatles

Sunshine on my shoulders makes me happy
Sunshine in my eyes can make me cry
Sunshine on the water looks so lovely
Sunshine almost always makes me high
'SUNSHINE ON MY SHOULDERS'
Written by John by John Denver, Dick Kniss, and Mike Taylor
Sung by John Denver

SPRING DREAM ON A WALK WITH THE DOGS

The little birds have come back!
I missed their chirping.
Our ever-vigilant watchdogs
Ignore their trespassing.
They instinctively know
Man is the real threat
To their home
And the only one
That can save it.

The grass and the leaves on our many trees
Are turning green
And Sally has bought the seeds
And we are ready for the Spring sowing.

The dogs have missed the long green grass.
They are fascinated with the smell
And bite off what they can.
I have never noticed
Our impossible, impulsive 'Blucifer'
So calm and focused on nature's offerings.

The sun is so wonderfully warm.
I feel recharged each morning
As I absorb the unclouded sunlight in my face.
How did I survive the springless scene?

So long sheltering from winters' cold;
So long, the heavenly warmth, just a dream.

The dandelions, our little wild sunflowers,
Were the scourge of a nature-disconnected generation,
Deaf and dumb to nature's plan.
Mere worthless weeds on their perfect lawn,
What would the neighbors say?
They must be gone!

Our little sunshine bathers
Are perched, nah, enthroned
On pedestals
Of glorious green stems
That reach up to the sky
To a beautiful bright
And pedaled yellow crown
With a golden centered eye,
Perfectly colored and rounded
To devour the sun's rays
And attract the pollinators gaze.

And as I am entranced
With these magnificent round yellow faces
Smiling to the sun,
I see beyond me a beautiful bee,
Coming, no doubt,
To fulfill natures plan:
Nature's table of flowers
Serve the bees
With their bounty
Of nectar and pollen.
The worker bees collect it
And return home
To feed the hungry colonies.

The sweet bee then produces honey.
They are home builders too
For millions of insects and animals.
They are saviors
To many of our leafy lung friends,
The sentinels, who feed the rivers in the sky,
Who would all die
Without the proliferous pollinating bee.

The bees, in natures' thank-you,
Provide the kind flowers
With the means to reproduce
By spreading pollen
From flower to flower,
Nature's miracle of fructification,
Without which,
Plants could not create seeds
And life would cease.

These bountiful-spreading little buzzing creatures
Are indeed the 'bees knees'
To the insects, animals, flowers and trees
Who owe their existence
To the largesse and generosity of the buzzing bees.

Sadly, these buzzing bounty-bearers,
The bee-key to the door of life,
Are dying out at a devasting rate*
But spoiled humanity only knows the bee's sting.
We have failed to heed Einstein's warning dire:
If the bee disappeared off the face of the Earth,
Man would only have four years left
And then, we would all expire.
Wow!

In just a few moments
In this sun-filled Spring morning,
Nature has revealed to me
The wondrous intimacy
And life-giving relationship
Of the birds and the bees,
The flowers and the trees,
Butterflies, bats, wasps,
The water and even the breeze;
And for a lifetime of oblivious ease,
All they were to me
Was but cause to sneeze.

How did I fail to grasp
For so long -
Natures lesson of the marvelous,
Miraculous mixture
And connection between
Plants, animals and mankind?

And then……
The first beautiful butterfly!
Natures' winged canvass
Of contrasting colors,
Van Gogh's portrait
Of beauty, style, design
And symmetry divine:
Bright royal purples
Blended perfectly
With yellows,
On the delicate
But magic and magnificent wings
With small colored button shapes
Sewn symmetrically
All along the wings' ends,
As if to hold the masterpiece together.
Their beautiful bright colors all amatch
For the bright flowers they befriend.

They are unique in the sky –
Nature's ostentatious
And paper-thin bow-tie shaped wings,
All ready for their prom dance in the sky,
All wings and barely a body
With two antenna -
Nector detectors
Or sex hormone spotters
And
One big eye
And 17,000 mini eyes.
They are the gods and goddesses
Or, at least, royalty
To the celestial kingdom
Of the sky.

They do not traditionally fly,
But flutter their symmetrical
Leaf-thin wings
And then float on the barely felt breeze,
Then frantically flutter once again
Before they once more float majestically
On Springs' warming breath.

These are the delicate and beautiful
Winged ballerinas of the sky,

Who glide gloriously
To a heavenly tune
Of an unheard symphony,
Floating and flitting
on the invisible stage of air
to a rhythm which only nature
Knows the chords.

Ohhh! Two butterflies oblivious to us
And everything else,
Wildly flitting and flirting together!
They stop us in our tracks!

So old, to just now
Begin to appreciate nature's
Spring dance
And the magnificence
Of nature's mating and romance!

And the resplendence of their transformation:
From caterpillar to butterfly,
Flightless to a marvel of the sky,
From unimposing little worm,
Grounded, then sky-bound,
Then to a colorful and triumphant
Treasure of the morning sky,
To inseminator of plant life
To the magical mating
Of butterflies in the celestial blue.
All before my aging but hungry eyes!

These magical marvels
Represent all that is Winter's death to Spring life,
From gray clouds and
An avalanche of cold white,
To the glory of warm colors bright.

From a cold grave
Devoid of the green fingers
Reaching upwards from
The seed-sleeping ground,
With but a dream
Of their rounded bright faces of life
Smiling upwards;
Berift of the buzzing
And chirping sounds of life;

Barren of the beautiful exchanges
Of life creating caresses
And lifegiving contacts rife.

Then!
From a dreary and dark world within,
To the light of hope and vision,
My caterpillar worm of a winter
Has magnificently transformed
To the colorful bright beauty of
The butterfly of Spring.

*'Bumblebees are going extinct in a time of 'climate chaos' – National Geographic' PUBLISHED Feb 6, 2020 'Loss of the vital pollinators, due in part to temperature extremes and fluctuations, could have dire consequences for ecosystems and agriculture.' By Douglas Main; The leading cause of queen-bee failure to produce enough fertilized eggs to maintain the hive is one of the top causes of colony mortality. They found the failed queen bees had higher levels of heat-shock and pesticide protein markers compared to healthy queen bees. See https://phts.org 'scientists find clues to queen bee failure'.

Photo by author

G. CONCLUSION TO 'DON'T FORGET THE BEAUTY'

THE JOURNEY TO FIND MOTHER

Mine was the journey
From a hardened heart,
To a children-inspired transfiguration,
To the sensitivity of a birth-mother
And manifested with a concern
For the children of the world
And then, outward to humankind
Where the love for my children
Fluidly flowed and blossomed
Into words
As from a dream.

At the same time,
Seeing through my children's eyes
And feeling with their heart,
Nature, lady-Lazarus-like,
Rose from its unmarked grave,
Where, for so long, she lay buried and ensconced, a discarded prop.

But now, she came alive,
Into a gloriously living breathing heaven
That, for so long
I was dogmatically told lay elsewhere
And we would have to venture through the door of death to discover.

So I was blind and without a heart
To see and feel her
Flowing through my being.
In my transformed essence
I discovered the connection,
Absent so long…
Of the mother-child relationship.
A mother that fed me
From the fruit of her bosom,
A bosom
That had been hidden
By the cement, pavement
And sky-scrapers
Of the crass culture;
By the mass market
That separated us from Mother Earth's breasts;

By a world in which greed
Inspired a slave trade
In which mother earth
Was divided and sold to the highest bidder;
By a culture who was bedazzled with technology
And brainwashed to believe
That nature was evil and dangerous
And by a male God culture
In which power, war and death
Defeated the feminine of love, birth and sustenance.

I had fallen in love with the mother
I could finally see, feel and hear.
But what I was hearing, was a painful scream!
I could see a sickening visage
Of a maternal being close to death,
Whose temperature continued to rise
Far beyond normal;
Whose pain was revealed
In the throes of violent storm-filled seizures.

The heaven I had just discovered
Was becoming a sick and angry Mother-God,
Who was now disciplining
Her disobedient children,
Whose hearts had been removed
By a malevolent lifestyle;
Whose eyes had been diverted
By a culture who substituted
Their eyes and their brain
For a screen, selling comfort, conformity
And the new techno-money god,
So they now were unable
To see, hear, feel or know
Who/what verily held, protected and fed them the precious milk of life.

CHAPTER IV

DON'T FORGET TO LOVE

*You fill up my senses ...like a storm in the desert, like a sleepy
blue ocean. You fill up my senses. Come fill me again.*

Annie's Song
Written and recorded by
John Denver

INTRODUCTION AND ACKNOWLEDGEMENT
OF MY WIFE, SALLY

'To Love', is for the most part, about the manifestation of love between my children and myself. This relationship is at the heart of what transformed me so I was finally able to see, hear, feel and understand as never before.

However, upon much review and thought, all of this magic, all of these miracles, all of this heaven, would not have happened and could not have been sustained, but for my marriage to the most marvelous of human beings, my dear wife, Sally. I could not have found a better wife. There could not have been a better mother for my children. She was the energy that ensured the children would have everything they needed to fully develop. She was the embodiment of love and empathy that this book is all about. In every chapter you read, she is there, even though she may not be mentioned. Whatever energy I did not have, she did. What I could not do, she was able to do. The marvelousness of a love union is that the partner's strengths complete whatever weaknesses the other has. We have always been a team that strived and worked towards love and goodness. Every day I thank God that I discovered the woman who has loved me and my children as no one else could ever do.

A. TRANSFORMING LOVE

MOTHER-IN-LAW - DELLA (GARCIA) REED, MY WIFE, SALLY AND HER DAD CHARLES (CHUCK) REED

MY GRANDMA 'MAYE' – SUSIE SILVA (TOP) AND GREAT GRANDMOTHER,
Juanita Encinias Silva and GREAT GRANDFATHER Miguel Silva

MY GRANDPA JESUS LOPEZ (KNIGHTS OF COLUMBUS), ON THE RIGHT

My Grandma Lopez with my dad and my mom. (Gregoria Lopez in foreground)
(They were celebrating his appointment as U.S. Marshall)

MY PARENTS, MARTIN LOPEZ AND GREGORIA (SILVA) LOPEZ

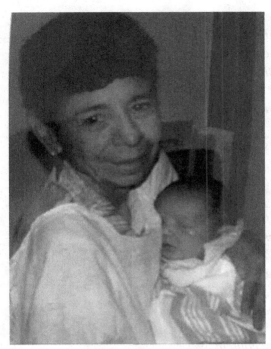

Della Garcia Reed (grandma) and Ali' (my daughter)

Best read while listening to PACHELBEL- CANON IN D MAJOR, By Johann Pachelbel

SEEDLINGS SLEEP AT TWILIGHT

Listen, hear and feel
The rhythmic whir of the electric fan,
*   The metronomic creak of the windup rocker*
*   And the string section of katydids chirruping.*
Together they perform a grand symphony
*   In the celebration of the approaching nightfall.*
A delicate and cooling summer breeze
*   Ever so gently whispers hope*
*   Of a sweet and cooling rain*
*   On the thirsty desert oasis*
*   Of the north valley of Albuquerque.*
The clouds are distant and, so far,
*   Reveal no sign of brilliant anger.*
They too will give me a respite.
Another round of Katydids chimes in,
*   Singing a different chorus.*

The shadows lengthen
*   As the sunlight dissipates into darkness.*
My mother-in-law,
*   The grandma, who loves Ali' dearly*

Lights a cigarette near the swings,
Away from the slumbering children,
Not to disturb their cool clean air
Which still hints with a smell of a rain shower.
Even she, always so frenetic
And ready to rock the silence
With her voice,
Quietly revels in this peaceful time.

My children, so small, so delicate,
Are dream-pods, as yet, without roots,
Still vulnerable if left unattended.
Like the unripe green pecans
That tantalizingly dangle
On the big pecan tree,
We must be alert and shoo the hungry birds away
Or our tree will have no mature pecans.

Neath the gaze of our smiling content eyes,
Our kids now sleep and dream.
Time slows as the shadows casually creep in.
My mind is at peace as my little ones rest.
The tempo of time has a soothing somnolence,
Like the effect of a soft blue-gray.
I can now dream about all they will be.
These are moments
Old fathers and grandparents love,
A time to rest, ponder and feel
Their connection to life.
There are no demands, no deadlines,
Only the feint pulse of slumbering time.

This soothing rhythm
Fills my senses and sedates my nerves.
This is a healing drug that is spawned
By the meeting of past and future generations,
Into which Sally and I
Are now joined.
From each end we are held
As if in a hammock.
We are supported by the memories
Of parents and grandparents on one side
And the dreams for my children
Lifting us up, from the other.

We fall if the knot is loosened
> *At either end.*
We fall if the tree of life
> *On either side, dies from lack of love,*
> *Or our failure to remember*
> *Or celebrate family gifts to us.*
In this wonderfully delirious time of approaching dusk
> *I feel so secure and peaceful,*
> *Holding old memories and future dreams*
> *And mystically elevated by them.*

In creating children, the knot was tied
> *And the chain of life was completed.*
A door I'd never passed through
> *Was revealed and opened.*
Behold, I now see the dream unfolding
> *And He who created me,*
> *Can smile and rest.*
My two little gifts from God
> *Are soundly asleep and dreaming...*
What a sweet and miraculous moment!
The incomparable beauty
> *Of their soft, silent and nearly still bodies,*
> *And the barely detectable rising*
> *And falling of their little chests!*

I am in a rare waking dream
> *When everything, nature and man*
> *Cooperates to allow my stirring soul*
> *And my senses,*
> *Starved for so long*
> *And now euphoric,*
> *To breathe in the beauty*
> *Of this precious Pachelbel symphony.*

(Respecting the connection to our past and our future is a critical message in these trying times. Mexico celebrates their connection to deceased relatives in the celebration of the Day of the Dead. Americans have converted October 31st into a day of meaningless celebration of ghouls and goblins, wearing scary costumes and begging candy. Respecting our future families by taking action now to protect them is a critical message of this book. My connection to past and future families is the critical inspiration of the above poem.)

ALI' THE LION / THE SPIRIT OF MY DAD WAS IN MY GIRL

After ten years of marriage, Alizandra (Ali') was born on March 26th, 1993. We thought that she would be our only. However, on July 12th, 1995, Amadeus was born. Their grand and great grandparents on the Lopez side of the family had all passed away. Friends and relatives were always telling us that they would have been so happy with the kids. The following events tell me that they <u>are</u> happy with our kids!

Ali' the Lion. We were living in Albuquerque, New Mexico and we had just celebrated Ali's first birthday. We were at the cat exhibit of the Albuquerque Zoo. Sally was holding Ali' and watching the lion who was unusually quiet. Too quiet for my girl. She began roaring at him to get his attention. The lion turned and looked directly at Ali' and she returned the lion's gaze. As they unwaveringly stared directly at each other, Ali' continued to roar at the lion. In response, the lion began to roar continuously, louder and louder as he kept his gaze on Ali'. Sally felt Ali's little heart pound more quickly. Though others were standing around, the lion kept a steady stare directly at Ali' and Ali' fearlessly returned the stare with her own roar. Like two boxers at a heavyweight weigh-in, neither was going to blink or look away first. Ali' was to be our lionhearted fighter. How could we have known to nickname her Ali' after the great and mouthy boxer Mohammed Ali'?

So we knew Ali' was brave in the safety of her mother's arms. How brave would she be on her own? We were soon to find out. Shortly after the above incident, we took Ali' to the children's part of the State Fair. At the petting zoo with all the goats, she was pretty much fearless as she interacted with them. We took her out to the carnival rides and although it was cold, windy and drizzling, she immediately started kicking and moving around in a way that tells us that she is really excited and could not wait. Keep in mind she was barely one at the time. We both expected that she might be a little fearful to ride any of the rides particularly if she had to ride them alone. Boy, were we wrong!

We took her to the "Car Ride" which is a series of little vehicles on a rail that travel in a circle. Sally took her to the ride, strapped her in, left her and the ride began. We didn't know what to expect. Sally was very concerned that Ali' might stand up or become afraid so Sally asked the carnie if she could remain inside the barriers. The young boy allowed her to do so. Ali' was so excited, according to Sally, she started leaning forward trying to push the ride to get it to begin. When it started, she waved and smiled as she went around. She was initially holding on the sides, I guess for balance, but she shortly was brave enough to put one hand on the wheel and start turning the wheel. Sally said that she was smiling so big that she could see her teeth, the few she had.

Ali' didn't want to get off. It was as if she had done this a million times! We discovered that Sally could have been a million miles away and it would not have made a difference to our girl. Della and Betty, Ali's grandmother and aunt, were right. This gal is going to love the carnival and the rides. She had no fear!

We then took her to what we thought was pretty much a kid's ride. It was an "airplane ride". Not knowing any better, I volunteered to go with her and have her sit on my lap, facing forward. Although Sally denies it, I still think she knew the nature of this plane ride. As I got on, I was naively feeling quite brave. Then the guy started the ride. It quickly became apparent that this was no kid's ride or at least not a one-year-old ride. I had wondered why no one else was on this ride but Ali' and me. As our "plane" left the ground and began circling, the centrifugal force increased tremendously. I was okay at first but near the end of the ride I was starting to get motion sickness.

According to Sally, Ali' had a big smile on her face and was reveling in every dizzying turn. As the G forces became too great, I realized I needed to make a fast exit from this so called "kid's ride".

I turned to the man at the controls and, in the manliest voice I could muster, I pointed to Ali' and told him: "I THINK SHE IS READY TO GET OUT NOW!" Sally claims I was looking pale while Ali' was looking in control with a smile from ear to ear. Everyone probably knew who wanted to get out. The carnie at the controls did not stop. Did he not know that he had a duty to protect children?

In my quickly dizzying brain I figured he was getting satisfaction seeing me suffer, particularly since he figured this sick old geezer was trying to blame it on his little daughter. As we went around again, I yelled to him, pleadingly and pathetically: "I THINK WE'D BETTER GET OUT NOW!"

At this point, my stomach was beginning to feel queasy. Unable to see Ali's face, I was sure she was getting sick too. Desperately, I even yelled at Sally: "WHY ISN'T HE STOPPING THIS THING?" After what seemed like forever, the guy finally stopped the ride. It took me an entire day-and-a-half to fully recover. What I found out from Sally was that Ali' had smiled throughout the ride. She had no ill effects at all. Where did she get this? Both Sally and I hate these rides. Did our girl have the right stuff or what?

Even though I was not feeling well, we knew we couldn't stop there. We took our budding astronaut to the little train that goes around on the track and put her in the middle seat. Although the elderly lady running the train, had told us she thought our girl was too young for the ride, she had not witnessed what we had seen. We disregarded the woman's concerns. It was not until later that it dawned on us that Ali' was far younger than any of the kids at this carnival ride show.

Of course, Ali' loved the train ride. At one point she put her head down and we thought she was getting ready to fall asleep. But no, she picked her head up and started looking around in excitement. She later told us she just wanted to see the train's floor. On exiting the ride, the elderly control lady said: "I guess she wasn't too young for this ride after all. She really enjoyed it."

During the train ride, Ali' looked up at the huge Ferris wheel where some crazy guy was yelling and she smiled. Guess what she was going to want to ride next? Thank god Sally had to go to her class or else I would have had to take our little lion on the Ferris wheel. Suddenly I knew how important it was to get to Sally's Spanish class! A second language is important you know! I am sure Ali' wanted to go on more rides but I kept reminding Sally that she did not want to be late to her Spanish class. We finally left. Thank God!

It seems all our concerns were baseless. We had assumed that because her "fraidy-cat" parents feared carnival rides, she too would fear them. We could not have been more wrong! Alizandra was so gleeful. She was going to love Uncle Cliffs", Albuquerque's own carnival place.

On the way home that evening, suddenly it all came together. Ali's fearlessness and daring behavior towards the lion was the lion in her. I then knew Ali' carried the heart of a lion. The lion growled at her when he heard her roar because he recognized his own. He caught and kept her gaze and she caught his because they knew they were one and the same. He roared in response to her roar because he felt compelled to show everyone he was the boss and not Ali', just as he might do if another lion had invaded his territory. As to Ali', nothing was more natural to her than roaring. It seemed to fit her nature perfectly. Then and now, she lets everyone know in a loud voice her wants and needs. We have "Ali', the Lionhearted" in our house. She has the lion's spirit and personality. She is the lion.

My Dad, Ali's Protector. During that same period, I dreamt about one of my high school classmates. I remember her as dark-complected, slightly overweight, sensitive and shy girl. She was not particularly popular. In the dream she had just received new spring clothes and was very excited about it. I awoke from the dream at 3:00 a.m. and the dream was fresh in my mind. I remembered that at our twentieth high school reunion someone told me that this classmate had moved to California, lost a lot of weight and had become quite outgoing and outspoken. They said that she had changed so much that I would not even recognize her if I saw her.

I felt that the classmate in the dream symbolized my father. As I thought about it, I remembered my father was very dark-complected with very thick facial features. He was also built stocky. I further thought of it and remembered that this girl's dad died in a car accident, I suspected was related to alcohol. My father had died at age 58 from a life of too much alcohol. Moreover, my dad had always expressed sensitivity to this family probably because their father died when his children were still young. He had always worried about me riding in a car with people who were drunk. He told me never get in a car when the driver was drinking and to exit the car as soon as I found out. In fact, I followed his advice one time and crawled out of a car window at the train stop, when I realized that the brother of the girl in my dream had been drinking or was acting drunk at the wheel.

The dream elicited everything about my deceased dad. At first, I only instinctively connected the dream to my girl, Ali'. I thought about Ali's tirelessness, drive and intelligence, which went even beyond her drive to eat. That was my father! The feeling came over me that Ali' had somehow and in some way inherited, shared or was being protected by my father's soul, a guardian angel, so-to-speak. If the classmate in my dream was my father, then the new spring clothes symbolized Alizandra. We had finally given my dad a granddaughter. Somehow, something significant in my father became part of who Ali' is. I believe my father is alive and living in and through Ali'.

'FERRIS WHEEL' by Ali' at age 7

TO LIVE BY HEART

I remember it was the spring when we took a long winding meandering, bumpy dirt road through a sparsely settled part of Los Lunas. We arrived at a barren sight that was to become the lot of land that would be the location of our little single-wide 78-foot-long trailer. Our surroundings were desolate and lacked the familiar signs of civilization. It was a nearly deserted desert community, devoid of pavement or stop signs. Dry brush and sand were certainly in plentiful supply. To the distant east there was a stunning view of the mountains. But everywhere else, we saw mostly sand. I felt like we were the only people living there.

I remember the first trip. I feared we would never arrive at our vacant little lot and if we did, I thought we would never find our way out. Certainly, we'd have trouble finding our way back to the empty space that we were to call our own. And so much has happened since then. That was the springtime so very long ago. Now this little place has become our home and the bosom of our transformed soul.

We eventually learned the route by heart. So now we can find our little house with our eyes closed.

Once the only signs of movement, if not life, around this formerly all-dirt road were tumbleweeds bounding boldly in the wind, as if to say to us: Nothing will hold you here. But we were young and in love and the world was beautiful with the expectation all would be well.

Eventually, time saw people come in to create a neighborhood. Grass, flowers, trees and critters slowly followed. The older neighbors gradually warmed up to us. They laughed when my wife built a sandbox for the toddlers. 'They have all the sand they want', the older folks told her with a smirk. The younger ones laughed. The laughter stopped when, lo-and-behold, the toddlers rushed to play at our house. And where, but the little box of, yes, just sand!

They laughed again when Sally broke off a branch from what looked to be a dead tree and planted it in our yard. Unfazed by the taunting and laughter, she told everyone that we would have a tree. For the longest time the dry stick stood in the middle of a mostly barren yard, like the forgotten prank of a child. The little sentinel pointed to the sky, silently and sadly signaling God to send rain. Other than the scant rainfall, I can't recall anyone watering it. Then one day it turned green and blossomed. The laughter stopped, replaced now by the future seeds of hope and love and what would turn out to be an omen.

To our modest trailer and yard of sand, now with the addition of a tree and a sandbox, children were always welcome and would always visit. There they could dance, play volleyball, or baseball. Occasionally, we pulled out our gloves and even boxed with anyone who considered himself a contender.

Though no courts were nearby, we pulled the tennis racquets out and tried to hit to each other on the dirt road. Without fences, you spent forever chasing balls.

We often ate together. I remember a boy who had never eaten at McDonalds. So we had to take him there. I recall laughter and just having fun. Eventually the local government put in paved roads and Ma bell even put in a public telephone, a long block from our home. The neighborhood hoodlums tore it down thrice, as if to say we don't need outsiders connected to our turf. Ma bell succumbed and removed the phone for good.

I later discovered that our neighborhood had a nickname – Little Juarez. But there was also a plentiful supply of blue eyes and blonde hair. The moniker was really about status. They were talking about the new arrivals to our country and cheap trailers.

There were plenty of trips to and from anywhere and everywhere. During these, sometimes bright and sometimes dark, mind-wandering journeys to and from our home, I had discussions with myself, with family and with friends. These were gab-sessions without rules or out-of-bounce lines. On these old roads I've seen Kimberly, the niece from my newly discovered family learning how to drive and nearly killing our dog, Critter. We had rescued Critter, my sister-in-law's dog, only to see her poisoned by a neighbor.

I've seen Ryzo, our wonder-mutt, open the refrigerator door, bring us cokes, and close the refrigerator door, on command. We sadly witnessed his unusual disappearance, a police officer, being the prime suspect.

During our trips, my nieces waxed spontaneous. There were jokes, serious conversations and plain silliness. But not all was carefree. Sally must have threatened to divorce me a hundred times, going and coming. As we wound and bumped around these old dusty paths, we came home to the theft of our wonder-mutt, to burglaries of what had value to the thief and to a house that had much sadness.

On these same roads, the neighborhood kids grew up. Some went on to live lives of crime, some to school and many got jobs. But there was always talking. If not with each other, a silent discussion with oneself. The voices were as rich, tragic or silent as the voice that a person heard within. And often the voices at home drowned out the voice within. For them there was much emptiness. Like a raft with a hole, their entire being continually leaked, so they could never fully experience that wonderful adventure down the beautiful river of life. Every day and night they fought to keep their head above the raging waters of life.

On these trips, we bared our hearts and enriched our souls. Always there was a voice. Always there was a subject. Always there was someone with something to offer. And then we heard the sound of a new voice! It was on these dirt roads to our little house, to the sandbox and now to the blossoming stick tree that we brought home little Alizandra, our first.

We were never fully conscious that we were but leaves on a tree, in a vast orchard of trees. Life craning its neck to the sun and at the same time, being watered or tragically, going unwatered and being baked by the sun until it withered.

But now I see landscapes, gardens, families and community. They are somehow linked to us and we, to them. Yes, they will flourish or die and in some way, we either helped or did not, to enlighten and to nourish the withering or blossoming spirit of the community which lives or dies within each of us.

So much of living or dying depends on whether others gave but a small part of themselves. And those brittle souls and tepid hearts who could not be loved, nor reach out to the sunlight, slowly withered on the vine.

As in any journey there are lessons of love and hate. Mine was this: One's only solace and salvation is to know that the real value is not in what you got from life but what you gave, what you shared and the lives that you touched and brightened. If you made this connection then death would feast on nothing from you. It would devour but the emptiest of shells. Because what remains is what you have given away and what others have received. And all that you have given, lives on as your loving gift, inconsumable legacy and living spirit.

In life's journey, you can now easily find your home and the road that leads outward and back, if your life has been the torch that has burned brightly for others. Your soul can now make the final trip home with its eyes closed.

At the end of life's road trip, you can declare without doubt that this was a fulfilled life. And the landscape of myriad minds, hearts and souls that you filled by your bright spirit, will grandly attest to the brightness of your existence. It is this that will have given meaning to the extinction of your last peaceful and life-filled exhalation.

So on the ultimate journey, your love lights and leads the way to your final home, whose now familiar route you have learned by heart.

(See 'Why A Human Love Must Not Hold One Captive' in Ch. VI. for complementary poem re death.)

MIRAGE MEMORY

In the distant journey
Through the vastness
And debilitatingly dry heat
Of times' dreary desert highway
I am mesmerized
By a distant stream of water
Flowing softly and serenely
Across the path ahead.
It shimmers as it flows
Beckoning me to come closer.
As I anxiously approach,
The mists from the phantom stream
Wondrously rise
And fully dissipate to the heavens.
But then another stream continues to flow
In the distance
Just beyond my hastening approach.

I am mystified and entranced
By the symmetry of the sight
Of this tantalizing, flowing,
Enticing illusion
That continues to draw me towards it.
Yet I am stymied and frustrated
That this oasis teases and mocks me.
As I reach out, it moves away.
As I thirst for its life-giving waters,

It callously denies my thirsty soul.
As I recollect its relation,
It softly says: "I am someone else,
Neither yours nor anyone's.
Neither does nature rule me,
For I am a dream".

I REMEMBER THIS DREAM!
It is a message of what could have been
For me so long ago,
When I drearily drifted
In a drought of self-centeredness
And depressing lovelessness
And
The titillating and tempting waters of love
Dreamfully wafted just out of reach.
I recall the birth and death of these streams:
Streams that elude those dying in deserts;
Moving closer but never arriving;
Nightmares of drought defeating deluge;
Eyes seeing, but tongues never tasting,
Emaciating souls ever weakening.

Many years ago
I reached the streaming waters
Foretold in my dream
And finally, they became part of my being
And I tasted and touched what had only teased.
I then joyfully reveled in liquid life.

I luxuriated in rushing waters
Caressing every hungry and starving pore
Of what was a fading existence.
Through my almost spent being
I sensed these streams
Rushing over my body,
A cascading liquid cool wave
Becoming part of me, moving me
Bringing me to life.

Yes.
These were the waters of love and happiness
That rescued and resuscitated me
From the brink of death.

I smile to recall this dream because
I awoke and my dream had become my life.
Massive clouds exploding with rain
On a starving despairing Sahara
And the river flowed over unprepared banks
And the earth roundly smiled to drink
After so long without.

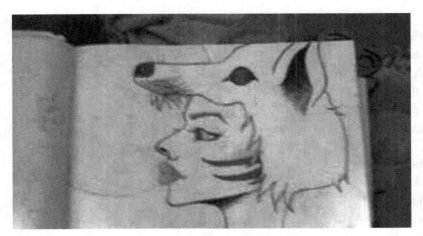

Drawing by ALI'

ALIZANDRA'S HEAD

I am drawn to her eyes,
Giant, almond shaped
And exotic.
They change colors
Like the season-changing colors
Of the beautiful Bosque.
Her windows to the world
Are big and bright
Circular pools
Begging to be bathed
In wisdom's waterfall
And nature's beauty.

I gloriously gaze
As these magic viewers
Peer from her tiny owl-head,
Now sparingly covered
With brief brown
Straight fine locks
That might shortly support a bow
And then to sprout
Rows of beautiful
Wild brown curls
With golden highlights.

My daughter's ears
Sally and contour outward
Far too big
For her little head.

The better to hear and take in
All the knowledge that awaits
And refined enough to detect
And distinguish evil and good
And poised to alert her
To the dangers
Ever lurking nearby.

In contrast to the wings
For ears,
Ali' has a precious, tiny
Bump of a button-nose
Suited to smelling less
Of the obnoxious air
That will surround her.

This delicate and precious
Petite work of art
Is permanently part of me now
And lives in the front
Of my memory
And in the heart of my soul.
Even when she is not
In my eyes or arms,
We are one.

'...And the people bowed and prayed
To the neon god they made...'
Written by Paul Simon and sung by Simon and Garfield
Sounds of Silence

CHRISTMAS MESSAGE

The experience of having children has given me a more universal appreciation of the meaning and message of the accepted rendition, representation or drawing of the birth of Jesus surrounded by nature.

We Americans have converted the birth of Jesus into an excuse and opportunity to celebrate things and money. How expensive and cool a gift can we get for our kids? The children measure the success of the holiday by what they got and the price tag. Congratulations to those parents who have their kids build, create or draw a picture for someone not so well off as they. Kudos to the churches that prepare and deliver meals to the low-income neighborhoods for Christmas.

Unfortunately, the wonder and beauty of giving, gets lost in the commercial translation. Along with the commercial celebration, Judeo-Christianity has connected the Christmas holiday with the re-enforcement of the follower's faith in a Messiah and all the Christian history that surrounds that concept.

Let me suggest an alternative viewpoint, message and interpretation that I humbly believe is more universal and involves a nature-based interpretation of the Christmas story. It does not involve faith in the divinity but does involve unconditional love, hope, and giving.

The telling of the nativity story involves a search for shelter, being turned away by innkeepers and finally finding a humble manger for the birth of the ultimate hope of mankind. It involves a search by three wise men from the east, guided by a bright star, adoration of the Christ child, the presentation of gifts of gold, frankincense and myrrh, and their refusal to inform Herod of the baby's whereabouts. Herod was killing first-borns, which included Jesus.

Whether you believe all of it or not, this simple event or the rendition thereof, has changed western civilization. Could it be that the Christmas' story's power lies not in whether you believe it or accept that the baby Jesus is the son of God? Could it be that the story itself has eternal meaning? Could it be that the truth of the Christmas message is in the brilliance and timeless wisdom of the metaphors themselves, unrelated to their factual authenticity? Please bear with me!

Might the message best be taken to mean that all of our children are the hope of the world; that we should live and die with the belief and duty to teach our children so they will be prepared to save the world from itself. Consider the following:

The Christ Families' Search for Shelter. Is it an over-simplification to believe that Jesus, Mary and Joseph are like so many in this world who are without the basics and must ask their neighbors to share what they have? Could those Innkeepers who turned the holy family away represent the same human beings that throughout history have chosen to look the other way rather than help those in need? Close to home, could those who turned the Holy Family away be a direct reference to our capitalist culture that finds no value outside of how much money it makes or saves us. The Innkeeper makes no money off a poor family who can't pay. This, not-so-veiled reference to the businessman, as the first bad-guy in the story, should make us think about the poor, oppressed, the downtrodden and how our country treats them.

Pope Francis' Encyclical, 'Laudato Si', essentially states that our failure to address the devastating effects of pollution on poor people and developing countries is a moral failure. In fact, he indicts 'consumerism' and the 'cheerful wrecklessness' that permeates the culture. Mmm! I wonder who he could be talking about?

I submit that the refusal of housing of the Holy Family is just another version of "what you do unto the least of your brethren, you do unto me?" I submit it does not have to be the Son of God for the lesson to be meaningful.

Wise men following the star and protecting the child. Is this just another way of saying enlightenment (symbolized by the star), is in risking your lives for the protection of infants and children, as did the wise men? Does it have to be the son of God for the story to have an effect or would any infant do?

How about a female child? I submit that the operative concept is that it was an infant, not necessarily the Christ child. Is it that difficult to believe that the author was sending a message and the baby Jesus represented all children, male or female?

How about future children? Pope Francis Encyclical, Laudato Si', strongly suggests that we have a moral duty to future generations.

The Manger scene traditionally had Joseph and Mary present for the birth. Their presence is symbolic of their cherishing, care and nurturing of the child-God. The universal message, I would suggest is to all parents to do the same with their children.

My Experience. I never quite fully appreciated the power and breadth of the infant metaphor until we had a child. The birth and care of Alizandra (Ali') and Amadeo changed that! Now when I think newborn, it evokes great hope, love, compassion, selflessness and giving.

Coincidentally, it evokes the timeless and eternal efforts of mothers going beyond fear, taking great risks to give birth, to protect and to nurture. I envision lionesses fighting to the death to protect their young. (I watch and listen to PBS of course)

I never fully understood or appreciated these feelings until Ali' came along. Now I can barely stand to watch those secretly filmed videos of nanny's abusing infants. The story of the baby Jesus powerfully evokes all these timeless emotions. There is even Herod to play the ultimate bad guy. Our world seems to have an abundance of bad guys to play Herod's part. But it is too easy to point to the other guy. We must all take responsibility for the evils in the world. Our willingness to tolerate the evil makes each of us culpable.

I think the helpless newborn metaphor involves even more than merely maternal instincts. It involves a calling that renders one's own life secondary to the child's life. The enlightening event for me was Ali's and Amadeo's birth. Through them, as with all births, the parents gain immortality. The mother and father lose themselves in the child and the child sees him/herself through the parent's eyes. The mother and father have a second chance at life through their child. Through Ali' and Amadeo, I am connected with the future. If I do not reach the mountaintop, then they might, and if not them, their children, and so on. My ideas, my values and yes, my genes will continue through them and in them. Death loses its grip on us through our offspring. Sound like the Holy Trinity concept, at least as far as the Father, Son and Holy Ghost being 'separate but one'? Are not we all separate but one with our children?

When it comes to the animal kingdom and protective mothers, this magnificent selflessness is not conscious, it is innate. In humans, it should be part of our being. Our children's lives and potential are more important than their parents. Not to be sacrilegious, but each of our children are little saviors and I submit, should be treated as such.

Nature's Lessons. Should we be looking to nature for moral guidance? The rural setting of the nativity and the animals in the manger surrounding the birth, certainly support this viewpoint. You will not hear this interpretation because western religions have always seen the worship of nature as antithetical to Christ worship. Nature is related to paganism and the worship of nature is akin to demon worship in the eyes of many. Pan, the pagan god of nature, comes to mind.

For me, the metaphor of a helpless child is even more powerful than the death and resurrection motif. It is better designed to elicit hope and quell our fears since it is tied to a natural maternal instinct. It also seems symbolic of the 'oneness' of the humanity notion which I address in this Chapter - *"Lost Gospels Explain Jesus' Main Message and my Transformation Better Than any Church Doctrine."* Maybe our male side needs the torture, death and resurrection story, because of its 'manliness' and bluntness. The crucifixion is more like a lopsided boxing match with lots of blood and gore. Men can relate! Birth and babies are just too sentimental and mushy to stimulate our masculine hearts and brains.

To put it succinctly, the Christmas story is that our hope is directly tied to the strength of our love and ability to give without expectation of receiving. No exception for Capitalism! Enlightenment and wisdom will be found in nurturing and protecting children not for any personal benefit or gain, but merely because selflessness, compassion and love are good virtues, in and of themselves. The message includes not merely our own children, but children everywhere. The Christmas message is empty, if we, like the selfish innkeepers, look the other way when childhood anywhere in the world is at risk.

The Modern Day Message. This message would not be complete or truthful if I did not address a modern-day setting and contrast it to the beautiful natural setting of the birth of Jesus. How would the Christmas setting affect us if it were portrayed, not in nature but in a smog-filled car-lot, not on natural earth but on asphalt or pavement? In the background, big factories and incinerators would be belching noxious and deadly smoke into the air and lungs of the little baby Jesus. Instead of animals, the little baby would be surrounded by pollution-belching vehicles that daily destroy the lungs of all the babies. In lieu of the pastoral scene, the birth would be surrounded by an animal-agricultural factory, torturing and killing millions of defenseless animals to satisfy our taste buds and polluting the neighborhood and the world. Instead of parents and wisemen, salesman and blaring ads would surround the baby, selling their life-destroying hotdogs, burgers and steaks, delivered by polluting vehicles for the comfort of the new family. Of course, front and center, there would be TV's blaring, VCR's recording and computer's efficiently communicating. Certainly, Joseph and Mary would be videotaping with their cell phones. The baby would drink or suckle chemically laden milk or soda from a plastic bottle. Instead of natural wood and straw, the baby's cradle would be an easily disposable plastic-covered bed. This way we could easily dispose of whatever did not suit our immediate needs.

Would this then be a more accurate and truthful rendition of the modern-day nativity scene? MERRY CHRISTMAS!

Curiously, the essence of this 'Message' was prepared before I had discovered that it was St. Francis of Assisi, who convinced the powerful Roman Catholic Church to adopt the crib with the baby Jesus, to bring the people closer to God by emphasizing His humanity. (See the PBS presentation:'A History of Christianity' and 'Christianity, The First Three Thousand Years' by Diarmaid Macculloch 3-19-20). St. Francis was the Catholic saint who truly believed what Jesus said: "Announce the kingdom! Possess no gold or silver or copper in your purses, no traveling bag, no sandals, no staff" (see Luke 9:1-3 KJV). Importantly, it was Francis who has been described as a 'nature mystic', one who finds God in the vast and beautiful fields of nature. Everything spoke to Francis of the infinite love of God. Trees, worms, lonely flowers by the side of the road - all were saints gazing up into the face of God. Mar 20, 2013 See 2013/03/20, the Washington Post.) So Maybe I am in good company my 'nature' interpretation of the Christmas scene.

THE APPEARANCES OF THE BLESSED MOTHER MARY AND HER MESSAGE, WHAT DOES IT MEAN?

Did you ever wonder why God chose to be so subtle and secretive about His presence and about the after-life? Why make it difficult to fathom the spiritual realm? What is accomplished by the secretive veil between life and death? When you pray would it not be refreshing for someone to answer in the language we are accustomed to? If we can make contact with a vehicle on Mars and receive photos from such a distant planet, why does it seem there is no easy link between God and humans?

I am not unmindful of the *faithfuls'* response to this query. If you have faith you can hear Gods answers, and/or, Faith is a prerequisite into heaven, and/or, the answer is a mystery, and/or, God is telling you and you are not listening.

In the movie "Contact", Jody Foster, the aspiring and godless astronaut, is speaking with a believer who happens to be in love with her. She, of course, believes that there is no proof of God - how can a rational person believe without proof? The believer tells her "Did your father love you?" She of course says yes to which he cunningly replies "Prove it!" I guess his message is you can't prove love so why expect to prove God.

But that is not entirely true. We can prove human love by 1)identifying the embodiment and sources of love; and 2) identifying what that being has given up and what they have done and said to us. (Yea. Probably some hearsay issues.) However, if the standard is 'preponderance of evidence' (more likely than not), this should be reasonably good evidence in any court to prove a person's love of another person. No faith is needed. Sure, there is always a chance that this is just evidence of a con job, but it is evidence, nevertheless.

Hey, even if you can't prove they love you, you can prove they exist! You don't have to rely on a two-thousand-year-old book of hearsay and double hearsay, from pre-enlightenment times, written after the purported source and authors have died.

I hear your response. God speaks to us through miracles... Well that is what this letter is really about. More specifically the appearances and messages of the Blessed Mother and what this means. I have reviewed some messages from her appearances. I have extracted and summarized the messages from Fatima.

The following seems to jump out at me in these messages: 1) That it is Mary that is the vehicle for the message, not Jesus or angels; (2) That she wants the world to focus on the immaculate heart; (3) That she asks that we pray the rosary; and (4) That her appearances are for the most part to poor people. (5) A vision of hell from Sister Lucia of Fatima

(1) **Mary as the Vehicle of the Message.** Most significant is that a woman infrequently mentioned in the Bible has managed to insert herself by appearances to numerous people. The great Christian/Judeo prophets have all been male: Jesus, Mohammed, Ezekiel, Isaiah, etc. So, what is 'God' saying by sending a mother. The most sage realize that the vehicle is the message. The mere fact that a mother is delivering the message speaks volumes.

In recent history the Holy Mother has appeared and spoken to hundreds of people. (I will put my skepticism aside, concerning whether they were true appearances or mere projections by the beholder. The appearance in Egypt is actually captured in a photograph.)The number, the nature and the quality of these appearances and messages is what is fascinating.

It seems significant that a female is carrying the message. It seems poignant that it is a mother with an immaculate heart. We know that symbols, metaphors and archetypes have a power beyond words. The mother image conjures up, consciously and I'm sure, unconsciously, notions of birth, children, unselfish love, nourishment and protection to the point of death. There can be no greater prayer than the life of a good mother.

The choice of the medium of the blessed mother tells us we must love as a good mother, with an emphasis on selflessness and love.

(2) **Focus on the Heart.** The heart is synonymous with love and giving. In our culture it is often the opposite of the mind.

(3) **Mary's Plea to Pray the Rosary:** Those who have prayed know the power of prayer. As for the rosary, the prayer most said on the rosary is the Hail Mary. *'Hail Mary, full of grace, the Lord is with thee, blessed are thou amongst women and blessed is the fruit of thy womb Jesus. Holy Mary, Mother of God, pray for us sinners now and at the hour of our death. Amen.'*

The 'Hail Mary' first conjures up the beauty of childbirth and the blessedness of a child. The second part identifies the motherhood of Mary and her power to change our lives. Symbolically speaking, it seems like a strong appeal to our maternal side and the power therein, as well as giving respect to the life that a woman carries. In what the Pope has called a culture of death, the prayer reminds us of the importance of human life.

(4) **Appearance to Poor People**: People oppressed or of little means have always been cognizant and receptive to a spiritual message. Had the Jews not been oppressed, they may never have left Egypt. We would never have had the Ten Commandments. Ideally the recipient of the spiritual message must not have been tainted and deafened by the luxury of things and physical comforts. Such would be absolutely inconsistent with the spiritual message. The messenger would be suspect. Query, have Americans forfeited their spiritual endowment by buying into the American culture that puts wealth, comfort, appearance and living for oneself only, over the values of love, giving, sacrifice and a life directed beyond the here-and-now, to the spiritual realm?

I read Mary's message to be saying we must be like the loving, giving and sacrificing mother to survive spiritually. We must pray to be saved and to have God speak to us. Moreover, we must cleanse ourselves of a culture that is antithetical to the spiritual.

So, in answer to the initial questions regarding the difficulty of fathoming the spiritual realm, maybe, like the radio contact with the voyager traveling in space, we must be on the right radio frequency to communicate and to receive messages. Before we can hear or see messages or visions from God, we must ourselves be on a spiritual frequency. The appearances and messages from the Blessed Mother, I think, are intended to mold our being so that we will hear and be able to communicate spiritually. Mary is essentially telling us what to do to tune in to the spirit.

You now know the spiritual frequency. Will we be able to cast off the clothing of the unclean, the carnal and the Profit-Above-All instinct at the door of the spiritual so we can transmit on the spiritual wavelength?

(5) **A Vision of Hell from Sister Lucia of Fatima.** The first of 'Three Secrets of Fatima, described in in her third memoir of 1941, and entrusted to the children during the apparition of 13 July 1917, was a 'vision of hell'. I suspect most Catholics would see that as a place you go after you die, if you did not have faith in God or turned away from God. Could it be more specific than that? Could Lucia have been seeing into the future, a view of the consequences of our destruction of nature - a hell on earth? It certainly would follow from our present day disregard and violation of everything the Blessed Mother stood for.

MY COMMENT ON THE APPEARANCE OF THE VIRGIN MARY AND HER MESSAGE

Where Does the Blessed Mother Fit? Catholics hold the Blessed Mother in the highest regard. Pope John the 23rd considered her responsible for saving him from death. Those of the Fundamentalist persuasion see her role as peripheral. Although the Bible recognizes Mary as "blessed", certainly Assembly of God would not pray to her, as would a Catholic. Would I, by acknowledging Mary's significance and influential role in God's plan, make me persona non-grata? All four of my conclusions are not inconsistent with biblical teaching. Yet, a Mary with God-like powers is not something you are going to hear any time soon in a fundamentalist sermon.

I have not retracted or omitted this essay because I believe it is of critical importance in living our spiritual life to the fullest. Our modern day lives often glorify the mind over the heart, things over people, the male over the female, adults over children, the workplace over child-rearing, vengeance over compassion and technology over nature. Our soul often seems devoid of the female and the maternal. My essay is about restoring this balance. Indeed, this is a central theme of this book. I think Mary's role, correctly perceived or otherwise, is to the same effect.

I further believe that there is a direct connection between our concern for nature and the strength of our maternal instinct. In spite of a Fundamentalist disagreement about the importance of Mary, this essay remains an essential part of the main message of this book.

**Gregoria Lopez, (mom), Theresa Lopez, (sister),
Martin Lopez (Author) and Martin Lopez Sr. (My dad)**

WRESTLING WITH MY BOY / REMEMBERING
MY FATHER AND HIS IMPACT

(Amadeo was seven years old at the time of the first writing.)

At the Lopez house, play-wrestling after dinner has become a regular routine. Amadeo looks forward to the fight, and for both of us, it is a way to unwind.

As I thought about our daily bouts, I was reminded about my father – an intelligent man requiring little sleep. My mom would tell me that he only needed four hours a night and during the last week of the particular election he was in, he would sleep only four hours .... the entire week! He was a superb county politician and an athlete-extraordinaire who was good enough to play second base for Air Force. In fact, he taught me everything about baseball. To him I am grateful for a Little League City championship when I was twelve. In every game, no matter who the coach was in the dugout, my dad would sit in the bleachers behind home plate and through me at the catcher's position, signal me who to walk, how to pitch to a certain batter and whether to speed up or slow the pitcher's pace. I'm sure our coach was annoyed by this but he knew my dad's credentials.

I remember one very memorable time when I was in high-school. I was on the Panther football team as a half-back and mostly saw the world from the bench. My greatest skill was the ability to avoid being hit by another player. I had some speed that was helpful and the inspiration that, at 125 pounds, most everyone was bigger than me, so I best avoid them.

We were playing in Bloomfield against a Bloomfield football team that always seemed to be full of big kids. Every year it was either Bloomfield or Kirtland that won the State Championship. So, it was always a big game. I do not think my dad much liked coming to these games to see me sit on the bench. As a coach and high-school football player he probably did not enjoy merely being a spectator with no control of the outcome. Moreover, he did not like the coach. (How could he like a coach who did not recognize his son's amazing talent!)

So, when I realized he had made the two-hour drive from Gallup to watch the Cathedral Panther football team play, I was surprised, delighted and saddened, at once. Since Bloomfield was so good it was highly unlikely that I would play. Had he come just to see me sit the bench? Or maybe he knew something I didn't?

I think by the end of the first half, our outmatched team was down by forty points. I was also told that our first-string halfback, Michael Landavazo, had been injured. Often, as I sat the bench, I would lose myself in fantasies or ideas, unrelated to football. For this reason, I hadn't noticed that he had been injured. (Maybe he wasn't hurt and they just did not want to risk his safety in a losing battle.)

In any case, shortly after the second half began, I heard the coach yell my name: 'Lopez! Come here!' I thought Damn! He had seen me daydreaming or not paying attention to the game and was going to yell at me to pay attention. No! He actually wanted me to play! 'Go in at the halfback position!' Shit! I was going to play in a real game! Oh god! Would I even know what to do? But I went out there like I knew what I was doing.

This 125-pound kid who ran funny but fast, got his chance to play and, remarkably, did not disappoint. I managed to make catches, run further and make tackles as never before. It was the best I ever played - one of the few times in fact, all in front of my father! He was so proud. He told me later: "If that performance didn't convince the coach that you should be playing all the time, I don't know what would!" He was not prone to exaggeration, so I felt good about it.

Apparently, the coach agreed. They awarded me the 'Cossack of the Week' award. I looked it up – 'a member of a people of southern Russia and Ukraine noted for their horsemanship and military skill.' In any case, it was an acknowledgement that I had a better game than anyone else. Knowing the coach, the award to me, was more an insult on how badly everyone else played. Moreover, my performance was against Bloomfield's second-team. After you are ahead by forty points you don't take a chance on injuring your good players. So, for one time in my life I was the best and my dad got to see it! These things are memorable.

(I missed the last part of the Monday practice in which I was honored with the award. During that practice, one of my fellow teammates, (Louie, I think) intentionally or inadvertently, struck my outstretched arm and dislocated it. I had to go to the hospital.) Well I got one great game in!)

Present or not for the award, it was that game my dad and I could always refer to and say I should have been the first-string halfback. (By the way, I have the video tape in case anyone doubts how good I was, at least, in that game.) Sometimes having evidence of being good is almost as good as playing first-team. You don't have to prove on a daily and weekly basis that you are the best. You just say: look at my video. It's not my fault that the coach doesn't appreciate great talent! This way the coach looks bad. I could then make the argument, at least in my head, that it was unfair that a quality player like me should be on the bench. Must be a bad and biased coach!

I am reminded about another memory of my dad. In every sport that I played, my dad would share with me what he knew. Even when I was quite young, he would play-box with me. I grew up watching Gillette's Friday Night at the Fights with him. It was our regular routine together on Friday nights. Sports were the glue that connected my father and me. Through sports I learned about life and right and wrong. His version was a little rougher than most fathers. For example, if you are rounding third base and the throw from the outfield was going to be close, and the catcher is blocking the home plate, it is acceptable to knock the catcher down. (While coaching eight and nine-year-olds, I got some angry glares from the dads of the kids I was coaching when I told them this knock-em-down 'wisdom'.

This rougher view of life was a consequence of growing up in Gallup - a rough and tumble mining and business town where many millionaires were made in numerous retail business. My family was not one of them. (I think my mom would have liked for my dad to have had a mind for money. But though he had an insurance business, getting rich did not seem to be his goal. He liked people and the politics that connected him with them. Friendships won out over money every time.)

Being tough and respected for it, was a goal of the Lopez family. Whatever toughness or that which I could feign, was a result of being the son and nephew of the Lopez family - a group who would never start a fight but would never back down from one. I was raised on the wild-west stories of my Uncle Grassy. I remember one, in particular, about how he took on three guys, one at a time, in a fight with only a chain that he did not use but placed it within reach. He warned his would-be gang attackers that if anyone jumps in to help, he would use the chain against all of them. Apparently, they concurred to this rule. One at a time, as my Uncle Grassy tells it, he beat them all. (Yes, it is hard to imagine that three guys who wanted to beat my uncle up would politely stand by, while Grassy beat up their buddies. Maybe tough-guys were more fair-minded in those days.) In any case I was convinced Grassy and my dad were the toughest guys in Gallup.

Grassy was also an athlete. He was a State Doubles Champion tennis player along with Dean Kirk whose trophy I had, and now my son has. Dean Kirk's nephew, Kevin Kirk, was our star Red Sox pitcher in Little League. I was the catcher during the championship year and he was the pitcher. We won the Little League City Championships together. The family torch had been passed.

I have had some time to think about it since then. The rest of my championship team seemed to have a large number of the children of parents who were my dad's political supporters and friends. I finally figured that, though my dad was not the official coach in the dugout, he was responsible for somehow attracting the best talent to the Red Sox. Two of the best pitchers and homerun hitters on our team, Angelo and Attilio Dipaolo, just happened to be the sons of a political supporter of my father. In fact, the summer after my Eighth-grade year, my dad sent me down to Atilio's restaurant and bar to apply for a job for the summer. I don't remember any interview but I got the job as a busboy. Mmm! It took me many years to finally appreciate that my dad was not only the coach behind the scenes, he was the one responsible for recruiting quality players for the Red Sox team. I had been oblivious to all these connections. He had somehow managed to put together a team that had enough talent to beat the great and mighty White Sox led by bigger than life, superstar pitcher and homerun hitter, Jimmy Horrocks. How did my dad not get him for the Red Sox? Must have been a Republican family!

I remember too, being told by my mom how my dad defended himself when the much bigger and taller deputy sheriff tried to push my father around. I grew up reveling in a family of tough guys and athletes but never bullies. I believed everything they told me. I wanted so bad to grow up like my dad's family.

The reality was that I was not connected by blood to my dad's family. I was adopted. I really think, my nature, was not very 'tough'. I was 5' 5" tall, weighed 125 pounds at my heaviest in high school, had a scrawny and unimposing frame and emotionally was not a natural fighter. Fighting was not in my nature. But when you are surrounded by a family of larger-than-life tough guys, guess what? I was intent on becoming a tough guy too and pretended as best as I could. I was a pretty good actor!

I remember my first lesson in toughness was when I was about 4 and my 3-year-old first-cousin and I were in the living room of the house of Grandpa and Grandma Lopez along with the brothers and sisters of my dad. My 3-year-old cousin actually bit me. Both his mother and my dad noticed. But nobody jumped up or seemed to get emotional about what had happened. Their only advice to me: Punch him if he does it again! Wow! I remember thinking that seemed rather extreme and I asked them again to be sure that is what they said. "Just hit him!" So, he bit me again and I punched him in the chest. He cried and it didn't happen again. It was that basic and primal! No talking, no sending him to his room, no yelling, no spanking, just a punch! That was the Lopez approach in a nutshell.

However, when it came to wrestling, I have a special memory of only one instance when my dad actually wrestled with me. It was something I would have loved to do. In the early years he was busy working or politicking. In my later teenage-years he was either inebriated or on-the-wagon. I remember him shaky and drinking atole (a cornmeal drink) that calmed his nerves after month-long binges.

Generally, he would drink outside the house and I would be asleep when he came home. Near the end of his life, he began binge-drinking with hard alcohol and was quickly rendered bedridden. We had little or no meaningful communications during this time. Moreover, when he was sober, he was on edge. Playfully and naively, I would come up behind him and without notice, grab him and he would get angry: 'You're lucky I didn't cold-cock you!', he would growl at me. Of course, being a kid, I would do it again and all would be repeated. During a time of my life when I was energetic and playful, my dad was not at all playful. He was essentially just holding on to life. I wanted so much to physically interact with the father who was a hero to me.

Don't get me wrong. My dad loved both my sister and I. He always took the opportunity to hug and kiss both Theresa and I. Even at ten years old I recall sitting on his lap. As long as he was able, he showed us his love. Recall too that my dad was 38 when they adopted us and 58 when he died of cirrhosis of the liver. His binge drinking killed him before his time.

My urge to roughhouse with my dad was not to be, except for one time. It was one of those days he was at home and had begun to drink but had not gotten to the point of drunkenness. His inhibitions had been lowered to the point he wasn't afraid of being a kid again. I don't know how it started. I probably goaded him with a threat and then grabbed him and we wrestled to the floor. I have no recollection what happened then or who controlled the wrestling. But the faded and delightful recollection remains. It was probably the last time I had much physical contact with him before he died. I vowed that if my son wanted to wrestle with me, I would oblige him wholeheartedly and that is what we do.

Our routine typically goes like this: Let's fight dad, he proclaims with reckless bravado. I am usually on the couch, the floor or the bed, generally too tired to do much of anything. But for some reason I can always find energy to wrestle with my boy. This was mainly because I didn't have to move from where I was seated or resting. If his laying down the gauntlet doesn't get my attention, he calls me a name that he thinks will get me mad or so he figures. You dummy! You stupid idiot, he yells at me.

These are the buzzwords that he has heard the kids use on the playgrounds at school. I don't know if anyone has called him a dummy or stupid, but for him, these have become fighting words. Maybe someone called him a name and that is how he knows how powerful those words are.

(Yes, I have thought that my acquiescence to such name-calling may be some kind of encouragement or authorization, but given the context, I do not think so.)

Anyway, I feign anger. With a furrowed brow I intensely stare right into his excited eyes. With my best rendition of Deniro, I ask him threateningly: What did you call me? With a daring inspired by a knowledge that I am too lazy to move from my seat and a desire to risk getting caught, he yells at me:

You stupid dummy! What are you going to do, old man? Now he has raised the ante beyond what is tolerable. I have told him never to call me "old man". I tell him I am going to get him bad. He laughs and screams. He again runs by me just within my reach and screams like a banshee as he passes. This goes on until I yell maniacally and jump up and grab him and drag him back to the couch like a lion snares and drags a wounded animal to their lair. He is kicking, fighting and screaming all the way back. He pleadingly asks what are you going to do to me? I tell him in a totalitarian voice. Just lie down and don't move. Or what will happen, he asks pleadingly and in a voice of surrender. Back in a comfortable position and with a firm grip on Amadeo I ask him: You called me what! And he squeals: Nothing, Nothing! I tell him: You are lying and I do not like liars!' In a show of bravado, he pushes the envelope and says I called you a stupid dummy. What? I scream, in a louder more threatening voice. "DUMMY!", he says in a voice between a giggle and a breathless scream.

Then my free right hand slowly and where he can see it, transforms into Senor Puno. (Mr. Fist). As the great Sugar Ray Leonard would taunt his opponents with a big wind-up, as if to deliver a bolo (roundhouse) punch, my arm begins to make circles, first small and then larger circles. And each time, like the Pit and the Pendulum, I would come menacingly closer. As my arm dangerously circles, I sing: Lanza lanza, pica la panza. (Swing, swing, poke the stomach!) All this was just as I remembered my dad playing with me. (My dad and I occasionally used to shadow-box.) Each time, the pendulum punch closes in and Senor Puno comes closer to his body. Amadeo screams with glee. He yells: No Senor Puno and struggles to get away. But I have got him tightly. I drag this out for suspense as Senor Puno comes scarily close. For him the excitement is wondering what Mr. Fist will finally do.

Finally, when Amadeo least expects it, Senor Puno begins to tickle him at all his ticklish spots. He screams and twists and yells: No Senor Puno No!! After he can hardly stand it and he says I'm going to wet my pants, I say: Que dices? Que dices? (What do you say?) If he is brave he says: "Nothing!" I turn up the tickle volume until between laughing and squealing he blurts: Perdoname Papi, Perdoname! (Forgive me daddy, forgive me!) Y que mas nino? (And what else child?) Por Favor! Por favor!! (Please! Please!) If he can take any more, I tell him: Y que mas? Te amo mucho papi, Te amo mucho!! (I love you a lot daddy, I love you a lot!) Y que mas? Sueltame papi Sueltame, (let me go!), said in pleading tones. The litany of submission and contrition is complete and I let him go.

Curiously Amadeo seldom speaks to me in Spanish. But in the heat of the battle and threatened with more tickling, his Spanish comes alive. The unspoken rule is that if he says he is sorry, tells me he loves me, and tells me to let him go, all in Spanish, I release him. He then runs like a tiger that has fought his way out of the trap.

Depending on his energy level and if he has any homework and how late it is, the scenario repeats itself. This is how the Lopez boys entertain themselves on a nightly basis.

(Update: At the time of this first writing, Amadeo is now 18 and I am 62. He is 5'9" and has no discernible fat on his body. I am 5'6" with no discernible muscle on my body. Yeah. We still sort-of rumble. But I no longer control the outcome. In fact, mostly for my protection, we have a rule that if it gets too rough, one of us can tap out, just like in cage fighting, and the other must stop. Amadeo does not always follow this rule. The difference now from the old days, is that the 17-year-old is an angry 17-year-old. Guess who he is generally mad at? He brings all that anger to the fight. Dad's feeble body does his best to avoid getting hurt.)

Since those wondrous days when our kids were fairly obedient and actually listened to us, many things have changed. However, Ali' and Amadeo have both won Tennis District Championships. Amadeo has won a Silver Gloves Boxing State Championship and a tennis State Doubles Championship.

Talk about 'rough and tumble', Ali' my daughter, early on learned gymnastics and was the tumbler for the high school cheer leaders at West Las Vegas. The job did not come easy. After a tryout, the 8th grade coach unfairly denied her from being on the 8th grade cheerleading team. (The gradeschool cheerleading coach was a former employee of mine and I suspect not happy with me.) This rejection did not faze Ali'. She tried out for the high school cheerleading team and made the team as an eighth-grader!

I remember another incident in which Ali' brazenly told the Tennis Coach, in front of the rest of the team, that Raven, her first-cousin and her, should be allowed to challenge the coaches' daughter and her partner for the number one position. Well, if the coach didn't like her before, he certainly didn't like her after she dared to publicly challenge his coaching.

The coach's bias revealed itself during the 'Finals' of the district tournament where Ali' had lost the first set and was down in the second set. Just as it looked like Ali' had lost, the Robertson coach, who Ali' had dared to humiliate, told us in the bleachers, where we were all watching, that Ali' had a good year and 2nd place as a Freshman is good. He then left. He had presumed that she would lose.

Sally, my dear wife, told him as he was leaving, in no uncertain terms: She hasn't lost yet! She is going to win! Ali', by all appearances was exhausted, having played three difficult matches in two days to get to the Finals. She was initially scheduled to play doubles with her first-cousin who dropped her at the last minute to play with someone else. She was forced to play in the 'singles' category, where she was not seeded. At the break, Sally and I told her what the coach said. I don't know if it was that, or her opponent calling her names, (I won't even mention the name. It was that bad!), but suddenly she came alive! She confidently began hitting shots that her opponent could not even reach. I remember the opposing coach desperately telling her student: 'Just one more game Claire, that's all! Ali' won every game of the second set to come back and tie the match one set to one! The opponent's coach then began desperately pleading with her star student: "Just one more set Claire!" Ali' soundly thrashed her opponent in the third set to take the District Championship. In all my years of watching tennis I had never seen such a comeback!

But my recollections of Ali's daring were just not in the sporting arena. I recall her telling the Las Vegas print press that the police were unfairly harassing them on the Plaza, (the center of town where kids would often congregate.) This girl was fearless! Ultimately high school was just too restrictive for her, so, as a sophomore, she left school, passed her GED, applied for college and was accepted. I would say Ali' was tough! The name of the greatest boxer that ever lived, fit her perfectly!

Both Ali' and Amadeo are as tough as nails. Their grandpa Lopez would be so proud of them. Neither are sheep, though I sometimes wish they were on some things. Curiously there is no genetic connection between my children and their grandpa Lopez. I was adopted. But somehow his hand has reached out over time and touched their lives to shape them into what they have become – tough!

AMADEO GOES TO THE BATHROOM LIKE DADDY

We were looking through pictures last night and Sally found one with Ali's curly short hair neatly combed. She was posing for a picture. She was standing up with a blue briefcase in her right hand, a white dress shirt on and a long neck tie. She was three years old. Sally remembered and told Ali' and later, me, that this was the day Ali' decided to dress up like Daddy. (Yes. I have to wear a dress shirt and tie to court.)

Then there was the day that I came home to Sally and Ali' giggling like little girls. (Okay, one was!) They gleefully informed me that Amadeo had learned to use the potty like daddy. Well Amadeo was about two at the time so I knew he had already been potty-trained. What could they have been talking about? Maybe he had learned to stand up to pee. They wouldn't tell me.

With great anticipation, they called Amadeo. Sally told him to go to the bathroom like daddy. The bathroom was not always off limits for the kids, even when Sally or me were in there. We infrequently locked the door. Even to this day (2008), our kids do not let Sally take a bath without bugging her for something.

Be that as it may, I was anxious to know how Amadeo "went to the bathroom like daddy." So I watched him. He first went to his little potty chair next to the toilet and sat on it. So it wasn't what I first thought. He then picked up a pencil and the lined pad of paper we had on the stand next to the toilet and began "writing" as if he knew what he was doing. Amadeo had seen me writing, while sitting on the toilet so often that he believed that daddy going to the bathroom and writing were one and the same.

Well now you know where and when I have found the time to write this book, uncleanly as it may sound to some of you. Writers will understand. Ideas and inspiration occur in different places for different people. My sanctuary, inspiration and muse were quite often to be found in the quiet of the bathroom, until my kids would discover my absence, search the house and eventually find me there…..writing.

Until tennis became a regular fixture of our lives, going to work in Ali's eyes, meant me leaving with my briefcase. But Amadeo had discovered my true joy…. Writing in the solitude of the bathroom.

AMADEO POEM TO HIS OLD MAN
by
Amadeo Lopez

12/11/11
Trish Maestas
English

SONNET TO MR. LOPEZ

You are the old man who complains a lot.
I am the young kid who's there to yell: Not!
You, the big lawyer who thinks he knows it all.
But without tennis will have a withdrawal.

You, who threaten to take my stuff away,
And me, the mad kid who just wants to play.
You come from work and loaf till end of day.
I escape from school to chill and zone away.

You try to disrupt me hanging with friends.
I ignore your bitching, your tone offends.
Though we argue and I cause you much strife
You are my father at the end of his life.

I swear to you to be all I can be
So we can live in peace and harmony.

GOD CONDENSED FROM...

God condensed from
> *Tens of thousands*
> *Of loving, sun-soaked*
> *Evaporating tears*
> *From the loud and uncontrollable*
> *Laughter of little children*
> *Who frolicked in the rain*
> *And woke the bored night.*

Ten thousand more children
> *saw their joy*
> *And joined the delirium*
> *And the tears of joy*
> *Transformed into a wall of water*
> *That roared into a river*
> *So Edens could spring*
> *Forth life and love*
> *In what were silent deserts before.*

The laughter grew louder,
> *Joyful tears furiously flowed*
> *And the white waters rose,*
> *Pushed forward*
> *To inspire a sublime sea*
> *Which vaporized*
> *Neath a saving sun*
> *And raptured upwards*
> *To a heaven of giant thunderheads*
> *That signaled the rain to fall,*
> *That woke the seeds of life*
> *And inspired a saving ship of life.*

The smiling sky responded
> *With an arced kaleidoscope of colors*
> *That spoke the light of hope.*

The tears born of a jubilant joy
> *Inspired a bright blue whale*
> *With my father's voice and eyes.*

This grand mammal
> *Who was made of*
> *The sacred silt of the sea*
> *Swallowed me whole.*

Safe inside these secure living walls
> *And through the whale's wide round windows of love*
> *My eyes could soak up beauty as never before.*

The mammoth liquid creature
      Carried me down to the depths of the sea,
      Touched the soft sand, opened its massive mouth
      And allowed me to frolic with the seahorses and shellfish
      Who sallied forth to see the great whale of love
      And greet me to their sanctuary.
There I joyously breathed in
      The wisdom of an ocean
      Of eons of life.

I returned to the inner sanctum
      Of the beautiful and bright liquid beast
      Who carried me to and through the hole
      At the heart of the earth.
Then through a wormhole
      I was whisked by a supernatural wind
That carried me to the full moon.
      Where I reveled in the sun's light
      And transformed into moonlight
      And danced on a moonbeam
      At the speed of light, until time stopped
      And I could see all as it really was and will be.

I voraciously breathed in this dream of light,
      Joyfully leaving
      A world of cold and darkness
      And I never wished to wake again.
And now I see my tears of joy and laughter
      Compose a serenade
      Of words and music
      Woven from my eyes and mouth
      Which becomes a liquid blue whale.
It is returning to earth
      With a smile and a hunger.
I hear it singing with a resonant voice.
      And the stars respond.
They miraculously shed a million
      Pent-up tears of timeless joy
      That evaporate
      And condense………

B. INSPIRATION

INVITATION TO THE CELEBRATION OF THE INDUCTION OF A CHILD INTO THE SERVICE OF THE SPIRIT, TO WIT: A BAPTISMAL

TO: 1"
WHEN: July 25, 1993
TIME: 10:30AM
WHERE: Trinity Lutheran
             4311 12TH NW
             Albuquerque, NM 87107
             344-9323 need directions

Dear:

You are hereby invited to join with us in a ceremony inducting Alizandra Olympia Reed-Lopez (Ali') into the service of soul soldiers of the spirit army, otherwise known as the rite of Baptism.

MUSINGS OF AN AGNOSTIC:

The notion of Baptism is often limited to celebrating the admittance of Christians into the Christian flock, (a dangerous thing in the early days). It has been symbolized and represented by Christ's Baptism by John the Baptist. It has been associated with Christianity, to the exclusion of it's more general, and to me, more relevant and wider significance, i.e., the recognition of the spiritual as a relevant part of our life. The term transcends religious preference, and has a living meaning. It signifies a way of living, inconsistent with the lifestyle now glamorized and glorified by the pitchman, whose emphasis is on the accumulation of things, garnering material wealth, and the absence of responsibility to one's fellow man.

The idea of a spiritual soldier is a militant concept, illustrated by the lives of Jesus, Gandhi, Martin Luther King, and Mother Teresa. It belongs to no particular religion and in fact, may be incompatible with religious bureaucracies' intent on enforcing blind faith to particular doctrines. Focusing on one's own life or a pet bureaucracy is not its main goal. The very essence of Jesus' life was one in which he gave up all material things and ultimately, gave his life in the interest of the greater good.

The spiritual is concerned with the question of why we are here, with emphasis on the "we" and not the "I" and on the greater good and not the personal good. This definition of spiritual recognizes that your life is given real significance by striving after goodness. It is into this way of thinking and living that I wish to introduce my child. It is into this way of life that I ask the Godparents to channel my child.

The celebration has a second significance: To share with you the reunion of a blood family separated for years and now united. I see no better time to celebrate this communion than at the time we celebrate the induction of our child into the spiritual family. The two celebrations will be symbolized and solidified by the appointment of my two brothers and their spouses as the spiritual guardians and trustees (Godparents) of Ali'. For years this blood connection has not been made public but the proverbial cat is out of the bag and we invite you to bear witness to the second celebration of this family reunion.

P.S.
Reception will follow the ceremony at the courtyard of the church. Bring your exercise duds! All challenges will be seriously considered and accepted by those who wish to test their athletic prowess.

Sincerely yours,
Martin & Sally

(*If my new-found family did not think I was a 'little different', this letter probably convinced them. They are all Catholics. If they had some issues about my 'baptism' concepts, they were polite enough not to mention anything.*)

BY ALI'

C. Optimism

<u>INTRODUCTION TO BIRTH ANNOUNCEMENT</u>

One morning about four or five a.m., shortly after Ali' was born, I woke and wrote what became the Birth Announcement. Although I later refined it, I wrote the essential announcement within thirty minutes. The "alien" motif seemed peculiar to many but appropriate for my situation. My instincts were telling me that I was experiencing something unique in my life. Something was telling me that this would be more than the birth of a child. Although a human being was giving birth to another human being, something spiritual and inexplicable was being sent with and through Ali' and it was not of human origin.

Indeed, looking back, it was to become a spiritual reawakening for me. My little alien brought with her the keys to a spiritual discovery and transformation that I had not experienced on this planet.

I think of Carl Sagan's novel and movie "Contact" when I try to explain the "alien" metaphor. Jody Foster played a scientist and devout atheist. No human words or experience here on earth could change her belief. Rather than divulge the ending, let's just say that an out-of-this-world experience opened her eyes to a different way of seeing things. And so it was with Ali'.

5-eyed girl by Ali'

RAM-GIRL BY ALI'

Elf by Ali'

D. Love Inspires A Bending of the Light – A Different Look

Big Eyed Girl in Trees and Clouds By Ali'

BIRTH NOTICE FOR ALIZANDRA LOPEZ

April 5, 1993
GREETINGS & SALUTATIONS:

A new visitor is amongst us! She was literally vacuum-jettisoned into the earth's atmosphere at 7:52 a.m. (earth time) on March 26, 1993 A.D., at the birthing room of Presbyterian hospital. The ostensible humanoid has an earth gravitational pull of 6 lbs. 10 oz. and measures 20 and ½ inches. (American human length increments.)

The little alien began her ejection procedures from the maternal earth vessel at 10:00 p.m. on March 25, 1993, just as we docked at our earth station in Los Lunas, New Mexico, USA. We arrived with an actual expectation of sleep. It was not to be. As the pace of the pre-ejection stages expedited, becoming consistent and inexorable, we ambulated vehicularly to Albuquerque where we rendezvoused with the earth physician and at 1:30 a.m., Mountain Standard Time, where we checked into the edifice known as "Pres" (Presbyterian Hospital). At circa 4:00 a.m. the port to Sally's outward voyage had become fully opened and all systems were operational for the little Lopez astronaut's exit from her life capsule and trip down the escape corridor for launch into the atmosphere.

Upon her arrival to Earth, we christened her with the appellation of Alizandra Olympia Reed-Lopez or Ali', as in Mohammed Ali', (the boxer.) Dr. De La Torre, the pediatrician thought the name was "very Greek." My nieces, who had already seen her, thought the name was more "geekish" than Greekish. They did not elaborate nor did I ask exactly what they meant.

The cranium circumference measured 33 centimeters and midsection at 30 centimeters. The brief brown wavy wisps of hair and wrinkled cranium were not unlike the hairdo of the aliens in the old TV series "V". Because of the vacuum, Ali' had a slight little cone-head and red markings extending from the center of her head and forming a shape similar to the Jewish headpiece known as a Yarmulke.

The earthling child's eyelids appeared quite swollen and puffy as she screamed her way into the highly oxygenated earth atmosphere. Beneath the swollen vision covers, were blue-gray viewers (two of them) extremely large and exotic, housed in large almond-shaped orbits.

Her facial color varied from crimson, when angry, to a light human skin color with russet cheeks. Her olfactory sense detector was but a small bulbous puffy button. The facial entry orifice to the alimentary canal seemed inordinately large as she shrieked in response to this new out-of-mother body experience.

What were most prominent were her huge fleshy cavernous and concave sound wave detectors. No separate weight or volume was taken by the Physician's Assistant of these little satellite dishes. After they viewed the child, some observers made reference to the names of Ross Perot, Clark Gable and Alfred E. Newman. The visiting family and friends seemed shocked as they loudly lamented, "My God, she looks like Martin!" I strongly disagreed. My hair is much longer, I told them. Notwithstanding these curious human comparisons, we expect she will shortly be called to star and debut in "Aliens 4", premiering in 1994.

To avoid lawsuits for intentional infliction of mental suffering and outrage, we have not enclosed a photo. If you insist on seeing her, you must sign a release of all liability and only then, will we allow you to see the video tape.

Seriously folks, Ali' is beautiful. Thank you for all the support you have given us during the nine months-plus pregnancy, and afterwards.

Special thanks for the (*gift received)* that you gave us. It was needed and it is being used. Any help in the future will be appreciated.

End of transmission.
Sally, Martin and Ali'

By Ali'

D. INSPIRATION AND MORE OPTIMISM

ANGEL DREAM

The innocence of a million sextupled
White fluffs from heaven
Are illuminated by the full moon
In an otherwise still dark morn.
The world is oblivious
To angels dancing and singing
To the beat of sweet tomorrows,
And waiting to be bathed
With the warm beams of morning light.

I am awake watching the restlessness
Of my own sleeping little angel
As she struggles to wake.
I hear a little scream
And she rolls directly
Into mom's waiting
And open bosom.
Searching mouth quickly latches
Onto the ready nipple
Of mother's left breast.
Breakfast is served!

The little fingers of Ali's left hand
tickle and caress
Sally's right breast as she suckles.
She then moves her hand
To her own left ear,
Feels inside
And caresses the contours,
Memorizing the ridges and valleys.

Bored, the restless hand
Scratches the quilted covers
And then waves in the air,
Searching……searching
With eyes still shut
For whatever little hands reach for
In their early spring dance with life.

My angel is so busy.
Not content to just
Take in mamma's sweet milk.
She must investigate
With her available arm and hand.

This one's gonna be a handful!

I wrote this shortly after my daughter was born. I was preoccupied with the negative. Writing this helped me, mentally and emotionally, to connect with family. Afterwards, I became far more optimistic about the future.

TO ALI': THE BRIGHT SIDE OF YOUR INHERITANCE

So many years, 40 and 2, to become a dad for the first time. I would joke that your first words will be "grampa!" So far, you have had the good sense to keep it to yourself. But I still worry about dying before I can see you fully blossom. I will be 62 when you are 20, if we make it that far.

I am told by some that they had children young and they wished they had waited. They have more patience and focus now, than before. They feel they are better grandparents than they were parents.

Others, who had children young, say, they grew up with their kids. It does not seem to bother them. Now their children are leaving home and they are still young enough to enjoy life without them. They have been freed to do what they please.

I guess, at my age, I better have the patience of a grandpa and not be in any hurry to have you leave the house. Don't worry! We won't kick you out! We will need someone to take care of us!

You, my child, are now all potential and dreams. Yet, I keep thinking "limits". How far can you go with Sally and my genes? Will you have knee problems like your Uncle Dave and me? Will you be more comfortable writing than speaking, like your dad? Will you have a lousy memory? Will you have no ear or interest in music?

When I should be dreaming of the moon, I am thinking Challenger disaster! When I should be seeing the stars, I can only see the ceiling! When I should be joyfully dreaming of the future, I can see only as far as this Friday's payroll!

Is this debilitating negativity to be your burden? Will I do to you what I have done to myself? Is it inevitable? If so, I will have failed. I will have given birth to pessimism, to hesitation, to fear, to cowardice, to weakness... to mediocrity.

You must strive to succeed at all you try. You must search; you must experiment, until you find that which you are better at than anyone else, that which brings you joy, and that which makes this world richer in some way. Failure must not be something you fear, but you must face it and say "What a great opportunity!" "I can and I will do this!"

I will hope and pray that you have your mother's energy and your daddy's focus.

You will not have to worry about looks. The Romeros, the Gutierrez', the Reeds and Garcia's are all good-looking people. But good looks are not the same as goodness. In your search for friends and one day, a spouse, you must be able to see the goodness beneath whatever exterior the person carries on the outside. That inner self is what should attract you.

From the Reed/Garcia side, you get great athleticism, work ethic and a talent for building. They built their own house and Betty and the rest of the family built a home for Desiree and her family. Sally, Jerry, and Eddy possess great hand eye coordination. Sally's brothers have powerful upper body strength. Jerry was so talented he worked out with the Ty Quan Do Olympians. I've never seen anyone hit a baseball like Sally's brother, your Uncle Richard. Always get him on your team. According to your mom, both Grampa Chuck and Grandma Della were very good skaters. May you fluidly glide through the ice rink of life like a world-class skater. Uncle Jerry, Eddie, your grandma Della and your mama, require little sleep and all the Reeds are hard-working. They built many houses for other folks. Your uncles' Paul and Jerry are both builders and contractors. So well built and so beautiful were the houses that your Uncle Jerry built, that some have graced the pages of magazines that feature the best and most beautiful of houses. Your Uncle Paul has become a very successful businessman. May you too learn to be a builder not a destroyer. (We can only hope that the builder gene trumps that lawyer gene.)

The Reeds were religious people who became preachers. Uncle Will, Grandpa Reed and aunt Blanch are all preachers. Will this moral/religious side inspire in you the likes of another Dr. Martin Luther King Jr.?

Ali', you are unique and blessed to also receive a family inheritance related to you in spirit, love and law, but not by blood: The Lopez/Silva families, through my dad and mom, your grandpa and grandma. They both spoke English and Spanish fluently.

Though neither Martin nor Gregoria, went to college, they both recognized the value of a good education. May you too be multi-lingual and live the dream they had by learning all that the world has to teach you.

Your grandpa Lopez, my dad, had his own business as an insurance salesman. However, his real talent was that of a politician. He was a politician-extraordinaire. Your Grandpa Martin went to Officer Training School and proudly exited the military as an officer. While others slept, he would read under his covers with a flashlight. Your Grandpa Lopez played semi-professional baseball with Air force. He was a man who needed little sleep and had an insatiable need for the company of people. May you inherit his ambition and great love of people.

Your Grandma 'Greg' Lopez had no children of her own but adopted both Theresa, me and later Chrissy. Every moment of her life was dedicated to imbuing us with a drive to succeed by giving us the best education and a respect for God. Your grandma Greg was an insurance secretary. She was a proud woman who worked hard her entire life so her children could have what she did not. May you inherit her pride and maternal instinct. May you have children and guide them as she did with Theresa, Chrissie and me. May you learn and respect the goodness and love which Jesus's life embodies.

You have an aunty Theresa, my sister. She had the writing talent. She has even written a play. I expect we might see a book from her one day. So Ali' start the beginnings of a future book now with a diary as soon as you can write.

You will hear about your great uncle "Grassy", a state doubles champion tennis player, a tough guy, a ladies' man and a son who dearly loved his mother. May you follow in his footsteps with the fighting spirit that made him a State Championship tennis player. May you too always love and respect your parents.

You will hear about your Great-Aunty Ida and Uncle Tony. He was a carpenter. Both of them were very religious and quite involved in the Catholic Church. Theirs was an unrivaled religious faith. When they passed away, they did so with the unfaltering belief that they were going to God. May you too come to believe strongly in something and dedicate yourself to it.

Speaking of religion, you have an Aunt, Sister Lucina, my dad's sister, who was a nun and taught me Spanish at Cathedral High. She could also put words together wonderfully. Language and writing skills, the foundation for good communication, is the key to connect with the world.

Uncle Tony and Aunt Ida's kids were so talented. I remember Auntie Elaine was part of one of the most talented group of cheerleaders at Cathedral High School. May you too be a talented leader. Vincent and Frances, both could play instruments, Frances, the piano and Vincent, the guitar. Oh, could your great-uncle Vince dance! But it is Vince's humor that is unforgettable. Ali' you must always be ready to laugh because if not, crying is the other option. Remember: He who laughs, lasts!

Hopefully you will meet your Uncle Gabriel, Uncle Davie and Auntie Dorgene. They were always so kind to me. And Auntie Dorgene was a superb artist. See the picture of nature's monuments of stone, right outside of Gallup, now hanging on our living room wall. That was our wedding gift from Dorgene. Kindness and talent will take you quite far.

You will hear about the very close-knit family of the Silva's: Auntie Tommy, Grandma Greg, Aunty Jenny and Auntie Virginia. Uncle Ernest, (her husband) and Aunty Tommy were excellent dancers. Uncle Ernest was talented musically and quick with a joke. He worked hard and saved his money so he and your Aunty Tommy could dance their dream. May you too learn to dance over the rough spots of life.

I would have loved for you to meet your great-auntie Jenny. She brought the gift of laughter wherever she went. Her sisters were different people when she was with them. She was so optimistic, vivacious, full of laughter and loving. She had the ability to transform the moods of others. May you be a vehicle of happiness and lift the spirits of all those around you.

You will hear about your great-grandmother, Suzie Silva, who we called 'Maye'. You carry her middle name (Suzie), as a reminder of her. She was a self-made woman, in a time when no one spoke of self-made and woman in the same breath. She was a woman requiring little sleep and had superhuman energy levels. Shortly after her marriage, her husband, your great grandpa and his dad, your great-great-grandfather, died in the 1918 flu epidemic. She was left to raise four girls with the help of her mother whose husband had been taken by the same flu epidemic. So 'Maye' washed and dried clothes by hand all night and worked at a clothing store by day. At one point in her life, she even ran a bakery in California. In addition to the Spanish and English languages that she spoke fluidly, she learned to speak the Navaho and Zuni languages. She came to own her own house and rental. You will marvel at the stories of Maye's unforgettable genius at cooking, not from recipes, but from memory. May you receive her energy and gift for sharing what she had on her table to all who came to her house.

Maye's deceased husband was an Encinias. You will find that you have an Aunty Trudy (Beverly) who has carried on Maye's indomitable spirit. Trudy has been a mother, housewife, businesswoman and politician. She too can set an example for you and all women in a time when a glass ceiling still exists for women.

Maye had a sister we called Gramma-Belle. She raised Eddy, Isabelle, Malda and Johnny. All were incredibly intelligent and extremely good-looking. You, Ali', must search for that unique intelligence that you have and develop it.

I must not forget about your great-uncle, Agapito Silva, (Gap), who fought in the Second World War and survived being captured and imprisoned by the Japanese. You must come to decide what is worth fighting and dying for and pursue and defend it with vigor. For as the great Dr. Martin Luther King once said: A human being who has nothing to die for has nothing to live for.

Of your genetic family, you have a daddy and his brother Dave, your uncle, that are lawyers. Your Uncle Dave has a degree from Harvard. Your uncle Pete is a very intelligent and successful businessman.

You have a great-Aunt Dolores, (Your biological Grandma [Molly's] sister. Dolores gave birth to two lawyers and an actress. Dolores had a magnificent mind and was a language specialist. Your grandma Molly (Amelia) has a Masters in the Spanish language. A second language will open up new worlds for you. Language is the doorway to a rich cultural heritage. Language is power, socially and economically. Pursue and develop a second tongue, and you will never regret it. Your grandma Amelia, was a teacher. A good teacher is worth their weight in gold. What I have learned from good teachers, changed my life. Always keep the teacher option open. There is a dire need for good teachers.

On the Gutierrez' side Ali', you have Great-aunts Fannie and Rita, who love to laugh, a trait that is indispensable for mental health. Aunt Fannie has written corridos about her brother's death. You may very well have inherited that writing gene. Never forget the power and satisfaction that the written and spoken word has. As soon as you get old enough I recommend doing a journal. Write down what inspires you before it slips away.

There is your Great Uncle Tony (TJ), who was always quick with a joke. Laughter is the best medicine.

Then there is your deceased biological grandfather, Dave Romero Sr. He served proudly in the military, was captured by the Japanese and miraculously survived the brutal Bataan Death March and a death camp. He, more than any other, is responsible for the financial success and security of the Romeros. This he did through focus, hard work, vision and determination. Where others merely saw dirt, he saw gold. His vision gave birth to the Romero Sand and Gravel business that grew and prospered. Your Uncle Dave has a transcript of your Grandfather Dave Sr.'s experiences in the war if you are interested in the details.

Interestingly, 'Gap' and Socorro, his wife and my birth father and mother, Dave and Molly Romero, were very good friends when Dave was alive. Gap and Dave were both prisoners captured by the Japanese. They had no idea that one would be my father and the other my Uncle. I wasn't born yet.

In life there will be connections and relations in the future that you cannot now even imagine. It is a very small world. Never think that the evil you do to anyone, distant or close, will not come back to haunt you, your children or your loved ones. Spoken more positively, the good that you do is never wasted. Whether or not you think it is noticed or appreciated, your family, your friends or someone, will benefit from your goodness. The world benefits by your acts of goodness and kindness.

You have received a rich and marvelous bequeathment of both blood, love, spirit and water. You should not worry like daddy, for few will stand on the shoulders of so many giants and see so far. Now is the time to dream.

THE BIRTH OF MY BOY

I was late for the birth of my boy. But it wasn't my fault! They had wheeled Sally into the operating room earlier than expected. So when I arrived the nurses and staff were telling me that I would not be able to see the birth of my baby; that they would have to ask the doctor if it was okay. It was a Cesarean, you know. Anything could happen! We are just thinking of your wife and the baby! If I feinted or collapsed, they said I was on my own.

I pictured me collapsing in a heap and the doctors and nurses going on as if nothing had happened. I laughed to myself. Yea, right! I told them that I had been there for the birth of my first child and even video-taped it. I was there when Sally had her miscarriage and I was on my feet the entire sad ordeal. I even watch as they draw my blood. I am not a fainter. I need to be there now!

I signed a few papers and they escorted me into a 20' by 30" room with white walls. They sat me on the right side of Sally, or about 8:00 O'clock, if her head was center-noon. The doctors had already begun. They had this white sheet hanging from above, reaching down to Sally's chest so it fully blocked her view of the surgery. Go figure! Maybe they thought if Sally were to see them cutting on her, she might pass out. Passing out seemed to be the big concern.

Sally gave me a smile and a look as if to ask what was going on. I knew what I had to do. She wanted me to tell her what they were doing. It fit right into my job description. She was apparently numbed so she was in no pain. But if she could not see or feel that she was giving birth, she wanted to, at least, know about it as it happened. So I became a live news reporter to my son's birth. This would be a first for me. The birth of Ali' was natural.

As I entered the room they had been carefully cutting the second layer of skin and stretching and attaching it to the side of her stomach. I don't remember that much blood. The nurses must have been swabbing it pretty well. Fortunately for my dear wife I had not arrived sooner. I am not sure Sally could have handled a graphic narration of the doctors skinning her alive. Being late worked this time!

In a matter of moments, I saw my boy and I told Sally he is huge. He has this gigantic chest and this huge head! Even though they told us that if he had gone to term, he would have weighed 10 pounds, I still never visualized him this big. Ali' was only seven pounds and neither Sally nor I are relatively big people. So his size was surprising to me.

In what I'm sure was a quizzical voice I told Sally: He is all white - white! That was the best I could describe him at the time. I did not know that when a baby does not come down the birth canal, the protective white paste that covers his body in the womb is not rubbed off. Amadeo was scheduled first class, - No head-squishing, time-consuming birth canal journey for him. You would have thought they would have forewarned one of us to expect this pasty-white appearance. Only later did Sally tell me that she had a little panic attack. She thought he might have stopped breathing. As usual, I was oblivious to her reaction and kept talking.

As they lifted him out of Sally, a lengthy stream of pee flowed from his penis upwards like a fountain that showered the doctor. I described it to Sally and she smiled. Well we knew the piping was in good order! I guess I never thought about unborn babies peeing in their own little mama cockpit. Now I know. That doctor got what he deserved for not telling Sally and me what to expect and for trying to keep me out of there. You go son! You've given meaning to the term 'Pis on you!' Way to show that doctor who is the boss!

Shortly after that, they cleaned Amadeo, who looked more like a Rocky or a Jake Lamotta after losing a twelve-round fight. His face, mostly his eye lids and eye brows, were awfully swollen. Boy did he give Frankenstein a run for his money. The bridge to his nose grew directly into his big and protruding brow which created an unnatural horizontal ridge just beneath his eye brows, like that of some prehistoric man. And such a serious look, like the weight of the world was upon him. I don't know what he went through in the womb but from his appearance, it must have been a rough, nearly-nine-month journey.

After a few years and some time to hold him, look at him and do a lot of dreaming, this is how I describe my boy: He's a miniature tank with a gigantic head. He has a barrel chest, wrestler's arms and big shoulders and but for his calves, normal size legs. These are Garcia, Gutierrez and Romero parts. He's got Sally's behind, large and curvaceous, unlike my non-existent butt. And I think those are Sally's legs. The giant calves and sturdy knees that have never snapped from the strain. Those hands are the size of baby Hercules, and I hope lightning-quick, like Uncle Dave claims his to be. The grip is powerful. I envision Babe Ruth, Boris Becker, or Jake LaMotta, the "Raging Bull". He also loves the water. Could we have a swimmer on our hands? His windows to the world and the windows to his soul tilt downward at the outside edges. They are drooping bedroom eyes, brown in color, exactly like Grandpa Chuck's except they are not green. His lashes are long, dark and curved. They seem particularly fond of the visual. Uh oh! I see a TV addict! His mouth is like mine and his little cousin David's, Pete's boy: Very meaty, like liver. The nose is prominent - a Reed/Garcia nose for sure. Nothing delicate about it! I see straight light brown locks, with golden highlights. He has blond cousins on the Reed side. His ears actually seem to fit unlike his sister's ultra-large ears. He has a large and heavy skull, Full of gray matter, we hope.

I think his upper body was built first. The big head and chest and with whatever material was left, God fashioned his skinny legs. He still walks with a waddle, like a person that is top-heavy. I think of his Uncle Jerry who is built like a "V", large shoulders and a small waist. A man who trained for the Olympics in Ty Kwan Do.

Amadeo is calm and laid back, save for one thing. My boy obsesses over food. He has got to have it. It is his tranquilizer, and he'll fight you for it. Fortunately, he has the instincts of the master hunter/gatherer. When he locates his food, he can eat it with a spoon in either hand. He may be military material. He zeroes in on food wherever it might be, even at a distance. Like advanced weaponry, he quickly locates his target.

With food in hand, he holds it up above his head, like a priest holding the host, apparently asking that this be a worthy offering. Once the food is in his mouth he savors it there for a long time.

He likes the kitchen like his great-grandma Maye. I see a chef or just a big eater. My son is still quiet but language is fighting its way out of this miniature and mostly stoic hunter. He is like I was - very silent, for so very long. He loves to do paintings, listen to music and of course, watch television. Uh oh! My son loves and craves daddy's toys: My camera, my remote, pagers, the TV... They are magic, like talismans to him. Not so unlike we male adults, I guess. He will fight you for them. But he is also a giver. He hears us talk and before we know he is even listening, he brings to us what we are talking about. He so much wants to please and be helpful, like his great-grandma Maye who never had a visitor that left hungry.

I am daydreaming now, but I see kindly nuns treating him special and he winning them with his charm. I see the living spirit of his great-grandmother Maye guarding his every move.

And there you have it: My take of Amadeo's birth and toddlerhood replete with inferences and dreams.

AMADEO SERVING/ PARENTS WATCHING, (seen right above his head.)

AMADEUS, MY BOY – THE DREAM EMERGES
(Amadeus translation: 'To Love God')

It is Sunday, 7:30 in the early morning.
For the third day in a close row
      We are on the road again.
Sally is driving
      And I am in the back with Amadeo.
The three other girls
      Enjoy the reclining cushioned seats,
      In the middle of the van,
      All asleep.
Too early for all of them.
Amadeo is stretched out
      Across the three seats in the back,
      Head on a pillow, on my lap.

All is so serene, so quiet!
Just the whir of the engine
      And the steady sound of moving air

Whistling through the not-so air-tight vents
  Of our old 91 Dodge conversion van.
We bought it because we needed space on wheels
  To take kids to tennis tournaments
  Throughout the Southwest.
It has since become a transporter
  Of tennis teams, laughter, conversations and dreams,
  teenager talk, plenty of rudeness
  And plain silliness.
Sometimes they even read
  Parts of the thick binder of good tennis form
  I make available to them on trips.
Okay...rarely does anyone read it!
But now they all sleep, except Sally and me.
I am reveling in yesterday's tremendous victory.
My nine-year-old Amadeo was a tennis genius,
  Gifted with accurate and powerful
  Strokes from God.
Even before the match
  His focus was that of a man
  On a mission.
Losses to both the Johnson brothers
  In tennis and then in baseball
  Had fueled a deep and driving desire
  To prove he was better.
The determination formed on his face
  And manifested in his resolute carriage.
He moved like never before.
We worried whether it
  Would fade or falter
  When one uneducated shot
  Careened astray?
Would it dissipate
  In a destructive display
  Of degenerative anger?

We had seen it before:
Hopes succumbing
  To the giant careless claws
  Of that explosive monster
  That has always lurked
  Deep within Amadeo's heart and soul
  And that would burst out at any time
  To snatch victory from Amadeo's clutch.

No doubt this inner demon
> *Was deigned from the dark*
> *Because his parents were so arrogant as*
> *To give him the famous name of Amadeus.*

Not the brilliant master music composer
> *And musician*
> *That the name Amadeus*
> *Should have secured in simple minds*
> *And certainly not a natural on the piano.*

No, Amadeus would not even visit
> *To touch the black and white melody makers*
> *To live up to his name.*

Oh, but hand him a tennis racquet....!

At two years old,
> *He held it like a natural,*
> *Like Mozart directing a masterpiece.*

A grand maestro.

And when he and his tennis baton with strings
> *Moved onto the tennis courts,*
> *This stringed tennis wand made magic.*

It was tennis music to those who knew,
> *A mystical melody of perfect timing:*
> *Twenty drums building*
> *To the explosive*
> *Crescendo*
> *Of A Giant Sound*
> *Of symbols*
> *Colliding*
> *In grand*
> *Unison!*

Then silence.

Over and over again,
> *Amadeo had converted*
> *The opponent into*
> *Part of the awe-struck audience,*
> *Riveted to a performance*
> *Of watching a tennis ball*
> *That the opponent*
> *Would never even reach.*

Like the great singer,
> *Reaching and holding a note*
> *Like no one else before!*

Breathtaking and heavenly!
Then the exuberant
> *And uncontrolled applause*
> *Of an audience on their feet.*
That is Amadeo and tennis.
From the beginning,
> *"To Love God"*
>> *Had no nemesis,*
>> *Save the angry demon*
>> *Buried within.*
So, the demon of dissonance
> *And the master of perfect tennis harmony*
> *Fought.*
Who would control today?
The Gods of focus and desire
> *Walked onto the courts today*
They were not to be denied.
Amadeus had the perfect symphony!

What child
> *Could play with such precision,*
> *Such timing and power?*
Wolfgang Amadeus Mozart
> *In the form of a little tennis player,*
> *Played today.*
The crowd left,
> *Like me,*
> *With their jaw to the ground.*
A perfect recital that elicited
> *Three curtain calls.*
It was a great day!
As I savor Amadeo's performance
> *In the tennis amphitheater of my mind,*
> *Our vehicle begins the climb*
> *To the city that*
> *Holds the honor or ignominy*
> *Of giving birth*
> *To the first uranium,*
> *Then plutonium bombs*
> *Which we used to destroy*
> *The people of*
> *Hiroshima then Nagasaki.*

Close to 200,000 deaths resulted.
Speaking of demons....
> *A few days before I had worried*
> *About the orange alerts...*
I visualized planes
> *Flying overhead*
> *As the children played.*
Could one of those planes end dreams?
Was one of them
a twin-towers nightmare?
Should I cancel the trip?
None of that bothered me now.
I was fully under the spell of my boy.
The early morning shadows
> *Mixed with my mood*
> *To give the landscape*
> *A different feeling.*
Even the trees all seemed to have
> *An individual and unique*
> *Look of their own.*
They were the winners
> *In the race to the sky*
> *And the battle to reach higher*
> *And touch the sun.*

Giant rock formations were jutting out of the earth
> *To make their own way*
Upwards to feel the warmth
> *Of the sun.*

And my boy was emerging
> *From the shadows*
> *Of anger and despair*
> *To give a great and unblemished*
> *Performance on the theater*
> *Of the tennis stage.*
The climb was just beginning
> *But for a brief moment*
> *This father's eyes*
> *Had glimpsed the magnificent*
> *View from the mountaintop.*

AMADEO AND BLUE, AKA 'BLUCIFER'

<u>A BOY AND HIS DOG</u>

Another early day and Sally tells me at 6:30 a.m. that Blue, Amadeo's handsome young German Shepherd dog, broke his leash and is out on the prowl. I gave Sal a ride to work and looked for Blue but did not see him. As I drove into the yard, I saw Blue near the back yard of our residence. I called him but he was happy with his freedom and refused to come to me. He bounded off before I could capture him.

Amadeo was still upstairs sleeping and I did not want to wake him up. Blue, on the run, is more of a danger to himself than others. He is still young, wild and unsocialized. Yeah, he can bark with the best at anything that comes near our house but can't seem to learn to come to the sound of his name. He ain't no Ryso, who was our first dog after Sally and I married. That remarkable little terrier, on command, was able to open the refrigerator door and bring us cokes and then, on command, close the fridge door. We, of course, attributed these remarkable skills to our uncanny ability to teach and knew it was time to have children to put our teaching skills to work. (Others had suggested that Ryso was just a smart dog. But they just did not appreciate how advanced our teaching talents were. There was no other dog that could do what Ryso could do. (We stand by our position that Ryso would have just been ordinary but for the Lopez education.)

But back to Blue. Although his big German Shepherd appearance is sometimes scary, he is not a biter, just a lunger, which is intimidating, but more likely to scare someone away than to injure them.

Blue is literally Amadeo's creation. In 2009, Blue's mom, Agent Orange, a Shiba Inu, athletic and smart, was still unneutered and in heat. While the rest of us were busy keeping male dogs out of the yard, Amadeo, had spotted a beautiful blond male German Shepherd. Somehow, he enticed it into the yard and Blue is the result. So Blue is the living proof that Amadeo has, God-like, created his own companion puppy. (Maybe 'Frankenstein-like' is the more appropriate term. As Blue has gotten older he has a new nickname – Blucifer the Beast. Ask Sally about the 'wild, crazy jumping dog, after her surgery.)

Amadeo is not very rational about his dog. Ask him, and like the mother of a newborn baby, he will tell you Blue is the most amazing and beautiful dog in the world. He will give you a history of how German Shepherds were the result of a German experiment to make the perfect dog. He concludes, without a doubt, that the experiment was a success. Just look at his dog! (Yeah! And just look at the Nazis!)

He will then yell at us how stupid our favorite dog Fluffy is. Fluffy is about 70 years old in human-equivalent years and is the only dog that is unleashed and unfenced. She has full access to the neighborhood. Don't tell Animal Control! Fluffy walks me to work twice a day and everyone at work knows her on a first-name basis. On weekends she comes into the building into my work area. So far, only the landlady has mentioned anything about it. I may need to read the small print in the lease. I'm working on making him a "companion" dog. I am sure I have some disability that would legally allow me to do so.

Fluffy is the senior dog that we bought from a young boy and his father selling dogs at Wal-Mart 12 years ago. The kids picked her out of a box of dogs when Amadeo and his sister were just eight and ten. Now that she is elderly, she gets no respect from our teenage kids, Ali' or Amadeo. They call her stupid, dumb, crazy and those are the nice things. No doubt, they are just jealous that their dogs are not refined enough to be off a leash or unfenced.

Of course, Amadeo is rough with all the dogs. He taunts Fluffy and yells at Agent Orange and Number 8. He roughhouses with his own dog who seems to take it well, no matter how rough Amadeo gets. My parents would have been appalled. If they were alive, they would have yelled at him: You're going to turn him into a mean dog by teasing him like that! The reality is that Amadeo does not know how to play gently. Everything explodes out of him whether it be play or conversation. He is a Silver Gloves State Champion in boxing and a Doubles State Champion in tennis. His nature is explosive. We are still working on harnessing it.

Anyway, back to the story. I went to work knowing Blue was out and about but I did not have time to look for him. I was running late for a client scheduled early. After my appointment I quickly left to pick up Sally for lunch. We returned home and still no Blue. I returned to work thinking the worst: He had bitten some little kid and was in the pound. We would shortly be getting sued. Or he ran in front of a car and was killed. Or someone ran over his long, broken leash that he was still dragging around and it yanked so hard, it broke his neck. Anyway, I was ready for the worst.

Sally picked me up about 4:30 pm and said that Amadeo had told her that the police were pursuing Blue and that Blue turned the corner and, just as he did, Amadeo was waiting and hiding in his car. He just opened the car door and Blue jumped in. The cop turned the corner and had no idea what had happened to the dog he was chasing. Amadeo, the hero, had eluded the cops again and saved his beloved Blue. It sounded plausible enough and I was just relieved that Blue was okay.

Later Amadeo 'clarified' to Sally: He was standing in the front doorway of the house and saw Blue running from a police car and Blue just ran into the front door of the house and the police just kept going.

I did not tell Amadeo that I had heard the stories from Sally and asked Amadeo about what happened. Now his creative mode revved to the max, he said that a police car was chasing Blue. He told me that over their loud speakers the cops told Blue: IMMEDIATELY SURRENDER OR WE WILL HAVE TO SHOOT! Blue immediately turned around and fearlessly ran at the police car that was bearing down on him and super-dog-like, just jumped over the vehicle. The police had to make a U-turn. By that time Blue had escaped by jumping into the van that Amadeo was driving and the officer never saw it. Wow! I had no idea that Blue had super powers!!!

Ever since Amadeo was very young he has always wound fantastic yarns. When he was in elementary school, he came home and excitedly told Sally how he was dancing on his school desk or how he punched the teacher out. No matter how many times he told her these incredible stories, Sally always believed him or feigned belief. I guess she just wanted him to feel that he could fool her.

We have come to realize the emotional benefits that pets bring to a family. The dogs have been great for the kids and yes Fluffy, my dog, has too some extent, kept me going. But we had never heard nor had we foreseen how a pet could stimulate the creative juices of a child. Well whatever story it is, Amadeo is always dancing on the creative and exciting edge of the truth. I think Amadeo has a career in writing comic books about the adventures of a boy and his super-dog.

Drawing by Ali'

'Miss Fluffy' (2004 – Jan 6, 2021) (Wardrobe by Ali')

Photo by Martin Lopez

<u>YOU ARE</u>

YOU ARE
THE FIRST STAR IN THE SKY,
A BLUEBIRD CHIRPING
IN EARLY MORN,
SNOWBIRDS RETURNING HOME,
THE FIRST MORNING RAY
THAT SIGNALS NIGHT'S END.

YOU ARE
THE SOLSTICE DAY,
LIGHT DEFEATING NIGHT,
THE FIRST DAY OF SPRING
THAT ENDS WINTER'S RULE.

YOU ARE
THE HARVEST MOON,
THE GREAT GOLDEN EYE
OF GOD GAZING
BRIGHTLY AND HOPEFULLY A'PEERING
OVER THE DARK HORIZON OF MY LIFE.
YOU ARE
THE FIRST KISS OF RAIN
ON CRACKING PARCHED TERRAIN,
REACHING A HIBERNATING SEED
IN THE DROUGHT
OF A ONCE DREARY
CHILDLESS LIFE.

YOU ARE
THE MAGNIFICENCE OF
THE SETTING SUN
IN THE NEW MEXICO SKY;
THE VAST AND GLORIOUS BRILLIANCE
OF A VIOLET INDIGO TRAIN
FLOWING MAJESTIC,
YOU ARE AN APPROACHING DUSK,
DONNING A PURPLE~ORANGE VELOUR,
ALL CAST IN THE WHISPERING WAKE
OF A SUN SILENTLY BUT ROYALLY
SALUTING ADIEU.
ITS MAGNIFICENT MESSAGE
IS THE GLOWING HOPE
OF A BRILLIANT MORN
AND THE DREAM
OF MANY MAJESTIC TOMORROWS,

ALL BECAUSE YOU ARE.

D. Children: Beauty and Love

EARTH-BORN ALIEN SURVIVES
Celebrates First Birthday

GALAXY GUARDIAN ASSOCIATION

The little Lopez "alien" christened with the earth appellation, Alizandra Olympia Susie Reed-Lopez, celebrates her matriculation to full-fledged earth-being, having survived 365 rotations of planet earth and the blue planet's oceans of 02 and H20 and assorted toxins and pollutants.

The transmogrification from alien, to earth-child is manifested mainly in her more earth-like appearance. She now ambulates bipedally, though still wobbly, not unlike the earthling American monster known as Frankenstein, (stiff legs and arms outstretched for balance). This mode of toddling is occasionally supplemented by the more familiar quadrupedal of earth's animal kingdom.

The top of Ali's cranium is now covered by the growth of extensive protuberances that humans refer to as hair. This follici gives her a very human look.

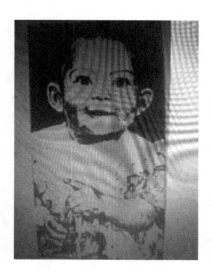

The two very large, cranially and laterally situated sound-wave detectors now seem much smaller with the growth of the skull. On the physiognomical aspect of the cranium, circular light detectors now have a very human and esthetic appearance: almond shape, slightly slanted upwards at the ends, chameleon-like in color: brown/green and hazel occasionally.

On the physiognomy, (face), the structure that filters and analyzes the air, known to earthlings as the nose, now displays a small bridge connecting it with the brow. Curiously it grows reddish upon detecting heat or cold or body generated heat. Her russet cheeks appear programmed to do the same.

The solid and liquid resource receptacle, frontally situated, (mouth and lips), now appears with a blush of pink in a human heart shape.

Inside this flexible entrance-way, small crushing and tearing devices have appeared, enamel in color. With their advent, Ali' now ingests more solid fuel for survival. She has indicated a preference for a variety of brassica oleracea (broccoli), and a variety of leguminous plants known as greenbeans. She also has a marked preference for the compressed hard thin-baked, crisp bleached and squared consumable, known to humans as crackers. In our reluctance to completely humanize Ali', we have banned the ingestion of the glucose carbohydrate, saccharum officinarum, commonly called sugar. This popular earth-made substance is apparently highly addictive and incrementally destroys the enamel cutting devices upon contact.

In lieu of the more direct and advanced mental communication, earthlings 'vocalize', with a combination of well-timed vibrations emanating from the mouth and throat. The sounds are shaped and cut by a unique, untamed and highly flexible animal which is housed within the borders of the tearing mechanism, resting on the mandible.

The fledgling child seems anxious to mimic these unique though primitive vocalizations, but has mastered but a few. Other than her maternal/paternal reference, (dada mama), her favorite words are the earthling-American term for spheroid: 'ball'. Her other favorite is a reference to the primitive ritual of immersion into a heated liquid of hydrogen and oxygen solution. She calls it 'bu-ba ba', (bubble bath). We hope to quickly inculcate her into a more frequent use of this vocalization method of communication that only humans have developed to any degree on the third planet from the sun.

We invite you all to share with us this human milestone, earthlings refer to as a birthday.

When: 1200 hours – earth military time (12 noon). Date: 3/26/1994. Place: Trinity Lutheran, 4311, 12th St. NW, Albuquerque, New Mexico 87107.

Solid and liquid resource materials of varying tastes will be served. Directions: Take I-40 west to 12th street exit heading north. The church is on the west side of the street and is north of Candelaria. For additional directions, call 345-2314 or 843-8888.

I sent this 'invitation' to my Aunt Tommie. When I went to her house, she asked me what it was I had sent her. I told her it was an invitation to Ali's birthday. She said: Youknow Martin, they sell birthday invitations at the store, pretty cheap.

She never had kids of her own. I guess she didn't know what kids do to you.

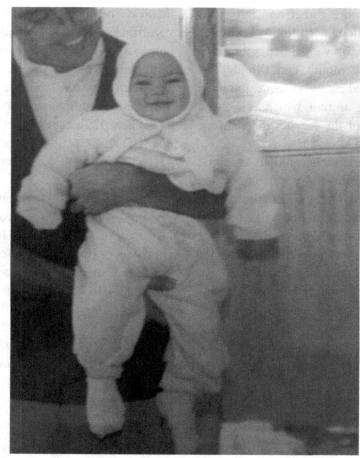

MARTIN, (AUTHOR) HOLDING ALI' (DAUGHTER)

DIRECTING ALI'

I lean over the crib

And gently lift and rest her on my chest and shoulder.

She picks up her proud head,

Turns it in the direction that I face.

Her body follows as I help her turn forward.

Head in front of mine, eyes in the direction of mine,

She is the driver. She will be my eyes.

Our day of play can now begin.

She leads, I follow. Where her eyes go, I go.

Where there is danger, I divert.

Where there is a concept, I name it and bring it to life.

When she is studious, I speak not, lest an idea be lost.

Where her hands want to touch,

She can hold and examine.

There are no time limits when children play.

An eternity of time brought this miraculous light

To the aging and arthritic eyes of my soul.

I will watch her; I will guide her; I will teach her

And direct her away from all danger.

She is the sunrise; She is the sunset;

She is the morning star.

She will....she must be better than me!

(This is a letter written by Ali', Amadeo's older sister, to Amadeo, I think, when Ali' was in her younger teens. I have not changed it any, other than typing it here.)

Dear Nature Boy,

I'm glad you were born, a miracle mom and dad say, you see, without you, childhood would be so lonely and silent Japanese films wouldn't be as humorous. Also, I wouldn't know what "pooning noobs in the wildernest" was. I'd probably assume it was some strange cult ritual. You taught me about people, myself, freerunning, courage, fighting, living off the grid, compromise, fagious, santa hats, computers, fishing hooks, homemade bombs, testing the limits of your taste buds against hot salsa and most of all, testing my patience. In the end I wouldn't be the person I am today if it wasn't for you.

Your sister,
ali.=]

ALI' HOLDING HER LITTLE BROTHER AMADEO

Holloween: The Boxer, (Amadeo) and the Nerd, (Ali')
(Amadeo became a Silver Gloves State champion. Ali' never became a nerd)

BY AMADEO (In highschool)

AMADEO, THE CRAZED GARDENER

By Amadeo (while in high school)

__SONSHINE__

Tiger, monster, head grower of grief,
Son, hope, dream belief.
A work in progress
An impossible dream
A nightmare
My death walking,
Strutting, overhead smashing!
A vision of perfection,
Athletic dream.

Or is it an artiste, that is
This new budding tree?
And is that the fine art
Of grafitti, that we see?
But not on
The inside walls
Of our house, pretty please!
The police were to be

The first connoisseurs
Of this artist's
Newly opened
Gallery!

Still,
A reason to live,
Though my heart is breaking
Over
And
Over
Again!

The embodiment of
A chance once more
To right wrongs,
To recreate history
Of uncles unheralded
For athletic prowess,
Their gifts to remain
An asterisk,
A forgotten family story.
A beautiful sounding bell
That no one heard ring.

They lived in an age
Where poverty entwining
Hid true talent inspiring.
Derision dominated
And diminished and deleted
The magnificent deeds
Of daring athletes shining
From front page news
To back yard bragging.

But alas! What do I see?
A farmer was emerging.
It was, at first, Mary Jane grass,
Don't ask, if for cash
Then …..
When Mom and dad cried:
…… 'Yabasta! *……..
A new garden appeared:
Onions, bell peppers,
Jalapenos and tomatoes -
A genesis, a creation of life.

A doubting and unreveling grandma
Disbelieving he was the creator!

A successful crop
All from a mere seed
To perfection of the finished deed.
A farmer had been born
who created perfect life,
From first planting simple seed
With love and by
Attending it's every need.
No monsters or devils
Need apply.
The creator of plant life
Has arrived.

We are still the obsessive parents
Watering this wild wandering human seed
Hoping that perfection
Blooms in the spring,

Then.. Before our eyes…

A moment to an hour,
Weakness to power,
Darkness into light,
Beauty born from fright,
Dazzling daybreak from
This long and bleak night.

From this weed emerges the flower,
Now fruit we devour.

Evolution from a wrong
Finally and ecstatically
Becomes the longed-for
Recognition of the right,
And a Pope chimes in:
Love nature and protect it
It is a moral obligation!
To fail, is a sin!
And before our eyes,
Our son becomes the light.

All this creative sonlight…
Embodied in the mixed,

Now magnificent wiring
Of my super lefty:
The Farmer, the Athlete and artist
My sweet and sustaining delight!

Enough!
In December of 2018, Amadeo graduated from the University of the Southwest with a Bachelor of Science in Kinesiology

Praying Mantis Reading Book, created by Amadeo while in high school.

CHAPTER IV.IV

CAN YOU HEAR THE MENTOR'S VOICE?

A. TRANSFORMATION

DID MY CHILDREN INSPIRE A MIRACULOUS TRANSFORMATION IN ME?

Was It God or Nature or Does It Matter?

The critical part of this book is my firm belief that I have had and am having a 'miraculous' experience through my children. With certainty, I can proclaim that synonymous with the arrival of my children, I became less self-centered and more empathetic than I had ever been before. My kids may argue with you about that. Many may read this and say if this guy considers this an inspired transformation, he must have been horrible before. There may be some truth to that.

Most all of the materials were done following the conception of my first child. I will let you read the poems and essays and let you decide whether my children were the genesis of a miracle in me.

Writing: Proof of Transformation? Certainly, I can tell you that I produced more poetry and essays than I had ever done in my life. But quantity does not equate to quality. Is what I have written, at a level, that I can claim is inspired? You tell me!

GLIMPSING HEAVEN. After numerous changes in the name of the book, I finally chose a title: *Glimpsing Heaven.* The 'Glimpsing Heaven' part is about the remarkable joy I experienced in finally seeing and experiencing the beauty around me through the eyes of my children. I used the limiting term "Glimpsing", to convey that so much of the 'Heaven' had been lost, blocked and destroyed by the calamity that our pollution is causing. We may never again fully experience the beauty of a pollution-free world.

'As Jesus Lived'. *(I have since amended it and eliminated the 'As Jesus lived' section)* The *'Don't Forgets',* (the beauty, the light, to love, and to fight), in **The Jumprope Song of Chapter II**, are on their face, simple directives to my children on how to live life. Most of this is based on my readings of

Jesus' life. I believe that the experiences the apostles had, particularly Paul, is the real God-experience. He and the other apostles were willing to die for their beliefs. That is a legitimate transformation. The last stanza in the poem – *'As Jesus Lived, So We Must'*, (since deleted and amended), should clarify that I believe that the example of Jesus' life is an example to live by. (This is to be distinguished from any dogmatic requirement compelling one to believe He is God.)

Many Causes? I submit that this book, through its poetry, essays and commentary, manifests something akin to a 'God' experience. So, does one go out and sire children to have this experience? No! I do not think that I would have experienced the same thing at a younger age or if we had not been deprived of children for ten years because of medical conditions. I don't know, if I had not moved to Las Vegas, N.M. and reunited with my birth family, whether I would have gone through this experience. *(See Ch. VII)* I do not know what impact the adoption experience had on me. If I had not been given up for adoption and/or not adopted by the Lopez family, I might not have been pre-disposed to experience this transformation. I don't know if I had been wealthy, whether I would have gone through this change. I just know that my 'mothering' experience with my children changed me.

Science. There is agreement that a baby causes chemical changes in the father's brain. *See YouTube, 'Babies'* for the chemical consequences on the father of a newborn. However, my focus is examining the nature, the how and why of my extensive transformation, and the development of empathy and love for more than my children. Are there other sources that explain or provide examples of a human transmogrification towards empathy directed at humanity and nature?

Transformations in Nature. Curiously, examples with transformation dynamics similar to a spiritual change occur in nature where animals risk almost certain death to reproduce and protect their offspring. For example, Salmon coming from the sea and braving hungry bears to swim upstream to spawn. After the journey and spawning their eggs, the salmon dies.* How about that for maternal instinct! Nature has given us some super examples on what it means to be a good mother. It means your children's survival is more important than your own. It means doing whatever it takes to enable your offspring to survive. (See *The Message of the Blessed Mother and its Meaning - Ch. III)*, for an example of the power of motherhood.)(See my *Christmas Message in Chapter III)* for a different take on the story of Jesus' birth.)

Just as nature has imbued mothers with the instinct to do whatever it takes for the survival of its young, so, all of us, must do the same. Just as the message of the Blessed Mother is to become a good mother, we must emulate her. This book is about the transformation we need to experience, to make our world livable for future generations.

Much of this book is written with the use of Christian symbols and imagery. Would I have gone through a similar experience if I had grown up in another culture and for example, had believed in Buddha? I think so but I would have likely utilized Buddhist imagery and symbolism to explain the experience.

Whatever the explanation for my transformation, I know that what I am seeing, experiencing and feeling around me is heaven. I also know that if we do not do something quickly, our children and their children will never experience this same heavenly beauty.

I ask you to read on and decide for yourself whether this was a real transformation, what brought it about and whether it was God or nature inspired?

*This is true of Pacific salmon but not of Atlantic salmon.

The Closest Essence to What Explains my Transformation.

B. WHAT EXPLANATION

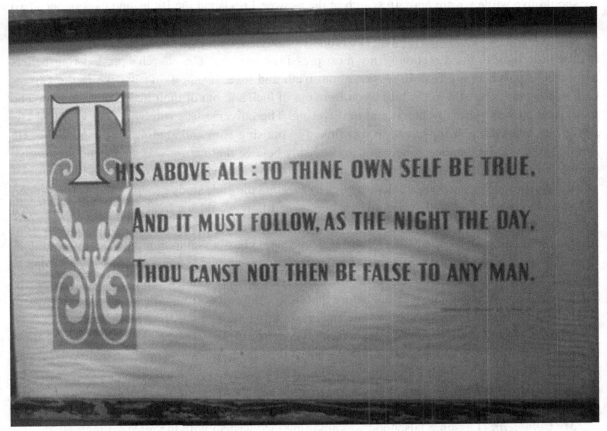

SHAKESPEAR'S 'HAMLET' on the wall of my dad's office in Gallup, NM

Jesus said, "If your leaders say to you, 'Look, the kingdom is in heaven/'then the birds of heaven will precede you. If they say to you, 'It is in the sea,' then the fish will precede you. Rather, the kingdom is inside you and it is outside you. "When you know yourselves, then you will be known, and you will understand that you are children of the living father. But if you do not know yourselves, then you dwell in poverty, and you are poverty." **The Sayings of Jesus # 3 of the Gospel of Thomas**

The philosopher Socrates famously declared that the unexamined life was not worth living. Asked to sum up what all philosophical commandments could be reduced to, he replied:
'Know yourself.'

"Knowing yourself is the beginning of all wisdom..."
The Buddha

JOURNEY TO DISCOVER JESUS' ESSENTIAL MESSAGE & EXPLANATION FOR MY TRANSFORMATION

After a remarkable transformation in my entire being, beginning with my wife's pregnancy, I searched for a reason why I had been filled with this mountainous emotional connection to my children, humanity and the wonder of nature surrounding and flowing through my being. My childrens' arrival into this world filled my heart and turned my mind towards the question why we are here and how we should live while we are here. In search of the answer, I revisited the Bible, and experienced two non-Catholic churches in Las Vegas, New Mexico.

<u>Church Did Not Hold the Answer.</u> The return to church did not explain the transformation in me. It shed little light in the direction of my most pressing concerns. The church's pre-existing beliefs and tenets squelched any real discussion about truth and love. If you didn't believe in the Christ-God as they interpreted it in the bible, you were out of luck and out of their heavenly kingdom. The interpretation was generally literal and unwavering. The universe was run by a God who had His hands into everything. Your salvation was linked to praising Him and abiding by the bible that He inspired. Darwin be damned if he could so foolishly believe that nature was smart enough to give birth to humanity. Creation was already explained in Genesis, Chapter one!

<u>Bible Trumps Reason.</u> I was foolish enough to question the bible study group: What would happen if Jesus was to come back? How would He see us and how would we treat Him? Would we even recognize him? I had hoped to inspire a conversation that revealed how far we were removed from what He said and how he lived. The leader of the group, (a businessman, not the pastor), told me in front of the group, in no uncertain terms, that the next time Jesus would come was already revealed in the last Chapter of the bible - Revelations. When He returned, that would mean the world had come to an end. So Jesus would not come back before that time – the end of time. Therefore, speaking about what could not happen was a waste of time and apparently blasphemous. End of discussion!

Who Is Out of the Kingdom? Speaking of the end of times, I reviewed the 'lists' in the bible of those who would not be raptured. All those out of the kingdom have been identified: *Revelations 22:15, NIV,* had identified the following: *"Outside are the dogs, (cruel enemies), those who practice magic arts and the sexually immoral, the murderers, the idolaters, and everyone who loves and practices falsehood.*

My Comment: (I assume falsehood was anything inconsistent with the bible's directives.)

"Corinthians 6-9-11, NKJV reminds: *"Or do you not know that the unrighteous' will not inherit the kingdom of God? Do not be deceived: neither the sexually immoral, nor idolaters, nor adulterers, nor men who practice homosexuality. Nor thieves, nor the greedy, nor drunkards, nor slanderers, nor swindlers will inherit the kingdom of God."*

Galatians 5-19-21, ESV directs: *"Now the works of the flesh are evident: sexual immorality, impurity, debauchery, idolatry, witchcraft, hatred, discord, jealousy, fits of anger, selfish ambition, dissensions, factions, divisions and envy; Drunkenness, orgies and things like these. I warn you, as I warned you before, that those who do such things will not inherit the kingdom of God.*

My Comment: (How about 'Science', which did not exist at the time? Would it have been considered 'witchcraft'?) *(How about a* country whose unabashed essence and ideal is to make more money than the next guy (Capitalism)? Is that in the category of 'selfish ambition'?)

Ephesians 5-5 ESV states: *"For you may be sure of this, that "everyone who is sexually immoral or impure, or who is covetous ('that is, an idolater), has no inheritance in the kingdom of Christ and God.*

My Comment: If covetous means greed, are Capitalists countries destined for hell?

1 timothy 1:9, ESV mandates: *that the law is not laid down for the just but for the lawless and disobedient, for the ungodly and sinners, for the unholy and profane, for those who strike their fathers and mothers, for murderers.*

Query: If your country enters into an unjust war and you support it, are you a murderer?

The above is a pretty broad-sweeping swath of folks outside the Kingdom. If 'practicing falsehoods', means disagreeing with the literal interpretation of the bible, I guess I am out of the Kingdom. Moreover, the 'list' leaves out my dad, (an alcoholic), my capitalist buddies and lawyers, greedy capitalists, and most everyone I know and many marvelous folks of the wrong sexual persuasion. Since my mom prayed to saints, was she committing the sin of idolatry? The 'revilers (those who assail with contemptuous or opprobrious language, address or speak of abusively) would probably include everyone in a democracy where freedom of speech is practiced and encouraged. Fits of Anger: Well… that is going to keep a bunch out.

Candidly, this Kingdom sounds more of a way to punish enemies of the tribe and control folks while they live, rather than any fair dissemination of justice. Of course, if they saw the Jehovah light and undid what they were, they had a shot at the big Heaven in the sky. Good luck homosexuals!

Speaking of homosexuals, at that same church, I foolishly dared to open up a discussion about homosexuality that quickly ended by reference to the Old Testament quote above. One of the women in the group later advised me that homosexuals were easily identified. They all had short appendages – short legs, short arms, short fingers and short anything else that protrudes from the body. Mmmm! And on the surface, she seemed to be an intelligent woman! My mind quickly referenced a line in the Billy Joel song: "Short People got nobody…" I guess she looks at them differently. As an aside, this homosexual spotter is a teacher at one of local grade schools. How scary is that!

All humor and derision aside, my adventure into fundamentalism turned up organizations that were not too far removed from the reasons I had reservations about Catholicism. The difference was that the Catholic Church utilized the Catechism instead of the Bible to keep the congregation in line.

The Old Testament seemed consumed with control, punishment and developing a narrow tribal mentality. It had very little to do with bringing out your better angels. In fact, if anyone was interested in beginning a war, particularly against a non-Christian country, the Old Testament was where you found support and justification. The Old Testament seemed more about fearing the devil for violations of biblical directives (see above), than bringing out the goodness in humanity.

The essential point I am making is that neither organization was able to offer an explanation why my children had animated my heart and opened up my eyes about living and dying. The truth had to be elsewhere.

The Lost Gospels. So, was there a source that could clarify what was manifesting in my life? A movie had referred to a religious text discovered in a bottle shortly after World War II. In one of my journeys to the "Religion" section of the bookstore, I discovered that indeed there existed non-canonical scripture imputed to Jesus and never spoken about in any church that I knew about. I purchased books on the subject: *'JUNG and the LOST GOSPELS', 'GNOSIS, THE NATURE & HISTORY OF GNOSTICISM', 'HONEST TO JESUS', THE GOSPEL OF THOMAS'* and other books that touched on the subject.

'…know yourselves…' or 'you are poverty' In the book, "Jung and the Lost Gospels" the last and most important paragraph, is the quote at the beginning of this essay and condensed at the beginning of this paragraph. To Jung it was a 'signal from the heavens', a 'synchronistic' solution following World War II and the bombing of Hiroshima and Nagasaki. According to Carl Jung, the discovery of these Gnostic scriptures tells us that "We have nothing to fear but unconsciousness. The Antichrists,

Behemoths, and unconscious projections, will vanish like waking from a nightmare when the process of *individuation* becomes operative." Wow! Modern-day Psychiatry met the ancient Sayings of Jesus and they were compatible!

Individuation: Jung believed that a human being is inwardly whole, but that most of us have lost touch with important parts of ourselves. He believed that through listening to the messages of our dreams and waking imagination, we can contact and reintegrate our different parts. The goal of life is individuation, the process of coming to know, giving expression to, and harmonizing the various components of the psyche. If we realize our uniqueness, we can undertake a process of individuation and tap into our true self. Each human being has a specific nature and calling, which is uniquely his or her own, and unless these are fulfilled through a union of conscious and unconscious, the person can become sick. Query: Are we living in a sick time?

To the extent that the Lost Gospels acknowledge that much of Jesus's efforts and words were directed to reuniting one's self, it helps to explain the first step in my transformation: Stop looking and listening outside ourselves for answers and look inwards! Or at least look outwards for the purpose of understanding what is inside of you. The Sayings of Jesus validated what had always seemed natural to me – Living and not denying what I was, rather than what everyone else was saying who I was. The *Sayings of Jesus* were telling me that I was on the right path.

The Relevant Lost Gospel Sayings: *"The Kingdom of God is inside/within you (and all about you), (The Sayings of Jesus # 3 of the Gospel of Thomas), not in buildings/mansions of wood and stone. Gospel of Thomas 77b (Cf. Acts 17:24,25 NIV)*

- *(When I am gone) Split a piece of wood and I am there, lift the/a stone and you will find me." Jesus says: "If you bring it into being within you, (then) that which you do not have within you [will] kill you." The Sayings of Jesus # 70 of the Gospel of Thomas."*
- *Jesus said: Become passers-by! Gospel of Thomas Saying 42.*

<u>Was I Looking In the Wrong Place?</u> The explanation for my transformation was to be found in the Dead Sea Scrolls, discovered in Nag Hamadi, in the Qumran caves at the base of an Egyptian cliff in 1945. Remarkably, it seemed that it had been written and directed to my concerns. My search for answers had led me to two different churches in Las Vegas, NM. I had not found an explanation for my question in these churches. Fortuitously, the question where to look for the answer to my query, was addressed in the Scrolls and an infrequently cited reference in the Bible.

<u>Not in Organizations of Men.</u> So the answer was: I was looking in the wrong place. I was looking in buildings/mansions of wood and stone. Or, in other words, I was searching in organizations of men. I needed to be looking inward and around me – at nature or *"God's Kingdom'*, (Under a stone is earth.) We should know by now that nature and man are inextricably connected. Looking inward should reveal our connection to nature. Looking to nature should help reveal ourselves.

'Become Passersby': So how was I to know the right route to the truth if it was not in joining those in buildings and mansions? So I looked to different interpretations. What does a passerby do? *He observes and gathers information. Then he keeps moving on to new areas (of study).* The admonition is to be as one who *"wears the world as a loose garment."* (St. Francis of Assisi).*To be a passerby is to be one who has let go of the world and all its things–to be a person who is spiritual. Don't be attached.* Create some emotional distance between yourself and the world. *In Buddhism, the root cause of suffering is attachment.**

<u>What It Means For Me.</u> As I understand this advice, instead of being able to wear the garments of culture loosely, the world's values and lifestyles inundate us and we absorb them and became infected with the world. My own take on this is that we must not become invested, infected or entwined with the values, lifestyles or organizations that we come upon. Rather we should see it, try to understand it but not become a part of it or controlled by it.

This is tough advice! But I suggest that our failure in completely ignoring the above wisdom, has gotten us into the end-of-the-world scenario we now face. We are now confronted with having to painfully peel off the deeply imbedded layers of material values that have permeated our being. Can we do it? Can we do it in time?

<u>Bible/Control:</u> Christian churches have always answered the important questions by directing one to the bible. It never directed anyone inward. That would be a sin in Catholic-speak. In Fundamentalist-speak, looking inwards into our imperfect being would profit us nothing. Moreover, we were likely to discover what the devil wanted us to know. The Catechism, for Catholics and the Bible for other Christians, held all the answers that we needed to know. Looking at it from the leaders' viewpoint, allowing or encouraging the flock to look inwards is the antithesis of power, authority and dominance of those in charge. That could not happen in a bureaucracy built on inviolable rules of control.

Bible - Be Like a Baby? More specifically, what did the Lost Gospels tell me about my specific experience - the remarkable transformation inspired by the birth of my children? In my search of the bible, the parable that was the closest to my experience was Luke *18:15 ESV*:

> *Now they were bringing the babies also to him that he might touch them; but when the disciples saw it, they rebuked them. But Jesus called them together and said, "Let the little children come to me, and do not hinder them, for of such is the kingdom of God. Amen I say to you whoever does not accept the kingdom of God as a little child will not enter into it."*

This biblical rendition of Jesus' words sounded more like another means of the church to put aside any independent thinking and compel acceptance to dogma without question or doubt. The interpretation, reasonably read, directs that we should become like babies and just accept what the church says! Well that interpretation/explanation just did not ring true for me.

Doubt vs. Faith. Part of my problem, according to the church and those who thought like them, was that I had failed to take things on faith in God. Sorry! That was antithetical to my being. I have always doubted what people would tell me unless it had some basis in reason, and in some cases, an intuitive connection. I have never been someone who takes things 'on faith'. The one thread throughout my existence has been doubt and questioning of what others blindly accepted. Post-enlightenment and in a scientific age, you would think, a refusal to take things on mere faith was a reasonable approach to living. Right?

I had always felt that even Jesus on the cross had his doubts: *'My God, my God, why have you forsaken me? (Matthew 27:46 NIV and Mark 15:34 NIV).* I recall a conversation with the pastor of the Lutheran church regarding this verse. I, ever the advocate, suggested that this verse is clear documentation of Jesus' doubt about God and his relationship with Him. The Pastor thought otherwise. To him these words were pre-ordained by the bible and had no other meaning. It sounded like he was saying Jesus' words were no more than an actor delivering lines foretold. He tried to persuade me that Jesus really did not doubt God. I proposed to him that indeed this was, at the least, a form of doubt about Jesus' connection to God. While at death's door to eternal life, the purported Son of God could not see or feel the light of God's love nor Heaven opening her gates to him. All he could feel was his life ending. It sounded like doubt to me.

In the summer of 2007, Time magazine published some excerpts from Mother Teresa's book of her letters. It was said this publication was against her will. Many of the letters were to her confessors and extremely private. The smiling apparently content holy woman had another side that was now revealed to us through a quite trustworthy vehicle – her confessions of doubt about her marriage partner – God. Through Saintly Mother Teresa, we should have now realized that the most holy amongst us question and yes, even doubt God's presence in their life. And yes, contrary to the Lutheran Pastor's interpretation, even Jesus in His dying moments, wondered whether God had given up on Him and whether He had been talking to himself all this time.

The Scroll Explanation. I now knew I was on the right path of searching inward and not being infected with the culture. But was there something out there that could explain what I had now been experiencing through the birth of my children? Everything else in this book describes and manifests how I have changed and the inspiration for that change. But certainly, I was not the only one who had come through this miraculous/mystical child-caused transformation and addressed it.

Was there some explanation that jibed with my circumstances? So how did the transformation through my children fit in to the literature or religion? Again, the answer was to be found in the Dead Sea Scrolls:

> *Jesus saw some little ones nursing. He said to his disciples, "These little ones who are being suckled are like those who enter (a) the kingdom" They said to him: If we then become children shall we enter the kingdom? Jesus says to them: When you make the two one, and when you make the inside the outside, and the outside like the inside and the upper like the lower and when you make the male and the female into a single one, so that the male is not male, and the female is not female, when you make eyes in place of an eye, and a hand in place of a hand, and a foot in place of a foot, and an image in place of an image, then you will enter the kingdom.*

(The Gospel According to Thomas, Logion 22.)

This Gospel posed the same issue as in the bible, quoted above, how a baby gets you into the kingdom. But becoming '...*like a baby*' was not the answer! The critical difference was that in the Dead Sea Scrolls, a mother was breastfeeding her child. So what does Jesus' explanation mean? With the help of Carl Jung's interpretations, I pursued an interpretation of *The Gospel According to Thomas, Logion 22:*

'*When you make the two one...*' In suckling her child, the mother becomes one with her child and the child becomes one with the mother. Other than the skin between them, they are one. The milk flowing from the mother to the child is not different than the blood flowing from the heart to carry life-giving nutrients to the rest of the body. The child instinctively recognizes that he cannot be separate from the mother or he dies. The mother's warmth and security reflect her need to be one with the child. The two have become one.

'*...when you make the inside the outside, and the outside like the inside*' The inside, where mother's milk resides in her, becomes the outside when it leaves her. The milk from outside the child becomes 'inside' as he consumes it and the milk from outside develops him inside. In this mother/child relationship they have made the inside the outside and the outside the inside.

'... and the upper like the lower': The upper may represent the spiritual/wisdom and the lower is the physical. We now appreciate the wisdom of breastfeeding in the short and long-term health of a child, including the baby's growth, the production of antibodies and brain development. Indeed, the child suckles the wisdom and health of the mother who represents the spiritual and wisdom. The oneness of the physical act of breast-feeding *(the 'lower')* makes the child smarter and healthier – *('the upper'.)*

'.. and when you make the male and the female into a single one, so that the male is not male, and the female is not female.' Where a mother breast-feeding her son, both innately recognize that the child's nurture is life to her since she bore him. There is no imputation of status based on male/female dichotomies.

'when you make eyes in place of an eye, and a hand in place of a hand, and a foot in place of a foot, and an image in place of an image,..'

"...eyes in place of an eye,..." One analysis: The eye symbolizes understanding ("I see.") So the experience of the Self or gnosis brings a new understanding. We must all try to see as others see if we were in their shoes or looking through their eyes.

"a hand in place of a hand,..." The old way of acting/thinking/doing is replaced by a new way.

"...a foot in place of a foot..." Your feet are for standing. Your standing point to see the world should change to a new standing point to see. This seems to supplement the explanation for "eyes in place of an eye". We must try to stand in the feet of others to understand them.

"...an image in place of an image..." An infant does not distinguish itself from its surroundings. They do not differentiate. In the child's mind he/she is just part of a greater whole. The infant's image is thus not as a separate individual but as connected with humanity. So our image of the world must transform as it is with an infant. We must try to imagine ourselves as intricately connected to the world of other human beings and act accordingly.

The mother suckling a child is a perfect symbol to illustrate Jesus' requirements to enter the kingdom and it finally has answered and illuminated, for me, the explanation how and what has happened to me.

The revelation was that we did not have to become like a baby to get into Heaven as *Luke 18:15-17* would suggest. It was not about being simple-minded or naïve in our relation with God, that would open the doors of Heaven. Remarkably enough, it was about the dependent relationship of mother and child, illustrated by the breastfeeding described in *The Gospel According to Thomas, Logion 22* that symbolized the relation we were to have with our fellow man. We were to exercise an empathy born of the realization that we were dependent on the rest of humanity and we should treat our fellow man with that always in mind.

The mother suckling a child works, because it illustrates oneness and empathy so well. So much of the world's problems emanate from the inability of mankind to see and feel others as part of them – (the absence of empathy.) We must see other's viewpoints (eyes) before ours, their way of acting, (hands) and viewpoint (feet) in place of ours and their being, an extension of ours (image). We must act towards others as if they were us. This explained my development of empathy. You do not destroy what is you. Or to put it colloquially, because mankind does not recognize its oneness, it has been cutting off its nose to spite its face. For a world on the verge of destroying itself, the message is beautiful, powerful and timely. Like the mother suckling the child, we must appreciate that mankind is one and develop empathy in our every thought and action.

So I finally had it explained to me and it fit perfectly. And remarkably enough, it was wisdom from the mouth of Jesus, through Thomas, devoid of an effort to make me join any organization. I had been drawn so close to my children's being and existence, that I could see and feel that dependence and oneness with the world that the child experiences and as reflected in *Logion 22*, quoted and explained above. The birth of my children drew out of me what had laid dormant for so long: maternal instinct. Empathy! Empathy for my children, mankind and now for the earth and all its beauty. Jesus, through Thomas, was saying that, like the mother breastfeeding her child, we, are all connected and dependent. We must always act and think with that in mind.

But What Explains My Transformation to Love Nature? Certainly, the inspiration from *Logion 22* is founded on the quintessential act of nature – breastfeeding. It is the ever-present act of sustaining life in the animal kingdom. No baby bottle necessary! Humanity is a consequence and a part of nature. *Logion 22* illustrates it. But is there more of an explanation?

NATURE IS THE 'KINGDOM'. But Thomas' answer did not completely respond to the philosophical question why nature was significant. The bible seemed to tell us that we could do what we want with nature, 'suppress' it and treat it as one might treat an enemy of the kingdom. Was there something more specific that addressed our natural surroundings as more than a mere stage or prop, to do with, as we pleased? I again turned to *The Sayings of Jesus #3 of the Gospel of Thomas,* also part of *the **Lost Gospels: "….the kingdom is inside you and it is outside you…" cited in full at the beginning.***

The connection had been made! In gigantic contrast to the bible's treating nature as no more than a disagreeable subject of a kingdom to be suppressed, Thomas identifies nature as a 'kingdom' in and of itself, and all the respect that goes along with that. And we are intricately connected to the 'kingdom' all around us, inside of us, and part of us, not superior thereto!

As if to address the very question whether those in power have used 'heaven' as a reward, after you die, if you obey their law/dogma, Thomas, somewhat humorously, tells us:

"If your leaders say to you, 'Look, the kingdom is in heaven/'then the birds of heaven will precede you. If they say to you, 'It is in the sea,' then the fish will precede you.

Jesus through Thomas then clarifies:

Rather, the kingdom is inside you and it is outside you. "When you know yourselves, then you will be known, and you will understand that you are children of the living father. But if you do not know yourselves, then you dwell in poverty, and you are poverty." The Sayings of Jesus # 3 of the Gospel of Thomas

It was a powerful and immediate message. This 'kingdom' or Heaven on earth, as I prefer to call it, was right here and part of us, rather than somewhere in the sky and only after we die,. It followed perfectly that we are directly responsible for our fellow man in this heaven on earth rather than living a life motivated by a heaven after death and only if we followed the Church beliefs correctly. I submit that Nature was the 'kingdom' the Lost Gospels were talking about.

Don't Destroy the Kingdom. I could come to no other conclusion that this heaven on earth or 'kingdom', was about how we treated our fellow man and how we treated nature. They were inseparable: "*…the kingdom is inside you and it is outside you..*". You could not or should not destroy or ignore the 'kingdom' on earth! Humankind was intricately connected with and part of this heaven.

The un-churched wisdom of Jesus from years gone by, had reached out over time and the message of the Gospel of Thomas jibed with what science and Pope Francis have finally come to appreciate – Nature is not less than us. If anything, it is greater than us. We did not create it. We are part of it. It is a kingdom and should be respected as such. It is evil to disrespect it or to treat it as less than God's Kingdom.

The <u>Four Laws of Nature</u> by Barry Commoner, (in chapter 4), now did not seem so novel. Jesus' use of the natural act of breastfeeding in *Logion 22*, to show unity, revealed how we are all <u>connected</u> to each other. Since this was the "Kingdom" /Heaven, which was in us and all around us, we were clearly connected to nature. Any act on our part, adding chemicals, technology or throwing waste 'away', damages this 'Kingdom'. Certainly, that we are living in 'heaven', means we are already living in perfection. The Closing Circle's law that 'Nature Knows <u>Best</u>', becomes perfectly clear. Living in perfection means that 'tinkering', 'tampering', and technologizing the work of perfection, reduces it. It becomes worthless and we learn that what we thought was 'free', is not, and our refusal to see our natural connection, has now converted our heavenly home into a living hell.

My life, and my poetry became infused with this feeling, realization and belief. This enlightened outlook converted the title of this book to 'Glimpsing Heaven on Earth'

There you have it. An explanation connecting my intimate experience of becoming a father and the transformation and infusion of my being with the ability and sensitivity to see, hear and feel what I had never experienced before. Imagine that! The answer in a bottle, hidden for sixteen hundred years, discovered by mankind a few years before my birth and by me personally, when my children were born!

*earlychristianwritings.com

CHAPTER V

DON'T FORGET THE LIGHT

A.   Love frees the light

1. INTRODUCTION TO 'THE LIGHT'

'THE GREEN ALIEN' BY Ali'
('The Light' is about seeing things differently, (in a different light.)

MY LIGHT

THE LIGHT LEAVES ME
AND FLOWS
INTO MY CHILDREN.
THEIR BRILLIANCE
BRIGHTENS MY NIGHT.
DEATH'S TROPHY
WILL HAVE NO LUSTER.
IN AND THROUGH
MY BOY AND GIRL,
MY FADING LIGHT
WILL SHINE FOREVER.

B. THE STRUGGLE

FIGHTING WINTER'S DYING LIGHT

Against the dark
And poisoned clouded skies
I see the barren winter trees,
All lined
In orderly measured degrees.
They shoulder
Straight and narrow streets
To destinations unchanged
And stand safe and secure
With their stiff sentinel salute
To the tired and toxic sky.
These monotonous rows
Challenge creativity
With their rigid
Straight wooden walls
That guard the road
And safely secure
The one-way route in.....
And militantly block
Any way out!

The soundless voice
From the sky
Speaks
With biblical
Certainty:
This is
The only path.
Do not question me!

These useless wooden
And cowardly scarecrows
Signal death with their dying leaves
And now wear
A frosty straightjacket

Of frigid cold degrees
That warns us
Of the coming
Bitter cold freeze.
Powerless, they accept
Their frigid fate.
Feet tied deep in the ground
They can only wait
Until the
Strangled
And now voiceless
Song of Spring
Comes to sing.

They silently stand,
Oblivious to time,
Prisoners of their roots,
Addicts to
A poisoned,
Dying
Supply
Of nourishing
Light to fight the night
And loving liquid
To fight
The coming blight.

Sewn securely
On their brittle branches
Are the slow-stitches
Of frozen death
Of powdered white.

This,
Their chosen bright apparel
Is a glistening pall
Of cold and sterile
That unfolds neatly into
The deceptive invitation

To a playground puerile
Of bright layers
Of reflecting light,
A brittle blanket
For the cold night.

These trees of cold feet
Calmly greet,
Their galling guests
Of symmetrical sparkle
And sleet.
They need no invitation
To roost,
This frosty family
Without couth,
And now
Onto cold bleak branches
The cold symmetrical sparkle family
Is unloosed.

And the trees, with open arms
Receive the cold and coothless snow -
A rush of cool crystals
In a neat leveled row.

And a vision far worse:
A saddened sorrowful spring
Will not speak
A-flowering
Of the life-giving love
Called leaves,
Sun-reflecting
Onto a sky of life abreathing.

Now a billion visions of green
Is a divorced dream
From their imagined Spring.
Instead,
Only death begins awakening,

Dooming a vision
Of the grand blossoming.
A haunting sad sound -
The cold wailing wind moans
As it ravages the
Once colorful bark
To bleak and barrenness
Within its mark.

Imagination's death
Devoured the life.
In its wake
See the sorry
Shadeless skeletons so stark.
Their wooden carcasses
Are now fit only
For burning
In ovens,
Hopeless and dark.

This would be me:
Forever imprisoned
In these dark dead streets
Of an orderly wooded sea
By bars of wood
On both sides -
Save for...
My salvation:
Warm beds of green,
Frequent watering
And ambitious doses
Of warm and enlightening
Sunshine streams,

Thus inspiring
A flower with wings.
A seed lifted out
With the winds of
Love and light.

Escaping
The cold wooden
Prison of a one-way life -
A jail of sterile
And sunless visions
And soulless imaginings
For a field
Of a billion flowers
And colors
All blossoming.

So before the final snow
On straight soldier stick rows
All standing solemnly
In a straight
And orderly line,
Guarding
The hearse-bearing streets
Where the singular stench of death
Powerfully and putridly permeates
This poisoned place
And dares to perforate your person
And your only protection is
A nose that knows
The flowery fragrance
That the clean air blows;

Before these barren
Wooden stick poems
Whose trite
Monotonous lines,
Predicting the death
Of lyric and rhyme
And foretelling
The bleak cold future
For their short and sad life;
Before I became
Part of them....

I escaped.
Their future
Would not be mine!
But.....
Would it be in time?

BY ALI'

C. The Darkness: What Holds Children Back?

And the people in the houses all went to the university… …
And there's doctors and there's lawyers and business executives
And they all get put in boxes and they all come out the same
And they all play on the golf course and drink their martini dry
And they all have pretty children and the children go to school….
And the children go to summer camp and then to the university… … …..
And the boys go into business and marry and raise a family
And they all get put in boxes, little boxes all the same…..
'Little Boxes' written and composed by Malvina Reynolds and sung by Pete Seeger

CAN NOTHINGNESS BE BENT?

As a New Year's project for myself I bought a book about Super String Theory, a sort of Physics theory about everything. The book is called The Elegant Universe. I was never much interested in science but I have heard that even when you are older you can better your mind by challenging it. Moreover, I had seen the documentary, "The Elegant Universe" on Channel 5 and it piqued my interest. I would read a little every day to slowly stretch the brain fabric of my science-resistant brain.

The book began with a brief history of great scientific discoveries. It included Einstein's theories of General and Special Relativity. Einstein was the ultimate brain because he explained gravity when not even the brilliant Isaac Newton could explain why it worked as it did. Although Newton could accurately explain distances, speeds and the forces of gravity, he died without being able to answer the question why gravity worked as it did. It took the brilliant Einstein, 500 years later, to solve the great mystery.

Without boring you with the full explanation of General Relativity, Einstein said gravity was mass warping the fabric of the universe. The fabric was composed of time and space. Imagine that - the universe being a 'fabric'. The greater the mass, the greater the warp. The closer the masses, the greater the warp. It is simply illustrated on a one-dimensional level by dropping a bowling ball on a mattress. Imagine the indentation. (The bowling ball is the force (the mass), and the mattress is the time and space.) Further visualize the effect of putting tennis balls on the mattress. Yes. They would roll towards the bowling ball. (Had to get tennis in there.)

What struck me was that space, which we have always considered just emptiness or nothingness, could actually bend! How does nothingness warp (bend)? Well I thought these were such remarkable notions I had to try to explain them to my kids, Ali' and Amadeo. So I did my best to explain to them Einstein's theories of General and Special Relativity. They loved the part that if you took a space trip and began approaching the speed of light, time would slow down. When you returned from this near speed-of-light journey, everyone else on earth would have died and you would have aged very little. They liked when I told them that, if for one year, you hovered by a tether to your spaceship near the horizon of a giant black hole just beyond its power to suck you in and tear you apart, and then returned to earth, you would be a thousand years younger than everyone or a thousand years into earth's future. Again, the power of the ultra-mass of a black hole to slow time down makes this possible. The mass of the black hole warps time!

We have always seen time as a constant, not susceptible to change. Now we have learned that speed and mass can affect time. Wow!

I left the kids without knowing the effect of this science lesson, one I had never received from my teachers. About a week later Amadeo, went to his sixth-grade class at (school name deleted). His science teacher was teaching the class about the universe. Amadeo asked him what was space made of? 'Just a lot of nothing', his teacher told him. Well Amadeo had just learned something else and he wasn't going to let this go. Amadeo asked: You sure it isn't something? Frustrated with Amadeo's obsession with something that was ridiculously obvious to the teacher (but scientifically incorrect), he raised his voice: NO AMADEO, SPACE IS MOSTLY A LOT OF NOTHING!!

Amadeo told me the story that night and asked: If space is nothing, how can it be bent? Whether the interaction with the teacher was accurate or not, I don't know. (Amadeo is sometimes quite creative in his recollection of history.) But it didn't matter. He had learned a basic concept about the universe and the teacher was oblivious to where Amadeo was going with the nothing/something essence of the universe. Amadeo had understood a part of Einstein's great General Theory of Relativity! Wow! And he had the guts to inquire into the contradiction? If the universe is essentially nothing, how can 'nothing' be bent?

Amadeo told me he did not push it because "you can never win an argument with a teacher". I was reminded of all the teachers I had that were more preoccupied with being 'right' than allowing the students to examine an idea. The notion that a student could teach the teacher was a scary thing. Hey, how can you respect a teacher that had to be taught by the student? I think it was worse in my high school since it was a Catholic school. I have to believe they were still suffering from Galileo's rebuke of the Churches' teaching that the Earth was the center of the universe. (Galileo said it was not.) And who was this Einstein guy? He wasn't even Catholic. How could we believe him? Science was a nice thing until it interfered with the Catholic dogma. As Galileo was banished to his house as punishment by the church, I think our teacher's punished Einstein and us by not bothering to tell us the whole story about Einstein's great discoveries.

Talk about only one interpretation and explanation of everything! Ever read the catechism? I recall my own frustrations with the teachers' inability to acknowledge another explanation of reality. All of us can recall teachers who could see only one way and squelched opposing views with sarcasm and sometimes discipline. I remember one priest whose best response to my argument was that he had a master's degree. How could I question anything he said?

My son was now experiencing a similar narrow-mindedness. But what was different was Amadeo knew he was right. Einstein's concept was more advanced than the 'nothingness' notion of the universe. Could any science teacher not have heard of Einstein's theories? Einstein's breakthrough occurred in 1915! Are science teachers still teaching a concept that has been outdated for almost one hundred years! What else are they getting wrong?

But more than that, how many opportunities are teachers missing because their approach is not to allow the student to argue and explain their point. How many great discussions never go anywhere because an inquiry is squelched, often dismissively? How many great ideas are never revealed because "you can never win an argument with a teacher?" Is that the kind of teachers we want educating our children? Maybe if teachers took an approach open to a student's ideas we would have students who grew up to be teachers who elicited great ideas from their students. Maybe it would have taken less than most of human history before we figured out what gravity was. Thank god that Einstein was not fazed by the math teacher that came close to flunking him out of college.

To those children and former students who know what I am talking about, yes, your teachers are worried that you might expose them as less intelligent than you are. Disregard their dismissive, insulting and belittling behavior. Recognize that they would have flunked Einstein and never appreciated what they had done. Fight against this dying of the mental light. Ask them questions that make your point. Don't worry if none of the other students understand?

Can you stretch emptiness? Well, until Einstein's time/space fabric concept, the world presumed there was nothing but empty space beyond our earth. You can't stretch what isn't there. Can you stretch a child's brain? Not if you presume there is nothing in there to stretch because you never learned that each child has Einstein potential in his or her own way. Einstein's nannies used to make fun of Einstein as a child because, before he spoke, he had to mouth the sentence. They considered him stupid.

So, it should be no secret why we are falling behind the rest of the world in education. We have bad teachers! Maybe we should pay them more and attract a better quality of educators. Of all my high school and grade school teachers, I can think of only four who were quality teachers – Coach Pat Graham, Sister Helen Francis, Fr. Columban and Sr. Lucina. The effects of what they taught me changed my life.

Let's demand that our legislators stretch their brains and the public pocketbooks to pay teachers a quality salary. Let's demand that we measure the size of a teacher's ability to impact and expand the fabric of our children's minds and eliminate the mentally vacuous teachers from our educational universe. As parents, let's not just try to get along with the administration, but stretch our boundaries of politeness towards the teachers, and make our expectations known to them. Let's recognize that the fabric of our children's brains is elastic and what we do, can be the force to make their brains grow. Let's expand our own horizons and make learning fun, and hire teachers that expand the universe of our child's minds. Let's be a massive force and make an indentation in the fabric of our educational system by not being afraid to speak out to make our world a better place to learn. Let us together become the giant gravity of the sun to make a dent in the universe of education.

CHAPTER VI

DON'T BURY YOUR SOUL IN A WORLD OF DESIRE

There is a house in New Orleans
They call the Rising Sun
And it's been the ruin of many a poor boy
And God I know I'm one

Oh mother, tell your children
Not to do what I have done
Spend your lives in sin and misery
In the House of the Rising Sun

House of the Rising Sun by Eric Burdon and The Animals
Written by Georgia Turner and Bert Martin
Arranged by Alan Price

("I gave her my heart but she wanted my soul…"
Don't Think Twice, It's Alright by Bob Dylan)

If anyone comes to me and does not hate his father and mother, his wife and children, his
brothers and sisters- yes, even his own life – he cannot be my disciple. Matthew 10:34-37 NIV
Luke 14:26 NIV

Anyone who loves their life will lose it, while anyone who hates their life in this world will keep it
for eternal life." **John 12:25 NIV**

WHY A HUMAN LOVE MUST NOT HOLD ONE CAPTIVE

YOU, HE, SHE, THEY ALL ASK:
WHY MUST THIS LOVE END?
WHY MUST WE WAKE FROM THIS DREAM
AND SURRENDER TO THE BITTERSWEET SORROW
OF A LAST KISS GIVEN SOONER THAN SHOULD BE?
I, WE AND YOU ARE BUT MERE INSTRUMENTS
OF A GREAT AND WONDROUS DESIGN
FROM WHICH WE GLEAM, IF EYES CAN SEE,
THAT UNIQUE CHARIOT OF LIFE
ONLY SOME CAN RIDE
DOWN THE WINDING NARROW PATH
THAT ONLY ONE OF US CAN TRAVERSE.

DESTINY UNFULFILLED, DEVOLVES INTO A FAILED FATE.
THIS FLICKERING DREAM LIGHT WILL NOT GROW BRIGHTER
WITHOUT THE RADIANT GLOW OF TORCHES
TO BRILLIANTLY LIGHT THE PATH
THAT IS SET OUT FOR EACH OF US.
THAT ROAD IS NOT ALWAYS MEANT FOR TWO.
THE GREATEST TRAGEDY IS TO GLANCE BACKWARDS
INTO A BLINDING LIGHT THAT REVEALS IN ITS ENTIRETY
THE FORK IN THE ROAD YOU DID NOT TAKE,
THE WANTON AND HOLLOW LIVES
LYING JUST OFF OF YOUR COMFORTABLE PATH
THAT YOU CHOSE TO IGNORE
AND IN YOUR COWARDLY LIFE, FEARED TO TOUCH.
THE LIGHT REVEALS THE MOUNDS PILED TO THE SKY
OF DECAYING BODIES AND VACANT SOULS
THAT YOU DID NOT NOTICE
AND THE ROTTING CORPSES AND UNSAVED SOULS

YOU FAILED TO SAVE,
ALL DROWNING IN A RIVER OF MISERY
THAT YOU REFUSED TO GAZE.

AS YOU GLIMPSE BACKWARDS
FROM THE END OF YOUR MISGUIDED PATH,
INSIDE THE SECURE WALLS, ADORNED WITH GREAT ART,
YOU LAY SURROUNDED, AND LITTLE COMFORTED
BY THE SECURITY AND WARMTH OF A LOVER
WHO SEDUCTIVELY CONVINCED YOU
THAT SHE COULD NOT WALK WITHOUT YOU
AND YOU BELIEVED YOU COULD NOT BE WITHOUT HER.
YOUR DREAM OF A LIFE ENDED SO QUICKLY.

AND NOW FROM THE COMFORTABLE BED
OF YOUR SELF-CENTERED EXISTENCE
IN WHICH YOUR LIFE AND SPIRIT
HAVE WITHERED TO NEAR NOTHING,
YOU SEE WHAT COULD AND SHOULD HAVE BEEN.
AND AS YOU SADLY SURVEY
THE FRIGHTENING WAKE
OF DEATH AND DECAY
OF THOSE WHO YOU COULD HAVE REACHED OUT TO
AND SAVED BUT DID NOT,
YOU ARE WEIGHTED WITH THE DEPRESSION
OF WHAT YOU COULD HAVE DONE BUT DID NOT

AND AS YOUR TIME NEARS,
YOU LOOK FOR THE LIGHT
TO GUIDE YOU HOME
BUT SEE ONLY DARKNESS
IN ALL DIRECTIONS.

DESPERATE YOU SEARCH BUT SEE ONLY DREAR.
AS DESPERATION SINKS ITS RAZOR-SHARP TEETH
INTO YOUR FADING FALTERING NOW EMPTY EXISTENCE,
YOUR LAST EXHUMATION DISSIPATES
INTO MERE EMPTINESS.

RAGING HORSE

WHAT NATURE
THE DEMON
THAT HAS SNARED
THE HEART
FROM MY SOUL?
WHAT COLOR THE LURE?
WHAT SHAPE THE HOOK?
WHAT DRIVES
MY SOUL
TOWARD TREACHEROUS NIGHT?

HOARDS OF
BUTTERFLIES IN SPRING
RECKLESSLY
CHASING MATES
OBLIVIOUS TO
THE RISK OF DYING.

THIS MIND,
THIS CONTROL,
THIS CONSCIOUSNESS,
THIS FLIMSY RIDER
FOOLHEARTEDLY,
MADLY,
AND BLINDLY ENDURES
TO ETERNALLY RIDE
THIS PRIMEVAL,
THIS GALLOPING,
THIS TRAGEDY
OF A BRONC,
NATURE'S
ETERNAL
AND MAJESTIC
DARK STALLION,
UNTIL
MAGNIFICENT RIDER
CRIES:
WILL THIS STEED
NEVER BE TAMED?

THEN,
FOR ONE WEAK MOMENT
WHEN WILL
MEETS WILL,
RIDER AGAINST BEAST,
HEAVEN MEETS HELL
AND THE RIDER
TEETERS
FROM NATURE'S
GOD-INTENDED
PRECARIOUS
PRECIPICE OF A MOUNT
AND THIS
HITHERTO OBEDIENT,
NOW MAD HORSE,
NOW MASTER,
NOW LOOSED
TO RUN,
TO RAGE,
RAMPAGING
AND
POOR RIDER,
DANGLING
LIKE A BALLOON
TIED BY A STRING
TO A CHILD'S HAND,
A MERE RAGDOLL,
FLAPPING,
SWINGING
PRECARIOUSLY
FROM TENUOUS GRIP

AND WEAK RIDER
FALTERS FURTHER
AND GRIP IS LOOSENED
FROM ITS FRAGILE HOLD
TO THE STRAP
AND KNOT,

THE SAME KNOT
THAT TIES AND THREADS
RELIGION,
THAT SENDS NOT,
MISSILES
TO ARMAGEDDON,
THAT VISELIKE
DARES TO GRASP
AGAINST ALL ODDS

AND THEN,
THIS ANCIENT STRAIN
BEGINS TO TEAR
THE FIBERS
OF THE RIDER'S
RAW AND BLOODY HAND,
AND THEN
THE WILL FAILS,
AND THE GRIP IS
IRREVERSIBLY LOOSED!
THE BRAIN
AND CONTROL
CONNECT
TO SAVAGE STEED
NO MORE!

THE MONSTER'S
POUNDING HEART
ENCAGED IN
BONE AND MUSCLE
ONCE REINED
AND MASTERED
BY MERE MIND,
NOW RUNS FREE.

I TOO
CANNOT HOLD LONG.

THIS WHIRLWIND RIDE
THAT MUST MAKE GOD

LAUGH
OR DESPAIR
BEGINS AGAIN
AND I THOUGHT
THIS HORSE WAS DEAD.
IT MUST
BE DREAMING
OF YOUTH.

A BREATH AHEAD

A breath ahead
      Of beacons' light
Two ships grope
      Through fog-filled night.

Near crag and corral
      Veiled vessels move
Fierce wave away
      From Deadman's Cove.

Dense clouds conceal
      Conspirator's flight
From half-moon's dim
      And strengthless light.

With darkness draping
      The devil's deed
The captain ignores
      What wise men heed.

A wicked wind blows
      Hard this night
A coast of scuttled crafts
      Attests her might.

The rapture of
      The siren's song
Risks impalement
      On rocks headlong.

Entranced by the
      Dream of Pirate's gold
Captain sees not
      The hidden hold.

So ships move blind
      Toward booty's lure
Risking craft and crew
      For the treasure's cure.

Neither Neptune's strength
      Nor Poseidon's power
Will deny
      This fated hour.

Hairs-breadth away
      These ships yaw as one
Sweet scend away
      From the morning sun.

Soaring, surging,
      The ocean writhes,
Waves explode
      From swelling tide.

For the nonce
      The stiff gales have died
Sate ships drift
      on the falling tide.

And more than two
      have met this night
As souls of past
      liaisons delight.

For in these ships
      Is tainted loot
Whose exchange forever
      Haunts their route.

A separate path
      Each craft will take
No farewell sound
      Will either make.

As they scurry
      To escape by night
A breath ahead
      Of beacon's light.

This was directed to a TV-dependent generation – 'baby-boomers'. I believe the general idea also applies to our internet-addicted Culture - Generation X and Y (The Millenials) and Generation Z. I have not yet done that internet poem.

TUBE POWER

IT LURKED BEHIND
ITS LARGE GLASS EYE,
WAITING FOR
THE ADDICTS CRY.

ONE KNOB TURNED,
ONE SOUL CONTENT,
ONE SOUL HOOKED
WITHOUT RELENT.

GREAT POWER GAINED
FROM THIS ONE SOURCE,
GREAT CRYSTAL BALL
TO PLOT YOUR COURSE.

ILLUSION OF SOLUTION,
NO FEAR OF CONTUSION,
CREATION OF LAUGHTER,
NO HUMOR TO MASTER.

FROM BIRTH TO DEATH,
LIFE WITH THE FRIEND,
TUBE POWER SIGNALS:
BEGINNING OF THE END.

LIFE THROUGH THE WINDOW,
NO BRAIN NEED APPLY
THE MIND SLIPS DEEPER,
THE RATINGS SOAR HIGH.

A TEACHER, A SITTER,
A MOM AND A PAL,
NO NEED FOR REFERENCES,
AND JOHNNY CAN'T SPELL.

THE CHILD LEARNS SOON
THE LESSON OF THE EYE
PROBLEMS ARE SOLVED
BY THE OTHER GUY.

A RIVETED VIEWER,
A BUYER FOR SALE,
THE EYE DISTRACTS,
THE AD MAKES THE SALE.

ASSAULTED AND PUMMELED
AND LEFT FOR DEAD.
THE PRISONER CRIES:
WHERE'S MY MILLION ED? *

WHEN LEADERS WE CHOOSE,
WE CONSULT WITH THE EYE.
PICK THE MAN WHO BLAMES
THE OTHER GUY.

POWER CONSOLIDATED,
VICTIM INEBRIATED,
NO RUSSIANS TO FEAR,
THE EYE CONQUERED HERE.

*This is a reference to Ed McMahon, who in my day, among other things, gave away big checks. (See Publishers Clearing House.)

CHAPTER VII

DON'T FORGET YOUR BROTHER REACHING UP TO YOU

A. INTRODUCTION

This Chapter addresses two points: The first is finding my blood brothers, birth mother and their families who opened up their hearts and their Las Vegas homes to my family. The second is the biblical admonition to take care of those who are not able to take care of themselves. The families' act of taking us in and my transformation made me more sensitive to this duty to my fellow man.

The family reunion is inextricably part of the transformation story. I had a most amazing thing happen in my life. As a curious adopted child, I had always wondered who my blood parents were. After my adopted parents had passed away, I began a search in earnest. In mid-life, I located my birth family. Through my brother Dave, they invited my family to come to Las Vegas, NM and live there. Sal and I both found jobs and I was inspired to start a tennis program for the low-income neighborhood.

This new location and new relationship created the perfect setting for the children-inspired transformation I underwent. Amadeo and Ali' were very young at the time. They fully benefitted from the transition and the time spent with the newly-found family, as did Sally and me.

This chapter addresses the amazing and wonderful consequences of the move.

Reunited blood brothers Martin Lopez, Dave and Pete Romero at Charlie's Spic and Span

B. A FAMILY PARTNER TO PROVIDE A SAFE JOURNEY TO THE LIGHT

LOPEZ FAMILY AT SALLY'S DAD'S GRAVE

Birth Parents – Dave Romero & Amelia 'Gutierrez' Romero

Juanita Chavez Gutierrez and Ignacio Gutierrez, my great-
grandparents on birth-mother side of family

1. Introduction to **Romero-Lopez Journey Towards Reunion – A Brother Reaching Out to a Brother**

I had to ask myself if the family reunion story should be part of this book or was it a separate story. The main premise of this book is spiritual/empathetic transformation through my children. I have to believe that the singular family reunion of relinquished child to blood family was a major part of my transformation. It was magic to see my toddlers reuniting with cousins that were so close in age. They now had the equivalent of blood brothers and sisters that had their backs and playmates to make life fun. The small town of Vegas and support of family may have been the essential part of my transformation.

The newly discovered family was also supportive of our nine-year tennis program and their children a big part of it. The incredible support, financial and otherwise, of my new family, made so much possible that would not have happened without them. I cannot separate the influence of my children in my transformation from the reunion of my blood family and their support.

The income and security of State jobs, no doubt freed us to do things we may not have done otherwise. A small tightknit town ensured that if our kids were doing something they should not have been doing, we found out. My brother Dave's status as the City Attorney and his blood relation to me, did not hurt our transition into the community and yes, getting a job. (One of the judge's bailiffs did not know that I was Dave's brother for a considerable period of time. It was not my habit to announce it. When he did find out, he was actually annoyed at me for not telling him. I guess he would have been nicer to me. I don't know.) My point is that it did make a difference.

So yes, my children caused a transformation in me. Yes, I was on in years when we had Ali' and Amadeo. That played a role. But I cannot minimize the security, safety and how my new status insulated my family from failure and yes maybe this inspiration might not have occurred but for our new home and new-found family.

So, with that in mind, here is an abbreviation of the entire reunion story.

INTRO TO LOPEZ 1999 XMAS NEWSLETTER. Nothing like a Christmas Newsletter to give you a feel of my new surroundings. This is a letter I would send to family every Christmas. I do not think anyone ever sent one back, but I would get a verbal critique every once in a while from a family member who thought I was off base. The letter is here because I believe it will assist you in understanding what contributed to my transformation. (You may even find it interesting regardless, or maybe not.)

LOPEZ' 1999 CHRISTMAS NEWSLETTER

Greetings:

In case you were wondering, the Lopez family has moved to Las Vegas, New Mexico, Sally and the kids in September of 96, and me, on April Fool's day, 1998. Las Vegas is where I would have been raised, but for a simple twist of fate. (I'll explain later.) Las Vegas sits at the foot of the Rocky Mountains where the grass-covered prairie begins, hence the name "Las Vegas" (The Meadows). Our house is 300 feet from the Gallinas River and five minutes from Storrie Lake. Numerous campgrounds, lakes and camp sites are within 45 minutes. Vegas began as a Spanish land grant and at one point was the capital of New Mexico. It has a rich and fascinating cultural and political history. And now we have become part of that.

We have also changed careers, and to some extent, lifestyles. Sally, who for years, worked with me at the law office, was hired at the hospital lab and now is a receptionist/clerk for the hospital. I now work at the District Attorney's office as an Assistant District Attorney. From not-so-frequent worshipers, we have now become active members of a small Lutheran church. Word travels fast here. Although I have never mentioned the church to the boss, he refers to me as the Martin Luther of the Chicanos. The magistrate judge sarcastically suggested to the Las Vegas Bar president that I missed the Bar party because I was too busy at a prayer group meeting. Such is a small town where Hispanics have always been Catholics and making fun of someone is acceptable.

Sally, although reluctant at first, realized most anything beat working for me in my Albuquerque law office. The Meadow City has grown on her. It has not been without pain. She physically has struggled with painful, debilitating illnesses. It now appears that she has made a full recovery. Even while suffering, Sally, her brother, Jerry and her sister Betty, literally tore down half of the house and remodeled it. You gotta see the job they did.

As for the kids, Ali' and Amadeo, have been in a Karate class for over a year. (Sally and I will need protection when we get old.) Ali' played her second year of T-ball and did well. I helped coach. The new coach thought that Ali' didn't speak English or preferred Spanish. He spoke to her in Spanish the entire season. Hey, I wasn't going to tell him different. She now knows baseball in Spanish. Ali' is now in first grade in a singular Spanish Immersion Program. Roughly 90% of the class is taught in Spanish and the kids are now expected to respond in Spanish. Ali' likes it. In May and November, she was "Student of the Week" for her Spanish.

Amadeo is now in his second year of Headstart. He looks forward to going and has a "girlfriend" named Tracy, upon whom he regularly showers gifts. He is still obsessed with his Power Rangers and seems to live his life through them. He is maturing. He heard that his daddy was singing Spanish songs with Ali' at her school for "Mostrar y Demonstrar" ("Show and Tell"). He demanded equal time! So within one week, on our way to school, he memorized three verses of "La Llorona". *(Weeping Lady).* The next week, we sang it to the class. He was quite proud.

Lastly, is "Rosa", our ever-alert mutt watchdog. As a puppy, she just appeared in our yard. Interestingly she bore a remarkable resemblance to the male dog we owned at the time. Undoubtedly one moral imperialist neighbor believed that if you sire'em, you raise'em. Rosa was ultimately a blessing. Ojo, her purported daddy, died shortly after Rosa arrived. Ojo is alive in and through Rosa and the kids have come to love her.

The big change is in the surroundings – from culturally-diverse city, to small, predominantly Hispanic community. For me, the best part is actually meeting people you know at the store, or anywhere, for that matter. Contrast that with shopping at the Albuquerque malls. Here people still greet you from their car or on the street. If you like your anonymity, don't move here. Blood, business or friendship connects everyone. It behooves one to speak highly of everyone, though not everyone does so. There are very few secrets. One of Sally's coworkers spotted me at Dicks Liquors one night and Sally had the news in the morning. (Fortunately for me, I was merely purchasing a sandwich... Really!)

As far as work goes, working for the State is different from private practice. I'll never adjust to secretaries that act as if they are doing you a favor when they do their job. And I can't fire them. That's the tough part! Loud tantrums are not unusual and even worse, tolerated. So much for political employees. As a newcomer, I may be more subject to this unprofessional treatment than those with seniority – a kind of hazing to get into the club. A version of "Carilla", *(friendly teasing),* I suppose. In the meantime, I'll bite my tongue and write memos. A good "Las Vegan" does not rock the boat, of course.

The good news is that my employer, new-found family and associates are tolerating me well, or at least giving that appearance. They continue to try to make a "Las Vegan" out of me. Little do they know my parents could not even make a "Gallupian" out of me. As I understand it, a Las Vegan always tells the judge they root for the judge's favorite football team – usually the Dallas Cowboys. A Las Vegan always tries to fit in. It means drinking with your fellow employees or buddies in celebration of whatever. Looking forward to and actually drinking to drunkenness is not frowned upon but ritualized and bragged about. A Las Vegan always gives and takes "carilla" (acceptable form of insult that is purportedly done to elicit laughter by making fun of another individual. In the 60's, we called it a "chop"). Hispanics are generally Catholics or fundamentalists or not religious at all. I guess I can claim I was conceived here, for what that is worth. But I have a long road to hoe before I arrive at the category of a true "Las Vegan".

Notwithstanding the above, I feel like I'm part of a big family here. Folks are willing to forgive my *'idiot-syncracies, (my former secretaries' term),* though they may make fun of them. Sal and I are frequent attendants to P.T.A. meetings and active participants in the Parents Spanish Immersion group. I am a member of the Domestic Violence Task Force. Eventually I hope to begin tennis programs within the grade schools.

When summer arrived, I became inspired to begin a summer tennis program open to all the kids of Las Vegas. Although, Las Vegas has produced superb tennis players, it had no public tennis program. Sal and I hired and trained six instructors and we taught tennis for the entire summer. Our biggest success was a shy 12-year-old girl whose parents said she had never really become interested in any extra-curricular activity, until this program. She liked tennis and progressively improved. In the final tournament, she tied for first place. Her success made the whole season a success for Sally and me. Buoyed by our achievement, we started an adult group of tennis players who met every Saturday morning, until it got too cold. I even found a group of tennis players, one of whom has a lighted tennis court in his yard. We played doubles after work through late November until I developed tennis elbow.

This Year's Thought: The fourth-century theologian Gregory of Nyssa, reflecting a long tradition of both Jewish and Christian thinking, said: "Whatever is the result of compulsion and force cannot be virtue." Is he correct? If so, did God give human beings dominion not only over the earth but also over themselves as individuals? Were the Creation stories parables of human equality, men and women both being formed in the image and likeness of God, and evocations of God's gift of moral freedom?

This Year's Best Movie: "The Green Mile" It involves superb acting by Tom Hanks, a larger than life Christ figure *(Michael Clarke Duncan)* and graphic depictions of electrocutions of men on death row. It hints at what we do with miraculous figures who threaten the status quo and what our country is doing to the black population.

This Year's Books: "**Contact**" (A distant journey to discover the power of experiential faith), "**God, The Evidence**" (An argument for God based on scientific revelations.), "**Honest to Jesus**" (An attempt to paint a picture of Jesus based on the latest techniques and research.) and "**The Word According To Eve**". (A female author's viewpoint of women and the Bible)

Finally, our family thanks everyone who has made our transition possible: To Della, my mother-in-law, who made my survival possible, under her roof, until I finally moved; To Molly, Dave and Pete, for providing me a home in Las Vegas; and to Auntie Tommie, who has taken us in whenever we are in Albuquerque. We have truly been blessed with a loving family. We look forward to sharing our abode with all family and friends.

Merry Christmas
And a Happy New Year

FIRST COUSINS' DOUBLES STATE CHAMPIONSHIP/CULMINATION OF A FAMILY'S LONG JOURNEY TO REUNION

This last May, (2015) David Romero and Amadeo Lopez won a State Doubles Championship and were instrumental in getting to the Finals of the Team Championship match for the Robertson Cardinals. On the road towards a team championship, the boys beat a NMMI (New Mexico Military Institute) doubles team that seemed invincible.

On this leg of the journey, the fathers took time from their regular jobs to watch, cheer, videotape, photograph and emote at every stage of this exciting adventure. Maybe you've heard that the dynamic tennis duo of Amadeo and David are first cousins and that their ever-present cheerleading fathers, Dave Romero and Martin Lopez, are (blood) brothers, raised in different parts of New Mexico. Don't be confused by the different last names and the different body shapes: one, full figured and the other, chiseled-in-stone. They are really related! (In case you are still not clear, the author is the one chiseled-in-stone!) Their boys have been playing tennis as a doubles team since they were quite young. (The doting dads have the videos and the pictures to prove it!)

This family victory nearly did not happen. In the beginning of the tennis season, the New Mexico Activities Association (NMAA) tried to keep this premiere team of primos-hermanos (first cousins) from competing by ruling that Amadeo was not eligible to play for Robertson after transferring from West Law Vegas. The NMAA claimed he violated the Transfer Rule which keeps athletes from going from one school to another by mandating that they sit out 180 days before they can play. They claimed his transfer from West Las Vegas to Robertson violated the Rule.

It is a rule that enables the NMAA to punish an athlete without any burden on the NMAA to show that there was any undue influence in the transfer. So even though the school Amadeo transferred from says they will not have a tennis team and he is transferring to one with a team, the NMAA decides to disallow him to play for the school he is transferring to. It is a rule that is blind to the needs of individual athletes and the connection between success in sports and in the classroom. Many are the casualties of a system whose families could not afford to hire an attorney to fight the bureaucracy that imposes these injustices.

The NMAA decision was devastating to Amadeo. While attending Robertson he missed five team matches and two months of practice with the team. In particular, he missed out on practicing and playing matches with his doubles partner David.

Lucky for this tennis duo that they found lawyers in their biggest fans. Dave entered his appearance and immediately began preparing for the hearing on the Injunction. This author helped prepare the well-documented and evidence-supported injunction to compel the NMAA to let Amadeo play. Dave filed the Complaint that demonstrated Amadeo's right to be able to play. The Temporary Injunction was granted immediately, allowing Amadeo to participate in his first match of the year. In the interim, the fathers requested a setting to make the injunction permanent. During that time, Amadeo and his dad endured a third NMAA administrative hearing in front of coaches and Superintendents who seemed not to grasp how the facts compelled a ruling in Amadeo's favor. Moreover, it appeared that at every level of appeal, the group of NMAA representatives hearing the appeal were fully under the sway of the head of the NMAA.

But legal enlightenment was about to brighten the first-cousins' path to their tennis destiny. However much the NMAA controlled the game on their home turf, it all changed once the ball bounced into the legal arena. A day and ½ before the scheduled Injunction hearing, Dave received the letter from the attorney for the NMAA, fully capitulating to our demand to let Amadeo play for Robertson. Amadeo was freed to fulfill a longtime dream of a State Championship with his first-cousin, David, a brother in all but last-name. Alleluia!

Overcoming the power of the NMAA was a wonderful family victory that will rank right up there in Romero/Lopez history with the victory of the first cousins winning a doubles state championship. Brother's winning a State Doubles Championship was done most recently by Placido and Emilio Gomez in 2009; Giorgio and Mario Fulgenzi in 2001 and 2002 and Garon and Warren Fulgenzi in 1983. The boys were in great company. Their predecessors were all quality players.

Of course, others have prevailed against the NMAA. But the Lopez/Romero victories in the court and on the court have another story that preceded it. That story may be as interesting as the legal and the tennis battle.

A Family Reunion. The NMAA barrier would have kept the boys from playing and winning a State Doubles title. However, this was but one, in a series of events, which history may never have even recorded. There is something unique about how these first cousins ended up even meeting and the story goes back 62 years.

Back to the Brothers. The journey towards family reunion began 62 years ago when a baby boy was conceived in San Miguel County and born in the Cradle Home in Santa Fe New Mexico. A few years later, a younger brother was born in Las Vegas, NM. Same mother and same father, but the first brother was brought up in Gallup, New Mexico and raised by Martin and Gregoria Lopez. The second brother was brought up in Las Vegas, NM by Dave and Molly Romero. Brother Pete of Pete's Fitness, was to come along shortly afterwards. Three boys, the same birth parents, one raised in Gallup, the two others, brought up in Las Vegas, NM.

Dave, and his younger brother Pete, grew up with a no-nonsense father who was a successful businessman in the Sand and Gravel business. As brother Dave tells it, Dave Sr. had learned the secret of turning sand into gold. The mother had a Master's degree and had a long tenure as a successful and popular educator. This author grew up with a father who was an insurance salesman but also was a very successful county politician. Maybe more significantly he played Semi-Professional baseball and Second Base for Air Force. Oh! He did play tennis and his brother "Grassy" was a State Doubles Champion. Mmmm!

David's dad, (Amadeo's Uncle Dave), my brother, would graduate from West High School where he played on a superb football team. He went on to Highlands University where he took a liking to politics and became the President of the Student Body. I attended Sacred Heart Cathedral, a Catholic high school in Gallup. I participated in all the sports but the school did not have a tennis team.

At Cathedral, I was a bit out of place. I think I was the only one in the school that did not accept everything I was told. I recall a priest reminding me that I always had the option of public school if I could not get the hang of this 'faith' thing. (It was that same insatiable curiosity that would ultimately lead me to search for my blood parents and finally end up in Las Vegas, New Mexico.)

In the interim, I would go to the University of New Mexico, (U.N.M.) for my undergraduate degree and in my spare time would play tennis and teach tennis in the City summer program. Both Dave and I were History and Political Science majors. In his spare time in college, Dave would take on all challengers in Ping Pong at the Highlands Student Union. Brother Dave went on to Harvard and got a Masters of Public Administration degree and then a law degree at the University of New Mexico. Pete was doing very well in college until he was called home to run the business when Dave Sr. became ill. Pete's life reminded me of the character, George Bailey, played by James Stewart, in the movie, *It's a Wonderful Life*. As you recall, George had great ambitions, but remained in his home town to run the family Saving and Loan. This is similar to what happened to my brother Pete. He was compelled to come home from college to run the business. He successfully did the job and like George Baily, married a beautiful and intelligent wife - Carla Romero, a college professor.

As for this author, I attended undergraduate school at the University of New Mexico and obtained a law degree at George Washington National Law Center in Washington D.C. At the end of law school, this Gallup-raised boy and the Las Vegas-raised brothers had not contacted each other. All I knew then was that I was adopted from a Santa Fe orphanage, (The Cradle Home) and my birth family was from Las Vegas NM and named Romero.

As you may know, once adopted, a new birth certificate is issued with the adopted parents' name. The adoption records are then sealed. This way, the birth parents cannot be easily traced by the adopted child. Helpful was the fact that the Lopez family did not keep an important fact from me. They had told me that I was from Las Vegas and according to the nurse at the orphanage, I was the 'Romero baby'.

With a law degree in hand, a prosecutor job in Espanola and an incessant curiosity, I located the "non-identifying" information at the Public Employees Retirement Association (P.E.R.A.). Go figure why it would be at this government agency! This 'non-identifying' information is available to all adopted children. With that information I found out that my birth father was a business-man with some education. My birth mother had a college education and was a teacher.

Armed with this knowledge, Paul Campos, (law school roommate and Best Man at my wedding) and I took a trip to the Las Vegas Clerk's office. I figured if I was born December 27, 1950, a marriage license might not be too far behind. I checked the marriage licenses for 1950. Bingo! In May of 1950 there was a marriage license for Amelia Gutierrez and Dave Romero. This was consistent with the nurse's identification that I was the Romero baby. But how could I be sure these were the same people identified in the "non-identifying" information? So I asked a clerk if she knew who Dave Romero was. To mine and Paul's surprise, she said: Yes! That is my uncle! He has a Sand and Gravel business and his wife, Molly was a teacher!

A businessman and a teacher! It was a match! But who was telling me this? I was talking to my first cousin! I had made the connection. Everything fit. I had the missing confirmation. I had located my birth family!

It was not long after this discovery that contact was made between the Romero family and the Lopez family. The Romero family was gracious. I was able to meet my birth father before he passed away and catch up with a lifetime of memories with my birth mother who is alive today. *(2021)*. After Dave and I handled a few cases together, we met extended family and accepted an invitation to move to Vegas. We were taken in with open arms. In 1996 Sally, my wife and our two little ones, Ali' and Amadeo moved to Vegas. Amadeo was a year-old at the time and Dave's boy was just a few months younger. I remained in Albuquerque to close down my private practice and on April 1st of 1998, I moved to the Meadow City.

Did the move alter the course of history? Dave and I often discuss how things might have gone differently if the Lopez's had never moved to Vegas. Dave has always enjoyed racquetball and golfing but was never a tennis player. He played football in High school. Pete was a bodybuilder, a runner and wrestled in high school. It is easy to see how David, with his dad's fast hands and superb hand-eye coordination may have become a champion golfer or racquetball player. With his natural speed, he could have been a star sprinter. With his size, he could have been a fullback or halfback on the Robertson football team or a Center on the basketball team, (which he was.) With all these influences and skills, David may have never picked up a tennis racquet.

But a tennis breeze was blowing in and the stars were aligning in just the right direction. In 1998, on a trip past the Highlands tennis courts, which were empty at the time, I told Sally: These courts shouldn't be empty. Let's start a tennis program. With this whimsical utterance was conceived an award-winning tennis program that lasted for nine years and included five years of coaching a West LV tennis team. Of course, the children of the two reunited brothers, Dave and Peter Romero were the first customers. One of those was a young David Romero. There was a three-month difference in age between David and Amadeo. They hit it off immediately. The makings of a State Championship doubles team had begun.

The first cousins were the beneficiaries of trips all over New Mexico, throughout the Southwest, Arizona, California and Texas, just to play tennis. On these trips the boys bonded and honed their tennis skills.

After high school, David received a full tennis scholarship to the New Mexico Military Institute. (Amadeo received a tennis scholarship to the University of the Southwest.)

<u>Amadeo, a Bumpy Journey.</u> The beginning of high school was quite uncertain for Amadeo. In 2009, as an Eighth-grader, Amadeo played on the Robertson tennis team. That year, in the Finals of the State team tournament Amadeo beat Michael Atkins 6 -1, 6-0, in the team singles match. (Atkins just recently became the 2013 State Singles Champion.) After that successful 2009 season, Amadeo somehow was derailed from tennis and for two years did not participate in high school tennis. (He did win a Silver Gloves State Championship during that time.) He changed high schools and went to West High school. But for two years it was not clear if he would ever play school tennis again. In his junior year, while playing for West High School, Amadeo ended up in the District tennis tourney in Taos. He found himself scheduled to play for the title against, guess who, his first cousin, David Romero, playing for the rival high school - Robertson.

But something was missing. Tennis was not as enjoyable for Amadeo as it once was. A decision was made, a risk was taken and Amadeo transferred back to Robertson High. The NMAA stuck its ugly foot out and tried to trip up the dream of two boys, long in the making, but two fathers were there to catch the boys, force the NMAA off the tennis court and give the boys the chance to fulfill the dream of a State title.

With the super coaching of Roman Fulgenzi, Juan Carlos Fulgenzi and Don Hasch, the boys began to look like a team with potential to go all the way. With limited time to practice together, the end of the season tournaments came quickly. The cousins did not disappoint. Playing inspired tennis, the team of Lopez and Romero beat every District and State contenders in two sets to win the State Doubles team title.

And now you know the history behind the headlines.

Comment: This is but one example of how the Lopez' family uniting with their blood family (Romero-Gutierrez), was inspirational. And I am forever indebted to my brother and the Romero family for the invitation that changed our lives.

I should note that before I pursued any steps in the direction of reuniting with my birth family, both my parents, Martin and Gregoria Lopez, had passed away. I never wanted my mom or dad to feel that there was any other mom and dad in my life but them. My mom, like many parents who adopt, was always sensitive to Theresa or me wanting to return to our birth parents. I never raised the adoption subject. However, my sister, Theresa, who was inclined to speak her mind more than me, and on more than one occasion, particularly when my mom was mad at her, would literally threaten my mom: I'm gonna go back to Lam Begas if you're mean to me! This would elicit from my mom, a sad and foresightful comment of resignation: Blood is thicker than water! Curiously, it was I and not Theresa, as far as I know, who searched for their blood parents.(Update: She did locate the identities of her birth parents.)

Second Comment (Thanks to Bruce Wertz for the information about the previous State Doubles Champions who were brothers.)

FIRST COUSIN STATE CHAMPIONS WITH COACH FULGENZI

C. RETURNING THE FAVOR

SUNSET VILLAGE & FAMILY

I prepared this article after our first year of teaching tennis to the Housing Community Children.

TEACHING TENNIS TO THE CHILDREN IN THE HOUSING COMMUNITY

In about 1996, Dave and the Romero family invited this new-found brother and his family to come to Las Vegas and even provided us a house to live in. Sally and the kids went up shortly afterwards. She quickly became employed and enrolled the two kids in Bible-school. She also enrolled Ali' in a Bi-lingual school.

I could not go up immediately as I had to close down my private practice. I arrived about a year later. Just shortly after I arrived in Las Vegas, we went passed the four Highlands tennis courts. It was a beautiful day in the later part of the afternoon and there was no one playing on the courts. I turned to Sally and declared: We are going to start a tennis program here!

I had taught tennis for the City of Albuquerque but had never before thought seriously about running my own tennis program, until that moment I saw the empty Las Vegas courts.

We began our program teaching tennis to the children in the Housing community. The Housing director was delighted that someone was interested in involving and directing a program to the Low Income 'Housing' kids. I can't be sure, but I believe my brother Dave, with his connections in the community, paved the way for us to begin such a program. I do know that I tried to begin a program in southern New Mexico, but the powers that existed, government and otherwise, were not at all interested. In little Las Vegas, New Mexico, my new-found family that had taken us in, were opening doors so Sally and I could share our skills with the kids in the Housing community. Wow!

I believe that my impulse to teach tennis was part of the unique transformation that my children had inspired.

The following is a brief rendition of our experience teaching tennis to the 'Sunset Village' children. It was written during the time Sally and I had begun the program:

IT IS NOT JUST A TENNIS LESSON. IT IS A LIFE LESSON

Intro To Sunset. The second part of the season, in 2000, began with our lessons to Sunset Village. They are often and patronizingly referred to as "Little Juarez". We began with the Sunset Village kids in August. To convey a not so untypical day, envision the following: The instructors are scheduled to meet and pick up the kids at the Center. (Yeah, the parents rarely brought them.) We arrive at the Sunset Village residence and the first thing you see is one of your eleven-year-old male students lying on the ground writhing in pain. You find out that his slightly built seven-year-old sister was attacked by some of the big eleven and twelve-year-olds. I do not doubt that the seven-year-old probably said something that she shouldn't have. You find out that the boy on the ground had tried to intervene on his sister's behalf when one of the girls kicked him in the groin. Fight over! The instructors console him and we gather the kids for practice.

A Chaos Attack. Three packed vehicles of kids come to practice. Some of the children are attentive and want to learn. Some grab a racquet and go off to the far court to hit to each other. For the latter group, it is demeaning to learn with the other kids. These are the teenagers and soon-to-become teenagers. For them listening and learning something new, means that they don't know everything. We had to tread lightly with them.

Within minutes, we have a huge exodus to the bathroom. A few of the kids are actually dedicated to learning and listen intently. They remain at the courts. As practice is winding down, the tall athletic thirteen-year-old with a temper, tries to start a fight with the same kid who took a low blow from the girls. The tall kid shoves the other to the ground. The Sunset Village supervisor/chaperone yanks the lanky boy by the shirt and pulls him away from the boy on the ground. She yells out his name: "You're going home now!" He argues but goes with her.

The Impact Sets In. As we pick up balls, a well-built twelve-year old boy, who generally does not like to listen, refuses to pick up tennis balls. Out of spite he hits two balls over the fence just to let everyone know that no one tells him what to do. He knows Sally has just picked up balls from outside of the fence. A chain reaction is occurring. It is like a pack of hyenas' first sight and scent of a wounded gazelle. These boys would have liked nothing better than to have beaten someone up or at least watch it happen. As Maricruz Rand, (one of the instructors) and I drive the boys back to their houses, the "F" word is spoken repeatedly. I reprimand them. Then the 'N' word is used. Maricruz is visibly disturbed. She turns and in her own way tells them she does not appreciate them using that word. The boys seem undaunted by our chiding. They discuss something involving the word f_g__ ts and laugh.

The foul language does not offend me. I have heard it all before. What bothers me is the inability of any of these boys to feel compassion for those they insult. They feel powerful with their put-downs. As the predator knows only its' hunger, the prey is only something to consume. It is only food. It's as if their parents had never told them what is acceptable verbal decorum. But far deeper, their actions and words reflect some unattended need. This is how they try to feel good about themselves and get attention.

We drop the kids off at the Center. They are not in a hurry to go home. No parents are waiting. Nor have any of the parents been to any of the practices. Besides the chaperones and Center supervisors, only one parent that I know of, plans to come and watch their kids play in the tournament.

MariCruz turns to me with a look of shock and says "what got into them?" I respond: "It's not what got into them. It's what's inside of them that just came out." Sally, my wife, drives up. Her look tells me that she has been affected by the violence and chaos she witnessed today. I'm worried that she will refuse to help me teach anymore. That would be a tragedy. The kids like her, far more than they like me. I'm more inclined to discipline, whereas she tries to distract them from unwanted behavior. I'm hoping she will be feeling better the next day. Sally reminisces about how the other kids appreciated her so much. We never had these problems with them. I remind her that we are not doing this for us.

She expresses a concern that the foul language and bold displays of disrespect will affect our two kids. We again remind our two children that this is not how we want them to be acting. We hope that they will see the actions of these kids as something that makes them look bad, not cool. Sally says we need to tell the bad kids not to return and we'll only work with the kids who appreciate what is being done for them. I agree and tell her that they need to know that their actions will have consequences.

But Time Heals All. After a good night's sleep, Sally is talking about letting the troublemakers play in the tournament. I guess she has forgotten how she felt the day before. The truth is she just cannot help but like the kids. She remembers growing up poor and all the stresses the family goes through. In her heart, she believes there must be a different standard for these youngsters.

Tournament 2000. Because we started the teaching season late and due to numerous delays because of disciplinary problems, we began the tennis tournament on the 13th of October. Curiously, a few of the children were afraid to play. I had to practically beg Sarahi' to play. She finally did and got a "Finalist" trophy. I guess she just feared losing. In another match, a shy eight-year-old was winning but her nine-year old cousin, Natasha was making a comeback. Danielle turns to me and with a look of seriousness, says: "I don't want to play anymore" Well... she kept playing and finally won. The toughest part of that match was keeping them civil to each other. They refused to shake hands at the end. But finally, they whispered something to each other out of my hearing, and they "high-fived" with their rackets. I deemed it a reasonable compromise.

Juana. One of the new girls taking lessons, (I'll call her Juana) lost, but revealed some natural talent. Then she stopped coming to practices. I am told that she went to live with her brother and stepmother. I later discovered that her stepmother had been convicted of trafficking in drugs and kicked out of this country. She was apparently in Las Vegas illegally. I was told that at a young age while living in Mexico, "Juana" had lost her mother. A jealous boyfriend had shot the mother once with a small caliber bullet and then, to make his point, shot her in the head with a shotgun.

The violence and tragedy reflected in "Juana's" story was not that unusual. Many of the kids had parents in the penitentiary. Many were being raised by single mothers or grandmothers. It seemed to me many were raising themselves. Was it any wonder they had difficulty focusing?

As you might imagine, crowd control was a problem. We had to reign in two of the boys who continued to steal the new tennis balls and hide them. They then began a clod-throwing war and hit one of the girls who was injured enough to cry. Strangely enough, this was the boy whose mom was present. The mom was preoccupied in a conversation with an unknown adult male. Of the two chaperones present, one was playing a match and the other was smoking in her car. I yelled at the boy and politely reminded the mother that there was a problem and that I could not referee the matches and watch her boy. After two days of tournaments, we treated the kids to pizza and awarded them their trophies.

We are talking about a group of youngsters that had already been disciplined twice. Their supervisor from the Village, disciplined the kids by suspending all sports for all the children for a week-and-a-half because the Sunset children were allegedly destroying property and refusing to respect the folks running the Center. I disciplined three kids by suspending their lessons for one practice. They refused to obey my request to return to the tennis courts and move away from the dumpster in the parking lot, an area that I considered dangerous. They responded to me by climbing up and jumping in the dumpster. The Sunset supervisors disciplined four kids on another occasion for refusing to go home in the cars that brought them. In a show of spite and bravado these recalcitrant youngsters walked home at dusk against the commands of their supervisor. And all this occurred within a month and a half!

As a tennis instructor and someone who has worked with kids all my life, you attempt to accommodate for different or unusual circumstances. You can't expect the same behavior and should not treat youngsters the same from different socio-economic backgrounds. Though, at the end of a week, and coming from a full-time job to teach tennis, you sometimes wish you could just teach tennis! Imagine instructing students who refuse to learn your name so they just call you "Mister". Imagine having to discipline them for spitting on the court or on each other. Imagine continually having to tell kids not to be insulting the other kids on the court and breaking up fights or shoving matches that would turn into fights, if not addressed.

Why The Disrespect? In these circumstances, patience and compassion must be your constant companion. Some children are not raised with the same diligence and dedication as other children. Many have only one or no parents in the picture. Many have grandmothers or aunts trying to raise them. Some have parents that are home but are effectively absent either because they can't or refuse to give priority to the rearing of their children. This may be due to drug or alcohol problems that take up all their energy. Some of the kids exhibit anger management problems and discipline problems. This manifests itself in a disrespect for everything and anyone that tries to limit or control their world.

A Success Story. Your choices are to say it is not worth it and walk away or stay with it. If you pursue the latter, you must believe deep down that you can make a difference. We have committed to the latter. Many years ago, when Sally first started teaching for the City of Albuquerque, she replaced an instructor who could not handle the rowdiness and lack of discipline that she encountered with her students in the South Valley of Albuquerque, New Mexico.

As an instructor for the Arthur Ash Junior Tennis Program, these were exactly the children that Sally was supposed to be teaching. Sally recalls one 11-year-old that she continually had to divert from the pool tables where she seemed to prefer to watch the boys play pool, rather than come to tennis practice. In the end, Sally's efforts paid off. Her student and another male won the city-wide tournament in Albuquerque and earned themselves a trip to Los Angeles to participate in a National tournament sponsored by the Arthur Ash Junior Tennis Program. Since Sally was their instructor, she earned a trip to California as the chaperone and coach. In California, Sally and her winning students met and were tutored by some of the legends of tennis, Arthur Ashe, Vic Braden, and Jack Kramer, to mention a few.

K-Mart Versus Cardin. Sally's students arrived in California with their ten-dollar sneakers and K-Mart outfits only to be met by kids with $100.00 shoes and lavish Pierre Cardin tennis wardrobes. It was obvious that the competition in California was raised on Country club tennis courts. These were hardly inner-city kids. The writing was on the wall. Although Sally's students acquitted themselves well, they lost. However, the magic of such a trip and dream opportunity will forever be etched in their memories. Sally and I learned that through sport and perseverance we could make a difference in someone's life.

Notwithstanding all the difficulties and roadblocks to learning, there are kids who want to learn and do the right thing. Many of them are living in conditions that do not make it easy for success. They may not become super-star tennis players but that is not the goal. With tennis, help, and guidance they may escape the pitfalls, roadblocks and traps that lead to disaster or a no-where life.

Success with children will not happen without the help of a lot of folks. Thanks to many individuals, organizations like the USTA and the NNMTA, Lawrence Quintana, City funds and Federal government assistance, the children who could not afford to learn a sport could now afford to participate.

Reaching The Projects. One of our goals was to reach all the low-income areas and introduce tennis to the kids in those areas. Though there exist pockets of poverty we call "projects" or "Low-income areas", we were only able to start a tennis program with the Sunset Village area. We would have liked to get the message out and bring in other "Housing" areas such as Esperanza and the Los Ninos area.

In our efforts to promote tennis, Sally and I tried and were successful in beginning a tennis team at West high school. They had no tennis team there for thirteen years. Moreover, The Sunset Village children attended West Las Vegas High School. Now the kids we taught at Sunset could continue playing a game they enjoyed. Many kids who had no interest in other sports, came out for our tennis team. That story is for another book. It was a big success.

Beyond Sport. Lastly but most importantly, we need to look beyond sport to rescue, nurture and guide our children. We must appreciate that we cannot afford to lose one single child to the ravages of poverty, apathy and despair, so prevalent in a time when violent video games, TV, drugs and alcohol have replaced parents and teachers. The churches must do what they were intended to do. They must actively reach out to those who are lost in our communities. Our City government must continue to put a high priority on the well-being of all of our children. We all must act as substitute parents and teachers to those who would get lost in the maze of mindlessness and despair. Never was it truer that we cannot afford to lose one child. The failure or the loss of one child diminishes us all.

Update: We did our tennis program for nine years and expanded it to the community. On two different occasions, (2001 and 2004), we received from the United States Tennis Association, Southwest Section (USTA SW), the award of National Junior Tennis League, (NJTL) Chapter of the Year. Amazingly enough, one of our students from our low-income tennis program, is now a Tennis Pro at a distinguished country club in Albuquerque, NM. We are in contact with many of the families whose children we taught and their children have been doing well. We like to think we had a small part in that.

D. Least of Our Brethren

Show me the prison. Show me the jail...Show me the prisoner whose face is growing
pale; Show me the alley, show me the train; Show me the hobo who sleeps out
in the rain... ....Show me the famine. Show me the frail, eyes with no future that
shows how we have failed.... Show me the country that bombs had to fall... Show
me the ruins of building once so tall..... There but for fortune go you or go I.
'There But For Fortune' written by Phil Ochs
And sung by Peter, Paul and Mary

This essay is inspired by a conversation I had with one of the businessmen at the Lutheran church.
I told him I believed Jesus was a radical. This shocked my fellow Lutheran and he was quick to let
me know that Jesus was not a radical. My comments below had no effect on his opinion. The picture
so often painted by Americans is of a God who so much looks and sounds like a businessman whose
ultimate goals are profits and power. You will see that my perception of God is far different.

MY GOD IS A RADICAL

My God is a radical! My God is for the little guy! I see him in Moses who led a revolution against Egypt and miraculously smashed the manacles that bound the Jews to bondage. I see him in Martin Luther King, who, with non-violent resistance, unlocked the manacles of slavery and the chains of discrimination. I see God in Mother Teresa who fed the bread of hope to those dying of hunger. I see him in Gandhi who broke the colonial chains of the British without the sword. Ultimately, I see God in Jesus whose life was about compassion and love; whose only weapons were words and actions with a message to free humanity to follow in his footsteps in the narrow and risky path of speaking out against hate, war and hypocrisy. I hear him speaking for those who are trampled, ignored, berated, spat-upon, denigrated, persecuted, jailed, hated, insulted, laughed at and killed. 'Blessed are the poor, *(Matthew 5 NIV)*, the hungry and the persecuted' *(Matthew 5:10 NIV)* is not an empty phrase, empty preacher's words or mere slogan. (There is no exception for Capitalism; No exception for our overflowing and privatized penitentiary system.)

It is a powerful and relevant message. At the very least we must respect the poor, not denigrate them. We definitely must reach out in any way possible to help them.

My God is justice, heavy on compassion: *Judge not lest ye be judged. And you will be judged as you judge.(Matthew 7:2 NIV) Let he who has not sinned, cast the first stone.(John 8:7 NIV); Love thy enemy.(Luke 6:27-36 NIV); Turn the other cheek. (Matthew 5:39 NIV)* (As I read it, there is no exception for Wars, (Old Testament excepted)

My God is biased towards the poor. He loves those without and barely tolerates those that have. He said to the son of the rich man, "If you want to be perfect, go sell your possessions and give to the poor, and you will have treasure in heaven. Then come, follow me." *(Matthew 19:21 NIV). This was clearly* an indictment of the search for wealth on earth. *Woe unto you rich. You have received your comfort.(Luke 6: 24 NIV)* How dare the money-makers ignore these words, distort them, revise them and secrete the essential meaning to say it merely directs us not to love money. It is hypocritical to distort His words so you can live better than others.

My God is not a pragmatist. He stores no grain from the harvest. *(Luke 12:16-21 NIV)* He gives it to the hungry. (Luke 12: 33 NIV) He admires the birds of the wild for they want not. *(Matthew 6:26 NIV)*

My God is a 'Socialist''. He tells us to love your enemies, do good to them, and lend to them without expecting to get anything back... *(Luke 6:35NIV)* He tells us to give to "the least of our brethren, *(Matthew 25:40 NIV),* not those who would make us a buck. *(Luke 6:35 NIV.)* Is not the essence of Capitalism antithetical to this idea?

My God is a pacifist not a general or a warrior. He is a militant whose values are beyond family and he asks us to risk our life for what is right. *If you love your life you will lose it. If you hate your life, you will have eternal life. (John 12:25 NIV)* He is the militant-pacifist, the Martin Luther King who asks us to risk our physical being for the cause.

My God is not obsessed with his body. Eat what they feed you he tells us in *Luke 10:8 NIV.* Not 'you are what you eat', whose presumption is that our essence is our body and the right foods are relevant. He tells us it is every word that comes out of our mouth that matters, not what goes in. *(Matthew 15:11 NIV.)* In other words watch what you say. Deception is evil. Words of denigration towards your fellow man are evil.

My God is not obsessed with accessories and carrying clothes for the week. Carry neither purse, nor wallet nor sandals, and greet no one on the way. *See Luke 10:4 KJB.* (Maybe if we abided by this, our excessive purchase of clothing would not be polluting the world.)

Knowing what Jesus has told us, how could anyone see Jesus residing in the Land of Plenty or in the luxury suites of our Hotel comfort-oriented Nation? That would be possible only with a watered-down, carved up, dressed up, sugar added and pain-deleted version of Jesus. It is hard for a people who want for nothing and yearn to have it all, to hear, live or even understand the true Jesus.

Who do you think the following parable was directed to?

*"And Jesus went into the temple of God, and cast out all them that sold and bought in the temple, and overthrew the table of the **moneychangers**, and the seats of them that sold doves. And said unto them, It is written, My house shall be called the house of prayer, but ye have made it a den of thieves."*

Ultimately, it is the fact that Jesus died for what he believed. Yes! History and men who sought control, preached that he did not really die, but rose from the grave. I prefer the man that acted and spoke knowing he was risking his life.

Now more than ever, our country needs to follow the example of someone with compassion for the poor, the persecuted, the imprisoned, the denigrated, the hated, the insulted, the laughed at and those injured or killed by our lack of empathy. (Think of the millions every year that are dying from man-made pollution so we are enabled to live comfortably.) We must ask if our system is fair to the least of our brethren. Or will we continue to live in a country where the only standard is whether it will make us a buck?

(Comment: No, I have not lived up to the standards Jesus has set.)

CHAPTER VIII

THE GREATEST WRONG IS TO ALLOW EVIL IN YOUR MIDST/ IF THEY ARE ATTACKING THE INNOCENT YOU MUST RESIST/REDEMPTION IS JUSTICE RENDERED TO ALL

……..How many years can some people exist
Before they're allowed to be free?
How many times can a man turn his head
And pretend that he just doesn't see?…….
………..How many ears must one person have
Before he can hear people cry?
How many deaths will it take till he knows
That too many people have died?,…..
….The answer is blowin' in the wind.

Blowing in the Wind written and sung by Bob Dylan

'…And no one dared disturb the sounds of silence…'
By Simon and Garfunkel
The Sounds of Silence

So I told him that he'd better shut his mouth
And do his job like a man
And he answered "Listen, Father,
I will never kill another."
He thinks he's better
Than his brother that died…..
….Take your place on The Great Mandela
As it moves through your brief moment of time.
The Great Mandela
Song By
Peter, Paul and Mary

THE ASHES

THE BLIGHT OF BURNT HUMAN BODY CHARS
RESTLESSLY SWIRL
IN THE INFERNO OF
THE NAZI CREMATORIUM
OR THEY ARE SET ABLAZE
IN THE MORE PUBLIC
PITS AND PYRES.
THE SMOKE AND THE HUMAN ASHES
RISE AND THEN ESCAPE UPWARDS
THROUGH THE TARNISHED
AND TIRELESS SS SMOKESTACKS
OR FROM THE PITIFUL AND PITILESS
PITS AND PYRES.
THE GROTESQUE AND HELLISH SECRET
IS THEN DISGORGED TO HEAVEN.

LIKE A BILLION BRITTLE BOTTLES,
ALL CARRYING A DESPERATE MESSAGE,
CAST INTO A VAST AND ENDLESS OCEAN,
EACH SCINTILLA OF SMOKE
AND EVERY HUMAN EMBER
CARRIES A BELATED AND
DESPERATE PLEA FOR HELP.

THE SMOKE SPREADS
AND THEIR ASHES ARE SPEWED
INTO A NOW DARK THICK SUNLESS SKY
TO FOREVER DRIFT AS A DEATH SHIP
ON THIS DARK SEA
ALONGSIDE THE DAMNED
WITH BUT A PITIFUL PRAYER
OF REACHING A CARING SHORE.

THE ASHEN REMAINS RELENTLESSLY RISE
ON AN EXPANDING SHIP OF SMOKE
AND SPREAD SLOWLY, TRAVELING OUTWARDS,
FORMING A LARGE AND THICK BURIAL CLOTH
TO COVER THE HOLLOW SOULS OF THE LIVING DEAD
WHO ROT DAILY BENEATH THE PALL

AND ARE RENDERED PARALYZED
BY THE FEAR OF BECOMING PART
OF THE FLOATING
SMOKE AND ASHES OF DEATH.

OVER THE TOWNS AND COUNTRYSIDE
THE SMOKE SEARCHES
AND THE ASHES DESPERATELY PLEAD TO BE SEEN.
THEY FLOAT GHOST-LIKE
AS AN IRREPRESSIBLE MEMORY
OF AN UNFORGETTABLE NIGHTMARE.

THIS HORROR WAS CONCEIVED AND SPREAD:
FROM HOLY PAGES BLAMING THE 'CHRIST-KILLERS';
FROM THE HOLY HALLS OF CATHOLIC LUMINARIES;
AND FROM LUTHER-BEGOTTEN BIGOTS,
ALL OFFERING JEWISH GOATS FOR A NATIONS' SINS
AND FROM A WORLD WHO DEMANDED CONFORMITY
OF THOSE WHO RELIGIOUSLY AND RIGHTEOUSLY REFUSED.
THEIR 'INFERIOR' EXISTENCE WAS NOW AN AFFRONT
TO THE MACHINATIONS OF THE MASTER RACE,
THERE VERY LIFE'S PRESENCE, WAS TO BE ESCHEWED.

THE HATRED WAS INITIALLY CONCEIVED IN A FALSE BATTLE OF GODS:
JEHOVAH VERSUS JESUS.
TORTURE, DEATH, DIMINISHMENT AND REMOVAL
WERE THE TYRANTS' TOOLS
TO INSTITUTE AND ENFORCE THE ONE TRUE GOD.
WHEN CATHOLICISM BECAME ENTHRONED,
IN THE ROMAN EMPIRE,
AND THEN IN SPAIN, PORTUGAL, MEXICO...
THE SEEDS OF THE FUTURE HOLOCAUST
SPROUTED AND GREW, WATERED WITH HATRED
OF THE EMBODIMENT OF THOSE
WHO THOUGHT, BELIEVED AND LIVED DIFFERENTLY
THAN THE POWER THAT BE –
THE LIVING JEW COULD NOT BE FREE!

THEY WERE COMPELLED TO FLEE
AND PRETEND THEY WERE CATHOLICS
SO THEY COULD SURVIVE THIS HATING SEA.

THE BLACK AND GRAY SPECTER OF A FINAL SOLUTION
UNSOLEMNLY SPREADS ITS FUNERAL SHROUD.
THE CHARRED RELICS FLOAT DOWNWARDS
AND THESE ASHES, SYMBOLS OF AN EVIL SACRIFICE
AFFRONT THE BEAUTY OF NATURE.
THE SOOT OF SACRED REMAINS,
BY THEIR TOLERANCE
TRANSFORMS THE SACRED TO EVIL.
THE STENCH OF THE SIN COMMITTED
TO CREATE THESE SNOWFLAKES OF DEATH
SICKENS THE SENSITIVE SKY OF MOTHER EARTH.
ON THE BUSIEST OF KILLING DAYS,
THIS SICKLY FLOATING SILENT SCREAM
OF SMOKE AND ASHES
BLOTS OUT THE CREATOR'S LIGHT
SO DAY DEVOLVES INTO DEMON-BLACK NIGHT.

WHAT EVIL DEITY OR DEMON
COULD PILFER NATURE'S PORTRAIT
OF PURITY, PERFECTION AND SYMMETRY?
WHO WOULD STEAL GOD'S GIFT OF LIFE-GIVING SNOW
AND REPLACE IT WITH A TRILLION ASHES OF DEATH
TO POLLUTE A SAD AND SICKENED SKY?
WHAT DISEASE WOULD STIFLE THE SUN
WITH THIS PROFANATION OF UNFATHOMABLE DEATH?
WHO WOULD MOCK AND PURLOIN GOD'S GENIUS
WITH AN EVIL SNOW OF BLACK AND GRAY ANNIHILATION?
FROM WHAT SOURCE OF EVIL HAVE DEVOLVED
THESE DEVILS WHO DELIGHT IN DEATH BY ZYKLON B,
A FUMIGATOR,
ONCE A HERBICIDE, KILLER OF PLANTS,
NOW TURNED ABETTOR OF MASS HOMICIDE.
A FOREWARNING OF THE MASSACRE OF MANKIND
BY POISON OF A PLANET?

WHAT NATURE THIS HELL-BEAST BORN OF HATRED
WHO DELIGHT IN DELIVERING DEATH
BY GAS AND FIRE?

AND WHAT GOD WOULD ACCEPT
THIS SAVAGE SACRIFICE OF INNOCENCE?
WHO WOULD CELEBRATE A REIGN OF HATE

BY FIRE AND LIES,
AS IF SETTING ADRIFT THIS ASHEN OFFERING
COULD BRING ABSOLUTION?
WHAT COULD CALL ITSELF A RELIGION OF GOD
THAT WOULD BE CONTENT
TO LOOK THE OTHER WAY
WHEN EVIL WAS MURDEROUSLY IN THEIR MIDST?

WHO WOULD BARGAIN WITH EVIL MANIFEST IN BLACK SHIRTS
AND IGNORE THE PLIGHT OF A CHOSEN PEOPLE
BECAUSE THEIR GOD DID NOT DIE ON A CROSS OF WOOD?

WHAT NATURE A CATHOLIC CONCORDAT
TO BE BLIND TO BLATANT EVIL
TOWARDS DESCENDANTS OF JESUS? *

IT WAS A DEAL WITH THE DEVIL
NO MATTER WHAT THEIR WORDS
TO THE WORLD, THIS ROMAN RELIGION
WOULD TRY TO CONVEY.

ONTO HOUSETOPS, DOORSTEPS AND SIDEWALKS,
THE SEARCHING FLOATING MEMORIES SPREAD.
GROWING, RISING, BLACKENING THE SKY DAILY.
THEIR VERY EXISTENCE CONDEMNS
THE SOULS OF THE MUTE AND THE DEAF;
MARKING HEARTS THAT HAVE HARDENED TO HEAVEN'S CALL;
MARKING EARS THAT DO NOT HEAR THE SHROUD
OF SILENCED SCREAMS FALLING FROM ABOVE;
MARKING LIPS, SEWN TIGHTLY TOGETHER
BY FEAR SPAWNED OF A DESICCATED SOUL.

THEIR ASHES, UNHEEDED, SOUNDLESSLY SPILL FROM THE SKY.
THEY ARE ASHES OF ONCE SKIN, BONE, BLOOD AND SINEW
OF MEN, WOMEN AND CHILDREN.
THEY LIVED, BREATHED, LAUGHED, LOVED
AND DREAMT OF ALL LIFE'S GLORIOUS POSSIBILITIES
FOR THEM AND THEIR CHILDREN.

THEY FALL FROM THE SKY AS LONELY REMINDERS
OF A DYING SAVIOR PLEADING:
MY GOD, MY GOD

WHY HAS THOU FORSAKEN ME?
THEY STAND, AS ONCE HE, STRIPPED AND SEPARATED
FROM POSSESSIONS AND LOVED ONES.

THEY DIE ON A CROSS
OF MILLENNIAS OF HATE,
WHICH IS NOW CONTORTED
INTO A COLD METAL SWASTIKA,
EVIL INNATE.

AND ALL THIS...
BY AMBITIOUS MEN WHO PUT POWER BEFORE LOVE,
EFFICIENCY OVER COMPASSION AND
SURVIVAL AND POWER, OVER THE SPIRIT.

IN A WAR OF VENDETTA AGAINST
THE 'MURDERERS OF GOD',
SUPPORTED BY LUTHER IN HIS
VILE PUBLICATION OF HATE AND LIES,
IGNORED BY A CHURCH,
TO SAVE CATHOLIC POWER,
THE 'PROMISED LAND' PEOPLE
BECAME THE SCAPEGOAT
FOR A HUNGRY DEVIL TO DEVOUR.

THIS CONTAGION OF FEAR
SCREAMED:
'RISK ONLY WHAT IS NOT DEAR!'
AND THE DOORS REMAINED CLOSED
TO ANY JEW WHO SOUGHT SHELTER
AWAY FROM THE KILLING STORM
BECAUSE THE DOORS
THAT OPENED TO THE ANNE FRANK FAMILIES
WERE FAR AND FEW
AND NAZI'S NOW NAMED THE JEW
AS THE CAUSE OF THE CALAMITY
THAT GERMANY WAS GOING THROUGH.

THE HEARTLESS POISON SPREAD
TO PERMEATE THE VERY SINEWS
OF THE EXECUTIONER'S
AND THE ONLOOKER'S SOUL.

IN THE BATTLE AGAINST THE GREATEST OF EVILS
SUBSUMED IN A SWASTIKA,
WHEN ONLY ACTIONS AND WORDS MEANT ANYTHING,
THE MEN OF THE CROSS
WERE RENDERED CRIPPLED, BLIND, DEAF AND DUMB.
THEY SPOKE ONLY CHRISTIAN CAPITULATION.
THEY DARED NOT SPEAK "MY BROTHER",
NOR SEE THE FACE OF JESUS AS A JEW,
LEST THE POISONOUS GAS
WERE TO FILL THEIR LUNGS TOO.

A SACRILEGIOUS SILENCE DROPPED
WITH THE POWER OF AN H-BOMB
AND SOULS WITHOUT HEARTS
DARED NOT FEEL THE VICTIM'S PAIN.
THE MUSHROOM CLOUD WAS TOUTED BY NAZIS
AS THE INAUGURAL ASHEN THUNDERHEAD
THAT WOULD LAUNCH A SAVING RAIN
THAT WOULD SAVE A SO-CALLED SOCIETY
STRUGGLING TO REGAIN THE PRIDE,
A LOSING WAR HAD DENIED.

WINNING THE WAR
WAS SEEN AS SALVATION.
NO ONE COULD FEEL FOR
THE SIX MILLION WHO DIED
FROM THE MUFFLED BLAST
FELT IN THE CHAMBERS OF GAS.

AND AGAIN, THE CHRIST AND CRUCIFIX,
VINTAGE CONSTANTINE, TURNED SWORD,
NOW ZYKLON B,
DEVASTATINGLY DIRECTED
AT THE CHRIST-KILLING HOARD.
AND THOSE WITH THE CROSSES OF WOOD,
DEVOID OF THE MESSAGE OF JESUS:
TO RISK YOUR LIFE
FOR LOVE OF MANKIND,
AND RISKING ALL FOR GOODNESS,
COWARD AT THE BEAST,
LEST IT TURN AND SNUFF OUT
THEIR SNIVELING AND HAPLESS SOULS.

IT BEGINS AND PROCEEDS
WITH DEGRADATION AND HUMILIATION.
IDENTIFY THEM AS AN 'ALIEN RACE'
'THE ETERNAL JEW',
NOT DESERVING OF GOD'S GRACE:
PUBLISH HATE-FILLED WORDS:
'ON THE JEWS AND THEIR LIES'
PAINT THEM AS POISONERS OF THE CULTURE,
RACIAL POLLUTERS,
PREVENT THEM FROM USING PUBLIC PLACES;
REPRESENT THEM AS RATS THAT CARRY CONTAGION.
PORTRAY THEM AS DAMAGED GOODS;
COMPEL THEM TO WEAR A BADGE;
IDENTIFY THEM AS LESSER THAN HUMAN;
MARK THEIR BUSINESSES
AS FULL OF JEWISH SHAME.
DESTROY THEIR BUSINESSES,
SYNAGOGUES AND HOMES;
ERASE ANY FAME;
IDENTIFY THEM AS LESSER;
AND THE ONES TO BLAME;
CALLOUSLY EXHIBIT THEM;
DESTROY WHAT THEY BUILT;
SHAME THEM, DISPLAYING THEM ON A WALK
IT'S CALLED KRISTALLNACHT!
THEN TO THE GHETTOES
THEN SEPARATE THE WOMEN AND CHILDREN
TO BE MURDERED AS USELESS.
THE REST TO BE WORKED TO DEATH, STARVED,
OR DIE OF A DEBILITATING DISEASE
FROM CONSUMMATELY UNCLEAN CONDITIONS.
THE REST ARE EXTERMINATED BY GAS.
SUCH ANNIHILATION, SUCH HELLATIOUS DEATHS!
WILL NOTHING TAKE OUR BREATH?

SEE YOUR BROTHER THE JEW, LIKE SHEEP TO SLAUGHTER
IN THE MODERN ASSEMBLY LINE OF MASS MURDER.
FEEL THE HORROR THEY MUST HAVE KNOWN
AS LIFE DISAPPEARED WITH EACH GASP
OF POISON AND BURNING GAS
UNTIL DESPERATION GRIPPED THEM AND

AS LUNGS AND HEARTS WERE SEARED AND SEIZED.
HEAR THEIR SCREAMS,
AS DESPERATION TURNED TO MOANS,
AS THEIR DREAMS WERE DEVOURED
AND THEN ... A PERMANENT SILENCE
THAT SIGNALED THE EVIL WAS COMPLETE.
INNOCENCE, BEAUTY, TALENT, BRILLIANCE
AND THE GIFT OF LIFE AND LOVE
AND THE POWER TO CHANGE THE WORLD
BECAME SMOKE, ASHES AND CHIMNEY SOOT.

A FEW MILLION HEARTS STOPPED.
UNTOLD MILLIONS
OF FUTURE DREAMS DID NOT FLY
ON WINGS, NOW WITHOUT HEARTS TO SOAR.

TEN TRILLION BRILLIANT WORDS
AND WONDROUS MUSICAL NOTES
WILL NOT LIFT OUR HEARTS TO THE SKY
AND SET US FREE.

HOW MANY FUTURE GENIUSES TURNED TO ASHES
THAT COULD HAVE SAVED US FROM OURSELVES?
WHO NOW TO LEAD US TO THE PROMISED LAND?
THEIR DEATH BORE ONLY A SAD SILENCE
THAT MUST STALK AND HAUNT OUR SOULS.

WHAT CURTAIN CLOAKS OUR INNER LIGHT
SO WE SEE ONLY OUR OWN SURVIVAL?
WHAT FORM OF AMNESIA WITHOUT ANTIDOTE
BLANKS OUR MEMORY AND NUMBS THE NERVES
TO OUR DYING NEIGHBOR?
HOW CAN WE FORGET
TREBLINKA*, AUSCHWITZ-BIRKENAU*, DACHAU*,
CHELMNO*, SOBIBOR*, BELZEC* AND MAJDANEK*?
IS OUR NATURE THE VERY CULPRIT AND CURSE?
OR HAVE THE FALLEN ANGELS TAKEN CONTROL?
PERCHANCE THE SIN OF ADAM AND EVE?

MAYBE DEMON-GODS HAVE DRAWN THE CURTAIN
BETWEEN THE SOUL'S SOURCE AND THE UNIVERSE
SO WE KNOW AND BELIEVE ONLY

WHAT WE CAN SEE, HEAR AND PROVE.
WHO DREW THE CURTAIN ON THIS SPIRITUAL LIGHT?

WOULD I HAVE RISKED MY LIFE FOR THEM?
WOULD I HAVE RISKED BOTH FAMILY AND FRIEND?
OR HAVE I TOO BEEN DULLED
TO THE MESSAGE OF THE FALLING ASHES?
ARE WE ALL CONDEMNED COWARDS,
CHAINED TO OUR COMFORTABLE EXISTENCE,
BLIND TO THE ASSAULT ON OUR SPIRIT,
DEAF TO THE MUFFLED MOANS BEYOND OUR WALLS?

ARE WE ALL OBLIVIOUS
TO A BESEECHING SMOKE
AND THE IMPLORING RAIN OF ASHES
THAT REACHES OUT OVER TIME
AND TEARS AT OUR SOUL?
THIS SEARCHING SMOKE AND ASHES,
A RESULT OF EVIL, TELL US WE MUST ACT NOW
OR OUR LIVES WILL HAVE MEANT NOTHING.
THEY TELL US THAT IN OUR HANDS
AND IN OUR HEARTS IS THE SOLE SOLUTION.
THE SURVIVAL OF THE EMPATHETIC SPIRIT
IS OUR SINGULAR CONSOLATION.
FAILING OUR INTERCESSION,
LEAVES ONLY OUR SOUL'S RUINATION.

THE ASHES OF JEWS CRY OUT:
THE SOUL'S REDEMPTION IS ACHIEVED
ONLY BY RISKING YOUR LOVE AND YOUR LIFE
FOR THE UNJUSTLY ATTACKED
AND THE UNFAIRLY CONDEMNED.

(Long after I wrote this I discovered I had Jewish ancestors from Spain. In college, I chose to do numerous papers on the Holocaust. For some reason that horrendous event attracted my interest. Could my Jewish ancestors have been speaking through me?)

In Pope Pius XIth Encyclical "With Burning Anxiety", about 'On the Church and The German Reich, written in 1937, the Pope never uses the term National Socialism. Adolf Hitler and the Nazi Party are not named. The effort to produce and distribute over 300,000 copies of the letter was entirely secret. The encyclical does not specifically mention the Jewish people. Although it does condemn the exaltation of one race or blood over another, i.e. racism. This encyclical was somewhat overshadowed by the anti-communist encyclical Divini Redemptoris which was issued on 19, March, 1937 in order to avoid the charge by the Nazis that the Pope was indirectly favoring communism. Please see the entire Encyclical.

See source for the following on the documentary 'the Accountant of Auschwitz' on Netflix:
Auschwitz-Birkenau 1,1000,000 murdered,
Treblinka: 925,000 murdered
Belzec 434,500 murdered
Chelmno 172,000 murdered
Sobibor 167,000 murdered
Majdanek 80,000 murdered
Dachau: 31,951 were murdered

'Only silence is shame'
The Ballad of Saco and Vanzetti
Written and performed by Woody Guthrie and by Joan Baez
Produced by Moe Asch

"I like your Christ, I do not like your Christians. Your Christians are so unlike your Christ."
Mahatma Gandhi.

"No servant can serve two masters, for either he will hate the one and love the other, or he will be devoted to the one and despise the other. You cannot serve God and money." Luke 16:13 ESV

1. *The Greatest Danger is to Ignore Evil in our Midst*

Violent ideologies inflict pain, a materialistic philosophy breeds the love of pleasure in direct contrast to Jesus' counsel, *"Man does not live on bread alone, but on every word that comes from the mouth of God." (Matthew 4:4 KJV)*

The question for me is whether our belief in traditional Christianity is ignoring evil in our midst. In my life, I have come to see a cavernous void between what Jesus has conveyed and what traditional Christianity has told us we must believe. I come up with the same answer Gandhi has given. Christians are so unlike Christ.

To put it in a nutshell, Christianity has become but a soulless appendage and a required garment of our American system. We wear it consistent with the materialism our culture encourages. We do not utilize it as a conscience to filter out evil and seek goodness based on the life and words of Jesus. Whether we call it Slavery, Colonialism, Native American genocide, Manifest Destiny, segregation and racist laws directed towards the black community, Patriotism, 'Just Wars', the Vietnam war, Holy Wars, Capital Punishment, biggest incarcerator in the world, Private penitentiaries, Capitalism or Free Enterprise, we can seem to justify most any evil. We rationalize all of it by claiming how strong our belief in God is. Our actions are secondary or irrelevant next to our 'strong' faith in God.

The fact remains that truly knowing Jesus need have nothing to do with Christianity. The idea that the God of the universe can be bribed with faith, piety, penance, offerings, rituals and traditions has widespread acceptance, and millions are shackled and controlled by the idea, which the clergy easily manipulates.

I submit that tradition and culture are powerful. Fear of being different and the punishments that our religious culture threatens, hellfire or otherwise, is often overwhelming. Combine this with the everyday need to survive, work and raise a family, it is extremely difficult to see the world differently and put those different viewpoints into action.

Certainly, we should recognize that we are destroying the world with pollution. We are benefitting from other's death and disease. This is the critical crisis of mankind's history. Our moral portrait will be determined by what we have painted. Will we create a beautiful masterpiece of love and action to save our beautiful gift? Or will our failure to love and to take action against evil, create a portrait of a nightmare of death, earth's destruction and the decimation of our children and grandchildren?

As far as the environment goes, I believe Pope Francis has stated it brilliantly – Protecting the earth is a moral duty. I submit that we owe it to ourselves, our families, present and future, and to God to take action against what is destroying us.

The evil is to say and do nothing. As the Joan Baez song goes, only silence is shame.

2. TRANSFORMED INTO BUREACRATS OF 'GOD' – Jesus/God Is To Honored and Adored, Not Emulated.

During my Catholic days, (high school), I did receive an invaluable clue about the nature of Catholic Christianity. I did not fully comprehend its meaning until I was transformed by my children, almost a generation afterwards. It came from one of the Cathedral High School priests, a lesson, I am sure, he didn't intend to teach me. I had asked father 'unnamed' why he was here teaching us and not out helping the poor like Jesus did. He told me that Jesus was God and he, (father unnamed), was a mere human. He could and should not aspire to do what only God could do.*

This caused me much dissonance at the time but I was not sure why. It took me most of my life to finally figure out what this truly meant. His 'excuse' for not doing God's work, as Jesus did, explains how so many could believe that 'praying', strongly believing, absolutely trusting, tolerating injustice around us, living a life incompatible with Jesus' words, was acceptable and not inconsistent with going to Heaven.

Not emulating Jesus, had now become justified. Much like Adam and Eve's ouster from the Garden of Eden for eating from the tree of Knowledge, I was being told that it was evil to try to act like God.

Acting God-like Equals Lesser Government Control. Consonant with this notion, the Church has to sell the masses on the idea that honoring, worshipping and praying to this God is the most important thing. And here is the reality of the priest's point - To actually require the masses to emulate this Supreme Being would somehow lessen His greatness and Godness. If we could actually do what Jesus-God did, he must not be so amazing. Lesser humans acting God-like means lesser control by a church/empire.

This explains to me why so many could live by praying and adoring God, instead of striving to do the good works that He did. This is why, for me, it is offensive to believe as the Lutheran church I attended, believed, that you did not need good works to get into Heaven. (See Ch.10, WRECKING ON THE HUBRIS ICEBERG where I address this issue.)

The Pagan Problem. A variation of this 'control' problem is an empire that would have numerous gods. By transforming Jesus and the 'Father', into 'the one true God, the powers-that-be, had one God, through whom they could mollify and control the whims of the masses by channeling them through one set of beliefs. It is much easier to control the masses when you have one object of honor and control. Just as you would not want 'Kings' in every town, you do not want a bunch of pagan gods whose beliefs compete with a one-male-God belief and conflict with the control of your empire/country. One God equals control. Many gods make control, supervision and brainwashing a problem. You gotta get rid of all these divisive gods! There is no power in division.

Jesus God? Moreover you have to somehow transform Jesus into one and the same as Jehovah God. Constantine the Great managed to do this and my Catholic mentors did the same through the 'Trinity',(three persons in one God), which was a source of much questioning for me.

Killing for God. The above is from the vantage point of the ruler/leader. How about from the vantage point of the masses. To me, the above explains a culture whose entire system is antithetical to 'loving thy neighbor and turning the other cheek. As long as you have an unadulterated and strong belief in the one God and all the particular beliefs that the particular church has brainwashed, I mean, educated you with, you get into Heaven. That is control! Loving thy neighbor becomes secondary to absolute faith in the 'trinity' God. This way of thinking is quite helpful when you need to take a country to war. Love thy neighbor easily takes a backseat to fighting for God and Country against the godless enemy. The patriotic directive from the Catholic pulpit, during the Vietnam War, to "Support Your Troops", now makes sense.

Father 'nameless' had clarified why and how Judeo Christianity believes that words, (prayers and faith), speak louder than actions. We, mere humans, cannot emulate God, but just pray for direction and honor His Godness. 'Goodness' is thus rendered subordinate to the belief in God.

The priest was living by the belief: Justification by Faith Alone: 'For by grace you have been saved through faith; and that not of yourselves, it is the gift of God; not as a result of works, so that no one may boast.'(See Ephesians 2:8-9 NIV)

CHAPTER IX

DON'T ALLOW YOUR GIFTS TO BE STIFLED BY THE WORLD

A. Catholic School

If I had a song
I'd sing it in the morning
I'd sing it in the evening
All over this land
I'd sing out danger
I'd sing out a warning
I'd sing out love between
My brothers and my sisters....
written by
Pete Seeger and Lee Hays
Sung by Trini Lopez and Peter, Paul and Mary, among others

Yo soy un hombre sincero   *I am a sincere man*
de donde crece la palma   *from the land of the palm tree*
Y antes de murirme quiero   *And before I die, I want*
echar mis versos de alma   *to share the poetry of my soul*

Mi verso es un verde claro.   *My words are a clear green*
y de un carmin' encendido   *and a fiery red*
Mi verso es de un cierro herrido   *My poetry is of a wounded doe*
que buscan el monte amparo...   *that seeks refuge in the mountain...*

Written by Cuban poet Jose' Marti
Composed by Josito Fernandez
From the lyrics of *Guantanamera*
Sung by Pete Seeger and The Sandpipers, *amongst others*

THE ROOTLESS WANDERINGS OF THE LOPEZ TREE

From 'secret', to Catholic believer, to skeptic, to science-based, to evidence-based, to rationalist, to 'meism' and finally to a 'child-inspired' view of the world.

In this essay, I attempt to examine the unique and hopefully entertaining paths, the gifts and curses along the way, that all contributed to the philosophy of this book.

I made my ignominious entrance into the world in 1950, at the Cradle Home, (Orphanage Adoption Agency), in Santa Fe, NM. My birth mother relinquished me, though she secretly carried me in her tummy, apparently well tucked away, during her wedding. I had been given the name of 'Eloy'. My purported birth-father's name was Dave. I was curious why I was given the name of 'Eloy'. So I asked my birth mother how she came upon the name 'Eloy'. She said that it was the name of an old boyfriend. Mmmm! (I have not yet done a DNA test but that will be for another book.)

From Well-Kept Secret to a Skeptic. Is this scenario how skeptics are shaped? A covered-up belch, a returned purchase of a dress that is no longer stylish, an embarrassing faux pas? This 'mistake' entered into the world belonging to no one and denied by all, lest the pregnant-before-marriage mother is discovered and accused of a mortal sin and stained for life. (Not even her husband's name, the purported father, was on the relinquishment document.) Now why would he not want anyone to know that he too was giving me up? Or can you relinquish what is not yours?

So well-kept was this 'secret', that one of the brothers of my birth-mother, upon being told that I was Molly's child, responded incredulously – I am her brother! I would have known if she had a child! I guess he thought I was an imposter who was trying to scam the family. I think his daughters finally convinced him that I was for-real. I guess my birth mother knows how to keep a secret.

Take him back! From documents I obtained at Public Employees Retirement Association of New Mexico (PERA), I discovered that a military family had 'adopted' me and took me to California to reside. Then the adopting male brought me back to the Cradle Home and said that his wife had become ill and was no longer able to take care of me. My family (Wife and children), get a big kick out of this story, particularly when I become 'annoying'. 'See! We are not the only ones that can't put up with you!' Wow! How do I win an argument after being twice given up? Must be a defective product!

Seriously, I often wonder, if I would have developed differently in a military family. My family, (the Lopez's), even though infected with the biases of their time, (Catholicism, Militarism and trusting government), they gave me a great deal of leeway to think my own thoughts. Other than the publication of "The Atheist", they probably were not aware what I was thinking. Athletics was the distraction from the more important issues of the day. It was also the glue that held the Lopez family together.

I also wonder how I might have turned out if I were raised by the Romeros – the father, a no-nonsense businessman and a mother who was a Masters-educated fourth-grade teacher and a devout Catholic. I suspect control and appearances were the priorities. My 'relinquishment' is the best clue I have as to how it would have gone. I shudder to think how my questioning attitude would have been handled by a dogmatic Catholic worried about appearances and a 'bottom-line businessman. I would have been in trouble!

Skeptics Don't Trust! Back to what did happen. Ultimately, this well-hidden and 'ugly secret', became a skeptic and thrown into a world of true believers. The true believers were my family, the Catholic school, students, teachers and a generation that believed what they were told. And they were told that the Catechism/Bible God was smack dab in the middle of this picture; that you should always believe and trust your government; that appearances were more important than reality and secrets more important than honesty. What the world told you about yourself was more important than who you truly were. Any expression of doubt about the status quo was met with reprimands, separation and derision. What a world!

I early-on realized that my uneasiness and disconnectedness was related to a consuming need to discover the truth about who I was, the world I lived in and how a Judeo Christian God did or did not fit. Catholic school was just not answering the questions that I had. This need to know was fueled by a deep skepticism that revealed itself more often as I got older.

During my younger years I worked at accepting the Catholic beliefs and attempted to abide by their tenets – mostly reciting a lot of 'Hail Marys', 'Our Fathers' and 'Acts of Contrition'. It was all I knew.

Even during my younger years, there was a strong undertow that was eating away at the very foundation of all I was taught. It would take a Notre Dame-trained high school teacher and a Catholic Daughters of America poetry contest to reveal the skeptic I now know I was. These two events, (I address below), were the final waves that washed away the last philosophical grain of sand to reveal that my entire view of the world and life was built on nothing but sand.

The Lecture. The time was the eleventh grade of Cathedral High school. The teacher was the Notre-Dame trained Pat Graham. He also happened to be my track coach. This incomparable teacher's topic of the lecture was something he might have been fired for if the principal had found out: Science vs. Catholic theories/the source of our being. (I am sure that wasn't actually the identified title and I am sure he didn't pass out any handouts on the topic. It was an English class. On second thought, the Catholic schools were so desperate for teachers, maybe they were just happy to have him, regardless of his liberal bent.)

Just because it was English, Coach Graham did not limit himself to any particular topic. Everything was fair game. We were discussing matter and energy in English class! I asked: "Does not everything have to begin somewhere?" Coach Graham's answer was No! In 1905, Einstein had brilliantly revealed through E=MC2 that energy and matter were not separate but all part of the same eternal dance. Matter and energy are in a constant cycle and... here was the kicker - they were eternal. No one had to create either of them. Matter and energy did not necessarily need a beginning or a creator.*

As far as I was concerned, I had split the philosophical atom. The God conundrum had been solved. The release of intellectual energy changed the direction of my life. So much for the traditional and comfortable belief that there must exist a God because He had to have created everything. If "everything" was always there, you did not need a God to create it. This is what nature did, and needed no help. The argument that *there was a God because someone had to start it,* that Dom 'the bomb' submitted as 'proof' of God, was now resolved in my favor. Nature did not need the help of a God! Catholics, who were afraid of the Bible, unless it suited their agenda, had apparently not indoctrinated me sufficiently in the creation story and God's central role therein. Einstein's great scientific discovery had now erased the need for a God, at least as far as I had understood it.

In a few words, my intellectual tether to God was lopped off. God made so much sense when you believed there had to be someone who started it all. Now that was all gone and I was adrift in a philosophical world where most everyone was firmly tied to a belief in God. Belief in God became purely a 'faith' thing. And I was not very good at that game. All those years of Catholic school down the drain! On the other hand, the door had been opened to experience the world through different lenses. What lenses would that be? Would the discovery of E=MC2 lead to a Hiroshima or a Nagasaki in my own life?

The Poem. It was tenth grade and the class was English, taught by the elderly but still witty and incomparable Sister Helen Francis. She looked and acted as if we were mere babies who were foolish not to hang on her every word. Now that I think of it, she was right. But I was too cool and aloof to appreciate her value to me. Besides, she was so ancient that she had taught my father and his brothers, at this same school. Moreover, what value could English Literature and poetry have for me? It did not help me more powerfully hit a baseball, more accurately shoot a basketball or run faster in track. As you can see, I was hardly an intellectual!

The assignment was to write a religious poem. It was motivated by a yearly contest sponsored by the Catholic Daughters of America, a group of Catholic females who encouraged religious poetry. They all must have assumed that the poem would be something consistent with our religious training. However, I recall no specific directive to that effect. In addition, the winner would have their poem published in *Sermons In Poetry,* a book containing the poems of all the winners across the country. (I later discovered most everyone that submitted a poem, had their poem inserted into the book.) Moreover, we would have the admiration of everyone who thought poetry was important. I was to later discover that did not include too many people.

I recall reading many of the poems that made their way into this Catholic Daughters of America book. They were all wonderful, loving and simple poems about angels, saints, God's love, goodness, Heaven and so on. The kind of ideas and 'inspiration' you would expect out of tenth-graders in a Catholic school in a Catholic Daughter of America Poetry contest. The substance of what I was to write was not to be pretty, as far as Catholic dogma went.

I had never written a poem before and it all seemed kind of frivolous. But for some reason this assignment piqued my interest. I wrote my poem, submitted it, and lo and behold, I actually won or qualified to have my poem go in the book! This story would have no significance except the topic I chose was "The Atheist":

THE ATHEIST

WHERE IS THIS GOD THAT YOU TELL ME ABOUT?
WHERE IS HIS DWELLING? I'VE NOT SEEN HIM ABOUT.
WHAT MAKES YOU BELIEVE WHEN LIFE TREATS YOU THIS WAY?
WHAT PROOF OF A GOD DO YOU HAVE WHEN YOU PRAY?
NONE BUT A DEATH, TWO THOUSAND YEARS PASSED.
THE WRITINGS OF MEN WHOSE LIFE-SPAN HAS ELAPSED.
YOU SAY THERE IS A LIFE AFTER THIS ONE.
THERE IS ONLY ONE LIFE AND THEN YOU ARE DONE. *

Effect. I will never know for sure how the teacher interpreted what this poem said about me and my faith. Maybe they interpreted it as a sad commentary on the Godless view of the atheist. Maybe they saw it for what it was - a not so subtle attack on basic Catholic beliefs. This would account for the less-than-loving treatment I later received from most of the penguins and priests that claimed to be my educators. It might have been worse but for my dad's sister (Sister Lucina), being one of the teachers.

The Meaning. I now see what I wrote as my first step in a search for God and his love, an affair that would truly begin by my poem, or as I view it now, tugging at the ponytail of God. It must have been a long ponytail or there was too much slack, because it took years to get a reaction. But importantly, the medium had now been discovered - poetry would be my connection to the divine and ultimately, my children the inspiration.

Although, at the time, because of the nature of the poem, (The Atheist), it appeared I had cut the connection with God. Indeed, it now seems that religious dogma failed in its attempts to connect me to the Catholics' view of God. But this was just the first step in a lifelong search. Science, rationalism and 'meism' were to take its place in the next few years as I went through college and law school.

But these 'educational' vehicles also failed to put me any closer to the light of God's wisdom. I would have to await the deluge and drenching of divine brilliance that later streamed through my being when my children arrived. It seems my children's journey here, opened up, for the first time for me, a pathway, a portal, a window, allowing the light of God to pass through me and reflect back to the Divine. It was as if Heaven's womb gave birth to another me via my offspring.

The Skeptic Finds Love. The above events, (my adoption, the lecture and the poem), established or revealed an important part of my nature - I was a skeptic in search of the truth but without the right tools or the correct utilization of the tools, to do the search. Obviously, the beliefs I had been taught all my life did not satisfy my need to understand. "The Atheist" had put into question Heaven, the Messiah, prayer, and the notion of immortality. This began the questioning and the emptiness. Until the birth of Ali', the puzzle was incomplete and my soul was lacking. In fathering and raising Ali' and Amadeo, something changed inside me. It has to do with an ability to care. The gnawing emptiness has since been filled with love, joy, creativity and focus.

Finding 'God'. In a different sense, I rediscovered God in the eyes and being of my two little children. Through their innocent eyes I could peer deeply into the soul and catch a glimpse of God and it was to be found in the natural world. 'God' would ultimately not be proven but rather experienced through the miracle of birth and the resulting love of a father for his children. Experiencing the miracle of children transformed me to experience the miracle of nature and my intricate connection thereto.

Just as the female nature of Sophia, (the Gnostics and some mystics' embodiment of wisdom), entices them to God, the experience of the birth of my daughter and my relationship with her, inspired my movement back into God's light. And this light brightly illuminated the beauty around me. It allowed me to peer into the future and see the destruction of all that I was now connected to.

Children-Inspired. For the most part, my children inspired this book. What I wrote came through a different person. Never before had I written so much in so short a period. All somehow motivated, not merely because of my new role, but because of a changed nature. Emotionally and intellectually, I was able to see what I could not before the birth experience. The complete significance of Ali' and Amadeo did not become fully apparent until I put all the letters and poems together for this book. As I reviewed them, the pieces fit and I saw the picture of my transition and transmogrification. From distant and external-God-centered, to me-centered and finally to child-centered. The glorious presence of 'God' had come into my life.

My being had finally been altered to allow me to see my place in the universe and in all of time. A dark veil had been lifted and light could shine in, (Perhaps the light of the Holy Spirit…) *(See Chapter I - "Let The Children Take Your Heart")* As a transmitter is blocked because it is on the dark side of the moon, the emergence of the Lopez spacecraft from night's shadow, into the light has enabled me to transmit. I can make contact with the spiritual side of my being. (*See Chapter III A:* "THE APPEARANCES OF THE VIRGIN MARY AND HER MESSAGE. WHAT DOES IT MEAN?)

Time Running Out Equals Inspiration. Fatherhood apparently does nothing for many. I suspect being fatherless for 10 years of marriage, turning 40, doubting we could reproduce and finally having children, all combined to change me and bring inspiration. The specter of time running out is inspirational, in and of itself. *(See Chapter III - "Rejected Letter of Ali's Birthday Invitation").* Combine it with the living breathing incarnation of your own seed and the nativity message is reborn in me. There can be no better antidote to the de-edificating, debilitating and de-motivating power of the faithless skeptic's nagging doubt about why we are here.

Blasphemous as it may sound to some, I had finally found the little baby Jesus, the gift of universal hope, inspiration, energy and focus in the conception and birth of my children. I had never fully comprehended or even thought much about the power of bringing a child into the world. *(See Chapter III - "Christmas Message")* I was awestruck and still am. How could one plus one equal so much more? But through Ali' and Amadeo I became as close to immortal as is humanly possible. Or better said, I would now live forever through them and their offspring.

Immortality through Children. Through my kids, I had become a part of and connected with the future. Through them I was given a second chance to do better and be more than I could have ever been without them. We have no permanent or secure place in the universe until we know our genes have a foothold, so to speak, in the soil of the great gene pool of history. As the mountain climber is secured by the peg of the climber above him and he, by the peg of the climber above him and all of them to the pegs of the climbers below, (my ancestors), I am now secure to pursue the climb to the mountain top, knowing that we are all in this climb tethered and secured together. *(See Chapter III A - "Seedlings Sleep at Twilight")* Pre-children, I felt I was the sole climber. But now, as part of my being through my children, there exists a foothold above me on the mountainside. That part of me will reach the mountaintop and pull others to the top. Death now loses its great power over my soul. For in my genes, must also go a part of my soul, or my unique life force, the better part in younger, more vibrant, more brilliant bodies and minds. *(See Chapter V - "My Light")*

I was now given the opportunity to do whatever was needed to prepare my children for the journey, particularly to teach them why and how the journey should be made. *(See Chapter II A - "Jump Rope Song")*

This then is my unique and personal journey of leaping over the pitfalls of conformity, bounding over the barriers to becoming, ignoring the attraction of popularity, avoiding being hooked on the lure of things and money and searching deeply within, to find my unique route to self-discovery. This book then, is that bright flag, finally unfurling, to reveal children inspired truths.

*And for those who subscribe to the notion that the 'Big Bang' started it and suggest there was a beginning. Cosmologist Alexander Vilenkin believes the Big Bang wasn't a one-off event, but merely one of a series of big bangs creating an endless number of bubble universes.

* According to the book into which my poem was accepted, it stated: 'The best of these are in the first selection of the poetry book...' Mine was in the last pages of the second part of the book. Oh well! Considering that my topic was the antithesis of faith and God, I was probably fortunate that it was even published. Now that I look at it, fifty years later, It seems less poetry and more a legal statement of an issue that happens to rhyme. (See my comments at the l beginning of the book.)

FIRST COMMUNION NIGHTMARE REVISITED

STILL WORLD OF SLEEP LIES STEEPED IN FEAR
DEVOURED BY A SEA OF EVIL, FED FROM HADE'S SPHERE.
WHERE DEEP IS FRAUGHT WITH FIEND AND FREAK,
WHERE HATE IS STRONG, ALMIGHTY WEAK.

IF I AM DROWNING AT NIGHT IN DEMON SEA,
NOVENA TO SAINT JUDE, PRAY FOR ME.
GODSPEED SHOWER HOLY LIGHT.
LIFT ME FROM BEELZEBUB'S BLIGHT!

FIRST-COMMUNION EVE, I LAY FROZE IN DREAD.
BED TURNED TOMB, BODY TURNED LED.
WHAT DEED DARE DRIVE DEMONS TO RUN?
AMUCK, UNLOOSED, SWIRLING AS ONE.

FOUL FORMS DESCEND, VILE WITHOUT END.
SWOOPING CLOSER, RISING AGAIN.
HELL'S DORMANT SOULS, NOW REVENANT,
FULFILLING UNKNOWN COVENANT.

ON PRISTINE BED, ONCE SAFE AND SECURE
AN INVERTED CROSS, HELL'S SIGNATURE.
EYES SKIM IN FEAR, DAMNED EVIL ADRIFT!
CHRIST SYMBOL STRIPPED OF SAVIOR'S GIFT.

GOD PIERCE BLACK PALL WITH LIGHT OF LOVE!
HAIL FIERY TONGUES ON WINGS OF DOVE.
DRENCH DREAD DEMONS WITH DAWN'S LIGHT.
FREE ME FROM FEARED CURSE OF NIGHT!

MOM, HEAR YOUR CHILD'S PLEA, FEEL HIS PAIN!
RESCUE ME FROM LUCIFER'S REIGN!
IN WHAT DARK DEPTHS WAS MY SOUL LINED?
OR CHANGELING'S SOUL AND I MERE RIND?

THOUGH DARKNESS SURELY BORE THIS BANE,
WHAT SACRELIGION WOULD EXPLAIN?
WHY I'M IN HELL THIS HOLY EVE?
WHAT DEED TO DRIVE THE DIVINE TO LEAVE?

FROM HADE'S BOWELS PRAYED MORN IS BORN,
SECURED BY CROSS'S UPRIGHT FORM,
GOD NAILED TO WOOD, WHAT IRONY!
PLEADING: WHY HAS THOU FORSAKEN ME?

THE RANKLED SHEEP BLUES RAP
OR
DEFEATED BY THE RELIGIOUSISMS

He is smothered by the smell of wool that surrounds him on all sides and by the pressing of silent and baying sheep against his soul-being as they zombie-like sleep-walk in rows by the hundreds of thousands. Some proceed to the precipice, some to the slaughter house and some to the gigantic confines of Christian corrals, to wait for apocalypse, the rapture and redemption.

Theirs is to accept without questioning, to listen without hearing, to watch without seeing, to know without understanding, to do without thinking and ultimately to throw their hands to the sky in sweet surrender to the 'God-is-all-powerfulisms', 'you-must-fear-Godisms' or otherwise 'they-will-go-to-hellisms', sweetly sold to the subservient, submittingly singing the syrupy sounds of Amazing Grace.

The smell of think-less dogma, devoid of catma, Ratma and Mahatma, wafts and permeates the hordes of herds and overwhelm the gnawing need to ask the nagging questions of why and how could God not love "them", the true believers, best? The Savior died so we can live, bark the circus carny, sheepdog agents of shouting shepherding pastors, righteous priests, speech-making soul-seeking evangelists. We are sold that: If you tithe, you will not writhe, but receive eternal life.

Yea! But what about the life of Jesus, his walk, his lessons, sessions, obsessions, lack of possessions, hate condemnation, war revulsion, his hippie communism, anti-capitalism, social welfarism, spiritual egalitarianism, poor-people promising heavenly election and anti-wealthism?

Is anybody seeing the full picture? No!!!!! His Father sacrificed the life of His perfect Son so we can be saved, is the stock response the clean-brained masses shout in solemn and scary unison. But how he loved and what He said about living – does this count for something, cry the seekers of truth?

These resounding triumphant truths of spiritualism and goodness are diligently drowned out by our Savior-obsessive, anal-retentive, animal sacrificial barbarisms of God-pleasing speechisms and ancient-tribal-neatly–categorized ritualism which now have become sacred-rites-to-get-to-Heavenisms.

The path to their Christian God is filled with the vulgar, violent, Constantine-co-opted "holy crucifix" ornament of His death, the cross miraculously appearing in the sky, per Constantine's eye, etched onto the 'Holy War' sword, winning the battle, and the last thing they saw before the enemy died. It is now dangled above doors, draped around naïve necks, touted at every stop-sign and stop-light of every corridor of the cowardly Catholic Christian compartmentalized and one-way mind.

The Christian roads and routes to soul-filled spiritual streets are blocked by cul-de-sacs of correction, blockades, off-limits signs, Christian computer filters, thick dogmatic walls of protective derision and "they versus us" moralism that is inviolable, unbroachable, insurmountable and unscalable by climbers, spelunkers, sailors of reason, logic and love.

Their fortresses stand surrounded, guarded, protected and armed by the vigilant guards of bible-thumping, evangelical bowing, kowtowing Rollers of Holy and black-robed frumpy friars of faith-is-all-you-needism. They stand and kneel fully drenched and dipped in the powerful liquid of deodorization and devil-bug extermination that dries to a solid coat of dogmatic I-know-what-is-rightism. They are fully injected and holy pill regimented with the Christian anti-inflammatory and antibiotic that kills and reduces the swelling of the "whys", the "hows" and the "how comes", that occasionally appear as bumps, bruises, rashes and lesions on the pallid skin of "Christian morality". No warning appears on the container that these beliefs were created by those who wanted to control them and formulated when science and reason were non-existent.

The "I-am-saved" blinders and "you are not" sun glasses guard them from the glare of the world of brilliant lights that they fear may luridly lure, snag and devour an unwary soul-starved swimmer sallying carelessly into the piranha-filled ocean bowl of the tempter-world.

But they see only through the Scriptural Book as filtered through the American-flag-wrapped-lenses that inexorably find interpretation through Old Testament lenses which always read that the United States of America is the new chosen people and to do what we please, for it is God's undeniable will. Other interpreters need not apply.

God blessed us. Manifest Destiny is our mantra. We can do no evil. Manifest Destiny justified the genocide of the "savages" that dared to live on our land in the way of our expansion and prosperity. We kidnapped black non-Christian families from their country, generously and with no charge, gave them a murderous ship-ride to a life of slavery – all needed to make an economic system work and winked at by "good Christians."

Jesus! Wake these somnolent and sleepwalking sheep! They are dangerous to themselves and to us. Their numbers are scary. They are a perfect meal for pandering politicians. All the politician has to proclaim is I have found Jesus and the lambs will stampede towards them. After that, anything that the leaders tell them, they will follow blindly, be it war, racism, incarceration or the death penalty.

The "true believer" speaks not of contradictions though they stand like barbwire in the horizons of reason and love. But who dares to say God's book is unclear or ambiguous, lest the wrath of the Bible-quoting clerics condemn you for committing a sacrilege and shun you, unless you repent.

Does not love trump faith as Christians are told in Galatians? Should not the path of love that Jesus walked, be our model rather than our level of faith in a political inspired, Constantine-created, dissenter banishing, Nicene Creed caricature of a God belief? In this biblical bigotry of blather, love loses to faith most every time. This so-called world of God could not be God-inspired. This cookie-cutting, fast-food-fixing hamburger restaurant makes it only one way which becomes the ego-centrism of us-and-theyism, that translates into support-your-troop-isms of wars and tramples the intent of the words: "turn the other cheek." To live by the sword, we die by the sword and the hatred and violence that we sow, we will reap, because our sheep-filled and thought-less religion will righteously and blindly herd us all to the precipice where, after we have destroyed our planet, we, our children and grandchildren, will, by force of their numbers, fall to their deaths.

Please, please stop blindly following these sheep!

B. SEARCH FOR THE REAL MIRACLES

WHERE ARE THE MIRACLES?

As a boy attending Catholic school, I grew up inundated with stories of miracles—the many that Jesus and the Blessed Mother performed; the transubstantiation that purportedly occurs at the mass when the water and wine become the body and blood of Jesus Christ and the multitude of miracles performed by the Saints. That is how they became Saints. Wow! (Sorry about St. Christopher and his buddies – all those St. Christopher medals, now just mere rabbit's feet. Some miraculous happenings were just too fairy tale-ish to be true – A giant carrying people across a river. Yeah right!) In all fairness, there were men who existed that had a disease, (Gigantism), that caused them to be giants and plausibly carried people across rivers. But that is no miracle.

Bombarded with tales of miracles through history and all around me, you would think I could appreciate the existence of miracles. But I just could not! After all, I had never personally experienced the miraculous. Miracles were always something that happened to everyone else in times gone by or, so subtle, I could not be sure it even happened. For example, in the Catholic communion, the blessed hosts and wine, were miraculously transformed into the body and blood of Christ. I guess only the priest could determine if the wine tasted miraculously better. Did it have a touch of a blood taste? If the host was the body of Christ, Christ must have been pretty tasteless. You would think maybe the host would glow or make you float in the air after you consumed it. (I know the Altar boy ringing the bell was the signal a miracle was happening.) But it was just too subtle a change for me. Hey, it was just pancaked bread without leaven. Yeah, we weren't supposed to chew it or it would be a sin. But where was the miracle? I later discovered that a few of the priests were 'alcoholics. So, for them, maybe the taste of wine was heavenly. But, having no addiction to bread, the transformed host did not taste any different.

Others would tell me about miracles. For example, I had a friend who was a police officer who became an investigator after he left the District Attorney's office. He told me he had gone to Lourdes and claimed that after looking up at the sun for a long while, it began to spin wildly and began to fall from the sky. Hmmm! I'm guessing part of the sun must have hit him in the head.

In the retina-damaged eye of the beholder, maybe the sun spun wildly and fell from the sky. I can tell you that after he told me that, I stopped recommending this guy. Do I want an investigator that stares into the sun and swears he sees it fall out of the sky? Do I want a witness like him? I must imagine that this investigator would likely face the following kind of cross examination by the other attorney: Mr. Investigator: Do you believe you did a thorough investigation to come to the conclusions you arrived at? Investigator. *Yes, absolutely.* You have faith in those conclusions? *Yes sir.* In fact, you are not prone to draw conclusions based on faith alone. *That is right!* Did you ever travel to Lourdes? *Yes. But that has nothing to do with this case!* In fact, you claimed to see the sun spin wildly and fall out of the sky? *Well.....Yes.* In fact you told that to numerous people? *Yes.* Now the next day the sun was still in the sky. *Uhhh....Yes.* After this incident at Lourdes, you never saw or heard reports from anyone that pieces of the sun had hit the earth? *No.* So how long did you stare into the sun? *Long enough to see it spin and fall out of the sky.* Did you wear special glasses that kids and adults use to watch an eclipse? *Uh....No.* Why do you think physicians unanimously advise not to look directly into the sun without protective glasses? *To avoid damage to your eyes?* Why do you think doctors unanimously recommend special eye protection in an eclipse of the sun? *The same reason?* Did you think it might be dangerous to look directly into the sun? *Nobody else had any protection on!* And they too saw the sun spin wildly and fall out of the sky. *Yes.* Are you familiar with all the effects of persistently looking into the sun? *I don't know...* And you still believe you saw the sun spin wildly and fall to the earth? *Yes.* And do you feel as strongly about what you saw at Lourdes as you do about your conclusions of your investigation in this case. *Yes.* Thank you, Mr. Investigator. No more questions. *

I guess when you believe strongly enough, anything becomes a miracle. I remember when I was younger we went to Mora, New Mexico, where we were told that Jesus appears outside the church. So, my sister, her friend and I traveled to what, at the time, was the poorest county in the nation. I envisioned a large group of people standing around and suddenly a light from the sky would appear in front of a wall of the church and everyone would see Godly figures, as in three-D. Well it wasn't like that.

We went and arrived in Mora when the sun had gone down. We went to the church. There was a light directed to a part of the wall, not one from out of the sky. It was a normal lamped light on a wooden post. So we moved around to a position to see this 'apparition'. Well indeed, I saw on the wall, figures, one resembling Jesus, some figures resembling sheep and etched figures on the wall that could have been apostles. This visual was right there on the stucco wall with the light shining at just the right angle. (Curiously my sister saw the devil as she had often seen in her closet at night.) The 'apparition' did not speak to us, bless us or give us any predictions about the future.

I was curious, so I walked around the side of the church, where I witnessed not-so-perfect crosses, etched in the side walls that you could see if a light was shining at the right angle. Maybe a lesser god of sorts did these! But the 'apparition' of Jesus in the front was impressive. This was an artist obviously knowledgeable in the effects of light on deftly-carved stucco. But a miracle......I just didn't see it.

In a small corner of my little skeptical mind, I would have loved to experience a miracle or see something that I could not explain by natural causes. Then maybe, everything that my Catholic teachers and priests were telling me would make sense. However, the Mora 'Apparition", Jesus or devil, was not more than a poor towns' way of bringing folks in. Kudos to the artist, but he/she was not supernatural.

It would be quite reassuring to be part of a group that either do miracles, witness miracles or are somehow connected to miraculous acts. Add faith in a creator to this favored group and you become part of the group that goes to Heaven and not hell. The stakes were high! Non-believers in miracles risked the eternal fires of hell. Choosing whatever needed to be done to go to Heaven was the inescapable choice. Being an Atheist or non-believer did not seem to have much popularity in my small world. And almost no one wants to be shunned. The saying: 'When you have God, you are never alone' strikes me as a saying for people that are afraid to be alone. They might have to think or look inward. They may not like where it leads them. These are fearful people. These are church-folk. They saw miracles. I did not.

I suppose they meant that with God or the saints, you always have someone to talk to. Curiously Catholics were not much for talking to God, at least the way I normally communicate. We mostly just prayed the standard 'Our Father' (The Lord's Prayer), Hail Mary, Apostle's Creed, Act of Contrition, the Rosary and the Sign of the Cross. I do not recall ever communicating with anyone human by reciting some rote verse. This smacked more of faith verses required by a bureaucracy. Hardly normal communication.

(There was one cool prayer that I don't think was part of the liturgy – The St. Anthony prayer: *St. Anthony, St. Anthony, please look around. Something is lost and it must be found.* It used to work –we found stuff, but not for the reasons they told us. I think it gave us focus.) I also recall making the sign of the cross in Little League right before I went to home plate to bat. Indeed, I had a very high batting average and made the All Stars two years in a row. Was it God or was I the product of a Semi-professional baseball player/dad-coach? My dad once mentioned that when he played ball, and they won, he would wear the same socks for the next game. I asked if he washed them. He told me that might wash the 'good luck' out of them. Mmm! In those days, at least in my community, there seemed to be a fine line between superstition and miracles.

All of these liturgical prayers were directed at making it clear that God, the Virgin Mary and the saints were in charge, not us.*1 We were subject to their control and God's all-knowing, all-seeing plan. It was not for us to know what that was. We all just thankfully accepted the consequences and knew if we obeyed the Catholic rules to Heaven and avoided those sins that sent us to Hell and Purgatory, we would arrive at the Pearly Gates at our end. But did it bring us something miraculous. I didn't see it.

Maybe I wasn't praying right? In my middle years I joined a Fundamentalist church. Maybe I would actually learn how to 'talk' to 'God'. This church had folks that spoke in tongues revealing God's message. The church even had interpreters for the 'tongue speakers'. That is because, to the rest of us, it sounds like gibberish. The interpreter told us what God was saying through the person speaking in tongues. A miracle? Quite entertaining but I had a concern that the 'interpreter' was not credible, just versed in saying what was acceptable in the church. I could be wrong. She was a very intelligent woman.

For me, when I tried to talk with God and listen for His answer, the response sounded and felt like a familiar inner voice talking back,... my own! However, I think that was an improvement over nobody talking back. At the very least, I was having a conversation with myself, hopefully a higher part of my being. I think it was probably a good exercise in getting to know oneself, but miraculous? No.

Looking back, I was not seeking scientific proof before I believed. I just wanted to experience a miracle. Just as the apostles experienced Jesus appearing and being with them after his crucifixion, I wanted to see, hear, touch, smell or taste a miracle. I was a doubting Thomas, I guess. Yes, I was not the accept-what-they-told-you kind of child. But it just never happened. No miracles for me.

Many of my classmates, inspired/brainwashed by the nuns and priests, were quick to identify most anything as miracles – the beauty of the universe and how perfect it was. (In an Intelligent Design sort of way, it is pretty awesome and amazing! It is difficult for we humans to imagine this complicated existence as the result of an accident.) Classmates and teachers would claim a miracle when they would ask God for something and, lo and behold, it was given to them. I suspect their stories were akin to those that gamblers tell – you only hear the winning stories. Never how much they lost. And of course, the church had an explanation for not getting what you ask for – If you did not get what you ask for it was because it was not part of God's plan and that plan, we could never comprehend. I grew weary of being told that whatever they (our Catholic mentors) could not explain was a mystery or you had to take it on faith. Or if you can't accept it, go to the public school. It all seemed like an insult to me and everyone else, i.e., If you can't understand what we are telling you, there must be something wrong with you!

My Church school mentors, of course would tell us about the daily miracle in mass of the transubstantiation – the water, wine and host (unleavened bread), transforming into the body and blood of Christ. There was that "faith" thing again. It was a miracle because the priests and nuns told us it was. To me it seemed perfect for a good comedy skit. (Watch me make this invisible rabbit appear out of this hat. Whalla! Trust me! The rabbit is appearing. You mortals just can't see it!)

Was anybody else buying this? Apparently most all of my colleagues were good at suspending judgment. TV and the movies had trained us well at this. Maybe for me, these guys, (old priests and nuns) were just bad actors or poorly cast. How do you suspend judgment if Moses is being played by Peewee Herman or the Virgin Mary looks like a cross between a sumo-wrestler and the wicked witch? For whatever reason, I wasn't buying it.

Or maybe I was hypersensitive to being conned because of my status as an adopted child? You know….always wary of peoples' motives. Whatever it was, I could not ever feel fully comfortable having my mind controlled by purported miracles that I did not experience. You would know or feel differently about a miracle, wouldn't you? I just never felt it. While others around me saw trees turn into snakes or their guardian angel materializing to them or worse, my sister always seeing the devil in the closet, I saw nothing of the sort. I did not experience one single miracle.

This non-accepting state of mind persisted through adolescence and adulthood until the conception of my daughter, Ali'. Alas, my first miracle was unfolding. The transubstantiation was going on in me. A heart of stone softened to become pliable, sensitive and infused with new life. I could feel. I felt love. I felt maternal and protective. I felt and gave off warmth. I was inspired and could inspire. My mind opened up to let in ideas and inspired words to express these ideas. Eyes that were blind to the plight of children around me suddenly opened and I could see the pain in the faces of all children and the crippling effect of the world on them. From my debilitating deafness, I could finally hear the cries of children who were born into a world without love. I could see the poorest of humanity dying in a world where callused hearts were rewarded with financial success. The Blessed Mother's compassion filled me and became understandable and poignant. Her message transformed and transported me from the god-lost shadows of self-centeredness into the warm glorious brilliance of God's light. I had experienced my first miracle born on the 26th of March, 1993!

----

*Of course I would object to this cross examination as irrelevant and unethically mixing one's religious beliefs in the truth process. A belief in God and the miraculous should not be allowed to affect the credibility of a witness. Still, whoever utilized the services of this investigator ran the risk that those who knew him would be reluctant to believe him.

*1 In Las Vegas, NM, I joined a Fundamentalist church. The Blessed Mother and saints were never mentioned. The belief was that they did not want us to get confused and think that there was another source besides God who was in control. My mother would have been so sad to not be able to pray to St. Jude, the saint of the impossible. I think too that the absence of the Blessed Mother figure, would be a bit disempowering for women. The Catholics got some things right!

PART 2

FACING HELL ON EARTH, THE FRIEND, THE ENEMY, ANALYSIS AND SOLUTIONS

CHAPTER X

DON'T FORGET TO FIGHT FOR NATURE

Although the title of this chapter, Don't Forget to Fight, is hardly intimidating. It sounds more like our spouse telling us to dress lightly, extreme heat is in the forecast. Keep in mind, this title was one part of the four prayer/directives to my children when they were young. (Don't forget the Beauty, Don't forget the light, Don't forget to love and Don't forget to fight. See Ch. 1.) But, unlike the Catholic Church and the consequences of committing a mortal sin in my day, a violation of these 'mandates', does not send you to eternal hellfire at the end of your life. It is more immediate than that! Our failure to love, respect and fight against natures' destruction, is now sentencing us to a hell on earth. We are now feeling the 'heat' and it is quickly getting worse.

A. WHO/WHAT IS THE FIGHT FOR?
DESTRUCTION OF FORESTS IS CAUSING POLLUTION, DROUGHTS AND PANDEMICS

Part II focuses on polluters and the mentality causing the destruction of our environment. Let us now talk about our friend, nature, specifically the forests.

I have addressed the destruction of our forests as a major contributor to pollution. The analysis has focused on how our arboreal giants filter the carbon dioxide from the air. In their absence, the air becomes more poisoned, i.e., polluted. The pollution heats up the air and our water.

Droughts ensue. Increased evaporation from the heated waters, means more severe tornadoes, destroying our coasts. At the same time, the heat is melting our polar ice caps. Consequently, our earth's ability to reflect heat back into space has now been reduced, so the heat is trapped in the atmosphere. We are now getting heated and acidified oceans, consequently destroying our coral reefs, the tropical forests of our seas. Sea levels are getting higher, thusly endangering our coasts.

In addition to the above, we have, only recently, become aware of the function of trees as water-fountains - taking water from the ground and putting it in the air through their leaves – (transpiration). *-1. "Take away the trees, reasoned biologists such as Antonio Nobre, then of the National Institute of Amazonian Research in Manaus, and the rains would die. The Amazon basin would turn to desert." (See supra.) "When we cut down the trees, we get less water in the sky, thus less rainfall and if enough trees are cut, you get droughts." (supra) "We now know that flying rivers traverse the globe and influence rainfall over huge distances. And we are learning that forests play a key role in supplying them, which means that, in much of the world, the loss of the moisture recycling from deforestation* *is a more imminent threat even than global warming.' (supra).* So we now have another reason, other than transforming CO2 into oxygen, why the forests are critical to our existence.

And recently, we have become painfully aware of another devastating consequence of deforestation. According to Christina Nunez, in 'Deforestation Explained':*1

"As the world seeks to slow the pace of climate change, preserve wildlife, and support billions of people, trees inevitably hold a major part of the answer. Yet the mass destruction of trees— deforestation—continues, sacrificing the long-term benefits of standing trees for short-term gain."

According to the World Wildlife Fund, (Nov 6, 2019), forests cover about 30% of the earth's land surface. However, humans are cutting these essential habitats down on a massive scale. This human-driven and natural loss of trees affects wildlife, ecosystems, weather patterns, and even the climate. *2

Unfortunately for mankind, forests are disappearing at an alarming rate. Between 1990 and 2016, the world lost 502,000 square miles (1.3 million square kilometers) of forest, according to the World Bank – an area larger than South Africa. Since humans started cutting down forests, 46 percent of trees have been felled, according to a 2015 study in the journal Nature. About 17% of the Amazonian rainforest has been destroyed over the past 50 years, and losses recently have been on the rise.

*We need trees for a variety of reasons, not least of which is that they absorb not only the carbon dioxide that we exhale, but also the heat-trapping greenhouse gases that human activities emit. As those gases enter the atmosphere, global warming increases, a trend scientists now prefer to call climate change. Tropical tree cover alone can provide 23% of the climate mitigation needed over the next decade to meet goals set in the Paris Agreement in 2015, according to one estimate.*3*

The Devastation Upon Us - Pandemics What has now become devastatingly clear is that destroying our forests presents an immediate and foreseeable danger to humanity – epidemics, pandemics and possibly, the Covid 19 pandemic.

There is a direct connection between deforesting and humans coming into contact with the creatures whose homes we have destroyed. (See 1 supra)

When I first began focusing on pollution, I was still quite distant from the consequences of our natural devastation. Cutting down a forest to make room for human residences and for wood to make their living quarters, seemed quite normal. Hardly evil! We could forgive cattle farmers for cutting down trees to provide grazing land for the cows. Nothing unusual about that! Who doesn't like a good hamburger? Or how about cutting or burning forests to use the land for a commercial venture, like, mining. Certainly, we had plenty of trees to take the place of this small patch of trees. Right? We'll just plant more trees elsewhere! Animal habitat? What's that?

Though our pollution was rising daily, along with the heat, politicians refused to step on the toes of big business, and risk losing an election. Barry Commoner, Al Gore, Jay Inslee and Bernie Sanders, found out the hard way.

The problem has always been, that no one was taking seriously the consequences of destroying our green-leafed lungs. It was a consequence that would happen in the distant future. Surely our government would take care of it!

Then came the Covid 19 Pandemic (Corona Virus)! Humanity has been devastated by this tiny virus of nature. The U.S. is no exception. (At this writing we have a higher incidence of Covid 19 deaths than any country.) Yet only a few seem to be making the connection between the destruction of nature and the rise of these killing viruses.

The question we seem to be avoiding, is whether humanity is to blame for the Covid virus? While our American leader keeps pointing the finger at China as responsible for the virus, are we missing the big picture? Has deforestation given rise to the pandemics we have been experiencing?

Well, according to Amy Vittor, MD, Ph.D, the connection has been made! This doctor is an expert in vector-borne (carried by blood-feeding animals like ticks and mosquitoes), disease and has studied deforestation and vector-borne diseases for decades. (zoonotic disease when the jump is from animals to humans.) She has linked deforestation to pandemics and viral outbreaks, such as Zika, West Nile, Ebola, SARs and Nipah. Now it seems very probable that a displaced bat from a destroyed ecosystem may have been the culprit for Covid 19.*4 Infectious diseases are finding a foothold all over the world as we encroach on nature's habitats.

According to the Scientific Journal of Nature, Ebola outbreaks were noticeably worse in areas that were recently deforested.

How is deforestation connected? Dr. Vittor explains what we are doing to cause deforestation - logging, mining, converting to farming. For example, the Nipah virus of the late 90's in Malaysia and Singapore, that resulted in encephalitis. Pigs were infected and people in pig farms became ill with the Nipah virus.

The Dynamic. After deforestation, logs cause accumulation of water. Mosquitoes breed in the water. Infected mosquitoes then bite humans. Walla! A virus in humans.

Lyme Disease. Those who have moved into the northeast United States have seen the explosion of Lyme disease. It has coincided with the rapid expansion of the suburbs. Where we have torn down much of the forest in this area, we have come into closer contact with deer and consequently deer ticks that carry Lyme disease. *5

Infectious diseases will increase because of the pressures we are putting on our diminishing forests. A growing body of scientific evidence shows that the felling of tropical forests creates optimal conditions for the spread of mosquito-borne scourges, including malaria and dengue. Primates and other animals are also spreading disease from cleared forests to people.*6 The article, written in 2016, stated: '*They are deeply concerned that the next global pandemic could come out of the forest and spread quickly around the world, as was the case with SARS and Ebola, which both emerged from wild animals.*' (So much for the Presidents claim that we could not have foreseen it and blamed China.) The article further stated: *Mosquitoes are not the only carriers of pathogens from the wild to humans. Bats, primates, and even snails can carry disease, and transmission dynamics change for all of these species following forest clearing, often creating a much greater threat to people.* The article further states: *Throughout human history pathogens have emerged from forests. (My emphasis)*

The Corona virus has brought us high fevers, damaged lung function, extreme aches and pains and death. Isn't it curious that nature has mimicked what we have done to nature – We have given a fever to the earth, by polluting and burning our trees down; We have destroyed our leafed lungs and consequently earth's ability to filter and clear her air; We have destroyed the habitats of entire ecosystems and in the process sickened and killed those who once lived there. This mirror-image 'punishment' almost seems scripted.

We need to begin to give more credit to the power and influence of nature and less to those in power who deny that we are the cause of our demise.

The **bad news** of this pandemic is as follows: 1. The public does not appear to be making the connection between the Pandemic and the destruction of the environment, particularly the forests. The powerful effect of the Corona Virus has caused the public to focus on the short term need to 'get back to normal'. I fear that because of the pandemic, we will be further tolerating the downward drift into devastation from pollution. I hope I am wrong!

As bad, is that the President (Trump), has taken advantage of our change of focus, to eliminate critical administrative environmental protection rules. Of course, the justification is that in these financially devastating times, businesses do not need any more limitations on their ability to make money. Along these same lines, the wealthy have received an exorbitant amount of 'stimulus' money.

I fear the further consequence of this pandemic will be that the public will forget or be more sympathetic towards the polluting industries. They may be led to believe that we should not limit these polluting industries because it will detrimentally impact our return to financial normality. You can expect that our president will take the lead in ignoring the ongoing environmental catastrophe as he always has done.

With the presidential election on the horizon, we must get out to vote and send a message to our representatives and senators that the protection of the environment must remain the priority.

On the plus side of this pandemic crisis, it is arguable that this is a perfect time to transform our energy into natural energy and recyclables. On the 22nd of April, 2020, the U.N. Secretary-General (Guterres) said the Climate change devastation will be 'Many Times Greater' than the Corona virus pandemic. He is urging governments to capitalize on their coronavirus pandemic rebuilding efforts by doing more to help the environment. W.H.O. did a survey in 186 countries that found that 'climate" and "environment" topped the list of concerns that respondents believe will most affect humanity's future. A recent Pew Research Center survey found that the percentage of Americans who say global climate change is a major threat to the well-being of the U.S., has increased, from 44 percent in 2009 to 60% this year. Among Democrat-leaning voters, 88% say climate change is a major threat, compared with 31 percent of republican-leaning voters who say the same. This 'awareness' is good news!

We must all recognize that this will be the most critical election in world history. Protecting the earth and mankind must be the priority issue.

*-1. 'Rivers in the sky: the devastating effect deforestation is having on global rainfall' South China Morning Post Magazine Published Nov. 8, 2019, https://wwwgoogle.com
*1 'Deforestation explained' 'DEFORESTATION AND FOREST DEGRADATION'. See https://www.nationalgeogr
*2. World Wildlife Fund, https://www.worldwildlife
*3. 'Deforestation facts and information -National Geographic.
*4 THINK AGAIN, Opinions, Analysis, Essay by Andrew Stern (https.//www.nbcnews.com) Amy Vitor
*5 'researchers estimated that 329,000 (range 296,000-376,000) cases of Lyme disease occur annually in the United States.' See CDC Centers for disease control and Prevention) Several neurological problems can take over a patient suffering from Lyme disease. They begin to experience memory loss, trouble focusing, depression, anxiety emotional tantrums, or total personality changes from day to night. See 'Human Lyme Disease Symptoms and Signs with Pictures' at 'ALLMEDICINEDATA.INFO
*6 see Yale Environment 360 DEFORESTATION, 'How Forest Loss Is Leading To a Rise In Human Disease – Yale E360 by Jim Robbins February 23, 2016

B. WHO IS THE FIGHT AGAINST?

1. IS IT US?

THE ZEPHYR

THE ZEPHYR *(From Gr. Zephyros, allied to zophos, darkness, gloom, the dark or evening quarter, the west. 1. The west wind, poetically, any soft, mild gentle breeze, as the flowers nodded as the zephyrs passed over them.)*

In the beginning…
A quiet calm……,
A peacefulness…….,
Just the sounds
And smell of
Sweet nature.
Then…………..
Just a breath
And then a sigh,
And an ominous breeze.
Then, very slowly
A terrestrial gasp,
And a tumult.
Then……..
The beginnings
Of the big-brained beast
Blew in,
Touted by God
As superior to all.

And the world,
Without antibodies
To counter
The human virus,
Began succumbing
As the human seed
Ceaselessly,
Began to infect Creation,
And suffering
From a sort of autism,
This virus was rendered
Numb to the needs
Of the natural mother
From whom it was fed.

The voracious virus
Began filling every void
Where it was not,
Copying nature
And destroying it,
Destroying those
Who opposed it
At the same time.

The callous wind
Carried
Its virulent traveler,
Filtering, spreading
And infecting
Every crevice
Of the body, heart
And then the soul
Of the once-virgin,
Mother's body,

Gaze forward now
On her broken
And bruised body.
Mother Earth
Lays beaten,
Sliced, swollen
And bloodied.

Like a
Mocked savior
She is treated with
Metal and cement
Spiked splints,
Asphalt
And cement dressings,
Crudely placed
Over her crusting skin,
Now painfully laden with
Puss-filled sores
And savage scars.

The virulent voracious ones
Impale her
With giant spears
In every side

Whose machines of death
Reach blindly
Upwards
To a darkened, thick
And stench-filled sky.

The putrid smell
Is a constant remnant
And reminder
Of their presence.

Their metal sharp tips
Poke the eyes
Of the dimming sun.
Tubes, moving and static,
Ride and dig downward
Sucking life from
All parts of her moaning
And writhing being,
And satisfied with their snacks,
They belch
Their odoriferousness
Skywards
Through cement
And metal tubes
Efficiently disbursing
The parceled poison
To a sensitive
And sickened sky.
The malodorous venom
Creeps upwards
And outwards,
Infecting everything
And all it touches.
The moving and sharp
Mother earth-piercing spears
Cut deep into the sinews
Of her muscle and lifeblood
And leave her trembling.
The poisonous emissions
Form a giant swirling storm cloud
Over the dying body
And cast a dark
And foreboding shadow

Over the children
That threatens catastrophe
Of diluvian proportions.

Mother's eyes
Are blinded now
And craters stand
Where once
The living light
To her soul
Had shone
Brilliantly.
But now
They are brutally
Burned out,
Taken and sold
For soul-less cash
As valuable trinkets
And lavish ornaments
By mercenaries,
Who fought wars
Just because
There was money to be made
And power to be gained.

They kidnapped
And ransomed God,
Toyed with
And tortured Him,
Forced Him to work,
Made Him a soldier,
Patented his style,
Sold his logo
And tattooed it
To each captive's brain
And became rich
And powerful.
Armed with a brigade
Of Apocalyptic thinkers
That blame devils for our evils.
They have Him an amulet
Protecting all who wear it,
Pontificated Him salvageable
And pronounced only Him
Worthy of worship.

With all enemies shunned,
Blacklisted, Blackballed,
Ostracized,
Excommunicated
Jailed
Deported,
Beaten,
Tortured or killed,
They became rich,
Powerful and famous.

With Father God
Debilitated
And now impotent
And Mother dying,
The vile ones,
Led by the money giants,
Violently abort
Mother's unborn children
With dull-edged knives
And torture their mothers
To make burgers and steaks.
They feed the babies
And their parents
As fast food
To the lackeys
Of the Oil cats
And pit bulls
Of pure power
Who now, emboldened
And energized
Are sicced
On a fevered, poisoned and
A stench-filled sky
That blots out the sun.
They further despoil the living
By feasting on newborns,
Mother's babies,
Sinking their eyeteeth
And permeating
The protective membranes
Into the tender sinews
Of their innocent souls.
Giant needles permeate

Into the womb of
The maternal vehicle and poison
The lifeblood of the children.

See Mother's babies
Dead and displayed
On their trophy walls.
They are poached
Devoured
And sold because of greed,
Though the last
Of their dying breed.

Now mother painfully dies,
Delirious
From a rising temperature,
Alone and discarded
As mere refuse.
Hear her moaning
As she mourns
For her dying babies.

Mother will not see
Her babies
But only hear
Their desperate moans
And plaintiff wails.

The children
Will find no home
And no milk they can drink.
They cry a million tears,
Each toxic with despair,
Each moaning:
I cannot dream
Of the sunrise!
I will not see the sunset!
The oceans of night
Are drowning us.

Hear the sighs,
So much fainter now.
Taste the moon's tears,
Bitter and poisoned.

They slowly rain
As hemlock
For the children,

The ears
Of mother-earth's children
Are gnawed to the quick
So they will not hear

Nor will they live
To know the evil
From the infected
Poisonous wind
That consumes all
Who are afraid
Or are too weakened
To fight.

Who are these virulent beasts?
Maternaless monsters,
Empathy-less creatures
Without souls,
Demons
With only God
And Nature
Left to taunt?
Why can they not hear
This sorrowful wail
Of life begging to live?

Who are these infected men
Without ears
That hear nothing
Through the din
Of the all-consuming storm
That drowns
The desperate sounds
Of the children crying?

Nothing will benefit human health and increase the chances for survival
of life on Earth as much as the evolution to a vegetarian diet."
Albert Einstein

Rich nations should move to '100 percent synthetic beef'
(Bill Gates: 'How to Avoid a Climate Disaster')

2. ANIMAL AGRICULTURE/MEAT AND DAIRY – TO DIE FOR

(Extensive citations and sources are to be found at 'COWSPIRACY', 'THE FACTS' (CTF)
and at article 'The Environmental Impact of Factory Farming: How Meat Production Harms
Our Ecosystems, Economies, and Health' by Paul Recupero on August 8th, 2020 (TEIFF)

There are **profound health risks** and costs to farmers, workers, consumers, and the public, as a whole, that are brought about by industrial animal production. *(TEIFF)* From a consumption standpoint, regular intake of cured and processed meat has been linked to potential carcinogenic effects in humans, along with an increased risk of other health conditions such as heart disease, stroke, and diabetes. Annual costs for these diseases in the United States amount to more than $33 billion. *(TEIFF)*

Our country daily feeds, feasts, dines and gorges on hamburgers, steaks, cheese, eggs and a variety of milk products, like ice cream. Yet, the meats are killer foods…not in a good way! They are carcinogenic, not unlike cigarettes. The World Health Organization has classified processed meats – including ham, salami, bacon and frankfurters – as a Group 1 carcinogen which means that there is strong evidence that processed meats cause cancer. Red meat, such as beef, lamb and pork has been classified as a 'probable' cause of cancer. *(See World Health Organization)* Of course, there is nothing on the package that warns us that these products are literally killing us. Who doesn't like a good hamburger? Is it worth dying for?

Warnings Should be Required. The Center for Science in the Public Interest is calling on the U.S. Dept. of Agriculture to require a warning label on packages of bacon, ham, hot dogs, and other processed meat and poultry products to inform consumers that eating those foods is associated with an increased risk of cancer of the colon and rectum (colorectal cancer). (See WHO) This is based on findings of the International Agency for Research on Cancer, which concluded in 2015 that processed meat is "carcinogenic to humans." Colorectal cancer is the second-leading cause of cancer deaths in the U.S., and will cause about 49,150 deaths in 2016, according to the American Cancer Society. *(Hicks, Cheryl. "Give up dairy products to beat cancer".) (The Telegraph. June 2014 Dairy may "give guys man-boobs") (Davidson, Garry. "Milk & Dairy For Guys With Man Boobs". Chest Sculpting. August 2016))'Cancer Warning Label Urged for Processed Meat & Poultry)*

So why is this not on the news every night? Why are we not being warned about this? And how does our meat and dairy habit hurt us in other ways? Does it cause pollution? Does it impact our water table? Does the rearing of livestock cause land degradation, through deforestation? Is the rearing of livestock responsible for decreasing human immunity to disease? Does it impact biodiversity? Are livestock responsible for the spread of dangerous pathogens? Is it the leading cause of ocean dead zones, habitat destruction and species extinction? Does it negatively impact the poor? Does it negatively impact the workers, and surrounding neighbors of these animal factories? Does it reduce the value of surrounding properties? Is the rearing of livestock immoral? The animal industry is a powerful and pervasive industry. The following review of factory farming should give you some answers. It should also alarm you.

My Comment: As you review the following article and the entire book, ask yourself: Is what we are doing, allowing to happen, or benefitting from, evil? Does it violate the tenets of Judeo Christian beliefs? Are the deaths and torture that we are causing or allowing to be caused to our fellow earth travelers, evil? Are the sales of meat without warnings whose consumption causes early deaths, wrong, unethical, even unlawful? Are we acting sinfully, to mindlessly and indiscriminately consume meat and dairy, gas and oil and plastics? From the vantage-point of our leaders, have we, the public, become the 'collateral damage' necessary to sustain and enhance a financial empire in the hands of a few? Are we being led to what we are told is merely a shower before our stay at the luxury suites but turns out to be a gas chamber, our death and the death of the planet?

And to those of you who believe these questions and comparisons are outrageous, examine the question in the context of how our meat and dairy industry is rapidly moving us to an end-of-world scenario, quickly approaching irreversibility.

Factory Farming/Cattle /Meat and Dairy Industry*
(Underlining and bolding are my emphasis)

How Big is the Problem? Industrial Agriculture, also referred to as factory farming, is the dominant food production system in the United States. *(TEIFF)* "Today more than 95% of animals are raised in factory farms according to the *American Society for the Prevention of Cruelty to Animals.* The surge in factory farming has been driven by these corporations' enormous political influence and weak environmental regulations. *(TEIFF)*

MEAT AND DAIRY, THE BIGGEST POLLUTERS

Another Big Secret. Guess what! The companies that bring you the steaks, hamburgers, eggs cheese and milk, are one of the biggest polluters in the world! *(CTF)*

The U.N. report states that the <u>livestock</u> sector is one of the top two or three most significant contributors to serious environmental problems. The findings of this report suggest that it should be a major policy focus when dealing with problems of <u>land degradation, climate change and air pollution, water shortage, water pollution, and loss of biodiversity.</u> *(See Executive Summary of the Steering Committee of the Livestock, Environment and Development (LEAD) Initiative at its meeting in May 2005 in Copenhagen.)*

Factory farming is responsible for an immense amount of the greenhouse gas emissions and deforestation that fuel climate change. Collectively, cattle emit 150 billion gallons of methane daily into our atmosphere, a greenhouse gas that is 86 times more potent than carbon dioxide. *(TEIFF)*

A UN report warns: **Rearing cattle produces more greenhouse gases than driving cars**. (*See UN News Centre Nov 29, 2006.)*

Atmosphere and Climate/ Greenhouse Gases. With rising temperatures, rising sea levels, melting icecaps and glaciers, shifting ocean currents and weather patterns, climate change is the most serious challenge facing the human race. <u>Animal agriculture</u> is a major player, responsible for more greenhouse gas emissions than the combined exhaust from all transportation. *(CTF)*

<u>Compare Animal Agriculture Exhausts With Transportation</u>. Transportation exhaust is responsible for 13% of all greenhouse gas emissions. Greenhouse gas emissions from this sector primarily involve

fossil fuels burned for road, rail, air, and marine transportation. **Livestock** and their byproducts account for **51% of all worldwide greenhouse gas emissions**. (WorldWatch Institute, a Washington D.C. environmental think-tank) *(CTF)*. They state:

Livestock's contribution to environmental problems is on a massive scale....the impact is so significant that it needs to be addressed. Worldwatch Institute found that the FAO underestimated and overlooked some direct and indirect livestock emissions including CO2 emissions from livestock respiration, methane emissions, and emissions from clearing land to graze livestock and grow feed. (for cite, see supra and 'Saving Earth' (ttps://www.britannica.com)

Cows and Methane Emissions. Every time a cow burps or passes gas, or their defecation is left in massive puddles, methane wafts into the atmosphere. *(CTF)* This can have a big effect on climate because methane is a potent greenhouse gas—about 28 times more powerful than carbon dioxide at warming the earth, on a 100-year timescale, and more than 80 times more powerful over 20 years. *(CTF)*

Pollution. Cows produce 150 billion gallons of methane per day. *(CTF)*, constituting 18% of greenhouse gas emissions" *(CTF)* The report estimates that livestock "is responsible for 18 percent" of total anthropogenic* carbon dioxide emissions, 37% of methane and 65% of nitrous oxide emissions. *(CTF)* *(anthropogenic–chiefly of environmental pollution and pollutants, originating in human activity.)*

"Methane pollution causes one quarter of the global warming that we're experience right now." *(CTF)* "Carbon dioxide may be the most prevalent greenhouse gas (accounting for 81% of emissions), but methane is much more potent. Over a 20-year period, it traps 84 times more heat." * *See article supra*.

Methane: A More Dangerous Heat Trapping Gas. Methane's chemical shape is remarkably effective at trapping heat, which means that adding just a little more methane to the atmosphere can have big impacts on how much, and how quickly, the planet warms.

Since the Industrial Revolution, methane concentrations in the atmosphere have more than doubled, and about 20% of the warming the planet has experienced can be attributed to the gas. *(CTF)*

Manure Causes Methane. The manure that cattle and other grazers produce is also a site for microbes to do their business, producing even more methane. There are 1.4 billion cattle in the world, and that number is growing as demand for beef and dairy increases; together with other grazing animals, they contribute about 40% of the annual methane budget. *(CTF)*

Land Use/Deforestation. Further, the amount of land used just to feed and fatten these animals for their meat constitutes 1/3 of global arable land on the planet and requires extreme deforestation practices. In fact, factory farming is responsible for 91% of the deforestation that occurs in the Amazon. *(TEIFF)*

The **main sources of emissions** were found to be:

- Land use and land use change: including forest and other natural vegetation replaced by pasture and feed crop in the Neotropics (CO_2) and carbon release from soils such as pasture and arable land dedicated to feed production. *(See CTF for actual Gigatonnes)*
- Feed Production (except carbon released from soil): *(See CTF)* This includes fossil fuel used in manufacturing chemical fertilizer for feed crops (CO_2) and chemical fertilizer application on feed crops and leguminous feed crop.

- Animal production:, including enteric fermentation from ruminants (<u>burps and farts</u>) and on <u>farm fossil fuel use</u> (CO$_2$) *(See CTF)*
- Manure Management: mainly through <u>manure</u> storage, application and deposition *(See CTF)*
- Processing and international <u>transport</u>: *(CTF)*

May Be Worse. A 2009 article in the <u>Worldwatch Institute</u> magazine by authors Robert Goodland and Jeff Anhang, then employed at the World Bank, claimed that the FAO report was too conservative and that livestock sector accounts for much more of **global GHG** (green-house gas) **emissions, at least 51%,** taking into account animal respiration and photosynthetic capacity of the land used for feeding and housing livestock.

The Monetary Annual Cost Borne by Society. These <u>are costs that are created by the operation of a business itself, but that the business does not pay for</u>; They are external to the production and market for the goods themselves. Rather, they are <u>passed off to the rest of the society in taxes, health impairments, environmental degradation, and harms to other industries</u>. The total annual cost borne by society as a consequence of this industry is in the tens of billions of dollars. *(TEIFF)*

As one of the main polluters on earth, the externalities of the factory farming sector that you and I are footing the bill for include:

- immense pollution of surrounding communities
- destruction of local economies and other business sectors
- "dead zones" in our nation's rivers, streams, and coastal systems
- air and climate pollution
- declining property values
- global water shortages
- the eradication of biodiversity (which impacts food availability and cost) and
- medical expenses for some in surrounding communities *(TEIFF)*

IT CONTAMINATES WATER AND SOIL AND AFFECTS HUMAN HEALTH:
"Agriculture plays a major role in pollution, releasing large volumes of manure, chemicals, antibiotics, and growth hormones into water sources. This imposes risks to both aquatic ecosystems and human health. In fact, agriculture's most common chemical contaminant, nitrate, can cause "blue baby syndrome", which can lead to death in infants." (See '10 things you should know')

Residents of <u>rural communities</u> surrounding factory farms report high incidents of <u>illness</u>, and their <u>property values</u> are often <u>lowered</u> by their proximity to industrial farms. *(See article 'Cancer and Industrial Farming, University of Wisconsin GREEN BAY https://blog.usgb.edu*

Water Contamination Caused By Factory Farms. Manure from factory farms contains more than 150 pathogens that leach into swimming areas and drinking sources, six of which account for 90% of all human foodborne and waterborne diseases. The EPA estimates that about 53% of people in the U.S. rely on groundwater resources for drinking water. *(TEIFF)*

In Kewaunee County, **Wisconsin**, which has seen a significant increase in new factory farms over the past two decades, a 2017 study found **fecal microbes in 60% of sampled drinking wells**. In a petition by Kewaunee county residents opposing the removal of certain clean water protections from a local "factory's" permit, the presiding Administrative Law Judge noted "the proliferation of contaminated wells represents a massive regulatory failure to protect groundwater" by the Wisconsin Department of Natural Resources. *(TEIFF)*

In addition to bacteria, a 2015 report found <u>water systems</u> serving seven million Americans in 48 states contained <u>high levels of nitrates</u>, which are linked to certain types of cancer. Viney Aneja, a professor in the Department of Marine, Earth, and Atmospheric Sciences at North Carolina State University, has found that ammonia, one of the main sources of nitrogen pollution, can end up in waterways as far as 50 miles away, and transported in airborne form hundreds of miles away. In 2003, an egg facility in Ohio reported emissions of 1.6 million pounds of ammonia, 44 times the health-related reporting threshold set by the Environmental Protection Agency (EPA). These health issues come with a host of financial costs. *(TEIFF)*

<u>Health Hazards Faced By Workers</u> *(TEIFF)* The pollutants emitted by meat factories contribute not only to the overall environmental impact of factory farming but also to negative health outcomes in their workers. With respect to the toxicity of the factories themselves, factory farm employees suffer from the ammonia emissions associated with the factories. These workers are mostly low-income minorities who are unaware of the health hazards they will encounter on the job. Numerous studies have found respiratory problems among workers, with as many as 30% experiencing asthma, bronchitis, and lung disease. Children attending nearby schools also have elevated rates of these chronic respiratory issues. *(TEIFF)*

DEAD ZONES IN THE OCEAN. According to Dr. Richard Oppenlander, Environmental Researcher and Author of 'Comfortably Unaware', *'Livestock operations on land has caused.. created more than 500 nitrogen-flooded dead zones around the world in our oceans, comprising more than 95,000 square miles of areas completely devoid of life.'*

In coastal waters, massive "dead zones" begin to form. There, nitrogen and phosphorus fertilize the rapid growth of cyanobacteria, algae, phytoplankton, and seaweeds. With so many aquatic microorganisms consuming, reproducing and respiring at once, they literally use up most, if not all, of the oxygen in the water.

Few aquatic organisms can survive in these oxygen-deprived, "hypoxic," waters. The species that rely on oxygen in the water to breathe and cannot get to oxygenated waters fast enough, die off, hence the name "dead zone." Those individuals that do not directly die from suffocation, face stressful conditions which can lead to entire populations of fish, crabs, and shrimp succumbing to disease. Even species such as marine mammals and sea birds that receive their oxygen from the air, rather than water, face starvation, sickness, and death due to a severe loss in the food sources they rely on. These large swaths of lakes, coastal waters, and ocean become aquatic deserts, devoid of life. *(TEIFF)*

The number and size of <u>dead zones has increased</u> dramatically in the past 50 years becoming more widespread as our agriculture has become more unsustainable and larger factories have confined even greater numbers of animals. Since the 1960s, the number of dead zones have doubled each decade, with more than 400 occurring today. *(TEIFF)* While everyone in the eastern United States lives close to a dead zone of some size, Long Island Sound and the Chesapeake Bay to name a few, the most recognized dead zone in the U.S. is a swath in the Gulf of Mexico that is approximately the size of the state of New Jersey. This dead zone appears annually, not far from the mouth of the Mississippi River, a water source that drains agricultural operations up and down the United States. This is an area that is still feeling the effects from the 2011 BP Oil spill, a disaster that was also caused by a lack of proper regulation and government oversight. *(TEIFF)*

<u>Economic Impact Of Dead Zones On Tourism and Fishing.</u> As a consequence of lost biodiversity and ecosystem services, the tourism industry alone loses close to $1 billion a year as a result of nutrient over-enrichment. To use the Gulf of Mexico as an example, the Gulf now faces serious economic

effects from its growing dead zone, especially due to its reliance on the seafood and tourism sectors, which generate 600,000 jobs and $9 billion in wages for the region each year. *(TEIFF)*

With respect to the seafood industry, the Gulf's fishermen have seen severe impacts to their livelihood, which is particularly problematic as the commercial fishing industry in the Gulf has accounted for 40% of our nation's seafood. The Union of Concerned Scientists estimates that the Gulf's dead zone has cost up to $2.4 billion in damages to fish stocks and habitat every year for over 30 years. *(TEIFF)*

In another respect, the impacts to fisheries and tourism lead to higher costs for consumers and markets as the prices for products that are more difficult to provide have continued to increase. *(TEIFF)*

ITS USE OF PESTICIDES MAY HAVE ADVERSE HEALTH EFFECTS: *"Large volumes of chemical fertilizers and pesticides are used to increase agricultural yields and humans may be exposed to these potentially-toxic pesticides through the food they consume, resulting in adverse health effects. Some pesticides have been proven to act as endocrine disruptors, potentially affecting reproductive functions, increasing the incidence of breast cancer, causing abnormal growth patterns and developmental delays in children, and altering immune function. (See '10 things you should know')*

IT FOSTERS ANTIMICROBIAL RESISTANCE / Antibiotic Resistance. *In addition to threatening public health with water and air pollution, factory farms are hotbeds for the development of antibiotic-resistant bacteria that affect humans "In addition to preventing and treating disease, antimicrobials are commonly used to accelerate livestock growth. According to Food and Water Watch, "80% of the antibiotics used in the U.S. are by agriculture". Over time, microorganisms develop resistance, making antimicrobials less effective as medicine. In fact, about 700,000 people die of resistant infections every year. By 2050, those diseases may cause more deaths than cancer.*

The Centers for Disease Control and Prevention (CDC) recognizes **antibiotic resistance as one of the greatest public health threats in the world.** A staggering 84% of all antibiotics used in the United States are used on animals needed in factory farms to counteract the health challenges rendered by the overcrowded, unsanitary, and stressful living conditions within these facilities. As antibiotics are overused in these industrialized spaces, the bacteria they are intended to kill become resistant to these drugs.

According to the World Health Organization, *antimicrobial resistance "threatens the achievements of modern medicine" and may precipitate "a post-antibiotic era, in which common infections and minor injuries can kill"* (See 10 things you should know)
. When antibiotic-resistant bacteria spread to humans through our food supply or through contaminated waste, they can cause severe or even deadly infections in people. A study in 2015 found antibiotic-resistant bacteria present in approximately 35 to 80 percent of raw meat from supermarkets. Europe has banned the use of many antibiotics in agribusiness, yet the United States has refused to take such action.

One study has estimated the total annual costs of antibiotic-resistance at $30 billion. Moreover, U.S. annual costs related to deaths, medical care, and lost productivity from E. coli, derived primarily from animal manure, amount to $405 million. Disgracefully, bacterial outbreaks lead to yearly recalls of meat in which animals that were bred to spend their lives unable to move in confined cages for the sole purpose to be killed, are merely thrown in the garbage.

Even with the current research to prove the growing resistance of bacteria and its link to factory farming, the Food and Drug Administration has yet to require factory farms to stop the use of antibiotics for animals.

Crossover/Destruction of Ecosystems = Spread of Pathogens. The growing livestock sector also places increased pressure on natural resources and the environment, making a significant contribution to global environmental change. Also of concern are the public health implications of livestock production and intensification. As pressure on our global resources increases, people and their livestock are pushed into ever-closer proximity with natural areas and the habitats of wild fauna. This increases the chances of emergence and spread, in livestock and people, of infectious zoonotic pathogens originating in wild animals. This then is one of the real causes of the Pandemic and future pandemics.

Land Degradation. *"The livestock sector is by far the single largest anthropogenic user of land. The total area occupied by grazing is equivalent to 26% of the ice-free terrestrial surface of the planet. In addition, the total area dedicated to feed crop production amounts to 33% of total arable land. In all, livestock production accounts for 70% of all agricultural land and 30% of the land surface of the planet."* (See supra at 'Land Degradation')

How It Degrades the Land: *"Expansion of livestock production is a key factor in **deforestation**, especially in Latin America where the greatest amount of deforestation is occurring – 70% of previous forested land in the Amazon is occupied by pastures and feed crops covering a large part of the remainder. About 20% of the world's pastures and rangelands, with 73% of rangelands in dry areas, have been degraded to some extent, mostly through overgrazing, compaction and erosion created by livestock action. The dry lands in particular, are affected by these trends, as livestock are often the only source of livelihoods for the people living in these areas"* (See supra)

WATER. Livestock's Major Role in Water Depletion and Pollution: The world is moving towards increasing problems of freshwater shortage, scarcity and depletion, with 64% of the world's population expected to live in water stressed basins by 2025. (*See Executive Summary supra.*)

The *livestock sector is a key player in increasing water use*. It is probably the *largest sectoral source of water pollution*, contributing to eutrophication, *dead zones* in coastal areas, *degradation of coral reefs, human health problems*, emergence of *antibiotic resistance* and many others. The major sources of pollution are from animal wastes, antibiotics and hormones, chemicals from tanneries, fertilizers and pesticides used for feed crops, and sediments from eroded pastures.

WATER CONSUMPTION. Meat and dairy products are highly intensive. Domestic water use in the U S is 5%. 55% is for animal agriculture. **(CTF)** Animal Agriculture is responsible for 20%-33% of all fresh water consumption in the world today. *(CTF)*

Animal agriculture water consumption ranges from 34-76 trillion gallons annually. *(CTF)*

The human population drinks 5.2 billion gallons of water every day. *(Cowspiracy)* Cows drink 45 billion gallons of water per day. *(Cowspiracy)*

Agriculture is responsible for 80-90% of US water consumption. *(CTF)*

Growing feed crops for livestock, consumes 56% of water in the US. *(CTF)*

To produce 1lb of beef, requires 1,799 gallons of water, 1 lb. of cheeze, 900 gallons and 1 egg requires 53 gallons of water. 2,500 gallons of water are needed to produce 1 pound of beef. *(CTF)* 477 gallons of water are required to produce 1lb. of eggs; almost 900 gallons of water are needed for 1 lb. of cheese. *(CTF)*. 1,000 gallons of water are required to produce 1 gallon of milk. *(CTF)*. **It takes 660 gallons of water is to produce a 1/3-pound burger**. *(CTF)*

Water's Critical Role. Water represents at least 50% of most living organisms and plays a key role in the functioning of the ecosystem. It is also a critical natural resource mobilized by most human activities. Freshwater resources are the pillar sustaining development and maintaining food security livelihoods, industrial growth, and environmental sustainability throughout the world. *(CTF)*

More than one billion people do not have sufficient access to clean water. *2.1 billion people lack safe drinking water at home.* (W.H.O. 7/12/17 News release Geneva.) **Much of the world's human population growth and agricultural expansion is taking place in water stressed regions.** (*See Boretti, A., Rosa, L. Reassessing the projections of the World water Development Report. Npj Clean Water 2, 14 (2019). https://doi.org/10.1038/s41545-019-0039-9)*

U.S. Livestock-Caused Damages. *Global figures are not available, but* <u>*in the U.S.,*</u> *with the world's fourth largest land area,* <u>*livestock are responsible for*</u> *an estimated* <u>*55% of erosion and sediment,*</u> <u>*37% of pesticide use,*</u> <u>*50% of antibiotic use,*</u> *and* <u>*a third of the loads of nitrogen and phosphorus into freshwater resources.*</u> *Livestock also affect the replenishment of freshwater by compacting soil, reducing infiltration, degrading the banks of watercourse, drying up flood plains and lowering water tables. Livestock's contribution to deforestation also increase runoff and reduces dry season flows. (See p. xxii of 'Executive summary' of the 'assessment of global livestock-environment interactions by [LEAD] initiative at its meeting in May 2005 in Copenhagen.)*

Meat and dairy products are <u>**highly intensive because of all the grain that is needed**</u>.

Water Depletion and Damaged Soils. The availability of water has always been a limiting factor to human activities in particular agriculture, and the increasing level of demand for water is a growing concern. Excessive withdrawals, and poor water management, have resulted in a <u>lowered groundwater table, damaged soils and reduced water quality worldwide</u>. As a direct consequence of a lack of appropriate water resources management, a number of countries and regions are faced with ongoing depletion of water resources. *(CTF)*

LAND

<u>Livestock or livestock feed occupies 1/3 of the earth's ice-free land.</u> (CTF)

<u>Livestock covers 45% of the earth's total land.</u> *(CTF)*

<u>**Species Extinction/Habitat Destruction**</u>. <u>**Animal agriculture is the leading cause of species extinction, ocean dead zones, water pollution, and habitat destruction**</u>. Animal agriculture contributes to species extinction in many ways. *(See Species Extinction below for more details.)*

<u>2-5 acres of land are used per cow.</u> *(CTF)*

<u>**Nearly half of the contiguous US is devoted to animal agriculture**</u>. *(CTF)* The US lower 48 states represent 1.9 billion acres. Of that 1.9 billion acres: 778 million acres of private land are used for livestock grazing (forest grazing, pasture grazing, and crop grazing), 345 million acres for feed crops, 230 million acres of public land are used for grazing livestock. *(CTF)*

<u>**Desertification. 1/3 of the planet is desertified**</u> with livestock as the leading driver. (Desertification is the process by which fertile land becomes desert, typically as a result of drought, deforestation or inappropriate agriculture.) "Nearly one fifth of the world's land is threatened with desertification") *(CTF)*

COST According to some estimates, industrialized farming, which produces greenhouse gas emission, pollutes air and water, and destroys wildlife, costs the environment the equivalent of about <u>$3 trillion every year</u>. *(UN environment programme -"10 things you should know about industrial farming" ://www.unenvironment.org.)*

WASTE

(The following two paragraphs do not include the animals raised outside of USDA jurisdiction or in backyards, or the billions of fish raised in aquaculture settings in the US.) (CTF)

Every minute, 7 million pounds of excrement are produced by animals raised for food in the US.
*Total manure produced in one day is 9.519105 billion lbs. *(CTF)* Total manure produced in one year is 3.475 trillion lbs. *This is the equivalent of over 6.611 million lbs. per minute.

The massive scale that factory farms are run, without any connection to the land, the hundreds of millions of tons of waste produced and subsequently spread on land cannot be absorbed and filtered by the environment. *(TEIFF)*

Unregulated Waste That Is Untreated. These "externalities" are the result of these factories operating virtually unregulated, which has led to the dumping of hundreds of millions of tons of untreated sewage onto surrounding land, ultimately making its way into waterways and surrounding communities. According to the USDA and the EPA, animal feeding operations produce approximately 500 million tons of manure every year, with the largest facilities generating 60% of that waste. It is estimated that confined animals generate 3 times more waste than humans in the United States, however unlike human sewage, this waste is never treated and merely disposed of on land. *(TEIFF)*

Animals produce enough waste per year to cover every square foot of San Francisco, New York city, Tokyo, Paris, New Deli Berlin, Hong Kong, London, Rio De Janeiro, Delaware, Bali, Costa Rica, and Denmark combined. (based off 1 lb. of waste per 1 sq, ft. at 1.4 billion tons.) *(CTF)*

*Total manure produced in one year is 3.475 trillion lbs. (From above calculation.) *(CTF)*

Waste Lagoons and Their Effect. *(TEIFF)* Prior to this toxic waste being disposed of on land, it typically spends time in storage systems. These systems are essentially lakes as large as 14 acres by 25 feet deep, holding as much as 20-45 million gallons of waste. While the waste sits, it emits pollutants and greenhouse gases, such as methane, into the air contributing to climate change. The holding systems also leak and spill into water bodies in amounts that have the potential to be staggering.

A number of manure lagoons have experienced catastrophic failures, sending tens of millions of gallons of raw manure into streams, rivers, and estuaries, killing millions of fish.

Property Values Can Diminish in the Range of 50% to nearly 90% due to Proximity to Factory Farms, resulting in catastrophic effects on counties. *(TEIFF)* The economic impacts of factory farming extend beyond the proliferation of dead zones, as the factories themselves have **severe consequences for local economies**. Based on the harm factory farms inflict on water, air, and public health in their vicinity, it is not surprising that they also impact local property values **due to the unpleasant sight and odor of farms**. Neighbors complain of intolerable stench with **constant worry of pollution to drinking water sources**. *(TEIFF)*

Another study determined that each factory farm in Missouri has lowered property values in its surrounding community by an average of $2.68 million. *(TEIFF)*

If you consider the fact that **there are an estimated 20,000 Concentrated Animal Feeding Operations (CAFOs) in the U.S.**, property losses may total over $50 billion. Often, the **longtime residents of these communities have their voices drowned out by the industry's cash and lobbying**. *(TEIFF)*

OCEANS

__3/4 of the world's fisheries are exploited or depleted__. *(CTF)* The __We could see fishless oceans by 2048__. *(CTF)* According to Lisa Agabian, <u>SEA SHEPHERD</u>, Conservation Society, *"The oceans are under siege as never before. Marine environments are in trouble. And if we don't wake up and do something about it, we are going to see fishless oceans by the year 2048, that is the prediction from scientists."*

As many as 2.7 trillion animals are pulled from the ocean each year. *(CTF)* For every 1 pound of fish caught, up to 5 pounds of unintended marine species are caught and discarded as by-kill. *(CTF)* As many as 40% (63 billion pounds) of fish caught globally every year are discarded. *(CTF)* Scientists estimate as many as 650,000 whales, dolphins and seals are killed every year by fishing vessels. *(CTF)* Fish catch peaks at 85 million tons. *(CTF)* 40-50 million sharks are killed in fishing lines and nets. *(CTF)* Right whales are one step from extinction as warmer waters push them northward into boat traffic. *(CTF)*

The UN reported that three-quarters of the world's fisheries are overexploited, fully exploited, or significantly depleted due to overfishing.

RAINFOREST DESTRUCION

Our rainforests are the planet's lungs. They breathe in CO2 and exhale oxygen.

<u>Animal agriculture is responsible for up to 91% of Amazon destruction.</u> *(See CTF and Dr. Richard Oppenlander, Environmental Researcher, Author, Comfortably Unaware)* 1-2 acres of rainforest are cleared every second. *(CTF)* The <u>leading causes of rainforest destruction are livestock and feedcrops.</u> *(CTF)*

<u>Destruction of the Species.</u> Up to 137 plant, animal and insect species are lost every day due to rainforest destruction. *(CTF)*

<u>Our Lungs for Palm Oil Profits.</u> 26 million rainforest acres (10.8m hectares) have been cleared for palm oil production. *(CTF)*

<u>136 million rainforest acres cleared for animal agriculture.</u> *(CTF)*

<u>1,100 land activists have been killed in Brazil in the past 20 years.</u> *(CTF)*

WILDLIFE

In addition to the monumental habitat destruction caused by <u>clearing forests</u> and converting land to grow feed crops and for animal grazing, <u>predators and "competition" species are frequently targeted and hunted</u> because of a perceived threat to livestock profits. *(See Cowspiracy and Deniz Bolbol, American Wild Horse Preservation Campaign for gravity of this targeting and hunting.)* *"It is the insistence of and the lobbying power of the animal agriculture industry that continues to see wolves killed, that continues to see an insistence that predators be maintained at a low level that does not benefit the ecosystems."* (Cowspiracy)

<u>Imprisoning and killing Our Wild Animals.</u> Our USDA is killing predators of wild animals to protect livestock. *(CTF)* Illustrative is the Washington Dept of fish & Wildlife killing seven members of the Wedge Pack from a helicopter after a series of calf and sheep deaths in 2012. (CTF)

According to Dr. Will Tuttle, Environmental and Ethics Author: *"We have basically completely stolen the world, the earth from free living animals, to use for ourselves and our cows, pigs and chickens. Fish in the ocean have even been more devastated."*

The widespread use of pesticides, herbicides and chemical fertilizers used in the production of feed crops often interferes with the reproductive systems of animals and poison waterways. The overexploitation of wild species through commercial fishing, bushmeat trade as well as animal agriculture's impact on climate change, all contribute to global depletion of species and resources. *(CTF)*

We now have the **largest mass extinction in 65 million years**. *(CTF)* The decline of the bee population is another example. *(CTF)*

The government has been rounding up horses en masse, and we now have more wild horses and burros in government holding facilities, 50,000 wild horses and burros in government holding facilities, than we have free on the range. (Deniz Bolbol, American Wild Horse Preservation Campaign) *(CTF)*

Ten thousand years ago, 99% of biomass (i.e. zoomass) was wild animals. Today, humans and the animals that we raise as food make up 98% of the zoomass.)*(CTF)*

Biodiversity. We are in an era of unprecedented threats to biodiversity. The loss of species is estimated to be running 50 to 500 times higher than background rates found in the fossil record. Fifteen out of 24 important ecosystem services are assessed to be in decline.

Reducing Biodiversity Through Deforestation. Livestock now account for about 20% of the total terrestrial animal biomass, and the 30% of the earth's land surface that they now pre-empt, what was once habitat for wildlife. Indeed, the **livestock sector may well be the leading player in the reduction of biodiversity**, since it is the major driver of deforestation, as well as one of the leading drivers of land degradation, pollution, climate change, overfishing, sedimentation of coastal areas and facilitation of invasions by alien species. In addition, resource conflicts with pastoralists, threaten species of wild predators and also protected areas close to pastures. Meanwhile, in developed regions, especially Europe, pastures had become a location of diverse long-established types of ecosystems, many of which are now threatened by pasture abandonment.

If anyone cares about wild horses and wildlife and public lands and the environment, you can't ignore the impact, the negative impact, that livestock grazing is having on our public lands in the West. (Deniz Bolbol)

HUMANITY

'The fact of it is that we could feed every human being on the planet today an adequate diet if we did no more than take the feed that we are feeding to animals and actually turn it into food for the humans.' (Howard Lyman, Author, Mad Cowboy)

Today, 70 billion land animals are abused and killed every year in unimaginably depraved conditions. *(TEIFF)*

Summary of The Missing Paragraphs of David Simon, Lawyer, Author of Meatonomic$: *"The most heartbreaking feature of today's hellish, industrial meat production systems is that none of the billions of animals who spend their entire lives as prisoners will ever experience the slightest affection from, or fellowship with, another living being. They will be stripped from their mothers just when the maternal relationship is most craved by mother and child. Some will never know a mother's touch or call, nor taste a mother's milk...." "There's no humanity whatsoever in these factory systems – that is to say, there's no evidence of any human attribute other than the shallowest desire to make a profit.*

It's hard to imagine a more perfect hell for the animals we debase and insult in this manner. It's an embarrassment to humankind that in our treatment of our fellow planetary voyagers, we have forsaken the best qualities of our species – compassion, mercy and kindness, for the basest – greed, cruelty and violence. Unfortunately, that's simply the bleak nature of the factory farming systems that produce almost all the meat, eggs and dairy consumed in the industrialized world." (CTF)

Comment. *(I have included this paragraph because it reveals how we so easily have lost touch with nature. It reveals how we have so easily lost and forgotten our maternal instincts towards nature and our fellow earth travelers. We apparently can no longer feel the painful cost of our luxuries. We have fully accepted the cost of capitalism - our soul!)*

Cows Over Humanity The way that these companies are operating is leading to a crisis that will cost Americans, and the planet, exponentially more as costs build over time. Some people wonder if factory farming is necessary to feed the world. In reality, the reverse is true. Feeding huge numbers of confined animals actually uses more food – in the form of grains and other plants that could be used to feed humans directly. This is represented in the fact that if every animal-based food item was replaced with plant-based alternatives, enough food would be added to feed 350 million additional people. *(TEIFF)*

It is painfully clear that this **system is an unethical and uneconomical** way to produce the food we need. In contrast, sustainably grown foods cost a bit more upfront but their beneficial impacts on society and the environment are built into their price, saving us from these additional costs in the long run.

We are currently growing enough food to feed 10 billion people. *(CTF)*. Worldwide, at least 50% of grain is fed to livestock.*(CTF)* Cows eat 135 billion pounds of food per day. *(Cowspiracy)* According to Dr. Will Tuttle, *We have roughly a billion people starving every single day. Worldwide, 50% of the grain and legumes that we're growing, we're feeding to animals.*

Are We the Cause of Children Starving?*)* Dr. Richard Oppenlander, Environmental Researcher and Author of *Comfortably Unaware and Food Choices and Sustainability*: *"82% of the world's starving children live in countries where food is fed to animals in the livestock system that are then killed and eaten by more well-off individuals in developed countries such as the U.S., the U.K. and Europe. (Also see (CTF)*

The Hidden Costs. According to David Simon, lawyer and author of *"Meatonomics"*, *"the hidden or externalized costs that are imposed on society, health care, environmental damage, subsidies, damage to fisheries, and cruelty, is about 414 billion dollars* (yearly). *If they had to internalize those costs, the meat and dairy costs would skyrocket…(*five dollar carton of eggs would go to 13, a four-dollar Big Mac, would go to eleven dollars.) *"Whether you eat meat or not, you are paying part of the cost of somebody else's consumption. (See Cowspiracy)*

The Taxpayer Costs of Industrial Agriculture. *(TEIFF)* From 1995-2013, taxpayers provided $292.5 billion in direct agricultural subsidies and $96 billion in crop insurance subsidies.

Direct **costs to Americans**, as taxpayers, for the operation and pollution of factory farms comes in the form of subsidies to these corporations, cleanup costs to water supplies and ecosystems, as well as new infrastructure for lost ecosystem services.

The federal government spends more than $20 billion a year on subsidies for farm businesses. From 1995-2013, taxpayers provided $292.5 billion in direct agricultural subsidies, $96 billion in crop insurance subsidies, and over $100 billion in subsidies to grow genetically engineered crops, many of which are used to feed the animals slaughtered for meat. While huge operations reel in these taxpayer payments, the smallest 80 percent of farms within that timeframe received on average a total $604 in annual subsidies. In 2012 alone, $15.8 billion in taxpayer dollars went to farms in providing crop insurance with an outsized majority going to the largest factory farms. This amount is expected to climb to $90 billion over the next 10 years.

Furthermore, the **USDA uses tax dollars to promote factory farming by providing and guaranteeing loans** used by these giant facilities. Between 2009 and 2015, the Farm Service Agency approved almost $50 million in direct or guaranteed loans for chicken operations in <u>Maryland alone</u>.

Finally, <u>clean-up costs</u> from pollution run-off caused by the agricultural sector as a whole are astronomical – with an annual price tag of nearly $2 billion. The National Research Council has estimated the total economic costs of agricultural runoff lie anywhere between $2-16 billion annually. One researcher has calculated the total cost of just cleaning the soil under U.S. hog and dairy farms at <u>$4.1 billion</u>. In comparison, <u>Kansas taxpayers</u> have paid $56 million to remediate leaching at dairy and hog farms.

THE HUMAN COST

<u>Brazil Killing Environmental Activists.</u> "[Dorothy Stang's] death prompted Amazon activists – more than 1,000 of whom have been murdered in the last 20 years – to demand Brazil's government crack-down on the illegal seizure and clearance of the rainforest to graze cattle, raise soy crops, and harvest timber." "More than 1,100 activists, small farmers, judges, priests and other rural workers have been killed in land disputes in the last two decades."

In 2019, 212 environmental activists were killed, a record number. *(CTF)*

Rachel Cox, a campaigner at Global Witness, reported: *"Agribusiness and oil, gas and mining have been consistently the biggest drivers of attacks against land and environmental defenders-and they are also the industries pushing us further into runaway climate change through deforestation and increasing carbon emissions," (CTF)*

Who Is Getting the Medicine? 80% of antibiotics sold in the US are for livestock.*(CTF)*

<u>Human Population Rising.</u> World population in 1812: 1 billion; 1912: 1.5 billion; 2012: 7 billion. *(CTF)*

<u>The Numbers of Farm Animals.</u> 70 billion farmed animals are reared annually worldwide. More than 6 million animals are killed for food every hour. *(CTF)*

Who's Consuming the Water? Throughout the world, humans drink 5.2 billion gallons of water and eat 21 billion pounds of food each day. There are <u>7.5011 billion people on earth</u>. Worldwide, cows drink 45 billion gallons of water and eat 135 billion pounds of food each day. *(CTF)*.

Why Do A Handful of Companies, Collecting Billions in Profit and Receive Billions in Taxpayer Money Go Unregulated & Pass Financial and Health Costs On To American Taxpayers? <u>Because today those who have the capacity to pump millions of dollars into the political sphere to elect officials are prioritized over those who do not.</u> *(TEIFF)*

Regulatory Issues In Factory Farming. Increase in Ag-Gag Laws. *(TEIFF)* Finally, in the past decade there has been an increase in ag-gag laws across the country. These pieces of legislation punish investigators uncovering what goes on in factory farm facilities hoping to bring to light the cruelty, abuse, and food safety issues. These laws were pushed for by agribusiness after investigators revealed animals beaten, kicked, mutilated and thrown. Luckily, courts in some states have recently found these laws unconstitutional.

The Government Accountability Office (GAO), found EPA's regulation of the industry woefully inadequate, determining that the EPA has allowed 60% of AFOs to go unregulated. (TEIFF)

The Clean Water Act's Loopholes. Lax regulations along with an extreme lack of funding to federal and state environmental agencies responsible for enforcing those regulations has led to a vastly unregulated industry that has enabled the environmental impact of factory farming to grow even larger over the years. The few attempts to strengthen regulations have been challenged by industry and their enormous power, leading to very little progress at proper regulation.

The Clean Water Act (CWA) is the source for nearly all regulation of factory farms in the United States, by controlling the amount of pollution entering U.S. waters, including rivers and wetlands. Under the CWA, factory farms are referred to as Animal Feeding Operations (AFOs) and Concentrated Animal Feeding Operations (CAFOs). AFOs are operations where animals are, or will be, confined for a total of 45 days or more in any 12-month period, and where crops and vegetation are not sustained in the normal growing season over any portion of the lot. **AFOs that meet the definition of a CAFO are regulated by the EPA under the CWA.**

To be considered a CAFO, a facility must meet one of three criteria delineated by the EPA in terms of capacity from large, medium, to small depending on species. For instance, CAFOs meet the large criteria if they house 1,000 or more cattle, 10,000 or more swine, or 125,000 or more chickens. To be considered a medium CAFO, a facility contains 300-999 cattle, 3,000-9,999 hogs, or 37,500-124,999 chickens AND also discharge pollutants into U.S. waters "through a man-made ditch, flushing system, or other similar man-made device" OR directly into U.S. waters. Smaller AFOs *may* be regulated as CAFOs on a case-by-case basis. There are roughly **450,000 AFOs in the United States, of which over 20,000 meet the criteria for CAFOs**.

Under the CWA, CAFOs that discharge pollutants into a "water of the United States" are required to apply for a CWA permit and must not discharge more pollutants than stipulated in the permit or run the risk of violation. As with nearly all environmental regulations, the role of the federal government is to set national guidelines and oversee the states' role in direct enforcement of those guidelines. Due to EPA's delegation to the states and each state's ability to implement more strict standards, regulation of these facilities varies from state to state. *(TEIFF)*

While CAFO operators are in violation of permits for discharges that exceed the amounts allowable in their permits, it is up to the operator himself whether to apply for permit coverage, or when they do apply whether they feel the need to meet the limits specified. Even when permits are obtained, the requirements are too lax and there is extremely little enforcement regarding the terms. *(TEIFF)*

Loopholes. On top of this, there are many loopholes. Facilities that have permits and perform certain land practices (nutrient management plans) have the ability to be exempt from any run-off discharges that occur during very heavy rainfalls, a problem compounded as climate change leads to more regular intense storms. The requirement for manure application within the property of the CAFOs themselves, do not extend to the application of manure that is shipped off-site. In some areas of the country, to escape the CWA, facilities ship up to 85% of their manure offsite where federal rules no longer apply to the application to open fields. Even more, the CWA does not address air pollutants or prohibit the use of manure lagoons susceptible to spills. *(TEIFF)*

Worsening Regulation & Enforcement. Given the extreme lack of funding to environmental agencies, regulators rely heavily on CAFOs self-reporting and, in many instances, EPA and state regulators do not even know if a CAFO exists. As such, CAFO operators typically weigh whether their situation poses enough risk of getting caught discharging to warrant applying for a permit. Moreover, in the few instances of inspection and enforcement, CAFO operators are frequently only given warnings, despite extreme unpermitted pollution.

In 2017... the EPA inspected only 0.6% of all (factory farming) facilities. With regulator's inability to investigate a large portion of operating CAFOs, it is not surprising that many operate without permits. A nonpartisan government agency, the Government Accountability Office (GAO), found EPA's regulation of the industry woefully inadequate, determining that the EPA has allowed 60% of AFOs to go unregulated. In 2017, of the 19,496 CAFOs in the country, the EPA conducted 125 inspections and concluded 18 enforcement actions, meaning that the EPA inspected only 0.6 percent of all facilities. This shows that already inadequate enforcement is dropping considerably more after administrative changes in early 2017, with pushes to slash EPA funding further.

Due to poor funding to environmental agencies, the GAO found that that no federal agency collects the accurate and consistent data on CAFOs that is prerequisite to effective environmental enforcement strategy, concluding that the EPA "cannot fulfill its regulatory duties to protect human health and the environment without accurate and facility-specific information about CAFOs." EPA has recognized this much itself stating: "EPA does not have facility specific information for all CAFOs in the U.S."

Decrease in Federal Protections For Wetlands. Another major rollback of environmental regulations, directly impacting factory farm pollution, concerns specifically which streams, rivers, wetlands, and other water bodies the EPA has jurisdiction over and may prevent pollution into, under the CWA. EPA's jurisdiction of waters had been uncertain since a 2006 Supreme Court case, by which the court attempted to discern which waters, the EPA may limit pollution into. In 2015, after a 4-year scientific review, the EPA formulated the "Clean Water Rule", which was meant to solidify which waters may be regulated by the EPA under the Court's decision.

A 41-member EPA Science Advisory Board states the rule "decreases protection for our Nation's waters and does not support the objective of restoring and maintaining 'the chemical, physical and biological integrity' of these waters."

However, once entering office, the **Trump** Administration **quickly rescinded that rule** and this past February released its revised "Waters of the United States." **This rule dramatically restricts the waters that fall under EPA authority, with the U.S. Geological Survey estimating that the rule removes federal protections for 1 in every 5 streams and 51% of wetlands.** A 41-member **EPA Science Advisory Board**, made up largely of Trump Administration appointees, states the rule "decreases protection for our Nation's waters and **does not support the objective of restoring and maintaining 'the chemical, physical and biological integrity' of these waters."**

Gutting protections for wetlands is very problematic due to their status as important ecosystems for humans and wildlife. These areas, along rivers and streams, intercept and naturally filter harmful industrial pollution, naturally reduce flood damage, and act as buffers to coastal communities at threat of increasingly harsher storms in the years ahead. With further ability to destroy wetlands, taxpayers will be on the hook to fund the replacement of services we currently get for free. This will require installing technology to purify our waters and building structures along our shores as sea levels rise and storms intensify.

By removing federal oversight of these waterways, the EPA's proposed rule leaves it up to the states to carry the burden of environmental regulations. However, states have unquestionably too few resources to even attempt to deal with these problems. In fact, fewer than half of the states have their own permitting programs to protect wetlands. This deficiency is known by industry leaders and is why they are lobbying the federal government to comply with their demands.

Lack of Transparency. In a massive effort to assess just how little regulation this industry faces, in 2010, organizations such as the **Natural Resource Defense Council (NRDC)** began sending

Freedom of Information Act (FOIA) requests to the EPA for its records on CAFOs. NRDC found that the EPA had data on 7,500 CAFOs in 40 states. By comparison, at the time, EPA had estimated 17,300 CAFOs nation-wide, meaning **more than half of facilities were completely unaccounted for by the entities that are supposed to be limiting their pollution.**

Trump Admin Limits Release of EPA Information. Even more, when it comes to state government data, the amount of information available varied considerably from state to state. **For 18 states, NRDC found data on less than 1% of estimated CAFOs.** Unfortunately, **in response to NRDC and other organizations' requests to EPA for CAFO information, Agribusiness filed suit to prevent public discovery of the lack of data on their operations, with EPA Administrator Scott Pruitt (appointed in Feb 2017) appeasing the industry by agreeing to limit future public releases of EPA's information. This lack of transparency makes it even more difficult to keep the environmental impact of factory farming in check.**

The Bottom Line. The public deserves to have more insight into what abuses are suffered by billions of animals in these factories, and the externalities impacting the economy, not less. It goes without saying that **improved regulations** under the Clean Water Act, along with an **investment and drastic increase in the EPA's funding,** is critical to ensuring that industrialized animal agriculture in the U.S. does not continue to devastate public health, our economy, and the welfare of animals.

Reducing The Environmental Impact of Factory Farming: What Can We Do as Individuals? *(TEIFF)* **Elect Environmentally Conscious Candidates… And Vote With Your Wallet, Too**

The need for the American public to elect officials who will extend stronger regulations, and even **ban factory farms**, is long overdue, so that our country's agricultural system can return to one led by independent farmers following sustainable practices. *(TEIFF)*

Along with increasing demands of those in office to stand up to this billion-dollar industry, we must also **use our power as consumers.** By cutting cheap fast food and supermarket meat and dairy from our diets, while choosing to **buy "pasture raised" or at least "free range" from local-independent farms** when we do buy meat, we will tell the factory farming industry that they must change the way they operate if they want to continue to make profits. Even more, from a consumer health perspective these products contain less antibiotic resistant bacteria linked to food-borne illness. *(TEIFF)*

Meat Alternatives. While these sustainably produced foods may cost a bit more at the store, they cost us all much less in the grand scheme of things. The power of consumers has been shown lately in the growth of the **alternative meat industry with the success of startups like Beyond Meat and Impossible Foods, and these massive corporations are taking notice.**

Question Factory Farming Norms. *(TEIFF)* The environmental impact of factory farming is clearly severe and wide-reaching. As consumers continue to buy cheap meat from unsustainable sources and federal and state governments continue to allow these companies such as Tyson, Perdue, and Cargill to operate unregulated, the current situation will only get worse for those left to deal with the consequences. It is also important to realize that due to the complex web that are ecosystems, we are likely underestimating the true extent of the damage. This has been seen in many environmental studies and models, including those of climate change, where each year scientists find new variables that reveal a bleaker outlook on the true damage. *(TIEFF)*

Along with the costs that American citizens face, these huge companies that have no connection to their animals, are **inflicting unbelievable physical and emotional pain on self-aware beings**. While these animals live their lives in extreme confinement unable to even turn around, there are countless examples of cows, pigs, chickens, and turkeys being abused and beaten, even chicks being thrown in meat grinders while alive.

*Along with increasing **demands of those in office** to stand up to this billion-dollar industry, we must also use our* power as consumers. *(TIEFF)*

As individuals we must start questioning why something is the way that it is, and why don't we do it a better way? Is this because we do not like to change, or to question ourselves despite newly acquired knowledge? We have to look at our own decisions as we all have opportunities to force the improvement of our agricultural system. We need to demand the necessary improvements through who we elect to office and in our purchasing power as consumers. Industrial agriculture and our diets must change if the world is to prosper. (TIEFF)

One Earth and Soul-Saving Solution – Veganism

According to Michael Pollan, Best Selling Food Author of 'In Defense of Food': *'I think a plant-based diet is the most sustainable.'*

Dr. Will Tuttle, Environmental and Ethics Author, and author of *The World Peace Diet: We have roughly a billion people starving every single day. World-wide 50% of the legumes and grain that we are growing we feed to animals. They are eating huge amounts of grains and legumes and in the United States it is more like 90% of the soybean.*

If we became Vegan, If we didn't kill all these cows and eat them, then we wouldn't have to breed all these cows, chickens and pigs, then we wouldn't have to feed them, then we wouldn't have to devote all this land to growing grains and legumes to feed to them, then the forests could come back, wildlife could come back, the oceans would come back, the rivers would come clean again, the air would come back, our health would return.

<u>Solutions and Reasons:</u> A person who follows a vegan diet produces the equivalent of 50% less carbon dioxide, uses 1/11th oil, 1/13th water, and 1/18th land compared to a meat-lover for their food. *(CTF)*

<u>Vegetarian Requires Less Land.</u> Land required to feed 1 person for 1 year: Vegan: 1/6th acre; Vegetarian: 3x as much as a vegan; Meat Eater: 18x as much as a vegan. *(CTF)*

<u>Safe and efficient Protein:</u> There is <u>15x more protein on any given area of land with plants, rather than cows.</u> <u>Soybeans</u> can be produced at 52.5 bushels per acre x 60 lbs. per bushel = 3,150 dry soybeans per acre. Soybeans protein content (dry) is 163.44 grams per pound.

The protein content per acre of soybeans is 163.44 g x 3,150 lb. = 514,836 g per acre. Beef can be produced at 205 pounds per acre. Beef protein content (raw) is 95.34 grams per pound. Each day, a person who eats a vegan diet saves 1,100 gallons of water, 45 pounds of grain, 30 sq. ft. of forested land, 20 lbs. CO2 equivalent, and one animal's life. *(CTF)*

According to Michael Pollan, Best Selling Food Author of *In Defense of Food: It is a brutal system on every level. A plant-based diet is most sustainable.*

Solution – Buying Organic Produce. Buying organic produce reduces the likelihood of being exposed to the unhealthy bacteria and antibiotics in animal products. Buying organic produce also reduces the amount of burning fossil fuels and would also decrease the amount of carbon dioxide and greenhouse gas emissions. Local organic farm animals are also treated better and are raised in a healthy environment without overcrowding. (*See article 'Environment and Wellness' supra*)

What Drives Animal Agriculture? The surge in factory farming has been driven by these corporations' enormous political influence and weak environmental regulations.

So Why Do We Keep Eating Meat? In light of the above, why not become Vegan? Is it our culture, our genes, our taste buds or the powerful meat industry with its annual sales in the US higher than the GDP of Hungary or Ukraine *(NAMI North American Meat Institute)?* When confronted with the damaging facts stated above, why would we make the choice of suicide and world-ending death to humanity?

In Cowspiracy, we are told by Bruce Hamilton, Sierra Club, Deputy Executive Director that, on our watch, we are facing the next major extinction of species on the earth that we haven't seen since the time of the dinosaurs disappearing.

Industry-created Fear. In Cowspiracy, Will Potter, was interviewed. The Journalist and Author of "Green Is The New Red" said:

The Animal Agriculture industry is one of the most powerful industries on the planet. "Animal rights and environmental activists are the number one domestic terrorism threat according to the FBI. He believed the reason for this was that they, *more than any other social movements today, are directly threatening corporate profits. When we tried to find out how factory farms and animal agriculture was polluting the environment, they tried to claim exemptions to that information, either under National Security terms or public safety, trademark issues, business secret...we have seen all these attempts to keep people in the dark about what they're actually doing. One of the largest industries on the planet with the biggest environmental impact, was trying to keep us in the dark about how they were operating.*

Through the Freedom of Information Act, we obtained documents from the Counter-Terrorism unit, that showed they were monitoring my lectures, media interviews..., my website, my book,.. You are going up against people who have massive legal resources. It is just overwhelming the amount of money at their disposal and you have nothing. That fear is a big part of the tactic, as well.

The Cost of Telling the Truth. Tellingly, those financially supporting *Cowspiracy* withdrew funding because of the 'sensitive' nature of the topic.

In the documentary, *Cowspiracy*, Howard Lyman, former cattle rancher and author of *Mad Cowboy*, was interviewed. He was on the Oprah show and addressed The Food Disparagement law. It was against the law to say something you knew to be false about a perishable commodity. He denied saying anything on the Oprah show, he thought to be false. He and Oprah were sued by the National Cattlemen's Beef Association. It took five years and hundreds of thousands of dollars 'to extricate' himself from the suits of the cattle industry. Both were found 'not guilty' in 1998. He states that if someone says what he said back then, they would be found guilty under the Patriot Act even though he told the truth because you would be causing a disruption of the profits in the Animal Industry. Through the Freedom of Information Act, he obtained documents from the Anti-terrorist Unit that showed they were monitoring his lectures, media interviews, his website, and his book, *Mad Cowboy*.

The Oprah Suit. In April of 1996, Oprah Winfrey's show aired an episode on food safety.

(Same show as above.) In one segment they discussed mad cow disease. Howard Lyman, a vegetarian and animal rights activist, predicted that the disease would eventually plague the U.S. beef industry. Winfrey declared that the discussion "has just stopped me cold from eating another burger. I'm stopped."

The segment was widely viewed as having contributed to a drop in cattle prices. Members of the cattle industry were furious, as was U.S. Energy Secretary Rick Perry, who was then the Texas agriculture commissioner. Within days, Perry wrote a letter to Texas Attorney General Dan Morales, urging the state to take legal action against Lyman under a Texas law that was less than a year old. Texas, along with a dozen states had adopted the "veggie libel" laws that made a person liable for making false statements about the safety of food. To his credit, Morales refused to file an action. However, members of the Texas cattle industry soon stepped in and filed a lawsuit against Winfrey and others, alleging more than $10 million in damages. The jury trial was in Amarillo, Texas.

The attorney for Oprah knew he had his work cut out for him when he started seeing bumper stickers in town reading "The only mad cow in Texas is Oprah." And T-shirts sporting Winfrey's face and a red line across it. Of the 60 people called in for jury service, *"there wasn't one of them that wasn't connected to the cattle industry in some way"*. The cattle industry was a massive employer in the region.

Winfrey admitted: "It was stressful. It was challenging. To be on trial, may I just say, is one of the worst experiences of anybody's life."

On February 26, 1998, the jury voted unanimously in Winfrey's favor.

As of 2018, the 'veggie libel' law was still on the books.

Are Our Environmental "Protection" Organizations Not Protecting Us? Why Not? In *Cowspiracy: The Sustainability Secret,* Kip Andersen, (Director), interviewed the heads of the organizations that ostensibly exist to protect the environment and reviewed their literature. Whether it was Oceana, Greenpeace, '350.Org., Amazon Watch…..Sierra Club, Surfrider Foundation, they had virtually nothing on animal agriculture. They all seemed ignorant or feigned ignorance when asked about animal agriculture being the biggest polluter and the cause of forest destruction.

When Greenpeace refused to speak with Kip Anderson., He interviewed the former Greenpeace board of directors, Greenpeace USA and Greenpeace Alaska Founder, Will Anderson who explained:

"The environmental organizations, like other organizations, are not telling you the truth about what the world needs from us as a species. The information is right before their eyes. It's documented, peer reviewed, papers and journals. It is there for everybody to see. But the environmental organizations are refusing to act. Nowhere do you find in their policies or do you find in the Greenpeace mission that diet is important, that animal agriculture is the problem. It is so frustrating. They are refusing, like other environmental organizations, to look at the issue. The environmental community is failing us and failing the eco-systems. And it is so frustrating to see them doing this.

Why Are So Few Talking About Animal Agriculture Causing Pollution? A handful of corporations now control the marketplace: Tyson, Perdue, Cargill, and ADM. The stranglehold these few companies are exerting on our food system has become even more excessive in the last few decades, as we have seen a staggering increase in the intensive confinement of animals and replacement of small family operations. (*TAIFF*)

The surge in factory farming has been driven by these corporations' enormous political influence and weak environmental regulations. (*TAIFF*)

It Hurt's Fundraising. According to Michael Pollan, Environmental and Food Author of *"The Omnivore's Dilemma"*: *"They've* (the environmental organizations) *focused-grouped it and it is a political loser." They're membership organizations, a lot of them, they are looking to maximize the number of people making contributions… And if they get identified as being anti-meat, or challenging people on their every-day habits, that is something so dear to people,,, that it will hurt with their fund-raising"*

Lobbying Power of Animal Agriculture. Animal Agriculture Dictates Federal Policies. According to Wenonah Hauter, Food & Water Watch, Executive Director: *"When you look at who is lobbying for this system of agriculture, the largest food producers in the country and meat producers become so large and wealthy, they can dictate the federal policies around producing food because they have so much political power."*

It starts at the local level with the Bureau of Land Managements, and it goes all the way to Congress, sitting there willing to allow this type of mismanagement of our public lands to continue. (Deniz Bolbol)

The Effects of Lobbying. *(TEIFF)* Lawmakers' failure to properly fund environmental agencies and ensure proper protection of the public is largely due to the industry's influence in the political sphere. **The Pew Commission on Industrial Farm Animal Production Executive Director, Robert Martin, found "significant influence by agribusiness at every turn: in academic research, policy development, government regulation, and enforcement." This influence has been obtained by big animal agriculture spending $40 million per year on lobbying and campaign contributions."** *(TEIFF)*

From 2008-2013 agribusiness, as a whole, spent $751 million lobbying Congress. In direct **campaign contributions over the past two decades, agribusiness spent $480.5 million (with two-thirds going to republican candidates). The Trump Administration, more than any other, has been a revolving door for lobbyists to take charge of the government agencies who are tasked with regulating those industries. The administration's first pick as EPA Administrator, Scott Pruitt, received $345,246 in campaign contributions from the oil and gas industry in his previous position as Attorney General of Oklahoma. In that position, he sued the agency he would eventually be picked to lead 13 times in efforts to roll back regulations.** Upon Pruitt's resignation in 2017, the next pick to lead the EPA, Andrew Wheeler, previously served as a lobbyist for the fossil fuel industry and is now tasked with ensuring these industries provide safe environments for the public. **The Secretary of the Department of Interior, David Bernhardt, previously worked as a lobbyist on behalf of big agribusiness.**

Given this Administration's ties to corporate America, it is not surprising that the Trump Administration has attempted to revise or eliminate more than 90 environmental rules since entering office. **Despite already woefully scarce funding, the Administration has proposed drastic budget cuts to the Agency each year in office**. These cuts would eliminate 50 EPA programs and enact immense reduction of more than 50% to science, research, and development. As such, the outlook to gain necessary regulation of the environmental impact of factory farming under the current Administration is bleak. While the Obama EPA had added CAFO regulation and enforcement to its priority list in 2016, factory farms were quickly taken off the priority program in 2017. *(TEIFF)*

Fear of Losing Funding. According to Dr. Will Tuttle, environmental and Ethics Author,

"They do not want to address the primary driving cause of environmental devastation, which is animal agriculture, because they are businesses and they want to make sure that they have a reliable source of funding."

The protection of the Animal Agriculture industry goes even further than our cultural and political influences. There exists in this country a legal weapon used against those who would dare threaten the animal agricultural industry. The Animal Enterprise Protection Act of 1992 (Pub.L. 102–346). The law amends the law and gives the U.S. Department of Justice greater authority to target animal rights activists. The AETA does so by broadening the definition of "animal enterprise" to include academic and commercial enterprises that use or sell animals or animal products. It also increases the existing penalties, and includes penalties based on the amount of economic damage caused, and allows animal enterprises to seek restitution. *(See Wikipedia)*

The law contains a savings clause that indicates it should not be construed to "prohibit any expressive conduct (including peaceful picketing or other peaceful demonstration) protected from legal prohibition by the First Amendment to the Constitution." However, by its own terms, the statute criminalizes acts such as "intimidation." And prosecutions under AETA require using evidence of otherwise lawful free speech in order to demonstrate a "course of conduct" as proof of purpose or possible conspiracy. *(See Wikipedia)*

In July 2014, two men were indicted for "animal enterprise terrorism" after releasing 2,000 foxes and mink from fur farms. Their lawyer announced plans to challenge the constitutionality of the law. *(See Wikipedia)*

ARE ENVIRONMENTALISTS THE NEW TERRORISTS? According to Will Potter in his book *'Green Is The New Red'* he effectively argues that in a time when so many people are going green, the FBI is using anti-terrorism resources to target environmentalists and animal rights activists. The courts are being used to push conventional boundaries of what constitutes "terrorism" and to hit nonviolent activists with disproportionate sentences. Potter compares what is going on today with the Red Scare and the 'McCarthyism' of the 50's. It is about fear and intimidation, using a word-"eco-terrorist" to push a political agenda and instill fear and silence.

He effectively states that the animal-rights and environmental movements directly threaten corporate profits every time activists encourage people to go vegan, to stop driving, to consume fewer resources and live simply.

Potter warns that the U.S. government is using post-9-11 anti-terrorism resources to target environmentalists and animal right activists.

CONCLUSION. In case it is not clear why I spent so much time on the issue of animal agriculture, it illustrates strikingly the theme that runs throughout this book – the extensive lack of empathy for humanity and nature and the dearth of the maternal instinct that prevents us from feeling the pain of our fellow earth travelers and taking action against the polluters. It further shockingly illustrates the power that money and politics has on anyone trying to address the issue of pollution and focus on the wrongdoers. The issue is a critical one, in light of the quickly occurring earth-ending pollution tragedy.

This is the mountain that our country needs to climb to see what we need to do to successfully fight pollution. But we refuse to make the first step because we refuse to see the pain our fellow earth voyagers are suffering. We are not willing to risk or give up our comfortable lifestyles or limit them in any way.

Government and The Monied Silencing the Environmentalists. Those making fortunes from the tragedy of pollution and aligned and supported by the government, are doing all in their power to silence those who are pointing the finger of responsibility at them.

Tragically, animal industries' earth ending pollution and our apparent inability to timely stop it or even address it, is symptomatic of what Barry Commoner, author of *The Closing Circle*, told us about Capitalism in the eighties: *The very system of enhancing profit in this industry is precisely the cause of its intense, detrimental impact on the environment.* By time we fully appreciate the impact, the damage will have been done. In the case of animal agriculture pollution, the industries' power, monetary, political and legal, is the ultimate pressure working to reduce the likelihood that we will be able to stop the pollution before it is irreversible.

Steak, burgers, bacon, ham, eggs and ice cream are just too good even though they are killing us. And it doesn't help that our government and the animal agriculture industry is refusing to tell us that meat causes cancer. Moreover, it is now a crime to try to save and protect the animals.

It should now be crystal-clear that animal agriculture is one of the greatest polluters in the world and by its very existence, is destroying lives and is a major contributor to the devastation that attends pollution. It is time to stop the villains that sell us meat and dairy!

We must cease to callously, carelessly and cluelessly be the devil-may-care cause of death, disease and earth devastation.

- *Much of the above is based on 'Livestock's Long Shadow: Environmental Issues and Options' It is a United Nations report, released by the Food and Agriculture Organization (FAO) of the United Nations on 29 November 2006, that "aims to assess the full impact of the livestock sector on environmental problems, along with potential technical and policy approaches to mitigation". The following article was also very much inspired by 'Cowspiracy'. (See Netflix) and (COWSPIRACY, THE FACTS)(Also see 'Environmental Effects of Factory Farming' Nov 27, 2019)(See Factory Farming (https://www.farmsanctuar)'THE ISSUES Factory Farming' (Also see Animal Agriculture.. (https://sentientmedia.org) 'Animal Agriculture: Negatively Impacting the World Around Us" by Grant L. Ingel May 19, 19) (Also see 'Environmental Effects of Factory Farming' Nov 27, 2019)(See Factory Farming (https://www.farmsanctuar)'THE ISSUES Factory Farming'*

Underlining is my emphasis.

PLASTIC COMPANIES, (OIL AND GAS) - THE POISONERS, POLLUTERS AND DECEIVERS FOR PROFIT THAT TOO FEW ARE TALKING ABOUT

The following information is taken, for the most part, from the article "How to Avoid Toxic Chemicals in Plastics", written on December 13, 2016. (See https.//www.madesafe.org)(I have relied heavily on the documentary/movie, A Plastic Ocean. See Netflix

Plastic Poison. Plastic is everywhere. Plastic is loaded with toxic chemicals that can harm our health. Plastic contains phthalates, chemicals that migrated from the plastic and find their way into our bodies. Phthalates are endocrine disruptors that are linked to reproductive malformations in baby boys, reduced fertility, developmental disorders, asthma, and increased allergic reactions. They've also been identified by Project TENDR (Targeting Environmental Neuro-Developmental risks) as "a prime example of chemicals of emerging concern to brain development."

Baby Poisoners. Bottle-fed babies are swallowing millions of microplastic particles a day, according to research described as a "milestone" in the understanding of human exposure to tiny plastics. Scientists found that the recommended high-temperature process for sterilizing plastic bottles and preparing formula milk caused bottles to shed millions of microplastics and trillions of even smaller nanoplastics. The polypropylene bottles tested make up 82% of the world market, with glass bottles being the main alternative. Microplastics in the environment were already known to contaminate human food and drink, but the study shows that food preparation in plastic containers can lead to exposure thousands of times higher. *(See published study in the journal Nature Food. Article is from 'The Guardian')*

Poisoned. These chemicals have been banned from cosmetics in the European Union, and some phthalates were banned from children's toys in the U.S. in 2008. Unfortunately, phthalates are still so commonly used in U.S. products, that studies show that these chemicals are present in the urine of 99% of people tested.

BPA & BPA Substitutes. The most famous toxic chemical in plastics is Bisphenol-A, or BPA, which is a hormone disruptor linked to a whole host of health problems. The good news is that the FDA banned the use of BPA in baby bottles and children's sippycups in 2012. However, it's likely still found in many other plastics.

The bad news is that studies are showing that its replacement BPS, another chemical in the Bisphenol family, may be toxic as well, showing some of the same hormone-disrupting effects as BPA. In addition to BPA and BPS, studies show that plastics leech synthetic estrogen mimickers into the food or liquids stored inside them, which are linked to cancer, infertility, heart disease, and other health problems. (*My emphasis.*)

PVC. Polyvinyl chloride, is widely known as the most toxic plastic for health and environment. In its production, it releases dioxins, phthalates, vinyl chloride, ethylene dichloride, lead, cadmium and other toxic chemicals. It can leech many of these harmful chemicals into the water or food it's being used to contain, which is how those chemicals get into our bodies. In addition to destroying the environment, killing animals in the wild, becoming part of the bodies of sea animals as the plastic is consumed by them, it is now believed that plastics give off methane during degradation. (See IDEAS Ted.COM 'Methane isn't just cow farts:....)

Plastic, the Polluter. 80 million tons of waste in America alone, every year, comes from plastic food packaging. By our plastic waste we are devastating the oceans' sea animals. They are sickening and dying by ingesting plastic. Guess who is ultimately eating the plastic-filled fish?

<u>Big Oil and Gas Lied About Recycling.</u> The makers of plastic, the nations's largest oil and gas companies, have known all along that there was no value in recycling, even as they spent millions of dollars telling the American public the opposite. The industry sold the public on an idea it knew wouldn't work—that the majority of plastic could be, and would be, recycled—all while making billions of dollars selling the world new plastic. Industry spent tens of millions of dollars on ads touting recyclability and ran them for years promoting the benefits of a product that for the most part, was buried, was burned or, in some cases, wound up in the ocean.

<u>Poisoning Cheaper Than Recycling.</u> Industry officials knew this reality about recycling plastics as far back as the 1970's. But instead of being truthful to the American public, they began the plastics industry's $50 million-a-year ad campaign promoting the benefits of plastic. The industry could not get past the economics: Making new plastic out of oil is cheaper and easier than making it out of plastic trash.

The oil industry makes more than $400 billion a year making plastic, and as demand for oil for cars and truck declines, the industry is telling shareholders that future profits will increasingly come from plastic. (*See npr https://www.npr.org 'How big Oil Misled the Public Into Believing Plastic Would Be Recycled" September 11, 2020 by Laura Sullivan.)(Also see 'Most plastic will never be recycled – and the manufacturers couldn't care less by Arwa Mahdawi The Guardian.*)

<u>The World's Worst Companies For Plastic Waste Pollution.</u> Changing Markets Foundation has revealed the world's worst companies for plastic pollution:

- Coca-Cola has the biggest plastic footprint on the planet with 2.9 million metric tonnes of plastic packaging produced per year. (*One tonne equal 2,204.6 pounds*)
- Pepsico comes in second with 2.3 million metric tonnes.
- Nestle' is the third-worst offender with 1.7 million metric tonnes of plastic packaging produced.
- Five of the eight companies with the biggest plastic footprint are American, with Nestle' (Switzerland), Danone (France) and Unilever (United Kingdom/Netherlands), the exceptions. (*See Forbes 'The World's Worst Companies For PlASTIC Waste Pollution by Niall McCarthy Sep 18, 2020 (https://www.forbes.com)*)

<u>What the Science Community Must Do.</u> A pair of environmental scientists are warning that the worldwide population could be facing another health crisis-ailments that impact people due to ingestion of microplastics. (*See their Perspectives piece published in the journal Science, A. Dick Vethaak, with Vrije Universiteit Amsterdam and Juliette Legler, with Utrecht University.*)

They point out that medical scientists do not know what microplastics might be doing to people around the world, nor do they even know how much of the microplastics wind up in human bodies.

They conclude that due to the amount of microplastics in the environment, it is crucial that scientists begin to study their impacts on humans.

<u>Solution:</u> Ban plastic. Classify plastics as a hazardous substance. Sue the industry for misrepresentation. Stop Putting it in the Ocean. Stop using it. Opt for metal and glass containers. Use aluminum foil. Demand safer plastic. Opt for stainless steel bottles. Remove what the store has wrapped in plastic and take the item, leaving the store with the plastic. Look for food products stored in glass over plastic and store leftovers at home in glass or ceramic containers. Avoid plastic labeled with the recycle symbol #3 that is made of PVC. Do not heat food or liquids in plastic or pouches.

<u>Follow Germany's example</u>. The government compels the manufacturers of plastic to recycle or dispose of the plastics. In Germany you take your plastic bottles to any supermarket and insert your

plastic bottle into a machine which gives you a 25 cent deposit and the retailer gets the plastic back which they can sell to recyclers. Pressure your government for something that Germany does.

Invest in a recovery technology for plastics. Do as has been done in Haiti. They created a 'Plastic Bank' - a recycling system in which people are encouraged to collect plastic to keep it from entering the ocean and receiving cash for the plastic. The 'Plastic bank' then converts the plastic recovered into a reusable sellable form of plastic.

In Europe, they have created the technology and machinery to transform certain plastics into diesel.

Do as Ruanda, (in east Africa) which has banned plastic bags. Avoid putting plastics in the landfill. Think ReuseRefuse Single-Use Plastics. Join the global Movement plasticoceans.org.

Canada will ban single-use plastic items by the end of next year as part of an effort to achieve zero plastic waste by 2030. *(See CNN by Simret Aklilu.)*

Japan requires stores to charge a fee for plastic shopping bags. 75% of customers stopped using the plastic bags.

California has passed a first-in-the-nation law requiring plastic beverage containers to contain an increasing amount of recycled material. *(Sep 25, 2020)* The plastics industry had waged a multi-million dollar campaign to defeat a bill which would have called for a 75 % reduction in single-use plastic packaging, utensils, straws, containers and other foodware dumped into landfills.

C. __THE OBSTACLES, THE APPROACH, SOLUTIONS__

1. The Cultural/Religious Roadblock

a. IN THE PEWS WITH THE FUNDAMENTALISTS

"…hate your neighbor but don't forget to say grace" (by Barry McGuire in Eve of Destruction.)

The following letter was sent to those in charge at the Lutheran Church I last attended. This letter essentially sealed my family's departure. I guess I can't seem to bow out of anything quietly.

WRECKING ON THE HUBRIS ICEBERG/TOO COWARDLY
TO SAVE THE LEAST OF OUR BRETHREN
(ARE WE LIVING THE BIBLE'S MESSAGE?)

We are surrounded by a myriad of organizations and religious leaders who identify their church and way of thinking as the only vehicle for the salvation of our souls. They profess that, better than any others, they have just the right doctrine to get us into Heaven. Often, either spoken or presumed, the message will be that the other church has either lost or failed to live up to God's word. For example, Martin Luther, founder of the Lutherans, in dramatic fashion claimed, amongst other things, that the Catholic Church lost its mantel of spiritual leadership when they attempted to extract money from the masses purportedly in exchange for indulgences. The Catholic Church would receive money to build churches and the family received the satisfaction that their loved-one would have a shortened stay in Purgatory.

Martin Luther argued, among other things, that the Catholic Church had lost its right to spiritual leadership by succumbing to the expedient of raising money for political reasons and claiming a power to give spiritual blessings for a price. This, along with the rejection of the Pope as final interpreter of scripture and his claim of authority over secular rules, motivated Martin Luther to post his "95 Theses" on the door of the Castle Church and begin a new religion.

We, like Martin Luther or Calvin, must continually question if the church is doing what it should, to keep this ship-full of souls headed in the direction of Heaven. We too, must ask if the church has surrendered its spiritual leadership by straying too far afield of our Lord's example and directives. This article, with some trepidation, ventures to give you a checklist to determine if your church is still spiritually afloat.

But first, an analogy. As in the wreck of the Titanic, made famous by the movie, the ship crashed because they thought it to be unsinkable, ignored the standard warnings, sped through the dangerous, iceberg-infested waters and failed to take the proper safety precautions. It appears they had committed the sin Adam and Eve committed – that of hubris or pride. They thought they could be better than God. Or at least that the Titanic was so superior that it was unsinkable. I believe that this perilous pride is revealed in how one views and treats his fellow man. We must not be blinded by a similarly righteous arrogance and lack of empathy that would cause our souls to lovelessly sail and callously collide with God and nature's ice symbol that shouts to slow down. You are not superior to nature or your fellow man! Your callous and ice-cold heart, born and bred of a loveless faith, will be met and punished, with your soul sent and drowned at the bottom of a salvationless sea.

For the men in control of the Titanic, this arrogance translated into a failure to carry a sufficient number of lifeboats on board to save all the people if the need occurred. Of course, safety is not a concern if you believe, without doubt, that your ship is unsinkable. Do the leaders of your church believe so strongly in their own righteousness that they fail to store sufficient lifeboats of salvation? In other words, do they speak and act as if it is about them, their families and congregations rather than those not so privileged in the world?

The movie portrays officers of the boat filling the lifeboats with desperate passengers. Unfortunately, they fill them far short of each boat's capacity, leaving many stranded and destined to die a horrendous death in an icy graveyard. Is your church any different? As the ship sinks, do the privileged members get first dibs on the lifeboats of salvation while those paying "coach" fees remain locked in their compartments? Is there someone on board that is bold enough to open the locked doors to salvation, though that person risks losing a place on a lifeboat? Or is risk not part of their equation for salvation?

Lastly, the movie depicts lifeboats sailing away half-empty. The half-filled boats of passengers ignore the cries and screams of desperate and dying men and women in the frigid waters. They return far too late to save what have become frozen corpses. They feared that too many passengers would desperately over-fill the boat and cause it to sink, killing everyone. Does your church have a save-yourself-above all mentality where no one dares to reach out and save their fellow man, fearing they cannot risk their comfortable seat on the lifeboat to Heaven? After all, by reaching out and pulling in a dying man or god-forbid, even swimming out to save someone, you might fall victim to a similarly frigid fate.

There is no question that the waters beyond the hull of our church-ship are treacherous. Yet Jesus categorically and at the risk of physical death mandates us to go overboard to save our fellow man. His', and his apostles' life and death, brimmed with this message. It is no coincidence that the apostles died an early and painful death for their beliefs.

His words also point us in the direction of His example: ***"Whoever seeks to save his life will lose it, and whoever loses his life will preserve it." Luke 17: 33 KJV.*** Does your church believe they can cruise into Heaven without risking anything on earth? The Lord's parables constantly emphasize outreach at risk to one's life and lifestyle. E.g., Leaving the flock to search for the "lost sheep", *(Matt 18:12-13 NIV)* Not even burying your dead should keep you from following in his footsteps. *Matthew 8:22* NIV) Neither family nor your own life, according to Jesus, should stand in the way of this commitment. **Luke 14:26 NIV,** states:

"if anyone comes to Me and does not hate his father and mother, wife and children, brothers and sisters yes, and his own life also, he cannot be my disciple"

"And everyone who has left houses or brothers or sisters or father or mother or wife or children or lands, for My name's sake, shall receive a hundredfold, and inherit eternal life. Matthew 19:29 NIV.

Even the wealthy man's son who had abided by all the commandments left saddened to hear what he needed to do to inherit eternal life:

"One thing you lack: Go your way, sell whatever you have and give to the poor, and you will have treasure in heaven: and come, take up the cross, and follow me." Mark 10:17 – 21 NIV.

It seems to me that many of our churches are like the owners, captain and first-class passengers on the Titanic. They have become oblivious to the needs of anyone but the high paying customers. Martin Luther, in a sense, was saying grace or salvation should not depend on your pocket book. *(I.e., his objection to the Catholic Churches' taking money from poor people to allow their deceased relatives to go to Heaven.)* * If Jesus' death purchased our revocable ticket to Heaven, the lives and deaths of

Jesus and his apostles, illustrate vividly the means to ensure the ticket is not withdrawn. Their lives were secondary to the cause of salvation. I.e., at the risk of eternal damnation, you are obligated to jump into the icy waters beyond the safe hull of your church lifeboat to save others. You must open the locked doors of the passengers paying 'Third Class' fees.

I believe that we have more than sufficient guidance in the Bible to answer the question whether one's church has failed to be the spiritual leader and has become merely a social club for its members. We begin with the question whether our leaders' actions manifest a strong faith or merely give lip service to the concept? The faith I am talking about is a living breathing faith. It is a belief and a demonstration of the belief that Christ's death on the cross has saved us from our sins. That is easy enough to espouse and I submit that most churches have found a multitude of ways to say it. However, the Bible has made it abundantly clear that salvation is more than a mere espousal of the belief. In *James 2:14 – 17*, NIV, it says:

What good is it my brothers, if a man claims to have faith but has not deeds? Can such faith save him? Suppose a brother or sister is without clothes and daily food. If one of you says to him: "Go, I wish you well; keep warm and well fed, "but does nothing about his physical needs, what good is it? In the same way, faith by itself, if it is not accompanied by action, is dead". (**My Emphasis**)

Is your church spiritually dead? I hear your answer. Well as long as we believe in Jesus as our savior we are promised salvation. I submit that the mere belief that you will be saved by Jesus' death is but to merely hold a revocable ticket to salvation. It ignores Jesus' complete message and events of His and the apostles' lives.

Moreover, that limited belief ignores the lessons of history. I am sure that in their own minds, the leaders of the Catholic Church believed that Jesus was their savior as they sanctimoniously sucked the last pennies out of the pockets of the poor under the guise that this was necessary for the salvation of the souls of their deceased family members. I am sure that those leaders and followers who pursued the Holy Wars and the Inquisition did so believing that their actions were consistent with God's holy word. As the church leaders and their followers burnt witches, I am sure they believed that by so doing they would ensure their own salvation. I am sure that the churches that participated in slavery, apartheid, massacre of Native Americans or looked the other way, were firmly convinced that their faith in the Lord was strong. I am sure that the Catholic Church in Germany, probably thought they were doing the right thing as they looked the other way, during the Nazi era, while Jews were being rounded up and six million were to die.

What was missing was a love and compassion for their fellow man. No one probably mentioned to them **Galatians 5:6 NIV**: which states:

For in Christ Jesus neither circumcision nor uncircumcision has any value. The only thing that counts is faith expressing itself through love. Love does not flow through the barrel of a gun, or by the sharp end of a sword or through the whip of slavery!

All these folks, I am sure, were firmly indoctrinated in the belief that Jesus, as their savior was their ticket to Heaven, notwithstanding that they were participants in enormous evils. It seems to me that the inexpensive, beguiling, and alluring notion that a loveless faith could save them, was as responsible as any influence the devil had in their mass evil. The message, as revealed in *James*, supra, is that our deeds reveal the quality of our faith. Jesus has made it categorically clear that if we want to be saved, we must walk the walk, not just talk the talk. That means opening your door and helping those in need, even though you risk becoming like them.*

Moreover, Jesus has made it clear that walking the walk must be more than a Foxtrot. In ***Revelations 3:15 – 16 NIV***, the Lord gives us a standard of behavior:

I know your <u>deeds</u> that you are neither cold nor hot. I wish you were either one or the other! So, because you are lukewarm-neither hot nor cold-I am about to spit you out of my mouth.

This is a standard of zealousness, the highest of standards. Merely believing is not enough under this standard. This standard requires action. Is your church in essence saying to the needy: "Go, I wish you well; keep warm and well fed?" However, they are doing nothing about their physical needs. What if anything is your church doing to seek out those in need and attending to their needs?

So you say that we will take care of our families, fellow church members, friends and business associates. That should be enough right? In ***Luke 6:32 – 35 NIV***, the Lord tells us loving people for our benefit does us no good. He says:

"If you love those who love you, what credit is that to you? Even sinners love those who love them. And if you do good to those who are good to you, what credit is that to you? Even sinners do that. And if you lend to those from whom you expect repayment, what credit is that to you? Even sinners lend to sinners expecting to be repaid in full. But love your enemies, do good to them, and lend to them, without expecting to get anything back. Then your reward will be great, and you will be sons of the Most High, because He is kind to the ungrateful and wicked. Be merciful, just as your Father is merciful.

In ***Mark 2:17 NIV***, Jesus further says:

"It is not the healthy who need a doctor, but the sick. I did not come to call the righteous, but sinners."

The interpretation: We need to direct our love to those who may not appreciate it and to those who need it.

Then who are the ones that are 'sick'? He tells us categorically in ***Matthew 25:31 – 46 NIV***:

"When the Son of Man comes in His glory, and all the angels with Him, He will sit on his throne in heavenly glory." All the nations will be gathered before Him, and He will separate the people one from another as a shepherd separates the sheep from the goats. He will put the sheep on his right and the goats on the left. Then the King will say to those on His right 'Come, you who are blessed by my Father; take your inheritance, the kingdom prepared for you since the creation of the world. For I was hungry and you gave Me something to eat, I was thirsty and you gave Me something to drink, I was a stranger and you invited Me in, I needed clothes and you clothed Me, I was sick and you looked after me, I was in prison and you came to visit Me.' Then the righteous will answer Him, 'Lord, when did we see You hungry and feed You, or thirsty and give You something to drink? When did we see you a stranger and invite you in, or needing clothes and clothe you? When did we see you sick or in prison, and go to visit you?' "The king will reply, 'I tell you the truth, whatever you did for one of the least of these brothers of mine, you did for me.' "Then He will say to those on the left, 'Depart from me, you who are cursed, into the eternal fire prepared for the devil and his angels. For I was hungry and you gave Me nothing to eat, I was thirsty and you gave Me nothing to drink, I was a stranger and you did not invite Me in, I needed clothes and you did not clothe Me, I was sick and in prison and you did not look after Me.' "They will also answer, 'Lord, when did we see You hungry or thirsty or a stranger or needing clothes or sick or in prison, and did not help You?' He will reply, I tell you the truth, whatever you did not do for one of the least of these, you did not do for me.' "Then they will go away to eternal punishment, but the righteous to eternal life."

There is a dicho (saying) in Northern New Mexico: *"Ojos que no ven, corazon que no siente"* (Eyes that do not see, a heart that does not feel.) We live in a world wherein we, as Americans, have the highest standard of living in the world. Yet we have one of the highest rates of child mortality of the industrialized nations. We have an enormously high percentage of our children living under the poverty level and families that have not enough money to care for their basic needs. We have the highest percentage of our population behind bars of all the industrialized countries. We incarcerate one of every four incarcerated persons in the world. Our nursing homes are filling at a high rate with isolated and lonely elderly folk. If we cannot see the least of our brethren amongst us we must be blind or have no heart to feel their suffering.

Clearly those blind or compassionless folks are in the cold or lukewarm category. Is your church one of those? Do they act as if there will be endless time in the future to do what needs to be done for the least of their brethren now? Do they believe that asking God to take care of the problem absolves them of their Christ-given obligation to actively take care of our needy? Do they rail against big government and welfare, yet at the same time heartlessly fail to help those in need? (It is no accident that the government took over the job of creating a safety net for those in need. The churches' failure to take care of the "least of their brothers" necessitated government intervention.) Is every war their country engages in, a war they support, regardless of whether there is a justification?

Is your church walking the walk or just talking the talk? As they talk and you listen, and daily, do nothing, you inexorably move to the side of the "goats" for the sin of failing to see Jesus embodied in the neediest of our brethren. Could our Lord have spelled it out any better for us?

"This People Honors Me With Their Lips, But Their Heart Is Far From Me." Mark 7:6 NIV

Are there telltale signs that the congregation's tongues of fire are no longer burning or are flickering perilously close to extinction? Are the leaders more concerned about keeping their members happy, rather than telling them that their lives, as they are living them, will keep them out of Heaven? This reticence manifests itself in a myriad of ways. Do your leaders emphasize faith in Jesus but omit to mention **James's** admonition that faith without deeds is dead? Do they fail to explain why the church ignores numerous mandates that tie what we <u>do</u> to our salvation? Do the leaders dare go out into the community and evangelize? Or do they try to find someone else to do it? Do the leaders of your church dare go beyond the comfortable confines of the church grounds to preach salvation? Or do they take comfort that if they get an expensive sign and invite people to their church, that is enough? Are the members of your church embarrassed to evangelize in the community? Do they claim that compassion or evangelizing just isn't one of their gifts? Would they rather sit and pray in the safe and secure confines of the church with their own members? Do they refuse to believe that Jesus and his apostles were all about reaching out into the community and sharing the Good News?

Do your leaders tend to make light of serious issues or as bad, avoid addressing them? Do jokes take the place of serious soul-saving discussions? Does the pastor find it humorous to say we had many tragedies this year including the confirmation of Martin and Sally, ha ha? Does he persist in the explanation that this is humor and we should have read between the lines to understand it? Does the pastor laugh off or reject outright a proposal to study the Bible topically? I.e., someone proposes a general topic of interest to them and the pastor enlightens the members about the different parts of the bible that pertain to the topic and how it relates. Is this approach rejected because it involves too much work?

Though I speak with the tongues of men and of angels, but have not love, I have become sounding brass or a clanging cymbal. 1 Corinthians 13:1NIV.

Are the leaders more concerned about the "bottom line", than the ultimate consequences of the church's inaction? Does your church cater to the ostensibly perceived "indispensable" members who either are self-centered, bigoted or have a heart of stone? Is this compassionlessness manifested by members referring to certain of their less fortunate brethren outside the church as "slime buckets"? Does it manifest itself by members thinking and voicing an opinion that certain non-believers are less than they? Are some so bold as to state that "I am more important than the non-believer"? Are the rest of the members afraid to tell that member that God wants us all in heaven and we are all important to Him?

Does this heartlessness sometimes reflect itself in disdain for laws that make racially motivated or hate-crimes illegal? Do some members revel in the tragedies of non-Christian nations, literally laughing at their pain? Do some members still have difficulty accepting the Civil Rights movement and the laws that protect minorities? Are members still apologizing and making excuses for the ancestors that owned slaves?

"And why do you look at the speck in your brother's eye, but do not consider the plank in your own eye?..." Hypocrite! First remove the plank from your own eye, and then you will see clearly to remove the speck from your brother's eye. (Matthew 7:3 NIV)

Do the leaders still blame the community for any particular woe that exists rather than become active to address a particular problem? Does the congregation still fail to see the greater evils plaguing the community? Do they forget to pray for the severe evils in our own community which include excessive drug and alcohol abuse? Are the leaders quick to condemn our judicial system, school systems and non-Christians, alleging they have committed an evil by keeping prayer out of the public schools? Do they refuse to acknowledge or are unable to comprehend that prayer still exists in the public schools and the Court-imposed limitations are for the protection of Christians as well as others? Is attacking homosexuals a popular theme even though there are enough sins and hell-rendering omissions within the congregation to address.

Are the leaders defensive when someone says Jesus was "anti-establishment"? (If Judaism was the establishment, limited to the privileged few and burdened with laws that benefited them and excluded the masses, Jesus' life and work was nothing short of a revolution that overturned a highly exclusionary religion and began a new one.) If the Roman Empire was heartless and ruthless to the poor, downtrodden and anyone that threatened this system, then, to preach anything that placed the poor at the high end of the spiritual spectrum, at the risk of death, was revolutionary. What Jesus and his apostles did was revolutionary! So why bristle when He is identified as such? Due to a passive neglect in fully teaching God's word, have we become like the Pharisees*or worse, the ruling Roman empire and have become part of the same kind of establishment?* Is this why the word, 'radical', 'revolutionary' or 'anti-establishment' scares some of us?

Do the leaders and members refuse to recognize the successful example of other congregations and the educationally studied good sense of instituting a bible study program for low-income children during adult services? Is the claim made that it would not benefit the immediate members and the other children might be jealous? Are you told that they are really looking for adult members, not children? Is your request to include all children still not accepted because the adults' need to have their kids with them in church? Do some members go on a Servant Event but refuse to institute what they should have learned, e.g., evangelizing in their own community? Is the annual day of planning canceled for lack of interest and lack of planning?

Logically, I guess, I should outline the specifics of what should be done to reignite the fire of the Holy Ghost within one's church. However, if the next step is not painfully obvious at this point, anything further would be an exercise in futility. The "plank" may be firmly embedded in the churches' eye!

Here's wishing you a blessed Christmas and an inspired New Year.

(I wrote the above before I decided to write a book about the destruction of the environment and my children's inspiration. The 'Titanic' theme remarkably reflected and explained a mentality of a segment of the culture that prevents people from recognizing and taking action against the destruction of nature.)

* The italicized addition was done recently.

*The excuse for not interacting with those outside the church was the fear that you would become like them.

*1. (Jesus condemns the Pharisees, not for what they did, but for neglecting 'the more important matters of the law, justice, mercy and faithfulness.)

(I have been lambasted by some who know of my criticism of the Lutheran church, including by my sister-in-law, Betty Reed, who I hold in high regard. Oh yea! She is a Lutheran. I guess she might argue that belonging to a church is akin to being hired by a company who pay you a salary. They demand you say only good things about them or stop working there. Otherwise you are a hypocrite. Or maybe belonging to a church and criticizing it is like criticizing your government for pursuing what you claim is an immoral and unjust war. You should love it or leave it. Otherwise you are unpatriotic.

But is there a different dynamic when it comes to criticizing a church? After all, the church is fighting a war against the devil! So, I must be working with the devil? Ironically, the Lutherans owe their beginnings to a Catholic monk who essentially criticized and condemned the Pope for taking money from the poor to build churches and promising the impoverished Catholics that their loved ones would be taken out of Purgatory and moved to Heaven based on their 'donations'. So my response is that Martin Luther set the standard for church criticism. I am just following in his lead.

On a less sarcastic side, my wife, Sally had taken the kids to the Lutheran church when she heard that they had a Bible school for the toddlers. I had asked her to find a church that would be good for the kids. This was even before I arrived in Las Vegas. The daughter of the Lutheran's Pastor became our go-to babysitter. The kids enjoyed attending and playing with the other kids. The connection had been made and I believed what was good for the kids would be good for Sally and me.

So you now know that my intent was not to join this church to criticize them. Both Sally and I liked what we initially saw.

Moreover, I was a participant in most of the activities and had even sponsored and spear-headed a children's outreach program. I submitted a grant and obtained $500.00 for the program. Based on the program, we have constructed a sandbox, obtained soccer goals, volleyball poles and nets, a child's basketball goal, a basketball, a tether-ball pole-and-ball and we have dug the hole for the basketball pole. I've passed out flyers and have invited scores of people to the church.

Like Martin Luther, my joining this church was done with good intentions. So forgive me Betty.

D. AN OUTLINE OF A DIAGNOSIS OF THE POLLUTION ENEMY, A REVIEW OF THE ISSUES, A BATTLE PLAN, AND SOLUTIONS

I was inspired to assemble the ideas for this essay because of a serious concern that it will not be an easy task stopping the disaster that is global warming. If we know what the obstacles are, we can better plan to surmount and overcome them. Sometimes we can go around them but often it requires going right through them. In any case, I have tried to identify the biggest roadblocks, including, the makeup of our brain and emotions, mindsets, the money mountains, political, religious and historical tendencies and the numerous countries involved. The task ahead of us is enormous. It is a world-wide issue. But a view of the battleground engenders plans of attack. So, I have included 'solutions' at the end of each identified obstacle. (The following review is what happens when the double-major degree of History and Political Science meets the lawyer's analysis, this author's skepticism and a coach's desire for victory.)

There's a lady who's sure All that glitters is gold
And she's buying the stairway to heaven
When she gets there she knows if the stores are all closed
With a word she can get what she came for
Ohohohoh and she's buying a stairway to heaven
By Led Zeppelin

(Comment: It is not a 'she'. The 'stairway' is the American Dream and yes, it is the wealthy that have bought it! Guess who has lost it?)

The Battle Against the Polluters and the Man-Made Global Warming Disaster, Why the Obliviousness and Inaction - The Culprits, a Battle Plan & Solutions

I. WHAT IS THE ISSUE?

A. Introduction - The Threat. Recently I have been writing and thinking of whether this country could act quickly enough to avoid the point where the devastation of climate change becomes irreversible. Unless we immediately reduce the burning of coal, oil and gas that are driving up global temperatures, a new UN report warns, the world will suffer tremendous consequences as early as 2040. Moreover, we now realize that animal agriculture produces more pollution than vehicle pollution.*.1 The world's leading climate scientists made the starkest warning to date: Our current actions are not enough to meet our target of 1.5C of warming. They said the obvious: We must do more before it is too late.

As of this writing, 4.6 million die per year due to pollution. *(W.H.O.)* As of Jan. 27, 2021, the Doomsday Clock was set at one hundred seconds to midnight', the closest it has ever been to apocalypse. According to the Bulletin of the Atomic Scientists one of the major threats is climate change. (See full quote in Ch. 11)

Lawrence Wollersheim, a scientist turned concerned author, writes in *Climageddon: 'Global Warming is not getting better. It is getting worse at a far faster rate than we are planning or preparing for.'* *(See full quote in Ch 11)*

B. <u>So Why The Carelessness to Earth-Ending Pollution?</u> With such ongoing, imminent and calamitous news, why are so many so oblivious to this impending devastation and the need for emergency action? Will we reach a point where the environment is so heated up that it irreversibly sets into motion a climate change that is out of control? Have we already arrived at that point? What is it that has molded, shaped and sculpted us to accept deception and be blind and oblivious to pollution-caused pain, disease and death? Is this dynamic of obliviousness, the same one that, in our past, has led us to acquiesce to entering wrongful wars and surrender control of our financial and political system to the financial giants? Is an inordinate amount of control by the wealthy now facilitating the financial powers to pollute the environment to the point of ending humanity? Are our brains not made to react and respond to incremental acts of disaster? What has happened to us as a country that facilitates our obliviousness…our carelessness?

<u>What Forces at Work?</u> I ask how our country is shaped and what forces control its actions or inactions. What is the nature of a public, blinded and deaf to the evil of death and destruction? What is at the root of our callous and empathyless political and financial leaders who form our perception and reactions to man-made pollution and its catastrophic effects?

How are we, the public, infected, blinded, made gullible, distracted or conformed to be influenced by a government/business that convinces us of that which is not true and not in our best interests? What is the nature of this confabulation and the confluence of influences that so forms our perceptions, tastes, reactions, emotions, thoughts and actions, such that we cannot see reality as it is, or feel the pain and suffering of others?

1. THE TOOLS OF CONTROL <u>Are our Brains and Emotions Formed So We Are Good at Detecting and Reacting to Threats that Are Obvious but Not to Those Slowly Emerging Over Time, Like the Climate Disaster?</u> In the movie, '*The Matrix*', the machines that took over the earth, magically and technologically transformed what was a dying and destroyed earth so it appeared and felt like the earth at its highpoint in history. Even the food tasted delicious. I cannot help think we are living in a world where we are blindly destroying nature and if we just opened our eyes and our hearts, we would be able to feel and witness the disastrous consequences unfolding. Yet we go on as if all is fine. And we didn't even need any 'machines' to do their technological magic on us! Of course we did get some help from our human money machines. (I will address that below.) So what is this all about?

<u>Immediate Threats Get Our Attention.</u> I am not a doctor or a psychiatrist and cannot tell you the details of our brains and how their inner-workings interact to make us who we are. However, I think I can say that we are very good at reacting to obvious threats. Like a mama-bear challenging any animal in their territory, we will fight and risk our lives to protect obvious threats to our family and community. Like nature's protective mothers, humanity will react to what they see, hear or smell and that which presents an immediate threat to them. For example, a terrorist attack in our own country will get our attention immediately, particularly if the government exaggerates and lies about it. But news about distant 'future' events does not trigger that fight or flight reaction. (Particularly when benefitting businesses and politicians lie to us about the danger.) So spewing poison into the atmosphere, rivers, lakes and oceans, is just too subtle. Hotter temperatures, increased forest fires, melting ice caps, more severe storms, worldwide loss of animal and plant species – None of these is enough for us to be alerted and acknowledge that what we our doing has earth-ending consequences.

We have been told for 40 years about this environmental disaster but only until lately has anyone taken notice. We hope it is not too late and our reaction is enough. We are being told that the longer we wait, the more difficult the task will be.

Climate Anxiety. A growing school of psychologists believe the trauma of the climate crisis is a key barrier to change. (*See The Guardian, 'Hijacked by anxiety': how climate dread is hindering climate action. By Jillian Ambrose.*) It is a sense of dread, gloom and almost paralysing helplessness that is rising as we come to terms with the greatest existential challenge of our generation, or any generation. An increasing number of psychologists believe the trauma that is a consequence of climate breakdown is also one of the biggest obstacles in the struggle to take action against rising greenhouse gas emissions. Lertzman says: *'In simple terms, the human psyche is hardwired to disengage from information or experience that are overwhelmingly difficult or disturbing. <u>This is particularly true if an individual feels powerless to affect change.</u>"* *"In the most extreme form this inability to engage presents itself as a complete denial of the climate crisis and climate science."*

Solution. A Compassionate Approach. The suggestion to our leaders is to act as a guide, not as a doomsayer or cheerleader. We need to show them the way to affect the crisis. Obviously denial by a president is the worst way to address the problem! "The answer lies in a "ruthless compassion" – for ourselves and others – that acknowledges the extreme discomfort in confronting the crisis while still taking responsibility for the present." "We have to help people to navigate these feelings by increasing our emotional resilience and emotional intelligence." We need to empower those we want to convince of the calamity and to take action. Easier said than done!

Solution: Spread the Word Loudly: (*"the worst evil that science has not been able to find a cure for in human beings is apathy. We all have to become organizers." (Dolores Huerta), legendary activist and co-founder of the United Farm Workers.*) I cannot change the way our brains are put together but we can speak to our friends and neighbors that we are under attack; that our children and grandchildren are about to be viciously attacked and their futures stolen from them. We must yell at the top of our voice: THE ENEMY IS COMING AND HE IS IN OUR MIDST! PREPARE TO FIGHT! Become an activist! Be wary of all in control who minimize the danger. They are aiding and abetting the enemy! Get to the voting booth and vote for the candidate that recognizes the immediate and catastrophic threat that global warming presents.

(*I can only hope that the Black Lives Matter movement may be the spark for the rest of us to begin to fight against pollution and for our future existence.*)

Solution. Framing the Issue Starkly and Rationally: The bottom line is that even if we are wrong about whether we should fight and invest against pollution, the worst consequence is world-wide economic depression. Compare this to the 'end-of-the-world' scenario if we fail to act. The logic is powerful! (See 'The Most Terrifying Video You'll Ever See' on U Tube)

2. Factors that Contribute to this 'Powerlessness: I will attempt to address the factors and players that contribute to affect this feeling of powerlessness. But I will not minimize the threats so they are less overwhelming, difficult or disturbing. However I have proposed 'solutions' so we know there is a pathway to resolution.

a. Our Capitalistic Democracy: Unless It Is War, Our Leaders Will Choose Safe and Conservative Choices over Radical Ones. Unfortunately this is true even though our pollution is moving us quickly towards world devastation. Radical choices will have to be made. (See The Closing Circle) The one exception is President Franklin Delano Roosevelt and the Great Depression. The reality is that this coincided with World War II, and that may have been the biggest motivator for radical change.

Our selection of a president, and our choices of Senators and Congressmen is heavily weighted by the fear that the 'best' candidate will not win. So we often choose second-best or third-best, to make sure they are elected. This is made worse by our electoral system that allows someone to become president even though they lose the popular vote by a million voters. (Trump vs. Clinton).

This dynamic is further exacerbated of late because our country has become so divided. Moreover, the power of the wealthy within our Capitalist matrix, ensures business choices: what makes the big-businesses money, over what is best for the country. This is exacerbated by a large section of the voting populace who are vulnerable to the deception of the politicians who are controlled by the moneyed.

So instead of making the radical choices to save the world from the polluters, politicians and the public opt for the safe conservative choice. President Trump's choice to be president illustrates the irrational choice in most all respects. Why would religious folks vote for someone who has no scruples, other than the 'profit-above-all' mentality? The Fundamentalists voted for him. Why would a working class vote for someone whose very essence is antithetical to helping the workers? Non-college working class voted for him.

Illustrative of this dilemma is the existence of our biggest polluter – Animal Agriculture. It is literally killing us and quickly destroying the earth. But no one, not even the environmental organizations are seriously addressing the issue. (See Animal Ag. supra.) Our country and the world cannot sustain this level of pollution. Yet I have not heard from the Biden administration, with any plans to address it. (Update: He has asked us to limit our intake of hamburgers to one per month.) Moreover, the choice of Tom Vilsac as U.S. Secretary of Agriculture, does not bode well for protecting the public from Industrial Agriculture. Vilsac's record as a former dairy industry lobbyist, a 'do nothing' Secretary with a shoddy record on environmental justice, gives little hope to those who realize the severity of the Animal Agriculture problem.

We will discover if President Biden is beholden to the public or the Animal Agriculture industry.

Solutions: Maybe, as Bill Gates has recommended, the solution is to switch to synthetic beef. By doing so we could utilize our refined capitalist instincts to make a change that would save the world. To expedite this earth-saving process, the government must provide funds for this venture, whose financial risks are many. Will Biden dare to slap the animal ag industry in its' financial face? See my Animal Ag essay supra For more solutions.

b. Christianity and the Minimization of Nature. Is there some philosophical/religious belief that is holding us back from the fight to save nature and humanity? Consider the following: First you utilize a religious book, Catechism, a Bible, or religious dogma that is premised on complete worship and honor of a male God whose actions and words appear to reveal a tribal mentality. Then, justify the destruction of nature by pointing to the 'Holy Book' that is clear that man is superior to nature *(Matthew 6:26 NIV)*1 and allows man to "rule over" nature *(Genesis 1:26 NIV))* and 'suppress' nature. These biblical directives have facilitated and justified the destruction of nature, in spite of the bible's direction to not defile nature. *(Jeremiah 2:7 NIV)*. At the very least, an understandable essence of man's duty to nature certainly has not been clear.

Fundamentalism and the Environment. The question for me is whether somehow Christianity has facilitated or is a cause of Christians ignoring and disrespecting nature to humanities' detriment? I submit that the Bible has made it easy and yes, has even justified using and abusing nature:

The Power to Dominate Nature. *Genesis 1:28-30 NIV: God blessed them and said to them. Be fruitful and increase in number, fill the earth and subdue it. Rule over the fish of the sea and the birds of the air and over every living creature that moves on the ground. Then God said, I give you every seed-bearing plant on the face of the whole earth and every tree that has fruit with seed in it. They will be yours for food; And to all the beasts of the earth and all the birds of the air and all the creatures that move on the ground-everything that has the breath of life in it - I give every green plant for food. And it was so.* (**My emphasis**)

Synonyms for subdue are 'conquer', 'defeat', 'vanquish', 'overcome', 'overwhelm', 'crush', 'quash', 'beat', 'trounce', 'subjugate', 'suppress'… (See Google). It sure sounds like fighting words to me! The Old Testament God appears to put nature in the same category as non-believers in Jehovah or a tribal enemy who have, historically, been shown little mercy. The above biblical directives grant man extensive power over nature, including the right to 'suppress' it if necessary.

I submit that is exactly what the world has done – We have demeaned and tried to crush nature without the wisdom or empathy to realize we are consequently destroying ourselves. Moreover, it seems that 'God' has been short of all-knowing when it comes to His knowledge of ecology. Or He got it wrong when he claimed man's superiority to nature. Respectfully, maybe the person getting the message from God, got it wrong? Or maybe the interpretation is as simple as God giving man authority and permission to protect themselves from all of those vicious lions, tigers and bears, oh my!

Authority Over All of His Creation/What Standard? Arguably the bible encourages us to be stewards. I.e., our duty to take care of creation. But what kind of care? What standard of care? This delegation of authority by God presumes that man is superior to nature. It suggests that man is like a king and nature is a mere serf in a kingdom where the King has whatever authority it takes to run the kingdom. (A leader generally has the power to kill, destroy or punish his disobedient serfs as well as his enemy. A Patriarch's powers include war-powers against any tribe who dares to stand in his way.) When considered in the context of man's right to 'suppress' nature, 'taking care' of nature includes destroying it when it does not suit your needs. I.e., the standard of protection of nature is a low enough standard of care to be non-existent!

Nature Less Than Man? *For God so loved the world, as to give his only begotten Son; that whosoever believeth in him, may not perish, but may have life everlasting…John 3:16 KJB* Unfortunately for nature, it does not have this guarantee of eternity. The Biblical presumption is that nature is less significant than man and akin to a non-believer. So, if there is any question about the quality of care towards nature, I submit that the Judeo-Christian inclination, based on the minimizing language towards the status of nature, will be for less care, even recklessness.

Enlightened man now understands or should understand that man is inextricably linked to nature. Ergo, the destruction of nature is essentially suicide of humanity. But a significant part of humanity holds onto its belief that it is superior to and separate from nature. This is Fundamentalism at its' worst. Unfortunately for the rest of mankind, Fundamentalists can cite it as the word of God.

Dire Consequences of Following Biblical Directive. In our efforts to 'subdue' nature, pursuant to biblical directive, we have endeavored to trounce and vanquish nature which we are told by God is less than us. Our attempts to technologically improve on nature, to our detriment, have been oblivious to the effect and damaging consequences of our technological creations and their use to facilitate the poisoning of nature.

Are We Part of the Cycle of Nature Which Includes Death and Decay or Above Nature and Eternal? Maybe because I am getting old and have to confront my mortality, I have had to think more seriously about my end and where that fits with anything else. Most friends and family seem to put their faith in the idea that at the end of their life they will go to meet their maker and deceased family and friends, if they had faith and followed the rules to get to Heaven. Certainly, the fear of Hell, is part of their picture of the afterlife. Hell has been a powerful tool to shape Christians to conform to the beliefs of the Religious leaders and bureaucrats. So to deny an afterlife of Heaven, is to ensure eternal hellfire or at least the absence of an eternal heavenly existence. (See Revelation 21:8 ESV: "*But as for the cowardly, **the faithless**, the detestable, as for murderers, the sexually immoral, sorcerers,* *idolaters, and all liars, their portion will be in the lake that burns with fire and sulfur, which is the second death."* (My emphasis)

Our Bodies Unnaturally Eternal? Christianity has removed the fear of death to some degree by a promise of Heaven but it has also ignored or simplified the question of where our physical bodies go. The main theory seems to be that, like Christ, we will be resurrected with the same body we had on earth. (*Luke 24:1-6, NIV John 20:25, 27, NIV Philippians 3:20-21, NIV 1 Cor.15:49 NIV and 1Corinthians 15:13, NIV etc., 1 Cor. 15:52 NIV, Philippians 3:20-1 NIV, John 5:28-29 NIV, 1 Corinthians 15:42 NIV)* Thusly, Bible-believing Christians, believing that their physical bodies are eternal, have avoided the critical issue of our time, that we, like the rest of nature, ends its existence, breaks down into basic parts and returns to earth as food for the continuation of nature, period! With our eyes in a Heaven and an inability to contemplate our mortality, we have skipped an essential part of our existence – We are here as part of nature and our death is just returning to the cycle of nature. To ignore that we are inextricably connected to nature, even at our death, ensures our blithe disregard of nature, which ultimately leads to our destroying it.

Earth is But a Stage. To put it simply, we have been indoctrinated that earth and our existence here, is pretty much a jumping-off area, a testing ground, so to speak. Earth is but a stage and if we get our lines right and recognize who is responsible for us getting the part, we graduate to the real 'Heaven' when we die. Although Thomas, speaking for Jesus in the *Lost Gospels*, directed us that Heaven is in us and all around us, *(Ch. 4.5)*, we have refused to accept nature as our Heaven. So we consequently fail to see nature as part of us and essential to our existence.

Solution: Emulate Native Americans. Our eternal being, as believed by bible-based Christians, and their belief in nature's non-eternal existence, have made it easy to ignore our connection to nature. Our not-very-significant and temporal existence is a tough concept for the humanity who believe themselves more important than nature. We have much to learn from the Native Americans, who grasped their connection to nature and nature's importance, long before Science weighed in on this essential connection. (Yea, well look what happened to him! This was my uncle Ernest's response when, as a youngster, I naively, tried to speak with him about Jesus. He would no doubt say the same thing about Native Americans.) Power has so often won out over wisdom!

Solution: Look inwards to enlightenment and 'Stewards of Nature'. We will have our work cut out for us to overcome this very strong dogmatic barrier to addressing and stopping the ongoing man-made environmental calamity. It is hard to respect that which one feels is lesser than them. Our inner enlightened selves will have to emphasize the biblical 'stewards of nature' argument to this large and powerful group.

Effect of Lutheran Argument that Faith Above All Eliminates Good Works as Essential Key to Heaven. As a former 'excommunicated' Lutheran, I was told that all we need is faith in God and that our actions do not make a difference in getting us into Heaven. Martin Luther, whose anti-Jewish beliefs and teachings, facilitated the Holocaust, is now reaching out from the grave to eliminate any motivation to do good works to fight the unfolding end of the world scenario. *(See Ch 9 -Wrecking on the Hubris Iceberg)*

The Dead Sea Scrolls and the Pope Scream the Solution. *Jesus said: ...."..the kingdom is inside you and it is outside you...."* **The Sayings of Jesus # 3 of the Gospel of Thomas.** *(See Chapter 4.4 for the entire quote.)* The point is that God's Kingdom includes both humanity and nature. There is no distinction. Destroying either is wrong. This conforms perfectly with Pope Francis' powerful holding that to destroy nature is a sin. *(See Ch. 4)*

Faith in Revelations. "*Now, it is the end of the last days*...*Revelation 22:12 NIV.* For these Fundamentalists, nature and its intricate connection to the fate of humanity, is of no significance. The 'End of the World' was predicted by God and all the signs seem to be there. All that matters is their faith in God and being saved to enjoy the eternal afterlife. Any claim of an end-of-the-world scenario and that man has the power to stop it, is met with an argument that the end of the world is predicted in the bible. (See *Revelations 22:12 NIV.)* It is God's will! We cannot undo God's will! These are the folks that are easy pickings for politicians who are willing to categorize themselves as 'believers' and their opponents as liberals, socialists, Godless or Communists. It would seem that these fundamentalists have little motivation to stop pollution? Again, easy picking for the masters of the money matrix.

The Solution – Follow in His Footsteps. The answer to the problem is to follow in Jesus footsteps and risk our lives, our comforts and our wealth, to save the least of our brethren. As He did, we must speak out against the evils in the world. Certainly, poisoning our environment for our comfort and convenience at a cost of the extinction of God's gift to us – nature and humanity, is the greatest sin. Pope Francis has detailed this in his Encyclical on the Environment. *(See Ch. 4 for my summary)*

c. The Fundamentalists' link to Political Power: They have rejected science, they literally interpret the bible, and have a preference for the harsh, tribal mentality of the Old Testament. This is the group that was critical to electing president Trump. They elected George W. Bush over a man who saw the light about our environmental calamity, (Al Gore). The Fundamentalist link in the American matrix is extensive. Their malleability to conform to a politicians' wishes presents a major obstacle to stopping the pollution. It appears that the growing group of wealthy businessmen and their politicians, hardly need much to place fundamentalists in their political pocket. This group, because of their anti-science bent, will be easy fodder for leaders who have no scruples and follow only the vile maxim. Fundamentalists are babes in the woods where the human money-machines dwell and these financial and political giants daily suck life from their Fundamentalist 'batteries'.

White, non-college, working class and White Fundamentalism strongly support the fossil fuel industry because they connect it with jobs and American power and patriotism. The scientific consensus is insignificant to them because politicians tell them the science is wrong. Fundamentalism comprises a powerful part of the emotional and mental state of this country. This will make the fight against the polluters and saving the earth an uphill battle. Fundamentalists are the perfect cogs and the ideal batteries in the Big-Business, Big-Finance and government's controlling matrix.

A Former President's Take On Fundamentalism. This anti-science and anti-rational mentality still has a powerful effect on many folks and is a major obstacle to fighting pollution. This anti-science, anti-rational mentality is particularly powerful amongst 'fundamentalists. My beliefs about the dangers of Fundamentalism have been heavily influenced by former President Jimmy Carter's book: *Our Endangered Values.* Carter's dad was a Southern Baptist minister. The former president was also very active in the church.

President Carter, in a refined and knowledgeable fashion, makes a convincing argument that the Fundamentalist values have fouled up our world. He defines a fundamentalist organizations as 1) *Male-dominated/female oppressed; 2) Having a preference for the past but retain self-beneficial aspects of the present; 3) They make clear distinctions between themselves and others and as true believers, they are right and those who contradict them are ignorant and possibly evil; 4) They are militant in fighting any challenge to their beliefs, often angrily and with physical abuse and 5) They are demagogues who view change, cooperation, negotiation as signs of weakness. In summary, they are rigid, dominating and exclusionary.* Carter does mention George W. Bush by name and states that "fundamentalists have become increasingly influential in both religion and government, and have managed to change the nuances and subtleties of historic debate into black-and-white rigidities and the personal derogation of those who dare to disagree." Gee! This sounds so familiar!

In the last quarter century former President Carter has seen the growth of a right-wing movement within American politics, directly tied to the attributes of like-minded Christian groups. He sums up the effect as follows: *"The revolutionary new political principles involve <u>special favors for the powerful at the expense of others</u>, abandonment of social justice, denigration of those who differ, <u>failure to protect the environment</u>, attempts to exclude those who refuse to conform, a tendency toward unilateral diplomatic action and away from international agreements, an excessive inclination toward conflict and reliance on fear as a means of persuasion.(My emphasis.)*

Has Carter captured one of the essences that will make the war against pollution difficult? Has our fundamentalism facilitated the masters of the matrix to take a strong and unrelenting hold? The election of President Trump, should be cause to worry!

<u>SOLUTION</u>: <u>Moral Duty to Take Care of Nature.</u> A bright light in the world of Religion seems to be shining through the Dark Age mentality. A pope, who studied chemistry, has dared to support science. (*See Chapter 4.*) Nature, our purportedly inferior enemy, has scientifically turned out to be the equivalent to an essential 'neighbor' and arguably one that is covered by Jesus' directive to love thy neighbor as thyself. Pope Francis has finally declared the moral duty to take care of nature and directed that it is a sin to destroy it. The consequence of treating nature as less than us is now resulting in the destruction of nature and the beginnings of the death of humanity. Will anyone hear the message of Pope Francis in time? Do American Catholics even listen to the pope? (See my conversations with a close relative below.) Will this be enough to throw a wrench into the support for our money-motivated machine? I am less than optimistic. However, one of the lessons is to utilize the arguments in the Pope's Encyclical, Laudato Si. The Pope actually gives us some very practical recommendations.

A Moral Solution to ***"Complacency and a Cheerful Wrecklessness"*** We live in what the Pope calls a ''Throw-away Culture'. In spite of the death of millions caused by pollution, we refuse to take serious steps towards stopping pollution. We have become addicted to our luxuries. Anyone that has attempted to begin a recycling approach in their own household, has quickly found out that no one wants to stop using things that have made life so comfortable. My admonishment to the family to: 'Stop using the plastic and take cloth receptacles to Wal-Mart' is met with a response as if I were from some other planet. My family is embarrassed to be seen with me using my dollar store bags. *(Sally, my wife, has finally come around. Amadeo, my son, bought her some better looking cloth bags to use.)* A close family member who is Catholic, would rather just show me that he has some paper bags in his trunk and suggest: Why don't we just file some kind of legal suit? As for suggesting that he share my Summary of Pope Francis' environmental encyclical with fellow Catholics, he said he didn't want to be seen as a 'devil'. (He is the Harvard-educated one.)*2 As for our fossil-fuel-burning, carbon polluting vehicles, no one figures that their small pollution will make any difference. Why should I inconvenience myself by turning off the car and go in to get my fast food? Why would we inconvenience ourselves with mass transportation? Why would we pay for expensive electric cars? As for getting the word out that eating steaks, burgers and Dairy is destroying our environment with methane pollution....I best just work by example by becoming vegan. Notwithstanding that our leftover food 'garbage', is thrown 'away', into landfills, and is poisoning our sky with methane, one of the worst of the greenhouse gases, we are reluctant to channel the edible leftovers to the poor. We are slow to learn to compost our food instead of putting it in the garbage to add to the poison. As you see, the change will not be easy. It must become a priority in our lives!

The Pope's critique was right on! We really don't care what happens as long as our little world stays the same. Our business and political leaders have managed to suck our souls out in exchange for comforts. We hate to do anything that might threaten our comfortable way of life. In so acquiescing to this comfortable existence, and because of the large numbers of us addicted to comfort, we have become the gigantic battery powering those in control of this money-powered matrix. This malignancy of powerlessness, fueled by the fear of losing our comforts, freezes us into a state of ignorance and inaction. Our inner Neo's will have their biggest fight with this group. Unfortunately, it is large. Comfort breeds contentment and a lack of concern for others. It is a most difficult impediment.

Solution: Least of Our Brethren. Notwithstanding this strong fundamental influence, I believe that our reference point should be in the direction of Jesus' actual words and life. Now that we know almost 5 million people die from pollution each year and the poor are the ones most severely affected, Jesus' words and life should powerfully influence our being. He provides the most powerful non-violent weapon against a world that seems numb to victims of pollution. "What you do unto the least of my brethren, you do unto me" (*Mathew 25: 40 NIV.*) These must be the motivating words that inspire us to fight the polluters and stop their devastation.

Solution: Vote for Leaders That Address the Environmental Problems. For example, our government must intervene to make the purchase of an electrical vehicle a practical and affordable purchase for everyone. Public Transportation must go electric and reach out to everyone. We must educate our politicians about the pollution dangers of animal agriculture and the plastic polluters.

d. Effect of Capitalism At the risk of sounding unamerican and unpatriotic, I must identify a feature of our system that acts as a powerful barrier now blocking the fight against pollution. In this country, we have placed on a pedestal and altar, a group whose sole morality is based on how much money they can make, no matter the means or the quality of the product. We have created a system that encourages making money even if it risks the entire economy and now, the entire future of mankind. *(See my essay in this chapter on Animal Agriculture.)*

Capitalism Encourages Deadly Products. As Barry Commoner so elegantly explains it in *The Closing Circle,* our system encourages the creation and use of a product even though, after the damage is done, we discover the effects of the product are sickness, disease and death. *(See Ch. 3 – Summary of the Closing Circle)* Moreover, capitalism encourages a producer to continue selling the deadly product until they make enough money to invest in another product.

Solution. Civilly and Criminally prosecute those who cause sickness and death. We must enact a law that makes the destruction of the environment criminal.

Humans Driven and Controlled by Money? How possible, even probable is it that we could live in a country where a group could have taken over and controlled our lives, without anyone realizing or caring that it is happening? *4 How about a small group of humans and organizations motivated only by making money in a system that gives them inordinate control over our lives?

Is Capitalism, Ultimately Motivated by 'Profit', the Evil? Is the failure of the political system to impose financial restraints and limitations on the power of money to protect the public, the cause of financial decimation on everyone else? Is this same dynamic at work and now protecting financial and business interests, often by ignoring the environmental devastation these businesses are doing? *(See Commoner's viewpoint in The Closing Circle on this issue.)*

The 'One Percent' in Control? *Just prior to president Barack Obama's 2014 State of the Union Address, media reported that the wealthiest 1% of Americans possess 40% of the nation's wealth; the bottom 80% own 7%.*3.1 The gap between the wealth of the top 10% and that of the middle class is over 1,000%, that increases another 1,000% for the top 1%.*

As of Q(uarter)3, 2019, the bottom 50% of households had $1.67 trillion, or 1.6% of the net worth, versus $74.5 trillion, or 70% for the top 10%. From an international perspective, the difference in US median and mean wealth per adult is over 600%. The average employee "needs to work more than a month to earn what the CEO earns in one hour. *3.2

<u>Effect and Impact of Wealth Disparity and 'Profit Above All' Mentality.</u> We exist under an unethical businessman-president whose unabashed goals and policies are skewed clearly towards letting the financial system do what they want, to make money. Arguably a far worse situation than in *'The Matrix'* wherein a set of intelligent machines ran the country through a simulated reality and used our bodies as energy sources. Inside the simulated reality, humanity did not suffer the pain, as humanity is now enduring, and will become worse in the future. I submit that the impact of President Trump's blatant alignment with the money-making community combined with a policy of denial of the pollution problem (manifested significantly by our cancellation of our participation in the Paris Environmental Accords and the major rollback of environmental rules), will be devastating to the future of mankind.

<u>The Mantra of the Architects' of Capitalism - The Vile Maxim.</u> Chomsky, in *Requiem for an American Dream,* identifies the principle architects of policy" as the people who own the society". The mentality of those in charge, who Adam Smith called the "masters of mankind", follow *"the vile maxim," "All for ourselves and nothing for anyone else."* Chomsky identifies these entities as the financial institutions and multinational corporations. They prosper by considering only the bottom line. That the destruction of the world lies in the balance is not of importance to them.

We have to ask ourselves: whether we too are infected with the notion that making money is more important than anything else. This mentality blinds us to see any damaging human consequences of the vile maxim mentality. To care about anyone is only a distraction to the profit mentality. We will have to ask if capitalism has bought our soul and if we make for even stronger batteries for the matrix leaders who are energized by those who think like them, or at least, do not oppose them.

<u>Profits Over Life and Health.</u> On the 17th of July, 2019, I read that 'El Chapo', infamous drug lord, was going to prison for life plus 30 years. At the same time I read that numerous drug companies were targets of multiple lawsuits accusing them of driving up opioid sales with false claims about the safety and effectiveness of their drugs. Law suits were also against the members of the Sackler family who own Purdue Pharma. *4

In those lawsuits, Plaintiffs' claim that responsibility for the drug epidemic runs wide across the drug industry with manufacturers intent on grabbing as large a part of the opioid market as possible with little regard for the unfolding human tragedy. The opioid makers are blaming the epidemic on doctors overprescribing drugs. Purdue has already been hit with a $600 million fine for a criminal conviction over its marketing of opioids, and in March the company agreed to pay $270 million to settle a civil suit by the state of Oklahoma. Two years ago, Mallinckrodt paid a $35 million settlement with the justice department over its opioid deliveries. The data reveals that sales of opioids were often focused on areas most blighted by the epidemic, including some of the poorest parts of Appalachia. At one point, the highest per capita deliveries were to rural Mingo county, West Virginia, where "pill mills" and pharmacies were raking in money by churning out prescriptions without question to anyone who paid cash. The practice drew caravans of drug users from hundreds of miles away. McKesson and five other companies, including the pharmaceutical chains Walgreens, CVS and Walmart, were responsible for the bulk of painkiller deliveries across the US.

McKesson, which is listed seventh in the Fortune 500, paid a record $150 million fine two years ago to settle federal accusations that it was making suspiciously large deliveries of opioids to places where there could not be a legitimate demand for so many pills. It was also among companies that paid millions of dollars to settle lawsuits by West Virginia's attorney general that they flooded his state with opioids.

A former head of the DEA division responsible for monitoring prescription drug distribution, Joe Rannassizi, has previously told the Guardian that he attempted to launch criminal prosecutions against McKesson and other distributors but he ran into the power of the industry's political lobbying and was blocked by justice department officials.

I mention the above because it is illustrative of the power of big business and their absolute disdain for life or the law when it comes to making money. Selling pills that kill people was of no significance to them. It also reveals in Rannassizi's statement, that government will not pursue criminal prosecutions against wealthy businesses who sell deadly drugs, though they would do it against non-americans, like El Chapo, or those who are not wealthy. How many poor people or people of color do we 'warehouse' and compel to work in penitentiaries for little or no pay, even though the evil they are charged with does not rise to the evil of the drug manufacturing companies? We incarcerate more people than any other country in the world. Being rich is not only a powerful drug, it is admired and it is a powerful obstacle, if not the most powerful barrier, to the fight against earth-ending pollution.

We live in a country where those in power and those who have money are impervious to our health. *(See Ch. 10 Hamburgers – to Die For)* Unfortunately, this attitude has carried over into the environmental arena where the consequences are literally civilization-ending.

The Solution –Learn that meat is killing you and animal agriculture is destroying the planet. Try becoming a vegan or a vegetarian *(See Animal Ag. In this Chapter.)*

The Solution - Grassroots Mobilization. We must present our representatives with the political direction we must go and then shadow them to ensure that they do what we want them to do in a timely way. (See my suggestions at the end of this book.)

The 'activist' solution: The 'first steps' 'essential to our chance of avoiding a climate-and ecological disaster" include ending investments in fossil fuels, animal agriculture and plastics, establishing stronger carbon budgets, making "ecocide an international crime" and designing "climate policies that protect workers and the most vulnerable and reduce all forms of inequality: economic, racial and gender."

We need a call-to-arms based on Jefferson's words: *'That to secure these rights, Governments are instituted among men, deriving their just powers from the consent of the governed.'* And when did he believe that consent should be withdrawn? *'That whenever any form of Government becomes destructive of these ends, it is the Right of the People to alter or to abolish it, and to institute new Government, laying its foundation on such principles and organizing its powers in such form, as to them shall seem most likely to affect their safety and happiness.'* * *(See my call to arms: We are Taking Back Our Country in Ch. 12)*

The Jesus/Ghandi Weapons.*5 We need to include Jesus' words, (…least of our brethren…) and Ghandhi's non-violent activism (see *Marching To The Sea… in Ch. 11*) combined with a plan for utilizing these Pentagon funds to benefit a significant other part of this country. (See *Summary of The Closing Circle Ch. 4.)*

Solution is to Sue. Maybe it is the lawyer in me, but I think we need to sue the dastards that are making a fortune but being deceptive about the damage that is being done. (See some examples of law-suits in *Chapter 4 – Jump Rope for Ecology.)*

Criminally Prosecute The Dastards. Finally, we need to see that the evil that is being done is criminal. Two presidential candidates have seen this, Jay Inslee and Bernie Sanders are recommending that the executives of the polluting industries be criminally prosecuted. The issue is stark and simple. Is the extensive and callous poisoning of our world towards the end of humanity by Big Business and facilitated by their political puppets, a lesser evil than El Chapo's evil?

Historical Solution - Roosevelt's New Deal. When this country was devastated by the Great Depression, President Roosevelt initiated programs whose focus was not merely to make money for a few but for everyone, including those who were unable to do it for themselves. We must be creative and not be afraid to step on the feet of the wealthy who have so extensively contributed to the devastation of nature. We must refine the Green New Deal so it carries the green (renewable energy) message by way of 'Evangelists of Green' throughout the world, to convert others to transitioning from coal, oil and gas to renewable energy, from animal agriculture, to a high-protein vegetarian diet. Funds from the Pentagon directed towards war, must now be redirected to the war to save earth and mankind from the devastation we have done to nature.

Reach Out to Your Neighbors. We must develop a mentality away from comforting ourselves and our country. We must convert our mindset towards doing all in our power to save the world from extinction. We, like Greta Thunberg, must reach out to our neighbors and educate everyone to the pending disaster we have created and provide the mental, monetary and emotional tools to change our hearts and minds to fight this battle.

Educate Our Children. We must insist that we and our schools, educate our children about the impending world disaster. (See my lesson plan in Ch 4) We must create a generation of 'green fighters' who put saving the planet above everything else.

Encourage and Mandate Capitalist to Invest in Green Energy. I have added this category because I believe if we wait for capitalist to transform from polluters to green businesses, the damage to the environment will be irreversible.

e. The Practical Economic Connections and Local Reliance: A few years ago, a close family member and I were traveling through oil country in southern New Mexico. As I recoiled to the oil stench, I could not withhold my comment how it all stunk so bad. 'That is the smell of money!', my brother condescendingly tells me. The truth is that in New Mexico, oil pays a significant portion of our school system. Moreover, one third or more of New Mexico government is funded by fossil-fuel money or invested in state owed enterprises. We are a poor state, so that is a powerful motive to let the oil industry do whatever they want, as the last Republican governor in New Mexico did. To some extent, this same dynamic exists in all 50 states. Such is the magnitude of the problem. The fossil fuel industry has inserted/insinuated itself in our financial future to their 'benefit' and ultimately to our detriment. (The same applies to the Animal Agriculture Industry.)

Solution – Push for Pollution Free Industry. This is where we need to actually push for pollution-free industry, wind-power, solar power, geothermal and electric vehicles and non-animal agriculture. Our government must be convinced to assist pollution-free industry so it is financially accessible to all. *(See Barry Commoner suggestions in this regard, (Ch.4) and my recommendations in Ch 13.)* Our capitalist instincts and our tendency to cater to big-finance will be the biggest obstacle in this change.

Even more subtly and more devastatingly is the impact of animal agriculture. It's pollution is greater than that of that from all the vehicles. *(See full analysis supra in this chapter)* Our addiction to meat and dairy, pushed by our animal agricultural industries may be more serious than our addiction to gas and oil. Few seem to think it is a problem or even see it as a pollution bad-guy.

Solution – Veganism/Sue the Deceptors. At least, demand of your representatives to label meat as deadly. Stop eating meat and dairy, which is killing you and polluting the world. Try the vegan foods. Enforce the rules, administrative and otherwise, that would prevent these industries from polluting.

Economic Influence on Small Communities. I had the good fortune to be in the audience of a City Council meeting of a very small cross-roads town in New Mexico in early 2019. The attorney for Allsup's was also present. The issue was the City's approval of a 24-hour convenience store that sells fuel under the Shell, Alon, ConocoPhillips, Exxon and "Allsup's On the Go" brands. It also sells prepared food items. The new station would probably put the present gas and convenience station out of business. That did not seem to concern the Council. I suspect the economic survival of the town was the priority. A bigger more well-known name might attract more business and might hire more folks in the community. I suspect this dynamic is present all over the country - big oil companies making offers communities can't refuse. And the meeting began with all rising for the Pledge of Allegiance. A message that patriotism was involved in what the City proposed.

Solution: Tout Economic Benefits of Investing in Clean Energy. Our lives, our economies, our life routines are supported by, surrounded by, and inextricably connected with stability, that insures a comfortable way of life. If you are an investor, or a small community, death, disease and destruction sometime in the future, is a hard-sell argument. Our argument must be that renewable energy will be good for the community and the country, right now! We have to push for wind-farms and solar energy. We must tout the economic benefits of clean energy and the investment in that direction. We must push for non-meat and non-dairy industries.

Moreover, for the business communities, we must somehow minimize the pain of their transition to clean energy. The government must facilitate a transition from gas and oil jobs to jobs involving wind or solar power. We must put a plan out there that will reflect a concern for the interests of our finances as well as human beings. I think 'Green New Deal' when I think of a plan. *(See Inslee Green New Deal Plan.)*

Solution – Loudly Insist on a New Way. So, we have another factor that has acted to block environmental activism – Local, City, State and Federal governments reliance on the profits of capitalist ventures. Politicians have become reliant on the moneys generated by big business and financing and so have local and state governments. Capitalism has led to capitulation in masse. The claws and tentacles are deeply dug into our individual and political being. We fear the ouster of business and finance will result in a massive depression. No one wants to take a chance. The Masters of Mankind sink their teeth deeper. The job of the human money 'machines' is that much easier when so many others volunteer to be batteries. We must be the ones that loudly insist that we try a new way so our children have a better chance to survive.

f. FINANCIALIZATION - Freeing Big Finance to Do What It Wants - An Economic System That Encourages Speculation. In the 70's, the dismantling of the organizations that had successfully controlled currencies, lead predictably to an immediate sharp increase in speculation against currency. *(See Requiem for the American Dream p. 35)* *"At this same time....you started getting a huge increase in the flows of speculative capital—an astronomical increase—and enormous changes in the financial sector from traditional banks to risky investments, complex financial instruments, money manipulations, and so on." (P 35-36 of Requiem...).* The 2008 recession was the consequence. We refuse to learn the lesson of what causes depressions and recessions. The 'Nanny State' mentality contributes greatly to investments that may be perfect for the short term for the investor but devastating in the long-run for mankind. Yes I am thinking of the 'short term' investments in fossil fuels and Animal Agriculture.

Solution: Pass laws that do not encourage dangerous investments by the moneyed, the politicians and the polluters.

g. Illustration of How the Moneyed and the Politicians Take Advantage. Consider the following illustration of the control of the machine by the moneyed and the politicians. The politicians take money from the Wealthy who have an interest in continuing pollution. For example, governor Rick Perry of Texas. He effectuates this through political action committees or wealthy individuals. *"he relies on a relatively small network of very big hitters, wealthy businessmen and their spouses who want something out of Texas government." (* Craig McDonald, director of Texans for Public Justice, a nonprofit research group that tracks the influence of money in Texas politics.)* The Contributors get appointments and political favors. These are people who have business interests and were appointed to positions with regulatory power over businesses. The consequence is the accommodation of various energy interests in the particular state. This results in violations of The Clean Air Act. For example, Rick Perry's 'job-killing EPA strategy that Republicans have used. There's a saying in Texas, according to Smith that "it's cheaper to invest in politicians than in pollution controls." Perry has been similarly critical of the EPA's effort to regulate greenhouse gases nationally. *See CLIMATE CHANGE THE NOTION: "Rick Perry's Polluter Cronies".* www.thenation.com. Perry has become a multi-millionaire while in public office.

h. Money's Powerful Effect, In Hands of Fewer. Multiply the above scenario to a significant number of political offices that exist and you have a picture of what is wrong with our political system and why the battle against pollution will not be easy. This is the essence of the American matrix. No, the Wealthy and their politicians are not machines with super-powers. Functionally, they might as well be. They exert power and influence over the non-moneyed masses that effectively minimize the influence of those without money. Large amounts of money are your tickets to the political power rodeo. Politicians are refined enough to tell their constituents what we want to hear. Whether it is the truth is another issue. We get our goods and services from the polluters who are protected by the politicians. The moneyed group in control continues to get wealthier and the wealth is, more and more, in the hands of the few. The heartless control by the Wealthy and their influenced politicians, exerts the power of a machine to control all of us. Until money is removed from politics, we will continue to dance to the tune of the wealthy.

Solution. Provide a minimal amount of money to each voter to be directed to the political candidate of his choice.

Solution? – The Pledge Not to Take Money From Fossil Fuel Execs. In 2017, a pledge was created: It seeks to build support for curbing climate change by making the fossil fuel industry as politically toxic as Big Tobacco. The vow requires lawmakers to not take contributions of more than $200 from fossil fuel executives or political action committees associated with such companies and instead prioritize the health of our families, climate, and democracy over fossil fuel industry profits."

On Capitol Hill, the argument has been slow to catch on. As of mid- 2019, Jayapal, co-chairwoman of the Congressional Progressive Caucus, is one of just 41 members who've taken the vow.' No sitting Republican lawmakers have so far made the commitment, including environmentally conscious members like Rep. Brian Fitzpatrick of Pennsylvania." The congressional tally of pledge signers includes about 10 percent of the 47 senators in the Democratic caucus: Dianne Feinstein of California, Jeff Merkley of Oregon, Ed Markey and Elizabeth Warren of Massachusetts, and Vermont independent Bernie Sanders." "A similar proportion of House Democrats – 36 lawmakers, representing around 15 percent of the caucus – has taken the pledge." "Signatories in the House are overwhelmingly either freshman lawmakers – like Reps. Alexandria Ocasio-Cortez (D-N.Y.), Ayanna Pressley (D-Mass.) and Ilhan Omar (D-Minn.)" Most Democratic members of the House and Senate are willing to take their chances with the public trusting them. They have largely stayed away from an environmentalist-backed pledge.

After voting last year to not accept donations from fossil fuel companies, the Democratic National Committee quickly overturned the donation restrictions on "fossil fuel workers" and "employers' political action committees" (Greenwire, Aug. 13, 2018).* (*See E&E NEWS Email:* chiar@eenews.net*See article 'Opposition to fossil fuel cash splits Democrats. E&E NEWS, Jan 30, 2019.)*

How the above plays out will tell us whether our representatives are willing to commit to forego the funding of the polluting fuel industry and take a real stand against the devastation of pollution. So far it does not look good for nature and the future of mankind.

<u>Specific Examples of Governance by the Wealthy/Must Act Quickly.</u> Guess what? If the Corporation is called Exxon, do you think the political candidate who is taking money from them will have any other interests but Exxon's when they prepare legislation or when they vote? Welcome to governance by and for the wealthy. Since fighting pollution and saving mankind is not a big-moneyed interest, we should quickly realize that we will not be able to win the battle against pollution until we break the hold of big money on our politics. This response must be timely. Otherwise, the increasingly hotter temperatures may cause the change in the atmosphere to be irreversible, one step closer to Hawking's end-of-mankind prediction.

<u>Solution – Research your Candidate.</u> The "Neo' in us must react with the outrage that this democratic insult deserves. Find out who the candidate really works for and vote your interest not the corporations. Find out where the candidate stands on the Green New Deal and renewable energy.

<u>i. American Matrix' Political Deception in Practice.</u> In the book, *What's the Matter with Kansas? How Conservatives Won the Heart of America by Thomas Frank*, the author made it clear that there exists a real dynamic in which politicians will tell their potential supporters that they are the good guy, (the patriot, they found God, the anti-communist) and the opponent is the bad guy, the liberal, the leftist, unpatriotic or the Communist collaborator. The truth of what the politician tells his potential voter may not be true, but the voter wants to believe that the politician thinks and believes what the candidate believes. This dynamic hides the real interests of the politician and his real benefactor.

<u>The Politicians Approach to Get Votes</u>: A politician can stay in power and retain control and respect if he/she can convince people that the evil opponent is responsible for all the bad in the world. You can paint the cause of the problem any color or give it any shape just so long as it is blaming the evil on a bad guy, usually his/her opponent. It is called scapegoating. Conservatives found the modern devil in 'The Liberal', the "Progressive" 'the Socialist' or the 'far left'. This manipulating method has been maximized by President Trump. First you deny that there is an environmental crisis, then you contort the recommendations to fix it, as anti-jobs and anti-business. You identify the opposing candidate as 'Socialist'. Whalla, the candidate who is trying to save the world is the bad guy. President Trump becomes the good guy.

It also, quite often, results in devastating results to the particular community. President Trump's denial that we are polluting the earth and consequently removing Obama's protections, is now resulting in extensive damage to this country and the world.

The <u>modern power brokers</u> are big corporations, Wall Street and Big Industry. The charlatans are the politicians who speak bible-talk to their supporters but are beholden to those with money. And then there are the desperate multitudes who want the simplicity of the stark, black and white, good and evil. Like hungry dogs, the public laps up the answers the snake-oil politician feeds them. The message is always coated with the standard wrappings of "I am humble", "I am one of you", "I am God-fearing" and "I will fight the evil Godless Progressives". Modern day charlatans readily provide the ostensible power and antidote to the powerlessness, anger and resentment felt by those who are outside the control room without a key. Support me and I will give you the key to expunge and destroy the cause of all your problems – the Socialists. Defeat him and you will have the keys to Heaven. Never mind that it doesn't get better here on earth.

Consider the 2004 Presidential election, and you will see the Republican candidate who came from money, avoided the draft and was a fraternity man at Yale. He was successfully packaged, bought and successfully sold as a down-home, God-fearing, good old boy that was just like us. Consider the consequences of George W. Bushes' stay in the Oval Office - the Iraq War, built on the lie of Weapons of Mass Destruction and the Great Recession that he contributed to. We suffered the effects of a recession that saw the money powers come out smelling and looking good, while the rest of the public suffered serious financial repercussions. (*See What's the Matter with Kansas...How Conservatives Won the Heart of America. By Thomas Frank*) And do not forget the movie-star president (Reagan) whose actions devastated the working class who have not recovered since. (Our country seems to be suckers for TV and movie stars.)

The above dynamic, of late, has been exacerbated by a racism that compels white workers and Fundamentalists to fear non-white, non-Christians, taking over their jobs, lessening their rights and infecting their religion. It behooves unscrupulous politicians to paint their opponent as someone who will 'help' these non-whites, non-Christians to the detriment of the white worker and white Fundamentalist. Does President Trump's characterization of the Mexican immigrants as 'Animals' and 'Rapists' make sense now?

Some Great Local News. As of March 13, 2019, the New Mexico Senate and House Democrats have sent a bill to the Democratic Governor that sets NM on the path for carbon-free electricity from renewable resources by 2030 and 80 percent by 2040. The plan is a 'mandate', not just an aspiration and is among the most aggressive, if not the most, in the United States. This and the Green New Deal that is now being formulated on the National level, are great news! At the end of March, 2018, the democratic governor of New Mexico, signed the bill. Will it be enough to break 'big money's hold? Maybe it is becoming too expensive to drill for less and less oil? Whatever topples the economic evil-doers and their Vile Maxim works for me. As for the Green New Deal on the National level, we will probably have to wait for passage until the makeup of the House and Senate changes. That has not stopped the mouths of the moneyed and their politicos from attacking it as Socialist and an attack on Capitalism and our way of life.

More good news: Albuquerque, NM as of April of 2019 and Santa Fe, NM, have made plastic bags illegal. It would seem that somehow, we have to convert the business polluters into the renewable energy business.

Good News from Nevada: In mid-December, 2019, Nevada regulators approved a proposal from the state's largest utility, NV Energy, to add 1,190 megawatts of solar power and 590 megawatts of energy storage. This will put the company on pace to get about 40% of its electricity from clean sources by 2025. That gets it most of the way toward meeting the state's 2018 law of 50% renewable energy by 2030.

Good News About Saving Our Lungs: Another Solution - Wind Power in NM: Energy developers are tapping into New Mexico's billowing wind energy potential with plans to double installed generating capacity from wind farms on the eastern plains. Generous federal subsidies and major improvements in wind technology have combined to make wind-generated electricity a low-cost option today for utilities and corporations seeking renewable energy. More than a gigawatt of wind capacity is now under construction or planned in NM.

Good News from California: The first commercial geothermal power plant in the US was opened in 1960 in the Geysers, California: there are more than 60 operating in the US today.

Good News – Suing the Dastards. In October of 2016, the Boston-based Conservation Law Foundation filed a lawsuit against Exxon Mobil for endangering Massachusetts communities along the historic Mystic river through its activities at the Everett petroleum storage terminal. (*As of Mar. 13, 19, the federal court rejected the corporation's motion to have the case dismissed.*)

Good News in our Country: The election of Joe Biden who seems to adhere to the belief that the pollution-destruction of the planet is a priority.

j. The Major Polluters: One of the major polluters is the fossil fuel industry: Coal, Oil and Gas. ExxonMobil is the fifth largest oil company in the world. It is an American company with headquarters in Texas. Chevron Corporation is an American company and is the fourteenth largest oil company in the world. Conoco Phillips is an American company and is the 31st largest oil company in the world. EDG Resources is an American company, the fourth largest in the U.S. I mention these because you may want to know who may be buying your senator or representative's vote and poisoning the path to truth.

The Pentagon, our country's war machine, is also our biggest polluter, (the biggest polluter in the world). The research shows the US military is one of the largest climate polluters in history, consuming more liquid fuels and emitting more CO2e (carbon-dioxide equivalent) than most countries. *(June 20, 2019.)(Science News: 'U.S. military consumes more hydrocarbons than most countries – massive hidden impact on climate' Lancaster University. See the Messenger.)* We live in a country that is continuously at war everywhere in the world. Our news outlets, other than PBS, give little attention to this issue. War makes the war-machine beneficiaries big money. All of this gives gigantic weight and prescience to the words of President Eisenhower, many years ago: *'Beware the Military Industrial Complex.'* Our war-machine, firmly entrenched, as the biggest polluter and as a money maker for industry, stands powerfully and directly in the way of the fight to end pollution. This is one of the human machines at its worst. (*See Commoner recommendations.*)

The Polluters: **The Toxic 100: Top Corporate Air Polluters in the United States:** This index identifies the top air polluters among corporations that appear in the Fortune 500, Forbes 500, and Standard & Poor's 500 lists of the country's largest firms.

Rank Corporation

1. Bayer Group
2. Exxon Mobil
3. Sunoco
4. E.I du Pont de Nemours
5. ArceloMittal16. Alcoa Inc.
6. Steel Dynamics Inc.
7. Archer Daniels Midland Co. (ADM)
8. Ford Motor Co.
9. Eastman Kodak Co.
10. Koch Industries
11. ConocoPhillips
12. Valero Energy Corp.
13. General Electric Co.
14. AK Steel Holding
15. Dow Chemical Co.
16. Alcoa Inc.
17. Duke Energy
18. BASF
19. United States Steel Corp.
20. Public Service Enterprise Group (PSEG)
21. Precision Castparts
22. General Motors Corp.

*"The Toxic 100: Top Corporate Air Polluters in the United States." Infoplease. © 2000-2017 Sandbox Networks, Inc., publishing as Infoplease. 19 Dec. 2018 <https://www.infoplease.com/science-health/environment/toxic-100-top-corporate-air-polluters-united-states/>of plastic trash. (See 10/1018 report by environmental group Greenpeace.)

10 Major Companies Responsible for Deforestation & Destroying Our Planet

1. Cargill, 2. Black Rock, 3. Wilmar International Ltd., 4. Walmart, 5. JBS, 6. IKEA, 7. Korindo Group PT, 8. Yakult Honsha Co. Ltd, 9. Starbucks, 10. McDonald's. *(See 'One Green Planet' by Earth. Org (https://www.onegreenplan)*

Pesticide Industries. The most powerful chemical industry manufacturers of pesticides are Dow-DuPont, ChemChina Syngenta and Bayer-Monsanto. *(See Toxics Action Center report at 'PESTICIDES'. toxicsaction.org*

Animal Agriculture. If cattle were their own nation, they would be <u>the world's third largest emitter of greenhouse gases</u>, after China and the US. Livestock are reckoned to be responsible for up to 18% of all greenhouse emissions from human activities. *(See 'Factory Farming' in Ch. 10 for details)* Worldwatch Institute, a Washington D.C. environmental think-tank, most recently reported that livestock emissions actually account for 51% of greenhouse gases. (See Ch. 10 'Animal Agriculture') Rearing cattle produces more greenhouse gases than driving cars, a UN report warns.* 5.

The 2019 Top Four Meat & Poultry Processors: JBS, Tyson Foods, Cargill and SYSCO Corp.

Solution. Stop Eating Meat and Dairy. Become vegan. Tell your congress persons and senator that you want us to move away from the business of animal agriculture. Demand meatless burgers.

Pollution From Clothes. The clothing sector represents around 3% of the world's global production emissions of CO2, (mostly because of the use of energy to produce attire. The hectic pace of fast fashion contributes to this figure as clothes are discarded or fall apart after short periods.)

The following information is taken for the most part from the article 'How to Avoid Toxic Chemicals in Plastics" written on December 13, 2016. (See https.//www.madesafe.org)

Plastic Poison/Polluter. Plastics are a major polluter. (Please see supra in this chapter explaining the problem and solutions.) Stop buying plastic. Use recyclable materials instead.

Pollution from Food Waste. According to the U.N. Food and Agriculture Organization, 30 percent of food is wasted globally across the supply chain, contributing 8 percent of total global greenhouse gas emissions. If food waste were a country, it would come in third after the United States and China in terms of impact on global warming. *(See '11 Billion Pounds of Food Wasted Each Year Could Feed 28 Million people) (wwwampleharvest.org/) July 31ˢᵗ, 2018.*

(Landfills. Landfills and sewage treatment centers, pump out tons of methane each year—about 14 % of the U.S.'s annual footprint. *5.2 The IPCC warns that keeping methane emissions in check is necessary in order to keep the planet from warming further. *5.2)

Solution: Stop 'throwing away' your food scraps that end up at landfills. Feed the hungry, compost, donate food, and volunteer in organizations that work towards using and not wasting food.

Good News from Vermont. Vermont is the first U.S. state to ban food scraps from being trashed. The law is part of the state's decade-long plan to send at least half of its landfill waste to other facilities where it can be recycled or composted. *(July 6, 2020).* The rest of the world needs to take notice.

Leaking from Gas and Oil Drilling sites. Methane also leaks into the atmosphere at gas and oil drilling sites.* *(See ftnt 8.31 from Ch 10 – Animal Ag.)* Recent studies suggest that oil and gas wells in the U.S. alone are producing about 60% more methane than previously estimated by the

Environmental Protection Agency. Worldwide, the energy sector contributes about a quarter of the annual methane budget. *.31) (See ftnt .31 *8.31 from Ch 10 – Animal Ag.*)

k. THE PROBLEM FROM THE VANTAGE POINT OF THE PUBLIC: Have Americans Become The Baby Batteries as in the Movie The Matrix? In the movie, *'the Matrix',* not everyone was converted to a baby but I could not help detect that the machines chose the babies to be their human batteries. Of course, a baby is completely dependent on its caretaker as to what they see, feel and understand about their surroundings. Moreover, the baby has no power to fight back if it is starved or abused or drained of energy by the machine. I thought if you wanted to transform and control a society and you don't have magical or super-technological powers, you best transform everyone into a baby-like existence, so they would be totally at the mercy of those in power. Well how do you do that Mr. Lopez? Not even the machines made everyone a baby in *The Matrix*.

I submit to you an explanation why the battle to save nature and humanity will be so difficult. The following is how I think this country has turned us into the equivalent of babies, subservient to the human machines: big-business, multi-nationals, the financial sector and those politicians who need big-money to survive and prosper.

Chosen People/Manifest Destiny. We Americans have been convinced that we are the new 'Chosen People' so any and all acts that may appear evil, are really actions consistent with our Manifest Destiny. Slavery, the devastation to Native Americans, being the largest incarcerator in the world and unjust wars, to mention a few, have become entitlements and badges of honor for a large segment of Americans. We have entered into an unjust war, alleged to be against 'communism', taking the lives of American boys, devastating the Vietnamese and their countryside with bombs and lied to the American public about it. Americans have become the bullies of the world and we have managed to rationalize it. (And these are just a few of the evils that we have justified.) We, the public, have become *'babified'*. We may have 'cried' about these conditions, but we have failed to change them. *(The recent anti-racist riots, monument-toppling and demonstrations may be an indication that we will no longer be treated like babies.)*

Addressing these evils and connecting them to the people of the United States will subject this writer and any others who dare to speak the truth, to the claim of 'unpatriotic' or worse, a 'crazy radical'. My response is that there is not enough time before the climate emergency will become irreversible, to take conservative measures. We must speak and act consistent with the extinction emergency that has begun and threatens to become irreversible. We must call it as it is, without sugar-coating.

Result of Severance of the Ties to the Means of Production. Through technology and finances, we have separated the public from the means of food production. This way we do not have to grow or raise our own food to survive. We just go to the store. Our tie to nature is thus severed and a wall is built between us and maternal nature. It is hard to love that with which you have no connection.

Create Capitalism. Create an entire system in which the seller is rewarded only by profit and a bottom-line mentality. This way it is not about the quality or health of what is sold, but whether it is cheap, tastes good or makes us more comfortable.

Reward Business Size. Make sure the big companies are advantaged by being able to make it cheaper. For the public, quality becomes secondary. The only issue is how and where can they get it cheaper.

Create Technology so we Believe that Entertainment and Comfort are More Important than Thought - Addiction Through the Box. Create ideas and interpretations that are entertaining and fun to watch. Addict the public to the visual/audio magic box in which entertainment, game shows, buying what is advertised and watching TV Sports is more important than thinking, wisdom, love and action. Like watching the Gladiators in the arena of battle during the Roman Empire, we are calmed and distracted. Movie stars, television stars and cartoon producers became more important than the critical issues of the day. (Maybe, this is why Walt Disney and Ronald Reagan, (movie/cartoon producer and one who became president), were so powerful in testifying for McCarthy's viewpoint during the Red Scare). I will let the younger generation decide if all the features on their phone and the internet, are having the same effect. I submit it was not an accident that President Trump's preparation for the presidency was the American TV series, The Apprentice.

Addict and Lie to the Public About Fossil Fuel Burning Mechanisms – Our Connection to survival and the world. Addict the public to fossil fuel energy for heating, cooling, lighting, and all our household and business items.

Using advance technological devices and advertising, lie to the public to think that their goods, be it, tobacco, opiates, gas-powered vehicles, gas, oil or coal for production, plastics, meat, dairy, are not deadly or dangerous.

Deceive the Public about Eating Meat by Not Compelling Producers to Post on their Product that Meat Is a Carcinogen. (*See Animal Agriculture in this Chapter.*)

Addiction to Comfort, Entertainment and Control, Blind to the Danger of the Product. Create businesses ostensibly for the public's pleasure that are fueled by destroying nature and upon which they become dependent. Feed the public chemicals, poisons and carcinogens and 'sugar-coat' them so the public accepts what they consume without thought. Live as if there are no consequences for destroying that which feeds your existence.

Create an inexpensive mechanism that can transport the person to any place they wanted to go, entertain them, sell them what they want and think they need and make decisions for them.

Fight wars that are ostensibly against a 'communist threat' but hundreds-of thousands of lives are lost and it is all a lie. Investigate the protesters. Teach history to our children so it always appears that we did the right and just thing.

Destroy the American Dream by encouraging people to go to college but put them into financial servitude for the rest of their lives paying back what they owe. Require a price tag to be educated, even though many are prevented from attending because they cannot afford it. Knowing that early education has a tremendous impact in later years, refuse to adequately fund pre-school and early-years education. Emasculate the working class by making it difficult to create Unions. Tax the wealthy at a far lower rate than everyone else.

Punish Those Who Disagree. Punish those who did not conform to the dictates of the person in power. Investigate and infiltrate those who dare to publicly express their disagreement with the powers that be. (Have an organization in power that practices spying and infiltration and war-making as part of your government. Make it a secret organization and try to punish those who attempt to reveal the undemocratic actions of the organization. Call it a 'National Security' crime. (I think of Dr. Martin Luther King Jr and more recently, Edward Snowden.) Punish, destroy, demean and deprive those of their land that stand in the governments' way. Brand those who are different and call them homosexuals, communists, anti-American and make it a basis to lose their job as 'security risks'. Bring forth presidents (Reagan) and entertainment company leaders (Walt Disney) to testify about the risk.

Protect the powerful Animal Agriculture industry by making Animal Rights and environmental activists the number one domestic terrorism threat of the FBI. (See *Green is the New Red,* cited supra.)

Lie to the public. Insure that poor people are stuck in low-paying jobs by making college out of their reach. Minimize unions so wages are kept low and the employer gets richer. Practice and encourage racism by demeaning all those but White Christians. Elect a president who caters to the lowest human instincts. Do not teach or make it mandatory to have schools teach ecology and the dangers of destroying nature.

Destroy Native Americans and put them on reservations. Then brainwash and destroy the culture and language of their children. Treat them like second class citizens. Enslave black people and then later imprison them at percentages well beyond their numbers in the population.

<u>Technology, the God and Nature the Enemy/ Technology Invincible.</u> Convince everyone that there is no evil or danger that technology cannot defeat. Make it God-like. Dazzle the public with the power and magic of medical technology, which defeats the killer germs and viruses, the evil and demonic bugs with which nature has dared to attack mankind.

The powerfully held mentality that nature is our enemy and technology is our savior, had a strong influence on me. I was raised on a diet of anti-biotics to kill those evil germs and viruses who were the devil-like enemies. (You could hardly blame a mother whose father and grandfather died of the Spanish Flu in in 1918.) We grew up with the idea that if we could clean up, wash it away or somehow eliminate or avoid nature, we would not get sick. *(See Ch. 4, To Love a Tree.)* As our disease-fighting abilities became more refined, we learned to believe that no matter what nature sullied us with, the technology would be developed to control and defeat it. Nature was the enemy and technology, the savior. We have lost the fear of destroying ecosystems (deforestation), and then moving in next door. We believe technology will protect us from those bugs, viruses and pandemics that plague other countries. This mentality is now killing us. (*See my summary of The Closing Circle in Chapter 4*)*6

We continue to believe that technology will solve any problem that we have or may have in the future. The unfortunate and powerful effect is to allow big business and big-government to continue to destroy nature and put dangerous products on the market because we have grown up to ignorantly destroy nature, the enemy, without the realization that there are serious consequences to be paid that technology cannot timely fix.

The latest chapter is that we are being told that we should go to Mars. Our government is funding and sending astronauts to Mars. The problem is that as long as this country thinks they have an 'out' they will not focus their mental and financial energies towards the planet that needs saving. We should be taking a deep look into the heart of nature and our connection thereto. Because of the technology distraction, we are not looking or connecting with nature.

Nature, the Bad Guy. The history of dislike and hatred of nature has been manifested by the diminishment of those who would worship nature, including their 'pagan' gods, such as Pan. The Catholic Church was behind much of this since there could be no other than the one God to worship. I don't think I would have heard much about St. Francis of Assisi, lover of nature, but for the fact that he had the 'stigmata', the wounds Christ suffered. The nature-connection was played down.

My experience with the conversion of nature into something evil is personal. My mother could never come to believe that my father's alcoholism was rooted in the genes he inherited. She truly believed that a woman had transformed into an owl and visited our house to cast a spell on him (mal-ojo). Really! One day, when I was young, my mom saw an owl on our front porch. She quietly walked to the kitchen and boiled some water and tip-toed back to the porch with the visiting owl and threw the scalding hot water on the poor feathered creature. She later told me, somewhere in town, a lady's face will be burnt. Yeah! Even though I was young, I realized what had happened was bizarre and cruel. It clearly revealed a level of mental and emotional dysfunction whose reality was not rational or science-based but pure superstition in which nature was the carrier of the evil. And the poor cats, especially if you were a black feline! They became another possessor or carrier of evil. God forbid they cross your path! It wasn't that long ago that we held onto, and to some extent, still do, the belief that if you were sick, disobedient, mentally ill or ugly, it was because the devil made you that way or you were possessed. Our entire Christian belief is built on a concept of human sacrifice – that God sacrificed his only son, Jesus, to save mankind. Those Mayans sacrificing virgins should not sound so strange. My mom's actions even make sense in this context. I.e., bad things just don't happen. Someone or some thing is evilly causing it. The evil-causer must be punished or at least, some animal must be sacrificed to appease the god that might retaliate against us if we ignore the evil.

The effect of these pre-enlightenment notions is still powerful now. Combine this with our adulation of technology, which has functionally become our god, the battle to save 'evil' nature is going to be tough.

I think Carl Sagan summarizes our mentality well:

I have a foreboding of an America in my children's or grandchildren's time – when the United States is a service and information economy; when nearly all the key manufacturing industries have slipped away to other countries; when awesome technological powers are in the hands of a very few, and no one representing the public interest can even grasp the issues; when the people have lost the ability to set their own agendas or knowledgeably question those in authority; when, clutching our crystals and nervously consulting with our horoscopes, our critical faculties in decline, unable to distinguish between what feels good and what's true, we slide, almost without noticing, back into superstition and darkness. The dumbing down of America is most evident in the slow decay of substantive content in the enormously influential media, the 30-second sound bites (now down to 10 seconds or less), lowest common denominator programming, credulous presentations on pseudoscience and superstition, but especially a kind of celebration of ignorance.

Query: Are we quickly reaching that point? Have we reached it? Is the election of Donald Trump proof positive that we have lost our critical faculties? What emotion, what moral approach, what reasoning, will convince these groups that pollution is destroying our world?

CONCLUSION: The Public Being Transformed into 'Babies',: The public has thus become like a baby, totally dependent on the businesses and connected politicians that provide them with the above entertainment, luxuries, food and energy, without which they could not survive. As in the "Matrix", the public has taken on the traits of immaturity, dependency and impulsiveness. We have thus become the 'babies' and, consequently, the 'batteries' for the Wealthy and their politicians.

A substantial part of our country would rather be entertained, controlled and/or 'saved', than face and take action against the devastation of pollution.

From a moral/religious view, we have recklessly and wantonly eaten from the tree of knowledge and with this knowledge, committed the sin of pride. We have come to believe that we are more important and significant than the rest of humanity and nature. We have fought wars against humanity and now against nature with whom we are intricately and inextricable connected. Oblivious to this connection, we are now destroying ourselves. We have essentially begun our exit from this Garden of Eden.

The solution is to act now and not wait for technology to solve our problem! We must recognize this disaster and that we have caused it. We must educate ourselves, our families and the world about our failure that is leading to our extinction. I have proposed solutions herein as have the democratic candidates for president. We must civilly and criminally prosecute those who destroy nature. You and me….we, must all become activists to save our planet and humanity from what we have done.

*.1 See cites at Animal Agriculture.

*1. (Also See Fowler, Harold. The Gospel of Matthew: volume One. Joplin: College Press, 1968 which addresses the bible's anthropocentricism.)

*2 Any critique of my brother is greatly mitigated by the fact that I know he will come around to my viewpoint and be instrumental in the fight against pollution.

*3 Electric vehicles reflect the locations of charging stations.

*3.1 Kristof, Nicholas (July 2, 2014) "An Idiot's guide to Inequality"; The New York Times.

*3.2 Marsden, William (January 26, 2014), Obama's State of the Union speech will be call to arms on wealth gap, retrieved January 26, 2014.

*4 10/21/20 See articles re the opiate suits. The New York Times: 'Purdue Pharma Pleads Guilty to Criminal Charges for Opioid Sales' by Jan Hoffman and Katie Benner: (Purdue Pharma is the maker of Oxycontin) "The Justice Department announced an $8 billion settlement with the company. Members of the Sackler family will pay $225 million in civil penalties but criminal investigations continue."

*5 (the references to 'Neo', the 'machines' and 'babies as batteries' is to 'The Matrix' film)

* 5.1 See UN News Centre Nov 29, 2006.

*5.2 See Cites in Ch. 10 animal agriculture

*6 The recent Corona Virus could easily push to the back of our collective minds the real and immediate concern about the environment and polluting industries.

CHAPTER XI

<u>LIVE THIS MOMENT AS YOU WOULD LIVE THE LAST</u>

INTRODUCTION TO 'LIVE THIS MOMENT AS YOU WOULD LIVE THE LAST':

NOW
IS
THE
TIME
TO
TAKE
ACTION!

A. EARTH'S LAST MOMENTS

(Until I sent the book to the publisher, I felt compelled to identify and update focal points or indicators of how close we are to a potentially irreversible calamity. The caring mother needs to know the predator is nearby, so she is alerted to take action to protect her children. The following should reveal that the monster is at our doorstep.)

"...the outlook for life on Earth is more dire than is generally understood. Well, the outlook is worse than even scientists can grasp." (See 'Worried about Earth's future? theconversation.com.)

1. DOOMSDAY CLOCK AT 100 SECONDS TO MIDNIGHT

As of January 23rd, 2020, the Bulletin of Atomic Scientists has set the Doomsday Clock at one hundred seconds to midnight. The previous 'two minutes to midnight' setting was the closest it had been to apocalypse since the height of the Cold War. At that time, the U.S. and Soviet Union had both just tested their first hydrogen bombs.

What brought the clock to this perilous time? Climate change, the threat of cyber warfare, the malicious spread of misinformation, nuclear-armed world leaders and, in my opinion, a reckless, ego-maniacal and lying President.

The point of this brief comment is that scientists are now recognizing that along with weapons of mass destruction, climate change has world-ending potential and the consequences are already upon us.

I submit that each of us need to reconsider the very real danger that our continued abuse of the environment is causing and will cause in the near future. We need to be placing a priority on ending our abusive relationship with the ecosystem. The consequences are far too severe and the longer we wait, the more difficult it will be to end the problem.

2. ANOTHER DIRE WARNING FROM A SCIENTIST AND WRITER

I am not a scientist so I can only direct you to the science and the scientific literature. Please consider reading the book: ***CLIMAGEDDON*** *The Global Warming Emergency and How to Survive It by Lawrence Wollersheim. Mr. Wollersheim is an experienced scientist and researcher. He previously worked for a think tank. I include quotes herein why he wrote the book and some of his well-studied conclusions:*

"Global warming was not even on my radar. By chance, I began reading a global warming book. The more I read, the more concerned I became.

After reading 10,000 pages of books and published studies, I became so concerned I stopped all research in other areas. By that time, it was clear to me that catastrophic global warming risks were still not adequately being explained to the public and there was a growing probability of the extinction of humanity in a significantly shorter time frame than was being presented by governmental authorities."

Please consider some of his critical findings and conclusions:

'Global Warming is not getting better. It is getting worse at a far faster rate than we are planning or preparing for.'

'Global warming has irreversibly destabilized several critical climate areas—and dangerous climate stability transition points have already been crossed.'

'We have been given inaccurate and incomplete predictions by the United Nations authoritative intergovernmental Panel on Climate Change (IPCC) for when the main consequences of global warming will occur, as well as how bad those consequences will be. In part, this is happening to protect national and corporate fossil fuel economic interests.'

'Global warming has irreversibly destabilized several critical climate areas—and dangerous climate stability transition points have already been crossed.'

'The most expensive and worst consequences of global warming will not occur in 40 to 80 years as we are being told. They are already starting and many will occur in less than half that time.'

'Continued global warming will create economic devastation at every level. Hundreds of trillions *of dollars will be lost by those individuals, businesses, and nations most uninformed and unprepared for the massive coming changes.'*

'There is a clear and final global warming battle line we must not cross and it is very near, and staying on the safe side of that line will be the greatest adaptive challenge humanity has ever faced.'

'There is still time left.

'If we fail to act effectively to reverse escalating global warming, there is enough time left to slow down and lessen its consequences, as well as partially mitigate the mass suffering, death and the collapse of our economic, political, and social systems.'

3. FAILURE ON A WORLD SCALE.

In 2010, leaders from 196 countries gathered in Japan and agreed on a list of goals designed to save the earth. The Aichi Biodiversity Targets laid out a 10-year plan to conserve the world's biodiversity, promote sustainability, and protect ecosystems. That deadline has arrived and the world has collectively failed to fully achieve a single goal, according to the United Nations' Global Biodiversity Outlook report, published Tuesday. *(See Jessie Yeung, CNN)*

4. UPDATE ON POTENTIAL TIPPING POINTS

(Tipping Points are critical thresholds at which small changes can lead to dramatic shifts in the state of the entire system.) On April 28, 2020, in the Yale University e360, and based on new research, Fred Pearce, wrote an article entitled 'Why 'Carbon-Cycle Feedbacks' Could Drive Temperatures Even higher'. I included a summary of the article because it should tell us that reaching 'tipping

points' that may be irreversible, means we need to act now! Climageddon, addresses numerous 'tipping points' and I have included them supra. We are witnessing the transformation of our friend the tree, who generally turns CO2 into life-giving oxygen, but now, because of the increasing heat and deforestation, our forests are beginning to put CO2 into the atmosphere. Please read my summary below.

a. From Carbon Sink To Source -Another Tipping Point reached?

1. Thawing Permafrost & Carbon Release Methane Levels Continue To Rise.

Atmospheric chemist Luciana Gatti, a researcher at Brazil's national Institute for Space Research (INPE), has, for a decade, been sampling the air from sensors on aircraft flying over the world's largest Amazon rainforest. They have discovered that '*Their collating of recent results showed that, perhaps for the first time in thousands of years, a large part of the Amazon had switched from absorbing CO2 from the air, damping down global warming, to being a "source" of greenhouse gas and thus speeding up warming.*'

"*We have hit a tipping point,*" Gatti proclaimed.

Her results were not the short-term result of the fires. They were based on measurements from before the upsurge in fires, and showed a long-term trend. She concluded the sink had become a source. "*Each year it gets worse,*" she said. "*We have to stop deforestation while we work out what to do.*"

'New research indicates that in parts of the Amazon, the carbon dioxide emissions from tropical forests are now emitting more CO2 than they absorb. Some scientists are concerned this development, which is not yet incorporated into climate models, could put the temperature goals set by the Paris Agreement out of reach." *2

"The scientists are warning that past climate models used by UN's Intergovernmental Panel on Climate Change (IPCC) have not fully reflected the scale of the warming that lies ahead as carbon sinks die." *3

The extra emissions, known as carbon-cycle feedbacks, could already be making the prospect of keeping warming below 2 degrees Celsius – all but impossible.

'Our planet's land and oceans currently take up about half of all the CO2 we put into the atmosphere. The gas dissolves in seawater and is absorbed by growing plants. Without these "carbon sinks," warming, to date, would have been twice as great. We would already have exceeded the 2-degree target. But the question now is whether the take-up will remain as it is, or diminish." *1

The good news: The extra CO2 speeds up plant growth. This fertilization effect means that forests absorb more CO2 as they grow, slowing the build-up in the air. The bad news is that the higher temperatures, also brought about by the added CO2, are pulling in the other direction, reducing nature's ability to soak up CO2. This happens because warmer ocean waters dissolve less CO2, while soils release more of the gas and some forests suffer heat stress and die or catch fire.

Both these feedbacks are in play. According to ecologists, the debilitating effects of the warming, especially when combined with deforestation, are becoming increasingly dominant. This is what Gatti has seen in the Amazon. And the trend is often happening faster than expected.

"Gatti's findings, while relating to the southeast part of the Amazon, the region's most heavily deforested area, suggest that the rainforest as a whole could be close to flipping from a sink to a source of CO2. The ability of intact areas of the rainforest to absorb CO2 have already halved since the 1990s, says Carlos Nobre of the University of Sao Paulo, Brazil's most noted climate scientist." "Passing the tipping point for the whole forest would release more than 50 billion tons of carbon, he said recently, which is the equivalent of 5 years of global fossil-fuel and industrial emissions"

"Non-tropical forests remain largely in carbon "sink" mode. But other tropical rainforests appear to be following the Amazon in moving toward becoming carbon sources"

a. Thawing Permafrost. "Another big concern is the impact of thawing permafrost. This frozen ground, which covers large areas of the far north, holds hundreds of billions of tons of carbon that could be released as the land thaws. How much and how fast is an unresolved question. But the signs are not good. One recent study in northern Canada found thawing had reached depths "already exceeding those projected to occur by 2090.""

"Writing with Zeke Hassfather, of the Breakthrough Institute, in a blog this month on the website Carbon Brief, he warns that many of the projections of the new models" end up with much higher CO2 concentrations by 2100." That means more warming. "The combination of high climate sensitivity and high carbon-cycle feedbacks could result in substantial warming, even under more moderate emissions scenarios," they say."

b. Methane Levels Rising. *"The growing concern about CO2 feedbacks comes on top of alarm about trends in atmospheric levels of the second most important greenhouse gas, methane. These are more than twice pre-industrial levels, and after a decade of stability until 2007 they have been rising again sharply. The National Oceanic and Space Administration (NOAA) estimated this months that methane levels in the atmosphere reached a record 1,875 parts per billion in 2019, after the second largest year-on-year leap ever recorded.*

"...the concern is growing that, even if technology can reduce industrial emissions, a warmer world will drive a continuing surge in methane levels and more warming as a consequence."

My Comment: The above concerns re methane pollution are even more worrisome because of recent EPA rollbacks by the Trump administration: 'The Environmental Protection agency this week finalized a rule that kills off Obama-era limitations on how much methane, a potent greenhouse gas, oil and natural gas producers are allowed to emit into the atmosphere—even though industry leaders didn't want the changes."*4

"Measured over 20 years, each molecule of methane emitted has 84 times more warming effect than each molecule of CO2."

c. Methane Breaking through the Melting Permafrost. As of October 11, 2020, it was reported that a 'Boiling' sea was discovered in Siberia, stunning scientists. The Russia's Tomsk Polytechnic University reported *"An unusually powerful methane emission" has been spotted in the East Siberian Sea"*. It was reported that it was the most powerful methane emission of its type that had ever been seen.*4.3

The Associated Press reported in 2010 that in the past few decades, as the Earth has warmed, the icy ground has begun thawing more rapidly, accelerating the release of methane – a greenhouse gas, 23 times more powerful than carbon dioxide – at a perilous rate.

As we fail to act aggressively enough, the nightmare will get worse.

d. All sea ice will disappear by 2035. *4.5 & 5 'canary in the coal mine': Greenland ice has shrunk beyond return, study finds "Greenland's ice sheet may have shrunk past the point of return, with the ice likely to melt away no matter how quickly the world reduces climate-warming emissions," new research suggests. "That melting is already causing global seas to rise about a millimeter on average per year. If all of Greenland's ice goes, the water released would push sea levels up by an average of 6 meters—enough to swamp many coastal cities around the world. This process however, would take decades." *ANOTHER SIGN – THE ARTIC IS ON FIRE! *7

As of July 6, 2020, the Artic is ablaze. Siberia, the proverbial coldest place, situated way up at the top of the globe in the Arctic circle, is experiencing record warming temperatures, melting sea ice, and massive wildfire – changes to the environment that even the scientists most urgently tracking the climate crisis didn't expect to see for another several decades. According to New York's David S-Wallace-Wells, "in a world without climate change, this anomaly, one Danish meteorologist calculated, would be a <u>1-in-100,000 year event</u>". Scientists say that the area is warming at three times the rate of the rest of the world, due to a phenomenon called "<u>Arctic amplification</u>," in which melting ice exposes more dark sea and lake waters, turning zones that were once net heat-reflecting into heat-absorbing. And temperatures rise even more.

The effects of that increase are myriad and terrifying. Melting snow creates dry vegetation for wildfires, which have reached record levels this summer, sending out giant plumes of smoke and releasing more greenhouse gases than ever before.

Perhaps scariest is the potential calamity of total permafrost melting: <u>Under this layer of ice</u>, approximately 1,460 billion to 1,600 billion metric tons of organic <u>carbon</u> are <u>trapped</u>. That is more than twice the amount of carbon currently in the atmosphere. With previously stable permafrost subject to never-before-seen heat, <u>if it is released, we could reach a tipping point beyond human intervention. (my emphasis)</u>

<u>My Comment</u>: The world has a fever. It is a good warning sign that we need to stop, take note and figure out what's going on.

e. Arctic Heat Wave. On June 20, in the small Siberian town of Verkhoyansk, north of the Arctic Circle, a heat wave baking the region peaked at 38 degrees Celsius – just over 100 degrees Fahrenheit. It was the highest temperature ever recorded in the Artic.

It was warmer there (in the Arctic), than it was that same day, in Miami, Florida. In fact, it was warmer north of the Arctic Circle than it has ever been, on any June day, in the entire recorded history of Miami, which has only once, in the whole tropical century for which temperatures there have been registered, reached 100 degrees. (*July 21, 1942*)

The City of Houston, has been hit by five "500-year storms" in the last five years…"

The IPCC says: to safely avoid 2 degrees of warming, that we must half our emissions by 2030. At the rate we are going, the planet has only a 0.3 % chance of doing so. If Donald Trump won reelection, the analysis suggested, those chances would fall to 0.1 % - one in a thousand!

At 2 degrees, it's expected that more than 150 million additional people would die from the effects of pollution. Storms that used to arrive once every century would hit every single year, and that lands that are today home to 1.5 billion people would become literally uninhabitable, at least by the standards of human history.

The point of Mr. Wallace-Well's article is that global warming is scrambling our sense of time. ' …until the arrival of large-scale carbon removal technologies, it also illustrates the fact that time – in the form of carbon emissions, which hang in the atmosphere for centuries – is irreversible. The warming effects will unfurl for millennia, with the climate stabilizing perhaps only millions of years from now. Climate change unwinds history, melting ice frozen for many millennia and pushing rainforests, like the Amazon, closer to their long-overgrown savannah states. *8

My Comment. *I cannot do the article justice, but it reveals how global warming is having a massive effect, even on our sense of time, which is quickly running out.*

f. Worst Case Scenarios Reached. A recent report confirms that ice sheets in Greenland and Antarctica, whose melting rates are rapidly increasing, are matching the intergovernmental Panel on Climate Change's worst-case climate warming scenarios. *8.5

g. More Signs - Terrestrial Water Availability Is diminishing "The amount and location of available terrestrial water is changing worldwide. An international research team led by ETH Zurich has now proved for the first time that human-induced climate change is responsible for the changes observed in available terrestrial water."

"The researchers note that the increased intensity of dry seasons is generally caused by greater evaporation (due to higher temperatures and radiation) rather than reduced precipitation." "In general, the reconstructed water availability data point to more intense dry seasons in extratropical latitudes. Affected regions include Europe, western North America, northern Asia, southern South America, Australia, and East Africa." *9

h. More Severe Storms. *10 Destructive storms come from rising warm waters. America and the world are getting more frequent and bigger multibillion dollar tropical catastrophes like hurricane Laura, which is now menacing the U.S. Gulf coast. *(8/27/20)*. The list of these catastrophic storms continues to grow: Harvey, Irma, Maria, Florence, Michael, Dorian and now Laura.

The Atlantic is increasingly spawning more major hurricanes, according to an Associated Press Analysis of NOAA hurricane data since 1950. The Atlantic now averages three major hurricanes a year, based on a 30-year running average. In the 1980's and 1990's, it was two.

The Atlantic's Accumulated Cyclone Energy – a measurement that takes into account the number of storms their strength and how long they last – is now 120 on a 30-year running average. Thirty years ago, it was in the 70's or 80's on average.

Scientists agree that waters are warming, and that serves as hurricane fuel, said NOAA climate scientist Jim Kossin. A study by Kossin found that, once a storm formed, the chances of its attaining major storm status globally increased by 8 percent a decade since 1979. In the Atlantic, chances went up by 49 % a decade.

Climate change contributes to creating more damaging storms by causing a rising sea level that worsens storm surges and making storms move more slowly and produce more rain, scientists say.

All of this means that we should get used to more catastrophic storms, according to Munich Re's Bove. In addition he said: "Climate change will be a bigger driver of losses in the future." *5

i. Droughts. Currently, more than half the West—nearly 1 million square miles—is experiencing acute drought conditions. *10.1. The epicenter is the Southwest, where drought conditions have mostly prevailed since about 2000, the start of a megadrought that could last for decades. *(See 10.1)* The current Western drought could soon rise to a crisis level, with federal water managers warning that Lake Powell and Lake Mead, the two key Colorado River reservoirs may drop to levels that could result in economically damaging cuts to water allocations in the Southwest and California. In the last four decades, severe drought caused $252.7 billion in economic losses and damage in the U.S. about 14 % of the total cost of climate disasters in that span. Only hurricanes, at $954.4 billion, and severe storms, at $268.4 billion, have caused more damage.

Droughts often damage or destroy crops and natural ecosystems like forests and wetlands. They also affect water supplies and can reduce water available for hydropower, and for cooling coal or nuclear plants. Globally, about 55 million people are affected each year, and worsening droughts could displace up to 700 million people by 2030, according to the United Nations. *(See *10.1)*

j. Time Running Out. The International Energy agency chief and one of the world's foremost energy experts, makes the following warning (June 18, 2020): *"..the world has only six months in* *which to change the course of the climate crisis and prevent a post-lockdown rebound in greenhouse gas emissions that would overwhelm efforts to stave off climate catastrophe. *6*

*1 See Yale Environment 360 Why 'Carbon-Cycle Feedbacks' could Drive Temperatures Even Higher

*2 By Fred Pearce, April 28, 2020

*3 Gatti's studies in the Amazon, A new generation of climate models that incorporate these findings into future projections of climate change; Recent revelations that ecosystems are releasing rising volumes of methane, the second most important greenhouse gas and of vital importance for temperatures in the next couple of decades.

*4 'Trump admin. Finally kills off Obama-era rule limiting methane emissions by Kate Cox 8/14/2020 (https;// news.google.com)

*4.3 Article: 'Sleeping giant' Arctic methane deposits staring to release, scientists find' by Jonathan Watts, editor, Oct 27, 2020. See the Guardian

*4.5 ('Sea-Ice-free Arctic during the Last Interglacial supports fast future loss' by Maria-Vittoria Guarino, Louise C. Sime, and Allstair Sellar, published 10 Aug, 2020, for Abstract.

*5 (see REUTERS Sat Aug 15, 2020 (https://news.google.com)

*6 (See The Guardian: Climate change 'World has six months to avert climate crisis, says energy expert. Article written by Fiona Harvey, Environment correspondent.)

*7 (Taken from The CUT. CLIMATE CRISIS/ July 6, 2020: The Artic Is On Fire, and We Should all Be Terrified, By Bridget Read @bridgetgillard)

*8 (See Intelligencer Life after Warming June 27, 2020 'Global Warming Is Melting Our Sense of time' by David Wallace-Wells)

*8.5 "Worst-Case Climate Scenario" – Ice Sheets in Greenland and Antarctica Loss Rates Rapidly Increasing" by European Space Agency on Sep 08, 2020. See SciTechDaily at https://scitechdaily.com

*9 See 'climate change is altering terrestrial water availability by Michael Keller, ETH Zurich 7-3-20

*10 Information taken from article entitled "Hurricanes have gotten more destructive. Here's why. (see nbcnews.com) by Associated press Aug. 27, 2020.

*10.1 National Integrated Drought Information System. In article by Inside Climate news: 'Droughts That Start Over the Ocean? They're Often Worse Than Those That Form Over Land'

*11. See REBECCA HERSHER • MAY 27, 2021, NPR. To see more, visit ttps://www.npr.org.

k. Earth Is Barreling Toward 1.5 Degrees Celsius Of Warming. *11* The average temperature on Earth is now consistently 1 degree Celsius hotter than it was in the late 1800s, and that temperature will keep rising toward the critical 1.5-degree Celsius benchmark over the next five years, according to a new report from the World Meteorological Organization.

Scientists warn that humans must keep the average annual global temperature from lingering at or above 1.5 degrees Celsius to avoid the most catastrophic and long-term effects of climate change. Those include massive flooding, severe drought and runaway ocean warming that fuel tropical storms and drives mass die-offs of marine species.

The new report from the WMO, an agency of the United Nations, finds that global temperatures are accelerating toward 1.5 degrees Celsius of warming. The authors of the new report predict there is a 44% chance that the average annual temperature on Earth will temporarily hit 1.5 degrees Celsius of warming at some point in the next five years. That likelihood has doubled since last year.

"We're seeing accelerating change in our climate," says Randall Cerveny, a climate scientist at Arizona State University and a World Meteorological Organization rapporteur who was not involved in the report.

Years with record-breaking heat offer a glimpse of the future. For example, 2020 was one of the hottest years on record. Last year, global temperatures were about 1.2 degrees Celsius hotter than the late 1800s, according to the WMO.

Millions of people suffered immensely as a result. The U.S. experienced a record-breaking number of billion-dollar weather disasters, including hurricanes and wildfires. Widespread droughts, floods and heat waves killed people on every continent except Antarctica.

Recent climate disasters underscore the extent to which a couple degrees of warming can have enormous effects. For example, during the last ice age the Earth was only about 6 degrees Celsius colder than it is now, on average. An increase of 1.5 degrees Celsius "is a very, very, very, very big number," Cerveny says. "We need to be concerned about it."

But with every passing year of rising greenhouse gas emissions, it becomes more and more likely that humans will cause catastrophic warming. The report estimates there's a 90% chance that one of the next five years will be the warmest year on record.

The United Nations warns that, as of late 2020, humans were on track to cause more than 3 degrees Celsius of warming by the end of the century.

In case it is not abundantly clear, we, no longer have the luxury of casually fighting the climate disaster. It is quickly reaching a point where it will be irreversible. Please take heed!

B. TAKING ACTION

"The ultimate measure of a man is not where he stands in moments of comfort and convenience, but where he stands at times of challenge and controversy"
Martin Luther King Jr.
American Civil Rights Leader

MARCHING TO THE SEA, UNITED TO MAKE US POLLUTION FREE

Gandhi led his people to the sea
To send a message to the British monarchy:
We don't need to pay you for salt
The ocean provides it for free.
The message to the colonialists
Was powerful and clear:
We have this natural resource, why pay?
We have nature and we'll keep our money here.
We will do it India's way.

Let us, a country
That would not tolerate
Servitude to a Monarchy,
A proud country that cut
The British colonial strings,
Let us dare, like Gandhi
To begin a unified march
Away from our mental and financial colonists:
The Advertiser Kings;
The big businesses that deal us bling.
Let us also tell our monied monarchs:
We're not buying the superficial things
To keep you rich and in control;
And to our military
Who sells fear to keep us under control,
We say:
War and pollution are no longer the goal;
To our government,
Who dares to steal our future Spring:
We will not be foiled by your cosmetic covering
That hides the death and devastation
Wrought by your poison and polluting.

How long till we march to the sea?
To the forests or the nearest tree?

Or the nearest river running free?
Displaying our Gandhian unity
Condemning the ecological calamity.
Revealing to all
Our strength and unity,
Filled with hope, joy and love
Where we reach our destiny?

Arm in arm,
Children, neighbors
Entire families
Singing in sweet vibrant harmony!

We have trekked through the poisonous
Rains and bitter snow,
Through the thunder
Neath the deluge from the storm.
We have now wondrously seen
The spring leaves turn green.

We ask how long
Before we wake from the dream
To witness our immense poisoning
And the death of
The poorest and most vulnerable beings?
How long before
We witness the nightmare of nature,
A hellish storm
A fiery Venus
Ala Hawking's predicting
A scorched-earth scene?

The winter birds now dream
Of a sweet and warm return to home,
Their song is of love and life,
Trees of leaves of ever-loving green.

Just after winter's blight
Feathered friends return to an abundance of trees
To perch up near sun's light.
Their music fills the once quiet skies
And nature takes off in full flight.
We march so Spring
Will not be a dream
But will be our yearly delight.

Sweet is the smell
Of the great orchards of apple trees.
The lakes and clear skies
Have returned to life
Or such is our dream.

Turning our heads,
Opening our eyes,
We've met and joined
With our neighbors from the South.
We join hands
And together sing.
A glorious song of diversity rings,
No colors to cloud our mind.
No cold hearts to steal the unfolding Spring.

We all arrive at the shore,
Where ships of newcomers we gloriously greet.
Our hearts rise to meet and unlock the Empath's door.
We see only their loss
Like the loving wife greets,
the surviving soldier returned from the war.
They sing in languages distinct,
But all to the same simple beat
The music and song merge.
We are all better than before.

Guitarists, drummers, pianists
Organists and folks with violins…..
The melody and beat converge
No disharmony to purge.
Their hearts lovingly learned
Nature's tempo of life,
And now come
Anxious to join the jamboree.

They dreamed of a place to work
To see their children sing and play,
Where the searching sea meets
The warm shores of what could be.

They've arrived to touch freedom's shores.
To them we must open our doors.
The sun now breaks through the clouds.
Feel the warm rays.
We live and sing in the bosom

And warmth of maternal light.
Please open your heart's door.
Turn your wanting ears
See the searching waves
Meet the shore.
Hear the music wherever you are.

Hearts must listen
To hear the beat,
Love the gifts growing up beneath our feet,
And hear the voice
Of a sorrowful sky asking why.

Feel the ebb and flow of nature's breath.
In sync we move together and meet:
The dream of nature, hearts and minds,
The symphony of sweet mystical sounds divine,
The unity
Of nature and man
Reveling in the glory
of enlightenment,
Nature's gift of sunshine.

To revel in this tiny earth paradise
Seek nature's great maternal advice
Teach all, listen and hear
And then risk all to reprise
Your role of fearless caretaker
Of the oceans, lands and skies.

Please join, arm in arm with me
As we take the first step
On this journey of unity,
Connecting humanity
With nature
On our journey
To the waiting sea.

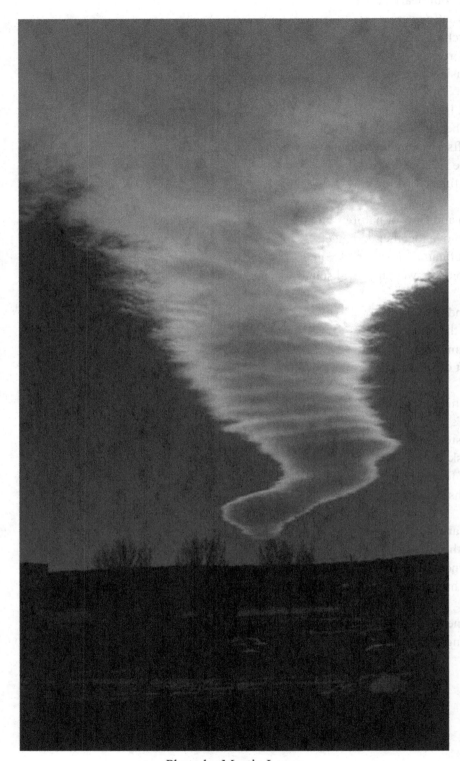

Photo by Martin Lopez

"When the people find that they can vote themselves money that will herald the end of the republic"
By Benjamin Franklin

'IF I HAD A HAMMER'
Composed and written by Lee Hays and Pete Seeger
Sung by Pete Seeger, Peter, Paul and Mary and
Trini Lopez

<u>WE ARE TAKING BACK OUR COUNTRY</u>

We're taking back what belongs to me and you
We're taking back our country true.
We're standing up and shouting out loud:
We're not the one percent crowd!
We're clicking in and taking control
Money won't buy our independent soul.

We choose clean air to breath
We demand clean water to drink
Your plutocratic greed
Makes it all badly stink
With every dollar you make
Mother-earth you forsake.

Our planet is family,
We will nurse her to health
We will take care of our children
We won't obsess over comfort & wealth.
This gift of nature we will not ignore
For the greed and comfort sold at our door

We're taking back our democracy.
You can shove your Plutocracy.
We are choosing our Mother Earth
Over your lust for monetary worth
We're stand'n up and say'n: No more!
Get a new doormat for your gilded floor!
Wake up and listen clear.
We know what you're doing
And we're stop'n it here.

Please join the movement to save mankind.

CHAPTER XII

SUMMARY AND CONCLUSION

CONCLUSION TO GLIMPSING HEAVEN / FACING HELL ON EARTH

"Will you teach your children what we have taught our children? That the earth is our mother. What befalls the earth befalls all the sons of the earth. This we know: the earth does not belong to man, man belongs to the earth. All things are connected like the blood that unites us all. Man did not weave the web of life, he is merely a strand in it. Whatever he does to the web, he does to himself. One thing we know: our god is also your god. The earth is precious to him and to harm the earth is to heap contempt on its creator."

by
Chief Seattle, Leader of the Suquamish and Duwamish Native American tribes.

CONCLUSION TO 'GLIMPSING HEAVEN, FACING HELL ON EARTH'

Thank you so very much for accompanying this husband/father/part-time poet, aspiring philosopher, retired trial attorney, X-tennis coach and now a (tree-hugger) dissident, on the journey that has brought us to this point.

As highlighted in Chapter 11, we are facing the devastation of our planet and humanity, and it has already begun. If we do not take action now, it is quickly moving to become irreversible. And according to the United Nations, World Meteorological Organization, 2019 is set to end the hottest decade on record. So it is not cooling off.

Through this book I have tried to trace my relationship with nature, from obliviousness to actual empathy. My children were the critical inspiration for this transformation. I have also tried to figure out the reasons why we have let this ongoing and worsening disaster continue without acting to stop it. The following also includes a summary of solutions. So let me begin my struggle to sum it up.

Breaking Out. My journey to the truth began by breaking out of the tightly knit tyranny of beliefs that prevent our growth as humans and now prevent us from feeling the pain of others, as well as being unable to see the consequences of our 'throwaway' lifestyle and the ensuing disastrous consequences that are already upon us.

It began when I was young and a skeptic in a time when most everyone else had an 'accepting' nature. It was a time when we had powerfully set in motion an all-out attack on nature, who we viewed as an enemy to be controlled for our benefit. We divided it up and sold it to the highest bidders. Then we paved over the earth so our vehicles could quickly and comfortably transport us and our technological tools to every destination. Then we drilled holes to extract the fuel for our hungry new technological monster machines to deliver us modernization and the American Dream. Then, with our technological superiority, we created high-tech toys and wrapped most everything in plastic for our convenience and the businessman's profit. We daily dined on meat and dairy, burgers, steaks, cowmilk and eggs. And after we were done, and it served our purpose, we threw our food scraps and plastics 'away'. We threw it 'away', like we did with everything else we had no use for. It was out of sight and out of our small minds because it was but mere 'garbage'. This was before we knew, (but should have known), that there was no 'away' in nature. Garbage went into where it should not be and now we are seeing, (or should be seeing), how it is poisoning us and destroying the planet.

Instead, we celebrated by devouring our death and disease-causing cattle by destroying their lives in the most inhumane way possible. Again we were oblivious to the powerful pollution that raising cattle caused. *(Animal Ag – Ch 10)*

Our businesses have been <u>driven by profit</u> and efficiency, oblivious to the damage to nature and future humanity. We were reluctant to learn that we were inextricably connected to nature. Due to a religious and cultural upbringing that taught us we were more significant than nature and living in a world where technology cured all, this superiority notion was reinforced. Although scientifically, the destructive effects on nature have been known for almost a half-century, that information was ignored and considered irrelevant. For those who knew, it was kept a secret. As long as we were comfortably addicted, watching and listening to the world with our technological toys, (Tube Power), life was peachy-keen, as we callously continued to poison ourselves and everything around us

As far back as 1824, Joseph Fourier, discovered the 'greenhouse effect", that certain gases (including CO_2) in Earth's atmosphere could trap heat from the sun instead of having it radiate back into space, thereby increasing the surface temperature of earth. We knew as early as 1956 that adding CO_2 to the atmosphere would increase infrared radiation absorbed, adding that industrialization would raise the Earth's temperature by just over 1 degree centigrade per century.

But apparently no one cared. We were about our daily life directed to working to achieve the American dream. We were told in the eighties by a candidate for President and a scientist (Barry Commoner), that our way of life was leading to ecological disaster. *(Ch. 4)* We refused to listen. He lost his bid and the argument that overpopulation was the problem, won the day. Losing Presidential candidate, Al Gore, warned us that the planet was heating up but again fundamentalism won the day. An Inconvenient Truth lost out to the wealthy fraternity boy that had 'found God'. We are now told by the leader of our country (Trump), that man-made pollution is a hoax. We seem to be unable to wake up to the reality that we are destroying our existence on the planet.

<u>A Comfortable Obliviousness.</u> I admit that I too, for most of my life, have been blind, deaf and dumb to the devastating direction we were going. I too was a comfortable hubris-filled passenger in first-class accommodations on the technologically superior Titanic ship, oblivious to the death-delivering calamitous iceberg of *'Nature Knows Best'* that awaited to end the voyage of humanity. We continue to live as if we are superior to nature's power to sink this technologically superior ship. *(See Ch. 10 WRECKING ON THE HUBRIS ICEBERG/TOO COWARDLY TO SAVE THE LEAST OF OUR BRETHREN.)*

Yes, I picked the right candidates, as far as civil rights, but I don't recall them worrying too much about the environment. Clearly there was more that I should have been doing but was not doing it. Even as a skeptic, I too worshiped at the foot of the technological god that could do no wrong. It certainly would fix any problem that we were to find ourselves in. And my attitude towards nature? I too, lived as if it were but a stage upon which we created our comfortable existence. My early life was pretty much a joyful and oblivious trip through the American dreamland, replete with all the future-killing devices that would bring us to the environmentally disastrous state we are presently in. In contrast to much of the developing world, I lived with all the benefits and pleasures of a technologically advanced system, where our whims could be satisfied with the touch of a button or the turn of a key. I lived unaware of the cost of this comfortable lifestyle. *(Ch. 6).* As in *The Matrix,* I was but one of many who were mere 'babys', serving as the batteries for the money machine's matrix of control.

Country of Deception. How could I have been oblivious to the environmental danger we were imposing by our lifestyle? I, like most of us, had not done my homework. It involved science, so I wasn't interested. But there was another factor. We were living in a country that has had a history of deception. I think of Vietnam, *The Pentagon Papers*, *The Fog of War* and our venture into Iraq based on the lie of 'Weapons of Mass Destruction'. I think of the tobacco companies lying about the dangers of smoking. I think of the report that the Stanford Research Institute presented to the American Petroleum Institute (API) in 1968 that warned the release of carbon dioxide from burning fossil fuels could carry an array of harmful consequences for the planet. I think of Exxon Mobil, the world's largest oil company, knowing of the severe consequences of climate change as early as 1981, only to spend millions of dollars over the following 27 years to promote climate denial. *(See Inside Climate News.)* I think of the oil and gas companies – the makers of plastic, knowing all along that the vast majority of plastics can't or won't be recycled (only 10%), but have told the public to recycle) (*'PLASTIC WAR' PBS 'Frontline' NPR).* I think of our country and the manufacturers of meat knowing that it kills us but putting no warning label on the package.

Government Investigations and Violations of Right To Free Speech. I think of the days of the 'Red Scare' when we attacked homosexuals who lost their government jobs because they were a 'Communist threat'. I think of all those who vehemently protested the Vietnam war who were secretly investigated. I think of the Black Movement of the sixties and J. Edgar Hoover, identifying the black leaders as Communists or Communist conspirators and justifying their investigations. I think of laws passed and used to prosecute those who dare to attack animal industry. Is it any wonder that people are afraid to speak up for what is right?

Why would our big businesses put dangerous products on the market without telling us? In Ch. 4, Barry Commoner explains that our capitalist/corporate system has a bias for making money over safety, so products go onto the mass market before their safety is fully known or explored. When death and illness ensue, denial begins, more die and get ill, the environment is devastated, and occasionally, the insurance companies pay for the deaths and illnesses. (*Google 'The World's Worst Environmental Disasters Caused by Companies' by Drea Knufken, June 21, 2010)*

The awful reality is that our politicians remain in office beholden to the direction of our big corporations. Both of these powers have combined to knowingly deceive us and, for the most part, have refused to acknowledge fault or even the existence of the danger or destruction of the planet and mankind by the continued use of pollution-causing substances such as gas and oil. At the same time government has investigated those who the military, or powerful industry portrayed as threats to National Security.

The Heroes and the Cost of Protest. During the Vietnam War, there were many who realized that the war was immoral. The college campuses spoke up. Many were the victims of unethical investigations by the FBI. Many faced the hatred and anger of an older conservative group who branded them as 'unpatriotic'. Some died for speaking their mind. (Kent State). Then there were those who dared to say no to the draft at great risk to their life and career. I think of Mohammed Ali', who may have lost the best years of his boxing career for his refusal to be drafted based on moral grounds. I recall my father telling me how foolish Ali' was for refusing to be drafted. "They would treat him like a movie star, just like they did with Elvis Presley. He would never see any active service." I am sad to think, that my father, a highly intelligent human being and a democrat, could not rise above being brought up in a 'business' town and his military background, to appreciate the moral issue involved. He was from a generation that trusted the government and its businesses. He was also a Catholic. Catholics and the clergy, as I recall from my days in Catholic School, 'supported our troops.' So many missed the moral wrong of this countries' actions!

I cannot go without mentioning the man that set the example for all of us – Dr. Martin Luther King Jr. He risked and lost his life fighting racial discrimination. The Civil Rights Act is the result of his leadership and sacrifice. (Ch. 8). We are in dire need of leaders and activists for the environment with the focus, daring and in-your-face activism that Dr. King displayed.

At the risk of insulting a large segment of the country, I must include the life of Jesus. I will never understand how a poor radical and dissident, who spoke to our duty to the least of our brethren, can be associated with a crass commercial culture who worships at the foot of the dollar sign. (Ch. 7) and Ch. 10). We must emulate His life, the empathy He preached and the wisdom in His words.

The Barriers. In *Chapter 10*, I have tried to identify the barriers to the fight against pollution and help explain and direct us to a solution to the ongoing and worsening environmental calamity. The picture reveals a dominant small group, who have grown more powerful – the wealthy few, who are connected to politicians willing to do their bidding in a legal and financial system that facilitates their empowerment. The work and power of these powerful few and their political agents has been facilitated by a weakened and spoiled public that have been indoctrinated, technologized, and distracted from appreciating that we are being led to oblivion.

Distrust those in Power. The lesson that must be learned, is to distrust those in power, including the big corporations, those who put profit above all, the PR machine, and the government that has sold to the highest bidder. The other critical lesson is to risk friendship, love and even your own life to vociferously speak out against and condemn those who would destroy us, the future of earth and our future families. (Ch. 6)

The False Enemies/Fighting the Fear. Some of the greatest evils in the world have been done to protect us from the devil, those godless Communists, godless Liberals and anyone that was not like us - non-white or non-Judeo-Christian. We must fight against the fears the world would impose upon us and distract us from the truth. We must look inward and find that moral compass that can guide us. We must bring our unique gifts to the battle to save our earth and our future. (Ch. 4, 4.4 and 9)

The Miracle of My Children. *(Chapters. 1 through 5.)* I may never have seen the beauty around me that was being so abused but for my great fortune to have married a wonderful wife who never gave up on our dream of having children. Sally was the perfect mother. Two little miracles finally arrived in my 'old age' and brought with them the new eyes and a softened heart that enabled me to see and feel the heaven all around me.

Transformation Philosophical / Religious Explanation. In Chapter 4.4, I addressed a philosophy of living and an explanation for my transformation. This was contained in the Lost Gospels, discovered at Qumran in 1945 and validated by famous Psychiatrist, Carl Jung's theory of individuation. They can be summarized as follows: Look inward to find the essence of yourself or suffer sickness; Be passers-by to avoid the poison of the material culture; Nature is the 'Kingdom of God' and empathy is the key to Heaven as symbolized by a mother breastfeeding her child. We have a roadmap of how we must change. Will we take it?

An Explanation for the Miracle. In *The Gospel According to Thomas, Logion 22. (Ch 4.4)*, Jesus', through Thomas, explained how a child will open the gates of Heaven. In answering the question how we get to Heaven, he, in some detail, illustrates what essentially is a mother breast-feeding her baby. Contrary to *Luke 18:15 ESV*, the answer to getting into Heaven, was not to accept everything like a little baby. Rather, the detailed answer marvelously symbolized how we should connect to our fellow man. We were to exercise an empathy born of the realization that we were dependent on the rest of humanity and we should treat our fellow man with that always in mind. It thusly illustrated the type of oneness and empathy we must exhibit to open the heavenly doors. For me, it provided the explanation that perfectly fit my situation. My closeness to the birth and the sustenance of my babies, miraculously connected me to mankind and nature by filling me with the ability to empathize. *(Ch. 4.4)*

We Are All Family. As remarkable, was a relinquishing birth mother and family that took in my family. This act may have made it possible for me to effectuate the clear and strong beliefs about the environment that I had finally developed. *(Ch. 7)* We, each one of us, must be that family that recognizes the rest of the world is our family and must be taken in and saved from the pollution disaster.

What I Saw When My Children Took My Eyes. *(Ch. 1)* With my children, came the emotional intelligence that inspired the realization that I had to protect them at any cost. My new eyes saw the predator at the doorstep. It was us. It was a country that lived as if there were no tomorrow. It was a culture that valued comfort and power at any price. The price was death, illness and the end of a future for our children and grandchildren who were heading straight into the jaws of a hell of our own making – a poisoned and heated-up earth. Hell was made from our own wastes and pollution, which now have threatened to make earth uninhabitable.

Fundamentalist Enablers. One of the enablers of this fiery future was a fundamentalism that President Jimmy Carter, the son of a Southern Baptist minister, wrote about in 'Our Endangered Values'. President Carter identified fundamentalists as 'rigid, dominating and exclusionary', and as such, one of the greatest threats and dangers to our democracy. *(Ch. 10)* The mentality of Fundamentalism is a major threat to the survival of mankind in the fight for the environment. We will not survive if we deny what is now more obvious than ever and supported by science. The religious indoctrination by non-science and a blind faith that refuses to believe that we have a moral duty to take care of nature, is the antithesis of empathy towards our fellow man.

Nature as the Enemy. This narrow-mindedness about nature was born and morally justified by a bible-based belief and a mindset that we could treat nature as an enemy and do whatever we needed to dominate and suppress it. *(Ch. 10)*

Fundamentalism Meets Evil in Person and Falls in Love. In 2016, the powerful and wealthy-few provided the monetary means and, along with white males, non-college working class and White Fundamentalism (Evangelicals), (8 out of 10 of them), provided the votes to elect Donald Trump. *(See Pew Research Center, U.S. Politics & Policy)* As president he embodies everything that has stood in the way of recognizing the impending ecological disaster, including a crass commercialism, a full acceptance of our comfort-making and wealth-making technology, the belief that making money was more important than anything else; a belief that dishonesty and deception are not evils but skills that maintain your power; the belief that power trumps everything else and the skill of doing whatever it takes to maintain power as the ultimate goal. President Trump has denied man-made climate change and has withdrawn our country from the Climate Accords, the one thing that might have slowed the world from its race to a suicidal end. This act may have been a tipping point towards losing the battle against pollution. Of course if you believe that Climate Change is a Chinese hoax, the President and his beliefs make sense.

Fight Against 'Love of the Things of the World' Or if you believe that the end is inevitable and all you can do now is get in good with your Maker, the battle to save our future will be lost. All around us we have been sold the seductive and the glamorous. Religious leaders have looked the other way or said it was okay. We have bought into it. Fight the system that has done this to you and your family. Anything short of this, is submission to 'the things of the world'. *1 John 2:15NASB.*

Faith Without Good Works Equals Evil. I have spent extensive time addressing Judeo Christianity because any moral belief that minimizes the importance of one's actions and highlights the strength of faith, is a recipe for evil. Torture, baseless wars, slavery, racism, sexism, massive incarceration, denying the importance of protecting the environment or most any evil, can be justified based on a strong faith. *(Ch. 10)*: A belief system that is devoid of the importance of one's duty to their fellow man, is a superb instrument of control by government. If we are to successfully fight the battle against pollution, we must free ourselves from any influence that tells us the destruction of nature, poisoning ourselves and polluting the world, is not evil.

Interestingly, if we look at what Jesus did and said, we cannot help but conclude that our actions toward our fellow man, particularly those at the bottom of our society, are critical to getting into Heaven. Jesus and his apostles made it perfectly clear that the strength of our faith is directly connected to what we do and fail to do for the least of our brethren. *(Ch. 10.)* At least 4.6 million per year die from pollution. *(W,H.O.)* We must act now to stop those deaths and the future deaths from pollution.

Technology, The New Savior/Nature the Enemy. The evil that is now killing us, was born of a belief that technology could cure all ailments and nature could be harnessed with no ill-effects. It was born of a system in which the wealthy have taken more control of our lives through their fortunes and by way of politicians, beholden to them. Concomitantly, with the rise of the Plutocracy, the power and control by the non-wealthy and middle class has been severely diminished. *(Ch. 10 and Requiem for The American Dream.)*

WHAT WILL SAVE US? The mindset born from the above factors, has blinded us to the darkness and disaster that is upon us and the devastation that lies ahead. What will save us and our progeny? Pope Francis addresses the cultural change that must take place: From a 'cheerful wrecklessness', we must convert to an empathetic sensitivity to nature, our poor and those who are being injured by our recklessness. *(Ch. 4)*

Barry Commoner provides us with the basic laws of nature and how we have violated them to our severe detriment. *(Ch. 4). The four laws of Ecology,* directed me to the problem and to solutions to 'Global Warming'.

Education. I submit that the only way to attack the problem is to educate ourselves about the problem. We must mandate the teaching of 'Ecology and the Politics to Save the World' from First Grade through College. (See Ch. 4)

We must take seriously Commoner's suggestions about what needs to be done and insist that our politicians effectuate it. The cost is in the billions. Where is it coming from? He, as President Eisenhower hinted at before him, points to the Military Industrial Complex. Commoner believes our investment in war needs to be redirected to fixing our economic system which presently fails to recognize our enormous debt to nature and the devastation this obliviousness has wrought.

We must change our capitalist and Nani-State mentality which is about profit and the vile maxim (It is just about us and no one or nothing else.) This is totally at odds with the way nature works. We must reconsider our 'Nanny-state' in which the super-rich corporations are deemed too big to fail, yet the rest of us are disposable. *(Requiem for the American Dream)*. We must conform our system and direct it to the serious problem at hand.

Fear and Respect. In *Chapter 9,* I address a world whose leaders control by fear. For me it was the Catholic world and the devil, through the nuns and the priests, who held the pitchfork of control. We were told to respect them. I had difficulty with both of those concepts. I used whatever weapon I had against it. We have reached a stage in history where we face the actual end of our species and a leader that says it is all a hoax. We have elected a president who represents the very worst of our society - The ultra-wealthy having inordinate power to make policy and the rest of us are left with minimal power. We must all stop fearing and respecting leaders and institutions that do not deserve respect. We must put fear aside and dare to challenge the system that is leading directly to destruction.

Will Capitalism, the Corporate clique and the Nanny-state conform to put nature, humanity and our future, before profit and the big corporation? We best pick the candidate that is willing to make the earth-saving choice. Are we ready to 'convert' to a way of life that gives up our easy throwaway existence and convert to renewables? Can we stop using plastics? Can our country stop burning fossil fuels? Will we stop our dangerous addiction to meat and dairy? Will we be able to stop wasting food that ultimately poisons the environment?

As I drive the highways in the Southwest part of this country, I am buoyed by the electric generating wind-mills that I have seen in Pastura, NM, and between Las Vegas, NM and Dallas and even in oil-filled Hobbs, NM. I am excited to see that Colorado is making it easy and cheap to install solar heating. And it is exciting to see electric cars and electric bikes. Yet, every time I get in the family car, I think about all the other pollution-spewing devices that are still leaving a gigantic pollution-print in the world. I remember living in Lovington, NM (oil country) and the foul smells emanating from the Navaho Refinery, which we were, unfortunately, downwind from. It made me miss the clean air of Las Vegas, N.M., my home town.

But Las Vegas, NM has its pollution too. When I go to Wal-Mart here in Las Vegas, I see plastic everywhere. I have never seen anyone else bring and use non-plastic bags for their groceries. (I finally saw two people. A clerk told me she had seen 20 people use non-plastic.) The cashiers are happy that I am bagging my own purchases in my non-plastic bag, but do not seem to have a clue why I would bring bags when they have all these plastic bags. I worry about what may be leaching out of the plastic into our foods. I worry about the oceans filling with plastic and the animals ingesting it. I was delighted with my trip to Santa Fe, where the store did not provide plastic bags, but provided non-plastic bags for 25 cents, if you did not bring your own.

Unfortunately, many see these 'plastic-free' 'stores and people as 'tree-huggers', an insult term that distinguishes these Santa Feans or local stores as 'elites' who have nothing better to do than obsess over irrelevant trees, poisoned oceans and dying animals. I sometimes think that it is a very small crowd here in Vegas that thinks there is a severe pollution problem that will impact all of us and our progeny. I hope I am wrong. But I can't help but think the rest of the country is about the same.

I am ecstatic that democratic candidates for president and senators are proposing a Green New Deal: Elizabeth Warren, Jay Inslee, Bernie Sanders, Alexandria Ocasio-Cortez, Senator Cory Booker, Senator Kamala Harris, Senator Amy Klobuchar, Beto O'Rourke, to name a few. Will we choose a leader like FDR, who had the empathy and courage to push through a radical plan that saved the country from the Great Depression?

'The Smell of Money'. This phrase reflects the reality that so much of our businesses, schools and government are funded by the taxes on the oil and gas industry. New Mexico is no different. Things will not change if our respect for the prevailing profit motive continues to trump the destruction of nature. Will the 'smell of money' close our eyes and stifle the sound of the scream of mother-earth until the stench of death overwhelms us? If my attempts to convince my Harvard-educated brother, are any indicator of success in the big picture, we are doomed!*

Combine the 'smell of money' mentality with the extensive lack of knowledge about how critical the problem is, add the feeling of powerlessness, and we have a picture of the state of our country vis-à-vis, the environment. The problem seems almost overwhelming!

Other Countries? That is just the U.S. I look at other countries and their apparent oblivious to the pollution disaster. In China, I see people wearing masks so they do not have to breath the pollution. In India, I see clothes manufacturers dumping their chemicals into the water and people getting sick from drinking it. I see the intentional burning of the Brazil rain forest so cattle ranchers can make money and it is apparently encouraged by their leader. The record of pollution is extensive throughout the world. How will we control them? Commoner's book, the Closing Circle has some suggestions that involve associating with other countries to produce certain pollution-free goods for the benefit of the world. We will need to see the biggest threat not in being defeated by another country in war, but seeing pollution as the world-ender, and work with other countries to stop it. The first step would have been to participate in the Paris Climate Agreement from which President Trump has withdrawn our country. A giant step backwards for our country.

Education. As a first step in the educational process, I have created in Chapter 4, a school curriculum in poetic form, with extensive footnotes about relevant ecological matters. See **"A POETIC EDUCATION ABOUT POLLUTION, THE PROBLEM and THE CONSEQUENCES, WITH FOOTNOTES"** Poetry, Science, Politics and Law! Go figure! I have provided a list of ways we can each fight pollution in our daily lives. *(Ch. 13)*. These solutions are a first step, once you recognize the danger and its cause. I have even provided an extensive cheer for the time we take to the streets to demand clean air.*(Ch. 12)* (Yes! I am a child of the Sixties!)

The Battle Is against Us. One of the great obstacles in this battle is ourselves. We have been suckling from the mammary of big business whose tit has provided sugar-sweetened 'milk' that has made us soft and the antithesis of self-reliant. Animal Agriculture tortures animals and pollutes the world while we gladly eat their burgers, steaks and dairy; Big business has given us chemically enhanced consumables without thought of the consequences. They have provided us with high-powered gas-guzzling, pollution-belching vehicles to which we are fully addicted. Television and advertising have trained us to believe that appearances and wealth are more important than substance. *(Ch. VI.)* We do not want to leave our comfortable lifestyles.

Finally, coal, gas and oil pollution equate to jobs. Loving nature is a hard sell to the family of anyone employed in oil, gas or coal production. Our government must step in to ensure that the work skills of employees in the coal, gas and oil related businesses will be used elsewhere as we move to renewable energy.

Will we succeed in recognizing the danger before it is too late? Writer and activist, Bill McKibben, wrote the 1989 book, *The End of Nature and* detailed the potential effects of climate change. It remains one of the most influential environmental books of all time. He believes that we can attain a level of $CO2$ to 350 parts per million (ppm).* He began the non-profit *350.org.*in 2008 and has enlisted the help of thousands of student volunteers around the world to mobilize public support for reducing humanity's carbon footprint. To get there, means building solar arrays instead of coal plants, planting trees instead of cutting down forests, ending animal agriculture, increasing energy efficiency and reducing wastes. Are we moving fast enough? His efforts and organization should give us hope and inspire us to get involved.

Or Are We a Virus? I refuse to believe that humanity is but a virus that consumes, destroys and moves on in search of its next victim. (Ch. 10, 'The Zephyr'). We are a country that has pulled together when we are or have been convinced that the danger was at our doorstep, but not before that. Apparently, the fact that 4.5 million human beings per year are dying as a result of pollution, has not sufficiently pulled at our heartstrings. So empathy may not work to ignite any fire. Apparently, the fact that the temperatures in the last four years, have been the hottest since temperatures have been taken, is not working. We instinctively know that it is an emergency if we, or our children, have a fever and it is critical to reduce it. But we fail to act when it is the earth that has a temperature! That our oceans are heating up, hasn't inspired us to make major changes nor the destruction of our under-water tropical forests, the coral reefs; That severe hurricanes, born of a heated ocean and increased evaporation, making them more severe, destroying our residences and taken lives, has not yet triggered the alarm. The forest fires raging in California, Oregon, Arizona, New Mexico, Australia, Brazil and elsewhere in the world, has not precipitated a reaction that Global Warming is here with a vengeance. That Europe, Spain and Portugal in the last four years, have experienced higher temperatures than ever recorded, does not seem significant to anyone.

What will it take? Our country has acted heroically when we have a knowledgeable and empathetic leader in charge. (I am thinking of President Roosevelt.) We have been responsive to the patriotic theme and a willingness to wage wars when we were convinced it was in our interests. We need to frame this environmental threat in the context of an enemy that will destroy us and our children if we do not take drastic action. (That the enemy is us, is a problem!)

There are huge obstacles to overcome to successfully begin and win this battle. You may say that you can't win this battle alone so you might as well not try. Moreover, you won't be around when it gets real bad! I submit that the biggest battle is to dare to say there is a problem and if any of my family or future families can be harmed, I will take action now. It must be your reason to live. As Martin Luther King said: "If a man has not discovered something that he will die for, he has nothing to live for."

The Example of the Native Americans. After growing up in the *Indian Capital of the World* and watching Channel 5, I am getting educated about the tragedy of the Native Americans in this country and indigenous people around the world. Our country and the Spaniards brutalized them and we are only now realizing how bad it was. But they have banded together and fought for their rights regarding their relationship to the earth. We, like them, will need to, first recognize our connection to the earth, and then be willing to do what is needed to preserve it. They have set an example for us. I have included quotes from Native American leaders that seemed prescient. They knew what needed to be done long before our scientists figured it out.

Seeing the Heaven Around Us. *Jesus said, "....the kingdom is inside you and it is outside you...."* **The Sayings of Jesus # 3 of the Gospel of Thomas.** *(See Ch. 4.5 for full quote).* I strongly hope very soon, as we experience the devastation of our pollution and the obliviousness that led to it, we will have a realization: We worshipped, had unquestionable faith and prayed for the guidance of an external all-powerful being to get us to Heaven, after our death. Yet we did not see that the Heavenly Kingdom was right here on earth and it threaded through our very being. *(Ch. 4.4)* We must realize the very gift of heaven is not separate from us, but intricately woven through us. Our abuse of nature is suicide and an affront to the creator. As humanity looks for Heaven elsewhere or fails to see their intricate connection to it here on earth, we will experience an earth-ending hell on earth.

"The LORD God took the man and put him in in the Garden of Eden to work it and take care of it." Genesis 2:15 NIV. This biblical provision, minus the biblical domination of nature admonition, must be our guideline.

Looking Inward and Through a Child's Eyes. The most difficult thing we must do is to look inwards and find our unique selves. We must love the children in our lives. It is through them that I believe we will find that empathy that will inspire us with the daring to stop those that would pollute us to death.

A Synchronicity of Sources. I believe that this book has brought together four disparate guiding sources that you would rarely hear in the same idea, all of them syncronicitously pointing in the same direction: Carl Jung, the Psychiatrist, (Ch 4.4), Jesus' words from the Lost Gospels (Ch. 4.4), Pope Francis Encyclical in Ch. 4, and the scientist, Barry Commoner (The Closing Circle) (Ch. 4).

Carl Jung, speaking to a world that viewed itself as defined by the world around them, directed them inwards in the search to find one's true self. He tells us that the failure to do so is sickness. This is his famous theory of 'Individuation'. Jung has captured our modern ailment perfectly and at the same time gives the direction to search for a solution. (Ch. 4.4)

The Lost Gospels cited in *(Ch. 4.4)* with Thomas speaking Jesus' words, remarkably mimics Jung's directive to look inwards to the self, otherwise you are mere 'poverty'. I submit this 'poverty' is the sickness that Jung speaks about and the cause is the same – failure to search inwards to find the self. We all are endowed with so many 'gifts' that are part of our being, but they wither and die if we do not fight to allow them to come out. So the richness of our humanity becomes 'poverty'.

In those same Gospels, Jesus through Thomas, tells us that the 'Kingdom' is here, now, inside us and around us. Nature's majesty and the obvious duty to respect it, was recognized in Jesus's time! The Pope tells us that we have a moral duty to protect nature and to destroy it is a sin. *(Ch. 4)* In a Judeo-Christian world that appears oblivious to nature and the damage we are doing, the head of the Catholic Church recognizes it and speaks it to the world.

And finally, we have a scientist and politician in Barry Commoner, to tell us in scientific terms the critical role that nature plays in our existence, the damage we are doing by ignoring nature, and daringly tells us what we have to do to fix it. *(Ch. 4)* The laws he reveals to us -The Four Laws of Nature, (Ch. 4), particularly our connection to nature, is directly or indirectly alluded to in the Dead Sea Scrolls by way of Jesus speaking through Thomas and also in Pope Francis' Encyclical. Do we need more moral directives?

Syncronicitous Messages of Solution. History rarely brings together, from so many different and powerful sources, a warning so clear and detailed. It is as if history or someone or something is saying: You may not believe science, religion or psychiatry, separately or alone, but they are saying the same thing: You must search for that gift of empathy within you, allow it to come out, connect with humanity and nature, hear the earth moaning, see it dying and find that courage to save it and humanity.

So, What Is to Be Done Now? Under the basic rule that David Hume, a famous political philosopher once advised: "...In every state, no matter what type—whether it's feudal, militarist, whatever it was, power is in the hands of the governed." They can, if they get together, take power. As long as they can be made to feel that they don't have power, then the powerful can rule. But if they come to understand that they do have power, then repressive and authoritarian governments alike will collapse." *(See Requiem for the American Dream p. 123)*

Recognize the Problem. We are now in a stage of human history where we're facing the end of nature, which includes humanity. *(See p 143 of Requiem for the American Dream.)* We must disabuse ourselves of what certain politicians, big corporations, PR folks and now a president, are selling us - to make people hate and fear each other, look out only for themselves, and not do anything for anyone else.

We must recognize that nature is not separate from us. It is inextricably part of us. Just as the blood that flows through our veins, the oceans, the streams and the rain are the same. If we pollute them, we are polluting ourselves.

Our trees are the lungs of the world. The CO2 we exhale is taken in by them and they exhale oxygen, so humanity can breathe. Our trees, through the leaves 'transpire' – they provide water vapor to the tree and then to the sky, enabling the tree to survive and rivers of the sky to flow and ultimately provide life-giving rain, so the life-cycle repeats. The Trees are an integral part of our earthen mother. Destroy them and we destroy the lungs and the bosom of life-giving waters that keep humanity alive. Moreover, the increase in heat that our pollution has already caused, is contributing to the forest fires destroying our wooden-leafed lungs and liquid life-giving sentinels. The smoke is adding to the pollution, exacerbating the problem. Stop heating the world! Stop burning our trees down! Start planting more trees!

The air, sky, clouds and weather are also part of us. What we breathe in sustains us. If it is something not intended, like CO2 or methane, it makes us sick. If we compel the sky to breathe pollution, it develops a fever. If it is not treated, it gets sick and will ultimately 'die'. Daily, we move closer towards Stephen Hawking's prediction of earth becoming a 'hothouse planet like Venus if we don't curb irreversible climate change.'

A hotter earth means the melting and disappearance of our white reflecting poles of ice. We then get higher oceans. If you live on a coast, you suffer severe consequences. This bodes the beginning of major human migrations to livable parts of the earth. Would we be able to accommodate?

Our oceans absorb the heat, our rich underwater tropical forests die. Hotter waters make the storms and hurricanes more severe. This combination of weather symptoms is mother earth's equivalent of seizures.

Secondly, nature is not a mere gift, with which we can do as we please. It is not here to make a profit for a few. It is not here to be abused for our own comfort and efficiency. The image of God must include nature. Man and nature are inextricably one. Humanity and nature must be seen together as the reflection of God. We are not separate from nature! We are not more important than nature!

We must see, hear, listen, feel, visualize, harmonize and intellectualize our connection with the earth. Failure to do so moves us closer to extinction. We must see her as a mother, a sister, and morally treat her as we are to treat the 'least of our brethren'. *See Ch. 4*, for a moral take on the environmental catastrophe and what should be done.

The Closing Circle by Barry Commoner, *summarized in Ch. 4*, provides us with the big picture of the problem and what we need to do to address it. He tells us that we must use the funds that go to our war machine (Military Industrial Complex) to fight the war on pollution. We must put back what we have stolen from nature. We must work with other countries, encouraging their production of natural goods.

Ch. 13, SUGGESTIONS TO FIGHT POLLUTION identifies specifics for those who want to know what they can do. Ch 11 - LIVE THIS MOMENT AS YOU WOULD LIVE THE LAST, lets us know that time is limited. If you need a 'fight song', 'We Are Taking Our Country Back', provides it. Ch.

<u>11's Marching to the Sea United to Make Us Pollution Free</u>, is some old fashion Gandhian activist advice to wake up the government.

So let us be heard and make 'Ecology and Saving Our Planet', mandatory education from kindergarten through College. Let us vote for those who recognize the environmental catastrophe around us and are daring enough to effectuate policy that addresses the problem.

So please let the children soften your heart, open your eyes and enhance your hearing, so you can tune in to the music of the soul. We cannot and must not obliviously drive our families into a disastrous future.

<u>Personal Solution</u>. We must recognize that power and strength within each of us and dare to tell the matrix leaders that we will no longer be their batteries. We must undo the influence of the matrix leaders who deceive us by telling us that all is fine and that Global Warming is but a hoax. It is not! It is devastatingly real! We must become the Neo's that fight the battle against this money-driven Matrix of control. We have been given the approach by a poor enlightened radical who lived over 2000 years ago. He taught us to love our neighbor and do not tolerate the evil that the world tries to impose on you. Dr. Martin Luther King Jr. and Mahatma Gandhi have revealed the activism needed to defeat those who would tyrannize us. If it is modern action drama that moves you, then look to Neo to battle our modern money-imposed matrix. Whatever approach you choose, your every action and thought must be directed to saving humanity from the death, suffering and devastation our pollution is exacting. Please begin now. Every moment we come closer to a climate nightmare that we may never be able to wake up from.

<u>Action Solution:</u> Stop putting our wastes into our skies, our waters and soils! Stop putting meat and dairy on your table! Immediately switch to renewable energy!

I hope the ideas in this book light a fire in each of us that will lead to action that is long overdue. I beseech you to think of your future families. Feel what they will have to endure in a world of devastation! Speak out against the powers that would silence you. Dare to make a scene. Be your own person. Know that this is the biggest issue ever and act accordingly!

And remember, it is not about the amount of money we have at our life's end that will define who we are, but rather, the seeds of goodness and wisdom that we have planted here on this marvelous and intricate garden of life. Let us choose to live and die for a way of life that will support a sustainable future for our living breathing mother earth and her children.

As of December 26, 2019, the CO2 in Parts Per Million (PPM) is 412.36 ppm. SeeCO2.earth.

A PERSONAL, EMOTIVE AND SYMBOLIC CONCLUSION

This author's journey through life was not so different from others, until Sally and I conceived two children late in my life. They changed me forever!

I had been brought up to believe that I was conceived of a male God, and to Him only I owed my existence. He created all, without the help of an earth mother. To believe that nature conceived and nurtured our being was blasphemy! As such, I was Mother-Earth-less, until I discovered the true source that suckles, secures and enhances my brittle being.

With this momentous discovery and experience, my heart grew and became sensitive, so I could feel what my earth brothers, sisters and children felt, and at the same time, feel the pain mama-earth was feeling.

My eyes became directed so I could see how she fed and cared for her children.

My being and soul were stirred, moved and enlightened. I woke up to the realization that all earth's children, were part of this magnificent natural wonder.

My nose delighted in the smells of the flowers, the rivers, fruit trees, and the freshness after a rain shower, but sickened to the stench of the sickness and death of a feverous mother dying because humanity cared not for her.

I reveled in the sun's power to bring warmth to my unenlightened and slowly freezing body, but saddened, from the death and destruction caused by the matricidal maniacs and the pyromaniacs, obliviously scorching our loving, little earth home.

My now newly agile and empathetic brain, filtered through my new-found heart, made connections previously ignored: We were part of nature, not superior. Our natural earth miracle was not a mere prop for our existence, not the dance-floor for our merriment. It was alive and intricately intertwined with our being. We ignored her to our detriment. When she was loved, she was delighted. When she was ignored and disrespected, she became sick and unable to care for us.

For my entire life, I, and most all of the big-brained beasts, have been oblivious to nature.

We had been regarding this living heaven on earth as mere roadway pavement for our vehicles of death. We have been treating our sky like a dumping ground for the gaseous wastes from the carbon, coal and oil we cut from the body of a mother whose skin, we had decimated, torn and treated as useless dirt and rocks. We have depleted our precious water and poisoned our skies with deadly methane because we are in love with our fast-food burgers, entitled to our steaks and addicted to our bacon and egg breakfast. Animal Agriculture and our politicians, made sure it stayed that way.

We have been poisoning ourselves and mother's ocean creatures with our convenient plastic containers.

We have been treating our leafed-lung and sky-river protectors, like lifeless wall materials to box us neatly in, along with our expected creature comforts, and away from unpredictable annoying nature.

We have been pouring and dumping damaging deadly waste over and into the sensitive pores of mother earths' delicate skin, until now, she is permanently scarred, feverous, and tremorous, from poisons injected deep into her stomach and spine. Severe infections without antibodies have now begun, as we have ripped the pale skin from her sensitive body and removed her heat-protective snow-white blankets; disease has taken hold of her being and her children are now infected with the inability to regenerate; her blood-pressure continues to rise along with her temperature; her beautiful body and soul is now threatened with the death of her life-carrying underground, above-ground and sky-bound arteries; her beautiful and protective bosom – the ocean and skies are being poisoned; Mother Earth is now on her deathbed and we can only think of pouring more poison into her dying mourning mouth.

Enlightenment and courage came when my children arrived! I was reborn, with a wisdom and connection as never before; Once you see what is voraciously consuming the future of the earth family; Once you are stripped of the culture that has empowered the death-makers to control the murder of Mother and her children; Once you have realized these are your children and grandchildren that will die, what do you do?

You tell the untainted truth to the world, no matter what the cost is to you or your reputation; You take action to undo the damage to mankind that has been done; You undo the buttons of be-what-you-are-told-to-be and do-what-you-are-told-to-do; you remove the stifling belt of this-is-how-it-has-always-been-done; You remove the monogramed 'hangnoose' necktie and diamond necklace of the 'I love things' lifestyle; You undress and burn the evil garments of the crass and careless culture that makes death and suffering seem normal and natural; You give eyes to those who blindly obliterate, so they can finally see their evil reflection in the mirror of decultured morality; You reveal the untainted light emanating from lives lived before and their self-less examples; You hold the unmasking mirror up to the world that reveals wickedness without restraint so we see the ugliness and pain that we have wrought.

Then you put on the armor of only-ness, and with armadillo-skin, you sally forth, boldly breaking apart the fierce and malevolent mold-makers of sameness; You embrace the natural essence of motherness, so it fills your every nature-connected pore; Then, through your primal eyes and nature's nostrils, you see and smell the monster at your doorstep, drooling to devour your cubs; You show your ancient protective natural teeth and growl, sending a message to the monster: You will never have my babies and I will defend them until death I am devoured!

Then, you stop craving and consuming the sugar-coated venom of the killing and crass culture. You hunt down and begin the battle against the giant poisoning predators who will not stop until their evil hunger is satisfied.

This then is my journey and where it has taken me. So join with me. Let us, lovingly and daringly emulate Dr. King and Gandhi and take to the streets, march to the sea and climb to the mountaintop, every step of the way, courageously, shining the light, through the darkness of these tenuous times.

APPENDIX/SOURCES/
RECOMMENDATIONS

Mindset:

Recognize that Global Warming and the severe consequences are already upon us. Scientists say climate change is getting worse and there could be "life-or-death consequences for our planet in the next 20 years. This report from the U.N. predicts that at the current warming rate, millions more people will die from extreme heat by the year 2040. *(See Intergovernmental Panel on Climate Change.)*

Though you may not be directly affected during your life, your family and descendants will be affected. What you do will have an impact. Failing to act, puts this monumental decision in the hands of those who do not care about the consequences of global warming. Consider the following ideas, sources, resources and activities that should help make a difference:

Environmental Attorneys: EARTH JUSTICE; Non-Profit Conservation Law Foundation: 'Lawyers for the Earth' 1-800-584-6460 Fax: 415-217-2040; info@earthjustice.org

Natural Food Store: Semilla Natural Foods, Las Vegas, NM 505-425-8139

Movies: An Inconvenient Truth; The Day After Tomorrow; The 11th Hour.

Inspirational Movie: *It's a Wonderful Life*

Documentaries: '*COWSPIRACY*: The Sustainability Secret (2014 documentary on NETFLIX.); 'PLASTIC WAR' PBS 'Frontline' NPR (Revelation that oil and gas companies – the makers of plastic- have known all along that the vast majority of plastics can't or won't be recycled (only 10%),but have told the public to recycle) (See google: '10 Environmental Documentaries To Binge-Watch Now'; See NETFLIX: 'Our Planet', 'Frozen Worlds', 'Jungles', 'Coastal Seas', 'From Deserts to Grasslands', 'The High Seas', 'Fresh Water', 'Forests'. 'I Am Greta' on Hulu (the story of teenage climate activist Greta Thunberg), *Planet of the Humans,* executive producer – Michael Moore (A skeptical view that questions whether biomass energy, wind power and solar energy are as renewable as they are portrayed.)

Books/Articles to Read: The Closing Circle by Barry Commoner, *The Politics of Energy (1979) by Barry Commoner,* Climageddon, the Global Warming Emergency and How to Survive It by Lawrence Wollersheim, *Green Is The New Red* by Will Potter (Potter points to our government aligning with big business and a major actor in actively trying to stop the Environmentalists.)*The End of Nature by Bill McKibben, (Falter) (1989) (the first book on global warming written for a general audience.)An Inconvenient Truth by Al Gore, Earth in the Balance, Ecology and the Human Spirit, by Al Gore; Das Kapital by Karl Marx, The Ecological Rift by John Bellamy Foster, Silent Spring by Rachel Carson, (documenting the adverse environmental effects caused by the indiscriminate use of pesticides.) Article: Capitalism, nature, socialism; a theoretical introduction by James O'Connor; David Brooks 'Weavers', Six Degrees: Our Future on a Hotter Planet, by Mark Lynas. Climate Shock by Gernot Wagner and Martin Weitzman (Princeton University Press; April 2016), Author Fred Pearce: The Land Grabbers, Earth Then and Now: Amazing Images of Our Changing World; The Climate Files: The Battle for the Truth about Global Warming; Why 'Carbon-Cycle Feedbacks' Could Drive Temperatures Even Higher; After the Coronavirus, Two Sharply Divergent Paths on Climate.... ;'Under A White Sky: the Nature of the Future by Elizabeth Kolbert, Pulitzer Prize-Winning Author of The Sixth Extinction*

Books About Animal Agriculture and Alternatives: *David Simon, lawyer, Author of "Meatonomics"; Mad Cowboy* by Howard Lyman; Dr. Richard Oppenlander, Environmental Researcher and Author, *Food Choices and Sustainability; In Defense of Food,* by Michael Pollan, Best Selling Food Author; *"The World Peace Diet",* by Dr. Will Tuttle, Environmental and Ethics Author; *'How to Grow More Vegetables...'* by Author and Biointensive Farming Innovator John Jeavons; *'Comfortably Unaware'* by Dr. Richard Oppenlander, Environmental Researcher and Author;*:'How to Avoid a Climate Disaster'* by Bill Gates.

Philosophy of Politics. Our Endangered Values by President Jimmy Carter

Non-Meat, Non-Dairy Organizations: Omega Creamery (Plant-based dairy) owned by John Schindler; *BEYOND EGGS,* Plant-Based Eggs, Hampton Creek Foods, owner Josh Tetrick;

Non-Meat, Non-Dairy Cites: www.COWSPIRACY.com

- *Merchants of Doubt: Naomi **Oreskes** and Erik Conway, How a handful of Scientists Obscured the Truth on Issues from tobacco Smoke to Global Warming.*
- *THIS CHANGES EVERYTHING CAPITALISM vs. THE CLIMATE by Naomi Klein*
- *DOUGHNUT ECONOMICS Seven Ways to Think Like a 21ˢᵗ-CenturyEconomist by Kate Raworth*
- *There Is No Planet B: by Mike Berners-Lee Green Is the New Red: An Insider's Account of a Social Movement Under Siege by Will Potter*
- *Losing Earth, A Recent History by Nathaniel Rich (How a coordinated campaign by lobbyists, corporations and politicians cast doubt on scientifically-backed public attack on climate change in the decade of 79-89.*
- *US food disparagement law: Eckley, Erika H & McEowen, Roger A. "Pink Slime and the Legal History of Food Disparagement". Agricultural and Applied Economics Association: Choices. 4ᵗʰ Quarter 2012 (New)*
- *We Are The Weather – Saving the Planet Begins at Breakfast*: Jonathan Safran Foer. *"Choosing to eat fewer animal products is probably the most important action an individual can take to reverse global warming..."*

Animal Enterprise Terrorism Act (AETA): "S. 3880 (109th): Animal Enterprise Terrorism Act". govtrack

- *The Climate Emergency, (Essay by Al Gore)*
- *The Uninhabitable Earth, Life After Warming by David Wallace-Wells*
- <u>*Plastic contamination.*</u> *How to Give Up Plastic by Will McCallum, A guide to changing the World, One Plastic Bottle at a Time*
- <u>*Human Consequences of Climate Change*</u>*. Dispatches from the New American Shore by Elizabeth Rush*
- *Storming the Wall, Climate Change Migration and Homeland Security by Todd Miller*
- <u>*A Study of five mass extinctions.*</u> *The Ends of the World by Peter Brannen*
- *Don't Even Think About It, Why Our Brains Are Wired to Ignore Climate Change by George Marshall*
- *Are We Smart Enough to Know How Smart Animals Are? By Frans de Waal*
- *The Imperfect Environmentalist: A Practical Guide to Clearing Your Body, Detoxing Your Home, and Saving the Earth (Without Losing Your Mind) by Sara Gilbert.*

Children's Books: *HEALING EARTH* BY John Todd.

Songs: 'Lonesome Friends of Scientists' by John Prine. (Does this explain why we don't care?)

<u>Moral Guides - Pope's Suggestions</u>: In the encyclical, Laudato Si', the Pope puts our moral duty to nature on the same level as our duty to our fellow man. (See my summary of Pope Francis' Encyclical in Chapter 4.)

Computer Internet Sites/organization cites

- *https://www.nationalgeogr; Bill McKibben - 350.org*
- <u>http://www.joboneforhumanity.org/climageddon</u> book support navigation <u>centerjobOneforHumanity.org</u>
- The Guardian *(www.theguardian)* – (A youth perspective on the environmental disaster.)
- http://www.joboneforhumanity.org/stop_sayingclimate_change_pledge; Common Dreams "Worst case climate projections likely": Study ""CommonDreams.org. November 9, 2012. <u>http://www.commondreams.org/news/2012/11/09worst-case-climate-projections-likely-study</u>
- *@upstreampolicy*
- 'Deforestation explained' 'DEFORESTATION AND FOREST DEGRADATION'. See <u>https://www.nationalgeogr</u>
- plasticoceans.org
- World Wildlife Fund, https://www.worldwildlife
- *Quora Digest": addresses electric vehicles, particularly 'Tesla'*
- *InsideClimate News Weekly; updated Climate Change Info.*
- *Waste360 Daily Wire*
- *Earth Day Network*
- *Union of Concerned Scientists*

- *Waste360*
  Jay Inslee
- *Society of St. Andrew: (addresses issues of food-waste.*

SAVING THE LUNGS OF THE WORLD: google 'tree planting organizations'

OneTreePlanted. One Tree Planted, https://onetreeplanted.org. One Tree Planted is a non-profit 501(c)3 organization focused on planting trees around the world. Anyone can get involved. One dollar plants one tree.

A Living Tribute
Plant-a-Tree Sympathy Cards
Pet Loss Memorial Trees
Green America Certified

- Plant a Billion Trees (https://www.nature.org/en-us/get-involved/how-to-help/plant-a-billion) (The Nature Conservancy's Plant a Billion Trees campaign is a major forest restoration effort with a goal of planting a billion trees across the planet. Trees provide so many benefits to our everyday lives. They filter clean air, provide fresh drinking water, help curb climate change, and create jobs
- **Deforestation.** Have less demand for products that lead to deforestation including meat, timber, soy, and palm oil. (Thank you Somini Sengupta, international climate reporter for the New York Times.)

Definite 'Do's'

- Stop eating meat and dairy.
- Recognize that the 2020 Presidential election will be the most critical election in our history.
- Vote for the candidate that recognizes that Global Warming has devastating consequences that are ongoing and will get more severe in the very near future.
- Vote for the candidate that dares to propose solutions that include prosecution of those who are complicit in the act of destroying lives.
- Consider the destruction to democracy caused by Corporations flooding the candidates of their choice with money and support the Democracy Dollars proposal of Andrew Young in which all voters receive $100 to donate to the candidate of their choice. This should diminish the influence that mega-wealthy individuals and companies have in our elections. In addition, we must pass a Constitutional amendment to allow our campaign finance laws to properly limit the power that the top 1% have.
- The most serious war we need to fight for our survival is the one against Pollution. We must begin transferring funds from the Military Industrial Complex to the War against pollution.
- Pass national laws, State laws and local laws requiring that Ecology in the Modern World be a mandatory course in grade school, high school and college. Offer scholarships to college for those who will major in Ecology.
- Demand of your political representatives that we must begin to direct money and invest in those energy industries that are pollution-free, are renewable and rely on nature. E.g., Wind Power, Solar Power, affordable electric transportation.

- Demand that your representative takes the pledge not to take money from fossil fuel polluting companies.
- Demand that your representative support the Green New Deal. (See example below.)
- Avoid meat and dairy, invest in industry that is an alternative to meat and dairy and demand that your representative vote to limit our use of meat and dairy.
- Demand that your representative, City, State and Federal, ban plastic.
- Tax Pollution.
- Demand an end to polluting industries. Tax or penalize them out of business.
- Demand that government assist businesses that make the move to ecology-friendly manufacturing and producing.
- Plant trees and begin programs to save the forests.

COAL, GAS, OIL, NATURAL GAS COAL AND METHANE: Limit the use of fossil fuels such as coal, oil, carbon and natural gas and replace them with renewable and cleaner sources of energy, all while increasing energy efficiency.

- daily decisions within your reach – like driving and flying less, switching to a 'green' energy provider and changing what you eat and buy.
- Revamp our subsidy system for the energy and food industries, which continue to reward fossil fuels, or setting new rules and incentives for sectors like farming, deforestation and waste management.

Political Agenda:

- Choose the candidate that has the best proposals. Consider the following proposal. E.g., Jay Inslee's Green New Deal – a deliberate phasing out of US fossil fuel production.

Personal

- Recycle: - Locate your local recycling center and begin taking plastics, metals and cardboards to them to recycle.
- Begin using natural materials instead of plastic
- Use solar energy, at least on your house
- Use & wash dishes instead of getting plastic stuff.
- Praise those who are reducing plastic use
- Stop purchasing water in PLASTIC BOTTLES.
- Conserve ENERGY – turn off computers, and electric appliances when not in use. Use energy efficient light bulbs and appliances.
- Use clothes lines and hang clothes to dry instead of using a dryer.
- Participate in your local utility's energy conservation programs.
- Eat Less Meat and fewer eggs. Become a vegan or vegetarian. Invest in non-meat and dairy.
- Packaging: Choose products packaged in natural materials. Try to avoid products in excessive plastic packaging.
- Use bar soap instead of body wash or shower gel.

- **Food**: Recognize that according to the Natural Resources Defense Council, the U.S. Environmental Protection Agency estimates that food waste makes up over 20% of our trash. About 95% of the food we throw away ends up in landfills or combustion facilities. They break down into methane, a potent greenhouse gas which contributes to climate change This comes principally from the energy used to produce the food, including emissions from livestock and fertilizer use and the greenhouse gases associated with the waste.
- Organizations/websites: *Society of St. Andrew, Gleaning America's Fields – Feeding America's Hungry, (endhunger.org). This cite references numerous organizations and studies on this issue.;. www.foodrescue.net,*
- *The EPA (environmental Protection Agency) has initiated the Food Recovery Challenge (www.foodrescue.net) offering their full support to any schools donating their surplus food.*
- Composting foods that can be organically disposed of at home is a great way to reduce the amount of food you throw in the trash. It's good for the environment, and can give you some fertilized soil for the garden. (For full article, google wikiHow: 'How to Dispose of Food', Sep 6, 2019)
- Eat less meat and dairy
- banning meat across an organization,
- Buy in bulk whenever possible, and when shopping, bring your own reusable containers and shopping bags instead of the plastic bags.
- Store refrigerated produce in towels or cloth instead of plastic bags.
- Use glass or steel food containers for leftovers instead of plastic. Cook at home more often!
- **The NERC-NEWMOA Fact Sheet list of ten "things you can do to make a difference:**
- "buy what you need and buy for durability"
- "borrow and share."
- reuse
- repair
- buy recycled
- don't waste food

Keep food out of disposal
- ask companies to label products with the carbon footprint

Ask your state or local government to act.
Keep learning about what affects climate change.
- sharing rides and using public transportation

Clothing. Buy less clothing and footwear! Opt for clothing made of bamboo grass, organic cotton, hemp, soy, recycled or up-cycled materials and used materials. Donate and recycle your clothes. Avoid fur and leather whenever possible. Look for eco-friendly products that carry 'eco-labels' from third-party certifications bodies, such as Demeter, Eco-Cert, ECO -INSTITUT, the Global Organic Textile Standard (GOTS), Oeko -Tes, or the Soil Association, as examples.

- *Recycle, donate, repair.*

Home Equipment. Replace air conditioners and refrigerators with ones that save energy and reduce hydrofluorocarbons (HFCs).

- "https://www.drawdown.org/solutions/materials/refrigerant-management" refrigerants
- Get rid of HFCs (chemicals used in fridges and air conditioning) 170 countries agreed to start phasing out HFCs in 2019.
- Praise businesses that are reducing their use of plastic by tagging the business and posting photos on social media. Tag *@upstreampolicy*, too, and Upstream, an organization fighting plastic pollution by advancing policies and corporate responsibility, will repost it.
- **Take a pledge to reduce your plastic use:** The Plastic Pollution Coalition's 4Rs Pledge entails *refusing* disposable plastic whenever you can; *reducing* your consumption of products with excess plastic packaging or parts; *reusing* durable containers, straws, bags and other items; and *recycling* the rest.
- Take *The Last Plastic Straw Pledge*, a commitment to refuse any plastic straws served with your beverage, encourage restaurants to only provide straws upon request and adopt compostable or reusable straws, and persuade restaurants to take the pledge against straws as well.
- Start your own cleanup or join an existing one. The Ocean Conservancy offers guidelines for *starting your own cleanup* of lakes, rivers or beaches. Take part in its International Coastal Cleanup, which will be held on September 15, 2018.

Join an Environmental Organization:

- Join the Earth Sharing Movement
- Support the Global Divestment Campaign
- Join or contribute to 350.org

Organize a plastic pollution event

- The Earth Day Network provides primers and toolkits for organizing community events to build awareness about plastic pollution.
- Host a screening for friends and neighbors of a documentary about plastic pollution such as "A Plastic Ocean," (Netflix), "Bag It," "Addicted to Plastic," or "Straws."

Support organizations that are fighting plastic pollution.

- Sponsor the Plastic Soup Foundation for your next sporting contest.
- Become a member of and/or donate to organizations that are working on plastic pollution, such as: Algalita, 5Gyres, Plastic Pollution Coalition, Plastic Soup Foundation, Surfrider Foundation, and Upstream.
- PlasticBagLaws.org as a resource for cities, states and communities that want to institute plastic bag bans.
- Join the global Movement plasticoceans.org
- To propose a plastic bag ban in your community, check out Romer's primer on implementing plastic bag laws.

- **'The big fat recycling lie'** **Where does all your recycling go? See Exponentialnvestor**
- *Ban polystyrene, (Styrofoam)*

<u>Bottled water bans</u>

- The <u>Ban the Bottle campaign</u> has suggestions for starting a bottled water ban in your community.
- *Plastic straw bans. 500 million straws are used each day in the U.S. Malibu, Miami Beach, San Luis Obispo, Fort Myers and numerous restaurants have stopped giving out straws unless customers specifically request them. As a result of the <u>Strawless in Seattle</u> campaign, Seattle too will ban straws in July, which could reduce straw use by a million a month. Inspired by Seattle, residents of Santa Fe are starting a Strawless Santa Fe campaign.*

Plastic-free restaurants

- Surfrider Foundation's <u>Ocean Friendly Restaurants campaign</u> helps restaurants reduce their plastic consumption. Encourage your local restaurants to sign up.
- The organization is also developing a <u>Global Plastic Reduction Toolkit</u> that will be a resource for proposing, passing and implementing legislation to regulate or restrict single-use plastics, highlighting successful examples in cities, states, and countries around the world.
- Surfrider's <u>Straws Suck campaign</u> encourages consumers to identify businesses that use straws by taking a photo of the plastic item and posting it to Twitter or Instagram with @ *SurfriderVan* and hashtag *#StrawsSuck* or *#RiseAbovePlastics*.
- *Dine at Plastic-free restaurants*
- Don't beat yourself up. Stay positive.
  Many of the above recommendations have been taken directly from Jacob Shwartz-Lucas' internet page: Progress, **Top 5 Ways to Fight Pollution, Why It Matters:**
- *Recommendations by Diego Arguedas Ortiz is a science and climate change reporter for BBC Future. He is <u>@arguedasortiz</u> on Twitter.*
- Change how industries are run or subsidized
- 'divest' funds out of polluting activities – such as avoiding stocks in fossil fuels, or banks that invest in high-emission industries. By getting rid of financial instruments related to the fossil fuel industry, organizations can both take climate action and reap economic benefits.
- Going car-free
- choose more efficient vehicles and, whenever possible, switch directly to electric vehicles,"
- give up flying or fly less.
- Virtual meetings
- holidaying in local destinations
- use trains instead of planes
- eat food that is both locally grown and seasonal. Even so, eating vegetarian still beats only purchasing local.
- Share with others what you do to lessen pollution. Be a community organizer.
- contribute to 'green' projects.

Printed in the United States
by Baker & Taylor Publisher Services